MW01486795

THE FENRIS WOLF

Issues no. 1-3

Edited by Carl Abrahamsson

TRAPARTbooks

The Fenris Wolf, issues no. 1-3

ISBN 978-91-986242-5-0

Trapart Books
P.O. Box 8105
SE-104 20 Stockholm
Sweden

info@trapart.net
www.trapart.net
www.patreon.com/vanessa23carl

The Fenris Wolf, issues no. 1-3
Contents

Editor's Introduction

Following the rapid success of the fourth issue of *The Fenris Wolf*, I felt more or less pressured into turning issues 1-3 into an anthology. I did have my doubts, as my life during that entire era between 1989 and 1993 was so imbued with *folie jeunesse*. Perhaps the material wouldn't be up to par today? Perhaps my editorial values were too relaxed at the time?

I had already toyed with the idea of making the issues in question available on the Internet, or as PDF-files. But I could also see that there would be a greater historical value in republishing them in a "real", tangible format. To really make *The Fenris Wolf* a series of journals, the way I had originally intended.

It's been highly interesting going through these old issues. Some of the stuff does seem a bit dated, while some of it is more relevant now than ever, and some of it even ahead of the times, still. Which is which, I leave to you to decide.

In this volume you can find all of the textual material from the first three issues. I also decided to include a new piece of writing in this anthology. *'Zine und Zeit* was written during the time I edited this book, ie during the summer of 2011. A lot of memories emerged and it dawned upon me that so much of this material stemmed from an era that was heavily influenced by a "Do It Yourself" ethos. To tie that pioneering entrepreneurial spirit in with magic and occultism is quite a fascinating area, and I hope you'll find this little text worth your reading while.

An editorial note: As the texts in this book stem from various minds from various cultures, there are obviously some stylistic inconsistencies. I have chosen to keep as many of these as possible, including possible "magical" language quirks, in the name of heterogeneous and creative integrity. However, for any spelling or typographical errors, pure and simple, I assume full responsibility.

Another editorial note: I have tried my hardest to reconnect with all the authors to again ask for permission to reprint their material. In all but a few cases I've succeeded. As time has moved onwards, so have apparently many of the contributors. If you read this and feel left out or over-looked in this process, I offer my sincere apologies and encourage you to get in touch. Thank you.

Old thanks: First and foremost, to *all* the contributors and facilitators. And especially to Anton LaVey, William Burroughs, and Stein Jarving who all left this mortal coil far too early. Also to Genesis Breyer P-Orridge, Tim O'Neill, Tom Halliwell and John Alexander, as well as to TOPYSCAN, TOPY Europe, TOPY US, Ordo Templi Orientis (especially Auga Odins Camp and Oasis), the Church of Satan, The Institute of Comparative Magico-anthropology, The Lumber Island Acid Crew, Maniac Repro, Carl Holmberg, Björn Sandén, Johan Kugelberg, Gunnar Lindqvist, Ulrich Hillebrand, Erik Pauser, CM von Hausswolff, Jan Ekman, Martin Bryder, Per Svensson, Leif Elggren, Roger Ekstam, Lars Lindblom, Kenneth Anger, Blanche Barton, Peter

Gilmore, Peggy Nadramia, Hymenæus Beta, David Griffin, Mikael Prey, Patrick Emt, Peter Bergstrandh, Michael Matton and Inger Lindman.

New thanks: Vera Mladenovska, Margareta Abrahamsson, Sofia Lindström-Abrahamsson, Fredrik Söderberg, William Breeze, Robert Ansell and the Edda and ICM networks.

In terms of dedications, I find it appropriate to reprint the one from issue no. 3: "This issue is dedicated with respect and love, not to the seekers, but to the finders."

Vade Ultra!

Carl Abrahamsson, Editor
Stockholm-Monstropolis, Summer Solstice 2011

'Zine und Zeit

Carl Abrahamsson

"The printing press, then only a century old, had been mistaken for an engine of immortality, and men hastened to commit to it deeds and passions for the benefit of future ages."

E.M. Forster, Abinger Harvest, *1936.*

"What remains, and remains undeniable to and by the most hardened objectivist, is that a great number of men have had certain kinds of emotion and, magari, of ecstasy. They have left indelible records of ideas born of, or conjoined with, this ecstasy."

Ezra Pound, Guide to Kulchur, *1938.*

Transmissions of esoteric knowledge have been handed down to us over the centuries in basically two fundamental ways: orally and in written/printed form. As for the oral transmissions, it's usually in their very nature to be secret and secretive. One could argue that general educational wisdom (stuff having to do with raising children, for instance, and conveying ethical codes) has been transmitted orally through multi-generations without these demands of secrecy, but it's equally true nowadays that even these invaluable everyday wisdoms can be found in printed form. Or on the Internet. That doesn't mean they become more tangible and applicable though. General human behaviour codes simply seem best transmitted orally.

As for specific, "real" magical knowledge, I would say there are absolutely strains and lines of wisdom that continue to be passed on – and who knows where they originally came from? I have encountered reliable "witnesses" possessing such knowledge, and I have myself been given some teachings from non-writing magicians that I know for sure don't exist in any duplicated form. Given their secret nature, I will leave those oral aspects right here. If you want eso-exoteric blabbermouths, please consult the Internet.

In terms of the written and in various ways duplicated word, it's literally easier to look at, and especially when it's "close to home". I think many of us share similar plug sparks in our esoteric engines: magical books would probably be the most common ground, ie books that either have a strong evocative potential or books actually dealing with magical subjects. Or a mix of these aspects. We hear of things, we read things, we investigate and become inspired. And then we read some more. The books can in themselves become genuine totemistic objects too, if there has been a substantial charge of inspirational-emotional energy in the reading process. This charge can last a lifetime (and possibly longer) and can also be fetishistically enhanced by, for instance, an autograph by the writer in question, or knowing that the book has previously been in the hands of someone important.

The esoteric journal or anthology containing various minds becomes a multifaceted gemstone, with condensed expressions of human thought. The market in general is swamped by a plethora of books containing all sorts of compensatory epiphanies and claims of revealing the inner mysteries of both this and that (Thank God(s) book covers pretty much correspond to the contents – it saves a lot of precious time!). But the journal, be it occult or not, has the potential of at least displaying one or two facets one can resonate with, be inspired by and, if one is lucky, allow to be integrated into one's own useable wisdom. It's a format that awakens curiosity and encourages taking a stand, pro or contra. A format that awakens further interest and makes you think and reflect. One crappy page of a book can be a reader-killer. If you happen to find one in an anthology, just flip to the next article.

Thoughts like these were going through my mind while originally working on the first three issues of *The Fenris Wolf* between 1989 and 1993. Essentially: to collect the writings of the people I had more or less access to at the time, and/or that I had been inspired by. "What has inspired me will very likely inspire others too." This is a fundamental link in the chain of the history of human ideas. Stuff that doesn't really work will of necessity be discarded. Powerful ideas and energies will be cared for and nurtured and passed on, perhaps even slightly improved. I'd say that this is one of the reasons why the history of persecuted ideas is so endlessly fascinating. If someone is willing to kill you because you have a dissenting idea in your mind, you can rest assured it's a good and vital idea. Many of the occult teachings and ideas have been occult for a very good reason: self-preservation. But when the time is right, the flower in question will eventually bloom.

Also, one very substantial thing that I learnt while working with various music fanzines earlier on: the world is malleable to a greater extent than what we're raised to believe – another very important magical insight. It's not impossible to penetrate new environments or cause change to occur in "conformity with will". It's not impossible to ask someone for something. Actually, my experience tells me that the answers to my requests have been affirmative and supportive more often than not.

These two aspects – a will to relay/transmit and a realisation that it is actually possible – became the cornerstones of my youthful folly in the wonderful worlds of garage rock, sleazy films, experimental art and worn-out anti-heroes. Chat and snap, cut and paste (I mean that literally), print or xerox, and distribute yourself (again, literally) at concerts and record stores. Very primitive stuff, but it worked. In fact it worked very well, and for each new issue, more doors opened. In my mind, there was already a formulation that what I was doing was magical in that sexy, supra-causal sense. As I drifted more and more into the hocus pocus quagmire, my first priority was not to secure a gallant robe or an extravagant wand to zap the cosmic forces. No, the first priority was to create an occult fanzine, through which I could weave my own magical spells. If you haven't guessed it already, it was the birth of *The Fenris Wolf*.

Have you been aroused by a blog lately? I'm sorry to say I haven't. I don't think I ever have, come to think of it. But when I flip through old issues of *Chaos International, Starfire, Nuit-Isis, The Cloven Hoof, The Black Flame,* old TOPY newsletters and fanzines or *The Cincinatti Journal of Ceremonial Magic*, I can feel a tingle that is sometimes decidedly more sexual than cerebral. Why is this? It's because the tiny magazine or fanzine in question has been charged with intellectual or magical energy, best summarized as a will to share radical, substantial human thought from a unique vantage point. This energy sort of radiates from the pages, no matter how poorly printed they are. I hope the first three Fenris Wolves emit that same good-will (some would say complete evil-will). I think they do, but I'm probably too partial.

The return of the book-book is apparent these days, no doubt a backlash against digiculture, e-books and toilet-paper paperbacks. For more on magical aspects of bibliophilia in relation to the grimoire tradition, please read Peter Grey's excellent piece in the fourth issue of *The Fenris Wolf*, "Barbarians at the Gates". It really goes without saying, but I feel compelled to say it again: tangible quality will last. Ephemeral digi-snippets of the "contemporary" will not last. If you want to share something and make some kind of impact while doing it, share it either straight ("live") into people's hearts and minds or in tangible, multidimensional forms. So far, the printed book has proven itself a worthy winner in this regard. I strongly suspect this will remain so for a long, long time.

And when this long, long time has passed, I suspect that the impression of our own written magical transmissions will be a fragmented jumble of disparate expressions, each with distinct suggestions on how to cope with an array of problems and challenges. That is, a more or less exact reflection of the times we were living in then (now), albeit garbed in esoteric lingo.

I think the historic hocus pocus traces will be obvious (in many ways, they already are). At about the mid-70s, a mere decade after the Aquarian psychedelic big bang, a huge release of creative energy settled in while we were (re-)evaluating those historic traces. Some have since preferred the conservative, museal, and cerebral approaches, while others have embraced a more anarchic, intuitive one, and then a zillion other approaches on top of that. However, what unites all serious expressions is that they will be regarded as serious down the line too.

One group or splinter fragment can't tell the entire story, as historians so well know. The more parts we have from the same totality, the bigger the picture, of course. First-hand sources have a tendency to die, but second-hand ones have so far lived on for thousands of years, through the blessings of diligent monks (and others who could write and duplicate texts) and primitive printing presses. The more first-hand experiences that will be correctly documented and relayed, the clearer the overall picture. And here's exactly where will-fuelled initiatives like magical publications, be they "order-biassed" or not, have a huge advantage over academic writing, as they not only can but rather inherently insist on expressing emotion and wonder as well as mere chronological, factual accounts and further bibliographic references. That holistic dynamic of enchantment is required to fully "get" the picture. History as such, esoteric or otherwise, is never objective in its creation.

If a piece of writing doesn't express some sort of subjective emotionality or a distinctly personal experience, we have to cock an eye on its validity as historic "meme". If there's a too chronological or too distanced an approach, we can be certain that there's been an adjusted editorial process in action, usually in the name of "objectivity". A "peer review" can just as easily be spelled "peer pressure". And this, paradoxical as it may sound, is of course always biassed and partial.

Don't forget that the biggest chunk of the word "history" is "story". The more subjective stories we have, the better we can create our own synthesis, our own individual *Gesamt*-evaluation.

Magical experimentation in various fields of natural sciences, arts, music, literature, etc, have later on become fundaments of "established" dogma in these fields. Perhaps what we have to consciously take into account now, is the importance of "scripting" the future through various magical publications and shared efforts. Some aspects of science seem to be catching up a bit, but the magical sciences will always be way ahead when it comes to human potential-research. I believe that all of the idealistic fanzines and small publications from these past decades will later on be looked upon as seeds, as sperm, waiting and waiting to fertilize some human mind-womb of the future. The ejaculatory process is swift and violent. Human development not quite so.

I can sense (vague, I know, but deliberately so) that there has been an increase in occult diplomacy during the past decade, circa 2000-2010. This has, according to me, very much taken place through an energy level increase in periodicals, books and human interaction (symposia, conferences, festivals, etc, not forgetting the integration of esoteric subjects and courses within academia, which has been a great step forward).

The Internet hasn't really turned out to be a garden of occult wisdom (not the same as "information"), but has certainly become useful as an extended address book and PR-tool. Traces of the networking and sharing of resources, as experimented with in Thee Temple ov Psychick Youth in the 1980s for instance, shifted shape and did indeed become a digitized storehouse of potential, albeit still dressed in the Emperor's new clothes. The exchange of pompous, masonic-looking certificates of mutual recognition has been replaced by a more thorough exchange of substantial information on grass roots levels, a merging of minds through tangible means, and a pragmatic occasional union based on tolerance. If the general objective is to further the individual in her attempts at elevation, of necessity tied in with a larger planetary need for survival strategies, then secteristic approaches and retentive affiliations might not be the best idea. Am I deluded when I claim that a new wave of occult publishers has been very instrumental in this Mercurial greasing process?

If Aleister Crowley hadn't worked so hard on publishing his occult writings in good, solid editions, he would very likely have been remembered merely through references from the gutter-press of his time – like a vilified footnote in the history of British debauchery. Crowley's ambitious efforts not only at writing but also at publishing his thoughts and ideas, and his Herculean labour of hustling copies (truly the "Great Work" for us all!), in many ways constitute the foundation of the extremely vital journal- and book-publishing environment we enjoy at the beginning of the 21st century. Which, in turn, will help change minds, perceptions and cultures now and in the future to a much greater extent than, I suspect, Crowley could ever foresee.

And let's not forget the magnificent entertainment aspect of occult publications. Idealism really is a lovely thing. There doesn't need to be a conflict between substance and lack of distance. No arena of human endeavour has been more touched by divine (?) madness than occultism. Delusions of grandeur in unchecked contexts create a splendidly entertaining stratification process. But when it's only spewed out in ugly and eye-draining Internet fora, who really cares? I see a very bright future for printed matter containing idealistic expressions, and one of many reasons for that view is that it takes real effort and real knowledge to create something that others want to touch and be touched by. Immediacy and complacency are usually very snug bed-fellows.

Within this spectrum of efforts, there is one very useable common denominator that is also one of the cornerstones of magical practice: You use what you have and you use it to the maximum. You can't use more than you have in magic. If you're deluded and think that you can, it will very soon be made clear that you can't. Ritual magic and its synchronistically sparkling mind-universe isn't a credit-based economy. You are what you are and you have what you have. If you can play with that, it's likely that you can change certain things to the better. That mere potential of change is of course also exactly what attracts the Napoleon-Cleopatra-contingent of "spiritual" loonies, ie those without a solid firmament of substantial self-knowledge. But today they are more likely to ram-rod online than to make books and magazines that require hard work and slightly more than an imagined crowd of admirers.

Looking back at the "post-punk" era and its spontaneous expressions, we find that the ones that have lasted, in the sense of still having a tangible "presence", are those with a genuine will to express something, and then an intelligence to express and shape that into a form that speaks to its desired audience. As we're mainly book nerds here on these pages, I will leave the immense spectrum of music. Suffice to say that the DIY-ethic, from the 60s and onwards (and with a particularly forceful impetus in the late 70s), has created a great many cottage industries producing truly unique musical works, packages, products, concerts, etc. Most of these instigators used what they had access to and nothing more. "Where there's a will, there's a way." Is there a lesson here, why those products today (usually) fetch a higher second hand price than a "top ten chartbuster" that was issued in a gazillion copies? Of course there is. And the same goes for books, periodicals and artworks.

Many thousands of years ago, the proper development of papyrus (Egyptian water reed) enabled a more elaborate and extensive writing process. A focus on religious and magical topics in writing was of course prevalent all over the Mediterranean hotbed of philosophy and spiritual speculation. The esoteric transmission may still have been oral, but as the Christian tyranny grew in fervour and indiscriminately killed off philosophers and burned manuscripts, the need for duplication and documentation became painfully obvious. The symbol of Alexandria's library burning (possibly the most vile act of terrorism ever) is relevant in the history of magical writing.

And then, there was... Well, I think you know that story quite well. And perhaps it's more interesting to start thinking about the future, now that we can safely study how the history of human ideas and creativity has been so eminently safeguarded by many wise women and men of various shades and shapes. Perhaps now it's our turn to face the future and leave something inspirational behind?

The magico-existentialist punches remain the same: Who are you? What do you have? What do you want to express? Find out in a genuinely honest way and you're half way there already. As for the future: Script it, and script it well!

The Strange Phenomena of the Dream

John Alexander

"If the doors of perception were cleansed, everything will appear to man as it is, infinite."

– William Blake

The more important the subject, it seems, the less we know about it. Why do we sleep? Why do we dream? Everyone dreams – some of us have better recall than others – dreams are not over in the space of a few seconds; we dream a total of about two hours per night. Dreaming, or the kind of sleep accompanied by dreams, is essential for our well-being – without sleep a normal man will die quicker than without food. To be deprived of our dreams, (paradoxical sleep) is more detrimental to our health than being deprived of orthodox sleep.

We have tended to regard sleep as an abnormal condition, and wakefulness as the norm. It is now considered that sleep is the prime condition – in view of the premature infant's addiction to sleep – with wakefulness intruding more and more with advancing years.

Interpreting dreams is as old as mankind, but modern thinking is based largely on Sigmund Freud's *The Interpretation of Dreams* published in 1899. In the same year the Icelandic philosopher Helgi Pjeturss began researching his ideas on the *Nature of Sleep and Dreams*, proposing a theory that dreams are a form of telepathic communication from other worlds.

The purpose of this brief article is two-fold: firstly, an examination of different views of dream interpretation; and secondly to introduce the theories of Helgi Pjeturss, whose work and ideas have not quite had the exposure as those of Sigmund Freud.

To primitive peoples dreams and sorcery are central to their beliefs. The Australian aborigines refer to the "Dreamtime" as the actual plane of existence, regarding the physical world as a kind of limbo shadow realm we pass through *en route* to the world of dreams.

The modern approach to dream interpretation, in the footsteps of Freud, is to rationalize as far as possible, to attribute dreams to the picture world of our own subconscious.

Psychoanalyst Dr. Ann Faraday writes in *The Dream Game* (London 1975): "The power of the dreaming mind to show us the thoughts of the heart that have passed us by during the day, with all their vast array of associated memories and fantasies, comes first and foremost from the fact that the sleeping brain is not having to pay attention to the outside world. Over and above this however, the dreaming mind is able to by-pass the prejudices and social pressure that so often prevent us from facing the thoughts of the heart straightforwardly in waking life. The dreaming mind cuts through the pretension and self-deception of the waking mind, riding roughshod over many of our most cherished illusions and showing our feelings for what they are."

This kind of dream interpretation, which seems the most acceptable for the modern reader, fulfills a valuable function in using dreams as a therapy – the "patient" is encouraged to work with dreams to uncover the traumas of the personality. But what of the dreamer transported to times and places alien to anything perceived in an awakened state?

"Brain-wave records indicate that the dreaming brain is even more active than the waking brain, which may mean that it is capable of more work in a given amount of time. Dreaming may show the brain running over the experiences of the previous day or two at a faster rate than in waking life, bringing to our attention all manner of things we have felt or perceived subliminally but have simply not been able to register consciously. This could also account for the dramatic vividness and exaggeration of feelings in dreams, both pleasant and unpleasant." (Faraday: *The Dream Game*)

Science is still a long way from any comprehensive understanding of dreams – in entering this veiled and unknown realm of symbols and alternative realities it is the mystics and the magicians who can help us open "the sun in the mouth", as the Egyptians defined the cosmic eye.

Carl Jung wrote, "in each of us there is another whom we do not know. He speaks to us in dreams and tells us how differently he sees us from the way we see ourselves..."

In *Man and His Symbols* (London, 1972) he cites a case study of a ten year old girl and a cycle of twelve dreams which she had recorded and presented to her father. Jung transcribed the relevant "motifs" as the following:

"The evil animal, a snake-like monster with many horns, kills and devours all other animals. But God comes from the four corners, being in fact four separate gods, and gives rebirth to all the dead animals. An ascent into heaven, where pagan dances are being celebrated: and a descent into hell, where angels are doing good deeds. A small mouse is penetrated by worms, snakes, fishes and human beings. Thus the mouse becomes human. This portrays the four stages of the origins of mankind. There is a desert on the moon where the dreamer sinks so deeply into the ground that she reaches hell. The girl becomes dangerously ill. Suddenly birds come out of here skin and cover her completely."

Jung identified themes of destruction and restoration, closer allied to primitive myth than Christian formulations. Jung recorded that he was greatly troubled by the dream sequence – dreams inappropriate for a young person approaching puberty, with a new life ahead. A year later the girl contracted an infectious disease and died.

Such dreams cut across plausible lines of time and causality – in this instance presents a case of extrasensory knowledge or perception transmitted in a dream state – even prophesy. The dreams suggest in their imagery a kind of psychic map for the poet/magician ready to enter an unknown territory.

For Jung, the dream-vision indicated a future – indications to fulfillment of present personal crises. For Freud, dreams were symptoms of sickness, indicating a past personal drama – symptoms of irresolution, repression or anxiety. In both the Jungian and Freudian scheme of things dreams are regarded as catharsis – a means to attaining wholeness. Jung's studies led to the formulation of what he termed the "Personal Unconscious" (in many ways similar to Freud's "Unconscious Repressed") and the "Collective Unconscious" – the area of the psyche where dreams and symbols have a transpersonal quality. These are patterns of symbolism that pertain to mankind as a whole.

There are others who claim dreams provide recollections of other lives; the spiritual teacher Paul Brunton, for example, describes as the Over-self: "Just as it is possible for the dream-mind to assume different personalities, each speaking and behaving according to type, it is possible for other hidden layers of the mind to dramatize themselves and speak as they might be expected to in their respective capacities. We are only on the fringe of discovering what latent powers the human mind possesses. The entity that controls can quite well be himself in another guise, not only because of the foregoing but also because of characteristics developed in former births and still living beneath the surface of this birth." *(Notebooks, vol II)*

Gurdjieff claimed in the *Work* that once you begin to pay attention to dreams, you interfere with them and so change them. Consequently the study of dreams as a psychological method of approach to oneself was discouraged. However Gurdjieff's student Dr. Maurice Nicholl wrote:

"*The Work* says there are many different kinds of dreams not recognized by western psychology... Most dreams are echoes of things seen during the day, sensations and movements... They have no meaning and are of no importance... There are also dreams that come from the centers we do not use – i.e. Higher Emotional and Higher Intellectual Centers... characterized by what can be roughly called dramatic formulation... The language of dreams is not our ordinary language... Higher intelligence is working on us and in us at every moment, only we cannot hear its words or understand its meaning." (Nicholl: *Psychological Commentaries on the Teaching of Gurdjieff and Ouspensky, Vol. I*)

The psychic and medium Edgar Cayce said that, "all dreams are given for the benefit of the individual, would he but interpret them correctly." (Edgar Cayce, *Readings 294 – 15*). It is the dreamer which is important, and not the dream. He referred to dreams as "scenes from the sixth sense" that provided visions of earlier incarnations. He said that such dreams must be interpreted as relevant to the dreamer's present situation, for they are memories relevant to the here and now.

The Taoist philosopher Chuang Tzu once wrote: "Beneath a tree I fell asleep and dreamt I was a butterfly, a butterfly flying about and enjoying myself. Suddenly I awoke and was myself again. I did not know whether it was me dreaming I was a butterfly, or whether I was a butterfly dreaming that I was he, sleeping beneath the tree."

The Nature of Sleep and Dreams

Helgi Pjeturss (1926)

After endeavouring for some years to understand the nature of sleep, I decided, in 1902, to take up a more special investigation into the nature of dreaming. The reason for my doing this was as follows: Psychologists write of visualizing an idea; that is, making thought visible, much as if this faculty of visualization were as normal to man as that of seeing. I found, however, that I had no ability to visualize. Ideas were to me something quite different from concrete pictures. I never once succeeded in seeing a face before me, unless I was looking at a face. My memories were never mental pictures. It took me considerable time to arrive at the conclusion that I had not a trace of the ability to visualize. But then, in comparing consciousness in the waking state and during sleep (that is, in dreams), I found an enormous difference. Thinking about a thing or a state when awake, was radically different from seeing the thing or experiencing the state: but dreaming about a thing or a state was the same as seeing or experiencing. The more I thought of it, the more remarkable it seemed that although in sleep the sense activities are practically suspended, the contents of the sleeping mind are very much as if the senses were working. In short, dreams are not, or only to a slight extent, thought and reminiscences, but are as it were, sentient and active life. There was my problem and it seemed to me that it must necessarily be of the greatest psychological importance. Time has proved that the problem is still more important than I had suspected, and is, in fact, of the most fundamental nature.

I set out, then, to find the cause of this difference between waking and sleep consciousness, and for years strove to find the solution. But my efforts were in vain: the hypotheses I formed had to be abandoned. At last it struck me, when considering thought-transference, that if words could be transferred from one brain to another, the same ought to be the case with pictures (the brain states accompanying the process of seeing). In the course of many years' subsequent study it has become quite clear to me, that at last I had found a clue to the truth. And the understanding of the nature of the dreams became the means for obtaining an insight into the nature of sleep and of life itself. For life is a vital charge, which is renewed during sleep. We can learn to observe distinctly the inflow of the vital current when sleep comes on, and how this current carries along with it the shadowy images of the incipient dream.

During sleep we establish contact with a dream-giver – a person whose brain and other nerve-states are transferred to the sleeper. What this person lives, the sleeper dreams, believing that he is himself experiencing the adventures of the dream-giver. What the sleeper obtains from the dream-giver, however, is more or less mutilated and distorted, translated, so to say, according to the sleeper's disposition and experience.

Dreams can be divided into groups according to the intimacy of the rapport between dreamer and the dream-giver. It follows, therefore, that the different stages of a dream can belong to different groups. When rapport is slight and transference imperfect, the pictures from the brain of the dream-giver are transferred to the brain of the dreamer much more easily than the stream of thoughts accompanying the pictures. In the brain of the dreamer then, these pictures, in accordance with certain laws of association, are erroneously interpreted, and the dream consists of illusions, the sleeper believing that he is in the dream seeing things known to him. These are the illusional dreams, corresponding to the *enypnia* of the ancient dream-expert, Artemidoros, whose *Oneirokritikon* is the most interesting work on dreams I have read. When the transference from the dream-giver to sleeper is more perfect, we have the vision-dream, the *Oneiros Artemidoros*: and, as a rule, what is seen in such a dream is foreign and unknown.

Here I arrived at a conclusion that was at first glance staggering. An analysis of the vision-dreams led to the inevitable conclusion that the dream-giver must be an inhabitant of some other planet. The human beings, animals, plants, buildings, landscapes, constellations, and other astronomical phenomena, seen very clearly in the vision-dreams, were such as do not exist on this planet or in its sky. Incredible as it may seem, there is no conviction I hold with greater certainty than this, that psycho-physiological contact with the inhabitants of other planets, is a normal phenomenon of human existence.

It is this unsuspected communication with the inhabitants of other planets – I am not referring to the planets of our own solar system – which has given rise to the occult belief in other planes of being. The stagnation which has for thousands of years characterized occult theories, is sufficient proof that an insight of the truth has not been attained. There will be no stagnation when the discoveries here indicated have received the necessary attention.

Another staggering result I obtained was the discovery of what I call the "Law of Determinants". For several years I had been endeavouring to trace how dreaming is influenced by happenings during waking life. At last I found, to my astonishment, that my dreams are influenced much less by my own thoughts and feelings than by those of the persons I have met in the course of the day. Such persons exercise so marked an influence on the current of energy creating the dream that they can properly be spoken of as Determinants. For more than 12 years I have been investigating this law, and am coming to the conclusion that it will be found to be a cosmic law of the most fundamental importance.

A Dark Storm Rising: Right-wing Christianity and its Paranoid Worldview of Occult Conspiracies

Tim O'Neill

Secret societies have always existed as historical and anthropological fact. However, the difficulty of obtaining valid information on them, for all but the most public groups, such as Freemasons, has led to a curious situation in which conspiracy hunters are free to range at will and invent whatever nefarious activity they wish to attribute to their favorite secret society. It is the impossibility of ever objectively proving that secret societies do all the horrible things that conspiracy buffs say they do, that lends conspiracy theory in general a hazy sense of paranoia. Often the sheer volume of suggestive "information" that conspiracy theorists amass tends to lend weight to their arguments, but most of these dedicated witch-hunters wind up with extremely complicated systems of pure inference based on such shaky documentation that the only people who would even begin to believe them are other conspiracy hunters!

In this closed world of paranoid assumption and frantic newspaper clipping, one group of theorists stands out as the most rabid and implacable... The "Christians". I put the word into parentheses, because most of these people are essentially right-wing extremists who stop barely short of outright fascism; yet most often their conservatism is cloaked by a Christian façade which tends to find the root of all conspiracy in Satan-worship and demonism. Secular conspiracy buffs are usually interested in matters such as the Trilateral Commission, the Bilderbergers, International Communism and the Rockefellers. This school I would term the "None Dare Call It Conspiracy" buffs, after the famous book by Gary Allen. Robert Anton Wilson, in his various *Illuminati* books, has examined this territory very extensively. He has also verged into the realm of the other major school of conspiracy hunting, the "Proofs of a Conspiracy" students, who follow John Robison's famous book of 1798. This book is the origin of all the occult conspiracy theories which attempt to implicate the Masons and Illuminati in an attempt to destroy "Christian Civilization".

The main competitor with Christianity for the role of state religion of the Roman Empire, during the first four centuries after the death of Jesus, was Gnosticism and its allied Mystery Religions. The distinction between Gnosticism and Christianity boils down to one simple yet far reaching matter. Christians vehemently believe that faith, particularly in God's mediators, the priesthood, supersedes any necessity for individual and direct contact with the numinous. As a matter of fact, Christianity has always been extremely nervous about its own mystics, even when they operate well within the bosom of orthodoxy. The fact that St. John of the Cross wound up in the prison of the Spanish Inquisition tells us quite a bit about the tolerance of mainstream Christianity toward the mystical or numinous experience. Gnosticism, in complete opposition to this conception, holds that religion is meaningless *without* direct contact in the spiritual realm, on an individual basis. Gnosticism never really developed a priesthood or orthodoxy, because its followers each had their own "school", their own interpretation of their mystical experience. Gnosticism was thus in a position where it could also never act as a unified political force. While the Gnostics were wrangling over tedious philosophical details, wealthy Roman matrons who were taken with the new Christian religion, gradually "sold" it to those who mattered; their husbands, the senators and generals of the Roman empire! Gnosticism also made the tragic error of limiting the experience of "gnosis", or direct knowledge of the spiritual worlds, to a tiny elite. Christianity brought itself to an extremely powerful political position by seeking both a popular base with the masses and the influence of the women of the upper classes. By the fourth Century, Christianity was the state religion of Rome and Gnosticism was well on the way toward being banned as a "heresy". That did not prevent Christianity from co-opting many Gnostic and Mystery Religion elements in the course of consolidating its power. With great stealth, Christian missionaries adopted many of the more superficial aspects of the older "pagan" beliefs, in order to speed the process of absorption for new converts.

By the sixth Century, the rooting out of Gnosticism as a serious rival to Christianity was well under way, and by the 12th Century, we witness the spectacle of the first Christian Crusade... Not against the Islamic "heathen", but against the Albigensian and Catharist Gnostics in the South of France. Using German mercenaries, the papacy slaughtered and plundered hundreds and thousands of innocents whose sole crime was not following the political and "spiritual" rule of Rome. The later suppression of the Order of the Templars and the great witch trials of the Middle Ages proved one thing; that the might of the Inquisition would not stand for even a *hint* of Gnostic belief to survive.

Gnosis, as a universal mystical experience was not about to simply die out. Too many people have experienced illumination without the intervention of priest or church in the course of world history for any mere political force to snuff out the reality of direct "knowing." The role of secret societies in the preservation of the Gnostic tradition is clear and still under-rated by most "straight" historians of religion. Under the cover of old folklore, popular songs, even games, the Gnostic wisdom survived. Often under cover of building trades, as in the case of the Masons, or camouflaged as small alchemical or humanist "study" groups, Gnostics met and continued their work in relative peace and quiet. The rise of the Renaissance Culture and its revival of the study of ancient texts even led to the "smuggling" of the Jewish form of Gnosticism, the Kabbalah, directly into the heart of the Vatican. Kabbalah was studied by Catholic priests as a "primitive" form of Christianity, when in reality it was a pure form of Gnosis. With the Protestant Reformation, Europe entered a period of sudden freedom from the chains of the Inquisition. Protestantism seemed to offer a hope for the Gnostics, and a veritable avalanche of secret orders descended upon Northern Europe. The Rosicrucians and their offspring, the Speculative Freemasons, are the best example of this sudden possibility in the air for a new Gnostic world-order. Protestantism, in the person of John Calvin, soon placed new shackles upon the population of Europe, but at least the death-grip of Rome had been broken for all time!

Gnosticism, as chaotic as it may appear from the outside, does have one central spiritual and political tendency which is fairly difficult to deny, since it is based on metaphysical reality. At the highest levels of the illuminative experience, all living beings are perceived as pure "monads"... Points of pure consciousness, beyond space, time, and even light. If this is the truth of the human condition: that all human beings are, as suggested in the *Constitution of the United States* (a document much influenced by Masonic and Illuminist ideals), *really* created equal, without need for priestcraft or state, then the European political order was nowhere near the potential reality. The great revolutions of the 18th and 19th Centuries certainly did have much Masonic and Illuminati influence behind them, but that is not to say that those secret societies *created* revolution. They essentially aided revolution as an essential aspect of the evolution of the Human Spirit.

If we were to search for the political aspect of the Gnostic belief system during the last three centuries, it would be found to be rooted in Continental Grand Orient Freemasonry (British and American Freemasonry is staunchly conservative and Christian), particularly in the Strict Observance and other Templarist forms of Masonry. It would also be found in the Bavarian Illuminati and all the other groups who attempted to act upon the metaphysical realities of the Gnostic experience in the political arena. Universalism, Anti-Imperialism, Libertarianism, Secularism and Anti-Clericalism all stem from the Gnostic *Weltanschauung*. It is no surprise that Karl Marx was a member of the quasi-Masonic "League of Just Men" before he developed his theories. The course of French, Italian and Sicilian Grand Orient Freemasonry during the period of the Great European revolutions, from 1789 to 1848, demonstrates a general Gnostic tendency that we can only term "antinomian"... A desire to replace centralized Christian Monarchy with individual determination in the spiritual and political realms... The power of the monad over the power of the priest and the king!

Now that I have essentially confirmed the basis of what the Christian conspiracy-mongers have been saying all along, it is time to examine why they say what they say and how they phrase it. The right-wing assumption that a well-organized international conspiracy to destroy Christian "civilization" was first widely broached in John Robison's 1798 book *Proofs of a Conspiracy*. He firmly believed that the Bavarian Illuminati had infiltrated Continental Freemasonry with the express intent of fomenting revolution against King and Pope. Robison is undoubtedly correct, and these groups were *factors* of revolution but certainly not the sole cause! They merely used the opportunity provided by centuries of pent-up popular hostility against oligarchy suddenly exploding into revolution. The great revolutions would have occurred whether the Masons and Illuminati had been there or not. These groups merely influenced the course of revolution toward the greatest degree of individual freedom, both spiritually and politically. Where Robison sees a plot to undermine Christian "order", the Gnostic sees great spiritual forces moving through the body politic, bringing humankind closer to self-realization.

Even before Robison printed his speculations, currents had been stirring in 18th

Century Europe that indicated that the Christian side had not been asleep. The formation of the Jesuit order as a virtual secret society in opposition to the Gnostic groups using the Reformation as "cover" (such as the Rosicrucians) was an open statement by the Papacy that Christianity could resort to mind-manipulation, secrecy, intrigue and assassination as well as anyone! As the Jesuits circulated through the royal courts of Europe and formed schools for the indoctrination of children, the Gnostics were moving on different levels. The foundation of Speculative Freemasonry in 1717 and the associated formation of the British Royal Society, demonstrated that the Gnostic interest was on two fronts... Antiquarian and scientific. By reviving an antiquarian version of an ancient Mystery Religion, the Masons were attempting to prove that the Gnostic Church had every inch the antiquity of the Catholic. The formation of the Royal Society was undoubtedly an attempt to create a secular, rational, scientific culture, far removed from the constrictions of Catholic dogma. The antiquarian side has had some influence, but the scientific has changed the world and seriously undermined the influence of Christianity amongst the educated classes.

By the time that Robison wrote his book, these massive forces had been battling each other for several centuries. His arch-conservative and fanatically Christian interpretation began to find serious supporters right about the same time that the Russian Revolution burst upon the world. Waves of anti-Masonic and anti-Semitic hatred were nothing new by the 1920s. They were often associated, because it was assumed that Masonry was a Kabbalistic plot (in truth, Kabbalah is but one aspect of Freemasonry). The famous discovery of papers being escorted by a member of the Bavarian Illuminati back in the 18th Century had sparked the first wave of conspiratorial hysteria, and the William Morgan Affair in the United States during the mid-1800s (it was assumed that several masons had kidnapped and murdered William Morgan because he had threatened to publish Masonic secrets) sparked a world-wide wave of anti-Masonic fervor. The third great wave of hysteria was the result of the Bolshevik revolution.

An outpouring of right-wing and rabidly Christian conspiracy volumes during the 1920s and 1930s demonstrated that the Inquisition was not as dead as everyone had assumed. The two classic conspiracy studies written during this period are still quoted from, *ad nauseam*, by contemporary conspiracy mongers. Nesta Webster's *Secret Societies and Subversive Movements* and Lady Queensborough's *Occult Theocracy*, brought the paranoid vision of Robison to new heights of imbalance! These two crusading defenders of Christian "decency" were accompanied by a third, less famous, figure, known only as "Inquire Within", or "Miss Stoddard", who claimed to have been high priestess of the Stella Matutina... (One of the many Golden Dawn offshoots during the first decades of the 20th Century.) A right-wing British newspaper, *The Patriot*, printed articles by all three women, along with anti-Semitic, anti-Masonic and anti-Bolshevik material of the most extreme rabidity.

Nesta Webster ultimately finds the Jews, in league with Satan, to be at the bottom of this dark anti-Christian force. The fact that she later gave her whole-hearted support to Benito Mussolini, and that she essentially accepted the scurrilous *Protocols of the Elders of Zion* as a genuine Jewish blueprint for world-domination, demonstrates, sufficiently, the cast of her attitudes. Her theory is burdened with wild suppositions, but the essential core thesis is simple: The Jews, Pagans, Gnostics, Communists, or anyone else with whom she diligently disagrees, felt themselves to have been usurped by Christianity as the dominant force in the world. Thusly, given her warped logic, they must be plotting the downfall of all that is good and pure! A much more insidious version of this intellectual "masterstroke" has it that such groups are genetically inferior and are therefore plotting to destroy the "rightful" Christian rulers of the world. That approach leads us directly to the crematoriums at Belsen, which would have undoubtedly horrified Nesta Webster, but given her pause for thought as to their ultimate utility.

Lady Queensborough harps upon one element that Mrs. Webster mentions only at the very end of her book... That Satan is the real force behind these secret societies and their infernal plots. Lady Queensborough's *Occult Theocracy* is more like the catalog of a schizophrenic's delusions than a serious historical study, yet the tendency to simply pile up mountain upon mountain of circumstantial evidence so common to this school finds its real origin point here. The paranoid style of conspiracy literature found its masterpiece in *Occult Theocracy.*

To the Jewish, Satanic and Gnostic menaces, "Inquire Within" adds the final touch. Her *Light Bearers of Darkness* and *Trail of the Serpent* adds the alluring powers of mesmerism, kundalini and sex magic to the already murky theories of her compatriots. The occultist element which Queensborough and Webster saw as a "front" for Jewish manipulation is here seen as a truly Gnostic menace, which rings somewhat nearer to the truth. "Inquire Within" also adds purely oriental elements, such as crazed Kali-worshippers and Thuggee to the mixture. With this trio of intrepid British conspiracy hunters, we find the stage set for our own contemporary version of Christian right-wing hysteria.

Fueled by the innate conservatism of the American Southwestern "Sun Belt" as exemplified in the growth of the John Birch Society, and a nascent trend toward alliance between Conservatism and Christian Fundamentalism in the "Bible Belt" of the American South, the 1960s saw the reissuing of all of these great conspiracy classics and a whole new wave of theorists working from that basis. The "Christian Book Club" in Hawthorne, California, began to reprint all the old titles and many new ones. The Millennarian influence with its dreams of Christians being swept up in instant "Rapture" just before Armageddon was another new source of conspiratorial theory. These authors tend to find the new menace in Humanism and Secularism as much as in Freemasonry and Illuminism. Tim LaHaye's *Battle for the Mind*, Martin's *Kingdom of the Cults* and Larson's *Book of Cults* all work this rich vein, however it is Salem Kirban, with his paranoid classics *666*, *1000*, *Satan's Angels Exposed* and a whole host of astonishing pamphlets who takes the cake! His vision of the world is based on a moment-to-moment fervent hope that God will imminently destroy all of these Satanic Gnostics and evil Humanists with the vengeance and fury of Holy War!

The Christian need for a scapegoat to explain both internal and external threats to their "God given" hegemony has been the omnipresent mark of a religion founded on the power of the Roman Empire and closely linked to mundane political power ever since. It is in the struggle to power that the early Church faced, that we find the essence of this psychological need to remain dominant at all costs. Christianity only seems to flourish in the presence of a tangible, or imagined, enemy, a phenomenon brilliantly chronicled by Norman Cohn in his classic *Europe's Inner Demons* and *In Pursuit of the Millennium*. This strange need for a scapegoat has paradoxically created a strong response from what was originally a weak and disorganized opponent – the Gnostic Religion. Today, the Gnostics are an important power hidden behind the mask of history; however they are by no means the all-powerful demons of right-wing Christian conspiracy theory. They are simply human beings with a different vision of spiritual truth. In that vision lies their persistence through the centuries and whatever power they may have to influence the course of history.

Bibliography

–∾– The Cardinal of Chile, *The Mystery of Freemasonry Unveiled*, The Christian Book Club of America, Hawthorne, California, USA 1957

–∾– Inquire Within, *Light-Bearers of Darkness*, The Christian Book Club of America, N.D. original edition, 1930

–∾– Inquire Within, *Trail of the Serpent*, Christian Book Club of America N.D., original edition, 1935

–∾– Webster, Nesta H., *Secret Societies and Subversive Movements*, Omni Publishers, Hawthorne, California, USA 1964

–∾– Miller, Edith Starr (Lady Queensborough), *Occult Theocracy*, The Christian Book Club of America 1980, original edition 1935

–∾– Robison, John, A.M., *Proofs of a Conspiracy*, The Americanist Classical Western Islands Press, Boston 1967, original edition 1798

–∾– McCabe, Joseph, *A History of Freemasonry*, Haldeman-Julius Publications, Girard, Kansas 1949

–∾– Winrod, Gerald B., *Adam Weishaupt: A Human Devil*, No Publisher or Date

–∾– Spenser, Robert Keith, *The Cult of the All-Seeing Eye*, The Christian Book Club of America, Hawthorne, California 1964

–∾– Cumbrey, Constance, *The Hidden Dangers of the Rainbow* (on the Aquarian Movement as a "Fourth Reich"!), Huntington House Inc., Shreveport, Louisiana 1983

–∾– Kirban, Salem, *Satan's Angels Exposed*, *The Rise of Antichrist*, *666* and *1000*, Salem Kirban, Inc., Huntingdon Valley, Pennsylvania 1980, 1978, 1970, respectively

–∾– LaHaye, Tim, *The Battle for the Mind*, Fleming H. Revell Co., Old Tappan, New Jersey 1980

–∾– Larson, Bob, *Larson's Book of Cults*, Tyndale Publishers, Inc. Wheaton, Illinois 1982

–∾– Cohn, Norman, *Europe's Inner Demons*, The New American Library, Inc., New York 1975

–∾– Lindsay, Hal, *The Late Great Planet Earth* and *The 1980's: Countdown to Armageddon*, both published by Bantam Books, New York, 1970 and 1981, respectively

–∾– Martin, Walter, *The Kingdom of the Cults*, Bethany Fellowship, Inc. Minneapolis, Minnesota 1965

Inauguration of Kenneth Anger

Carl Abrahamsson

The following essay was written in 1989, shortly before I met Anger the first time and while I was writing a thesis at the University of Stockholm on Crowley's influence in his work. Later on in this same volume you can find the interview done at our first meeting, in Los Angeles in 1990. Also, The Fenris Wolf 4 *(2011) has a transcript of a talk we had at the Danish Film School in 2008. – Ed.*

Kenneth Anger is one of those artists, like all truly great artists, who can be admired and appreciated on many different levels. You can see his films and enjoy them at face value, for their richness and beauty in colours, composition and movement. And you can see them as the magical gems, the potent talismans they also are. You can regard them as parts of the lifework of a Thelemic Magus, and as such objects of inspiration for us from someone who's relentlessly and lovefully involved in his own Great Work, and has been so since an early age.

Although Anger is often associated with the Avant Garde of American 1950s-1960s cinema, the "Underground", the "New American Cinema", his works are surely among the few that are timeless and have a value outside of this association. Now, why is this? What makes his films so appealing, both for students of cinema and for students of magic? Is the statement that Anger is the greatest Thelemic artist ever a "correct" one? What are the connections to Crowley and how do they show in Anger's films?

All this is currently a subject of study at the University of Stockholm, and this small article could be seen as a sketch for that work. I hope you'll find this piece enjoyable and that perhaps you'll find more details and love the films even more the next time you have the good fortune of seeing them...

I

Kenneth Anger was born in Santa Monica, California, in 1927. He grew up in Hollywood and, as a young child, attended tap-dancing classes together with celebrities like Shirley Temple and others. In 1934 he had a part in a Max Reinhardt & William Dieterle-collaboration called *A Midsummer Night's Dream*, in which he played a "changeling", a half human, half fairy creature.

In Beverly Hills High School he had friends like Miriam Marx, Groucho's daughter, and the general atmosphere of Hollywood and associating with people with enormous access to information and gossip, like Miss Marx in particular, shaped the young Anger into someone with a deep love and fascination for the dream-factory and its inhabitants. He's got one of the world's largest collections of hey-day stills and a vast selection of Hollywood memorabilia.

During the 50s he lived in Paris and worked at the French Cinémathèque as well as writing articles on films and life in the golden days of Hollywood. The articles were insights into the seamier sides of the seemingly all-glamorous lives of the Stars. Alcoholism, drugs, "depraved" sexuality, suicide, murder and other interesting aspects of stardom were all covered unscrupulously, but definitely with a sense of style and wit.

In 1959 the articles were compiled and published in France, under the title of *Hollywood Babylone*. It was published in the U.S. in 1966, however in a pirated, but hugely successful version. In 1975 the official edition came out and, a good thing for Anger, became tremendously successful too.

In the early 60s it was time for him to move back to America, to continue work on his films and to indulge in the newly arrived Age of Aquarius, with its psychedelic sensibility. These were prosperous times, with awards, successes and associations with many interesting people, such as Bobby Beausoleil and the Rolling Stones (more on them later...).

Anger has always been a keen traveler and in the early 70s he had his working- and living-base in England. During the 70s he shot what has become his latest publicly shown film, *Lucifer Rising*, released in 1980. And since then he has continued to make films, although not for public release, and to write. *Hollywood Babylon 2* was published in 1984 and has become another major hit.

Anger is not a very extrovert person, judging from the small amount of information available in film magazines and some compilation books. He lets his films speak, and speak they do, although not in an obvious manner or "language" to the "layman". He considers his magical life the most important thing, and the films are just one part of this. They are his "Magical Weapons", as he himself describes them. Some magicians are more inclined to keep to themselves (seemingly apparent in the case of artists working mainly with pictures. Anger is one example, Austin Spare another), whereas others aren't (prolific writers seem to be more extrovert, Crowley being the prime example...). This should naturally be respected, but it is also always a source of rumours and reputations not always true to real life. But perhaps that is what he wants...

II

Anger started making films at the very early age of seven. The family had a 16 mm camera and he used to get spare film to use for himself. His grandmother encouraged him in his fascination. In fact, she worked as a wardrobe mistress at United Artists and knew a lot of people in Hollywood. Among these was the German director Max Reinhardt, and she managed to have the director take a look at the young Anger (whose name was then something else...). Eventually he got the role as the changeling in the expressionistic *A Midsummer Night's Dream*, something which affected both his filmmaking (although a bit later on) and his interest in Hollywood.

Anger on the shooting: "They used real dwarves for the elves (they got them from a circus). The little girls who played fairies wore shredded cellophane – that's all they had on. Once the cellophane moonbeams on the set caught fire from the hot arc lights, and all these little girls got their asses singed. But nobody got hurt."

His first own film was one called *Ferdinand the Bull* (1937) and during the early 40s he made films with titles like *Who has been rocking my dream boat?*, *Escape Episode* and *Drastic Demise*. Most of these were recollections in cinema of material in his dream-diaries.

In 1947, on a weekend when his family was away to attend a funeral, he turned the house into a studio and, with the help of some sailor friends and a budget of just over a hundred dollars, he made the now legendary *Fireworks*. It depicts the homosexual fantasies of a young man, played by Anger himself, who seeks a companion, but gets beaten up by a gang of sailors. The film is very beautiful, shot in black and white and tinted blue. It has a distinct dreamlike atmosphere and was shot on a one-to-one ratio, that is, the takes that were used were the only ones shot.

He managed to get it screened in the San Francisco art circuit and the film got the attention it deserved. Through these and other new contacts, *Fireworks* was awarded prizes in Brussels, Cannes and Paris. Experimental Cinema's grand old man at the time, Jean Cocteau, expressed his liking for this powerful film (some say because it reminded him of his opium dreams). He claimed that "it touches the quick of the soul and this is very rare".

Cocteau invited Anger to Europe, and he went there in late 1949, to stay for four years. Before leaving he completed a film called *Puce Moment*; which is a short version of a never completed project called *Puce Women*.

He worked on many projects during this stay in France, but only a few were completed, which is a shame. A film of the Cocteau ballet *Le jeune homme et la mort* was made as a demo film for a 35 mm production, but this one was never made, and the demo version has never been shown. Also, scenes were shot for an Anger production of *Les chants de Maldoror* but due to lack of funds, this project couldn't be completed, which is really tragic. A cinematic vision of Lautréamont by Anger would have been really interesting...

In 1950 though, he made a film called *La lune des lapins*, but it wasn't really released until 1972. One quite significant thing about Anger is that he seems to be constantly revising his films. For instance, *La lune des lapins* was re-released in 1979 with a new soundtrack, and this has been the case with most of his productions, like with *Lucifer Rising* and *Inauguration of the Pleasure-dome*.

"Someone like D.W. Griffith (with *Intolerance*) never had two prints that were the same. Every print he'd be juxtaposing and re-cutting it." (Anger in *Film Culture*, 1966)

While in Paris he also edited Eisenstein's *Que Viva Mexico*, according to the director's original script and comments, something which could be seen as a homage, since this was one of the first films that made him realize the complete power of cinema. His grandmother had taken him to an outdoor screening, a double-bill of *Que Viva Mexico* (the Sol Lesser 1933 *Thunder Over Mexico* version) and *The Singing Fool* with Al Jolson, and this was also something that changed his life

Eaux d'Artifice is the name of the film made in 1953. Anger shot it in Tivoli in

Italy and it's a beautiful display of cascading fountains, carved rock faces and a midget dressed in 18th century clothing, apparently lost in Tivoli's lingering labyrinths.

In 1954, back in California, he went to a masquerade party and became so inspired that he convinced his friends at that time (among others Samson DeBrier, the authoress Anaïs Nin, and Marjorie Cameron, the wife of the famous scientist and magician John Parsons, who was once going to be Crowley's "magical son") to play in a film version of it.

He wanted to combine his memories from that night with mythology and ritual, and *Inauguration of the Pleasuredome* is the result.

Filmed over a short time, with the party's participants (many have various roles in the film), it stands out as one of the most beautiful films ever made. The basic setting is a party held by Lord Shiva for Kali, Pan, Isis, Osiris, Astarte and others. Yage is served and frenzied pleasure and power-play, expressed in many hallucinatory superimpositions and effective montage, become the results of the magnificent party.

Anaïs Nin writes about the film and the shooting in her diaries (Volume 5): "There was a distortion. Love became hatred, ecstasy became a nightmare. Those who began with a sensual attraction ended by devouring each other." The film has many levels, not just of celluloid, but also in its mythological and magical contents. It is a truly personal vision of Anger's own blend of Thelema, various mythologies interconnected and a very special sense of humour. Anaïs Nin again: "We all felt we needed to know the meaning of Kenneth's dream, so that we could act in it. But he did not confide in us. The scenes seemed disconnected, and the characters changed costumes and personalities. There was chaos because the theme was unknown."

The film was presented once in Brussels on three screens, but the most famous version is the *Sacred Mushroom Edition*-one from 1966, which also includes a prelude called *Anger Aquarian Arcanum* – a display of some of Crowley's paintings and Crowley reading Coleridge's poem *Kubla Khan*.

Another good friend of Anger's at the time was the sexologist Professor Alfred Kinsey. This man had acquired a great deal of old pornographic films from police archives, and Anger had helped him look through and review them all. Professor Kinsey knew of Anger's interest in Crowley and was himself interested in the erotic mural paintings that Crowley had made in the villa at the Abbey of Thelema in the 1920s. So, in 1955, they went together to Sicily, where the Abbey was situated. Anger removed the white paint that the locals had put on over the paintings just after Crowley had been "evicted" from Italy. This took three months and Anger also shot a film called *Thelema Abbey*, for British television.

In 1963 his next big project was completed, a 30 minute film called *Scorpio Rising*. Anger had returned from Europe and traveling in the early 60s, to find a new kind of culture emerging, a youthful one, filled with machines, violence and rock'n'roll... The Age of Aquarius with Scorpio Rising.

All of these things are depicted in Anger's presentation of a Brooklyn motorcycle-gang and their love for, and affectionate work with, their bikes. Scenes from their garages, a party and a race are inter-cut with scenes from an old Jesus-movie called *The Road to Jerusalem* and scenes from Laslo Benedek's *The Wild One* with Marlon Brando.

All this to a soundtrack of perfectly fitting classic rock'n'roll-tunes by Elvis Presley, The Surfaris, Ray Charles, The Randells and others.

"When I came back, I spent the first part of the summer of 1962 at Coney Island on the beach under the board-walk. The kids had their little transistors, and had them on. It's one of the things that I call a magical happening, the way it worked out, because every single song that I used in *Scorpio* came out at the time I made the film." (*Film Culture*, 1966)

This theme, of youth and a new culture of machines, was continued in *Kustom Kar Kommandos* (1965), and after this Anger started working on a film based on Crowley's poem *Hymn to Lucifer*, called *Lucifer Rising*, as well as completing the *Sacred Mushroom* edition of *Inauguration.*

He was now living in San Francisco in the midst of everything going on there in the mid-60s, and he also made friends with the Rolling Stones. They became quite interested in magic, especially Brian Jones, Mick Jagger and Anita Pallenberg... "Brian was a witch too. I'm convinced. He showed me his witch's tit. He had a supernumary tit in a very sexy place on his inner thigh. He said: 'In another time they would have burned me.' He was very happy about that." (Anger in *The Rolling Stones - The first twenty years*)

The original idea was to have Mick Jagger as Lucifer and Keith Richard as Beelzebub, but for some reason this didn't work out. Another musician, one from the San Francisco in-crowd fave band Love, Bobby Beausoleil, was the next one to play Lucifer. A lot of material was shot, but after some disagreement, Beausoleil took off and stole the shot material. Anger put a curse on him, and Beausoleil's car broke down just by Death Valley, where he then met Charles Manson and his Family. They buried the reels in the desert and Manson later tried to get 10.000 dollars from Anger for the kidnapped celluloid. They're both in prison now. Beausoleil for the Hinman murder and Manson for organizing the Tate-La Bianca murders. Later on, Anger and Beausoleil became friends again, and a soundtrack for a later version of *Lucifer Rising* was recorded by Beausoleil in prison.

But at the time of the theft, in 1967, Anger was naturally extremely depressed and even put in an ad in *The Village Voice* in October, stating his death as a filmmaker and burning several of his old prints before the eyes of Jonas Mekas and many others of his underground filmmaker friends.

However, luckily for us, he took up working again soon after this and edited *Invocation of my Demon Brother* (completed in 1969), which consists of material from a performance ritual he did in San Francisco in 1967, some odd bits that were still around from the original *Lucifer Rising* and scenes from the Rolling Stones concert in Hyde Park in 1969. Mick Jagger improvised the soundtrack for the film on one of the first Moog synthesizers.

He also made a film of Brian Jones' funeral in Cheltenham in July 1969, but this is one of the films he's never shown publicly. And, as mentioned earlier, he traveled a lot with a new cast (including Marianne Faithful) and shot *Lucifer Rising*, which was completed in 1980. In it, we can see Isis and Osiris joining forces to awaken Lucifer-Horus, the bringer of Light. This film can certainly be seen as the most explicitly Thelemic one, with Crowley actually appearing in (subliminal) pictures, and with students holding the

Stele of Revealing and Anger doing a ritual as the Magus.

Since the release of *Lucifer Rising,* Anger has been busy traveling around, showing his films and giving lectures, as well as completing the second volume of *Hollywood Babylon*. He is currently working on a film version of the two books for Edward Pressman Films. This will surely (and hopingly) become a success on a similar scale as the books, which will in turn bring him more money to more projects. Let's all hope...

III

When discussing Thelema in Art, you must be clear in realizing that this could have two meanings. An artist unaware of "Thelema", yet completely and successfully engaged in his work, could naturally be seen as "thelemic", as well as one very much aware of it all. In Anger's case, we have an example of a brilliant artist, thelemic both in method and aim. This is a very rare combination, and certainly a very interesting one.

All of his works are descriptions/interpretations of what's going on around us now, in the early stages of the Aeon of Horus. And, as with Crowley's poems for instance, these observations are often presented in a mythological and magical context, sometimes difficult to grasp at first sight, but always very clear in structure and shape once you get to know them properly.

Fireworks is not merely a homosexual fantasy. It's also very much a statement of clarity of one's own sexuality, an initiation into the Self, something necessary to everyone aspiring for magical development. It is said to be partly based on Crowley's *Liber 671* (*Liber Pyramidos*), which is basically just that, a ritual of Self Initiation. "It's very rare to have spiritual insights before you're thirty... I started when I was seventeen or eighteen." (Anger in *Film Threat,* no. 14)

Inauguration involves various mythological deities: Isis and Osiris, Astarte and Hecate, Shiva and Kali, Lilith and Pan, all at the same party and ecstatic ritual. Shiva is the master of ceremonies and prepares by dressing up in rich jewels. He controls the party, while Kali/The Scarlet Woman overlooks the power-play. The women cling to Pan, who's been given poison by Shiva. Astarte tries to reach for the moon, and Hecate, also associated with the moon, is angry and raving, since the Yage was stolen from her.

The truly fantastic thing about *Inauguration*, apart from the fact that it is so bombastically beautiful, is that every screening seems to tell you more, to show how everything is interconnected, to give us visual stimulation while studying Crowley's *Magick In Theory and Practice*, *Liber 777*, and other major thelemic works.

Scorpio Rising is a magical comment on the newly born Age of Aquarius with its Scorpio attributes: sex, electricity, machines, violence. A brilliantly edited display of people dedicated to a "sub" culture, their kinds of rituals and their kinds of gods: Brando and Hitler on one side and Jesus on the other. Anger: "The Age that ended in 1962 was the Piscean Age, the Age of the Fish, which was the Age of Jesus Christ. Where the Piscean Age was ruled by Neptune, the planet of mysticism, the Aquarian Age is ruled by Uranus, the most erratic planet of all... It's the sign of the unexpected, revolution, for one thing... The last 2000 years were based on renunciation, sacrifice and guilt. The fight for the next generation, the next 25 years, 50 years, just the beginning of the fight really, is skinning off the shell that's left over from the last era." (*Film Culture*, 1966)

The 1966 version of *Inauguration*, the *Sacred Mushroom Edition*, was, as mentioned, presented together with *Anger Aquarian Arcanum* and is such a powerful display of Crowley, mythology and the power and force of magic, that it surely must have made a lot of people "aware", not just in a psychedelia-induced way, but also in a magical sense, unparalleled in force to any other work of cinema in history.

And *Lucifer Rising*, seen by some as Anger's "Magnum Opus", is definitely the most effective of his films in displaying the thelemic mythology. Beautifully and relentlessly edited, it presents Isis, Osiris, their ritual, nature's response and the birth of Lucifer-Horus, the bringer of Light to the world in the new Aeon. Rituals are taking place at magical and Pagan sites in Egypt, Germany and England, all in celebration of "the crowned and conquering child". This film is also by far the best and most suggestive homage ever to Sergei Eisenstein – a working result of his theories of montage.

And, naturally, you could consider and label all of Anger's films and all of his writings "Magickal", since they are all part of his life. Which is "Magick".

I will end this short essay with a quote from Crowley's *Magick*, which I find illuminating in studying Anger – the filmmaker as well as the Magus...

"Every man that becomes a Magician helps others to do likewise. The more firmly and surely men move, and the more such action is accepted as the standard of morality, the less will conflict and confusion hamper humanity."

An Interview with Genesis P-Orridge

Carl Abrahamsson

The following interview with Psychic TV and Temple ov Psychick Youth mastermind Genesis P-Orridge was done at Times Square Studios in London in the summer of 1988, in a break between sessions for the Tekno Acid Beat-*album. Temple Records' involvement with the British Acid House scene gained Psychic TV very positive reviews and a good response worldwide, which was quite a change in regard to P-Orridge's musical endeavours on many levels. On other levels, however, British media's focussing on smearing P-Orridge in every possible way was still in full swing. – Ed.*

Why is it, do you think, that people can't, or won't, understand what Thee Temple is doing?

Why would so called professional journalists get themselves into the position of deciding in advance what they're going to like? Which is what they actually do. They've made up the story. Why would someone, who would probably, in other circumstances, say that they're an intelligent person...? I mean, who are they trying to serve by going out looking, preferably for victims without the power to strike back or speak back, and then do their very best to distort, destroy and hurt those people?

The psychology of that behaviour on a mass level is very disturbing. It's far more disturbing than what we may or may not be doing in private for our own philosophical reasons. That's the bit that's scary. Not what we're doing or not doing. How do they justify it to themselves when they go home? What do they do when they're lying in bed or watching TV or having a coffee? How can they just sit there, knowing that they do not care about the truth? Or are they so utterly perverted and morally corrupt that they actually believe there is a justification for that behaviour? Do they actually feel so totally right that they're the equivalent of a Fundamentalist Muslim terrorist? Or the equivalent of the person who assassinated John Lennon? Because that's the level they're at in terms of behaviour. They're no different to the "Son of Sam", who'll invent a glossary of terms, a pseudo *raison d'être*... In order to justify random violence, which is what they're doing. It's just random media violence.

It's terrorism basically. Blackmail and terrorism. And if one actually took these people to a rational court of law and prosecuted them, those would have to be the charges... Intimidation, protection racket, blackmail, violence and abuse, child abuse. When they attack families they're also threatening them as well. I'm sure, if you went up to them and said: "Do you enjoy being a child abuser?", they'd say "What are you talking about?

You're mad...". That's what they're doing. That's what *Sunday People* are doing with us. Caresse (P-Orridge's oldest daughter. – Ed.) has to go to school, and depending on what they invent and fantasize, she may well get intimidated by other people at school.

Does she have a private tutor?

No, she goes to the normal primary school. That's the bit that's really disturbing. Why do they decide to pick on us? Because we choose not to be secretive. That's the irony. I'm sure they'll try and imply that we're all very secretive. But, as you know yourself, anyone who wants to send in five pounds can get the same information from us as anyone else. And has been able to for seven years...

So we've not exactly been secretive. Far from it. What we try to do is make available more information of an esoteric or behavioural kind to give people more options as to what they can choose to be like. They may choose to be totally "normal". There's nothing wrong with that. But they may also choose to be less normal, given that they find out what else is possible. I think that they are scared, presumably of our power, that it may be growing. It's one of the great ironies of Western civilization that honesty is one of the things feared most: All the churches and religions in the West fear honesty, because they're based on intimidation and the threat of infinite violence when you die, which is a very bizarre thing to base a religion on. Eternal violence to your spirit and soul.

I think we're very honest people. And I think that terrifies a country that is conditioned into dishonesty. People at the very top of the pyramid are dishonest, totally, and corrupt. And also privileged enough to do whatever they want in private and cover it up afterwards, whether it would be Watergate or visiting prostitutes or whatever. Occasionally they hand over a scapegoat to the media, in order to cover up a much larger amount of corruption and cesspool behavior. But primarily the privileged ruling classes of all types are allowed one morality and the rest of us, who are not "true" human beings – according to them we're a lower breed – are not allowed to do what they don't tell us to. So, if they say "You're not allowed to have gay sex", 99.9 % of the population are legally not allowed to, by that 0.1 %. And if we don't like that decision we're physically intimidated by armies, police, courts, the press, mass-media and economic threats as well.

So, if you really look at the whole process, it's political. It's about political control. And obviously, we have for 20 odd years spoken out very clearly against control – political, behavioural, social and economic. It's not very surprising that one or two puppets of the powers that be have been trained and placed in those positions because they're so stupid. They can be convinced that they are a part of a moral crusade.

Would Thee Temple ever take sides in a party-political stance?

We would never support one or another party, because we go on a pragmatic level from the cause itself, whether it'd be animal rights or children's right or whatever. This week it could be rhinos and the next it could be a community nursery. One of the things that always surprises me is how few people have bothered to note how much overtly political action we take, both in our relationship with the media and in our day-to-day life.

Psychic TV get quite a lot of good reviews and a lot of attention. Isn't there ever anything positive on Thee Temple?

In Britain? In the world, yeah... We've had good positive response in America and Japan and Germany, all over. But at the same time there's also usually an anti-response, because what we're doing is deliberately challenging the status quo. And we're challenging inherited moral values, saying "I refuse to accept that you, the authorities, the educational system, my so called elders, my social parents, know implicitly what is or is not right and wrong". We tend to follow the American Indian philosophy that women and children are sacred and should never be abused and attacked. And that everybody, male, female, child, animal and the ground that we walk upon are a part of a food chain and a survival chain. You cannot separate any of those elements at all. As soon as you attempt to separate them, there is somewhere a form of death.

If you build a concrete city over the land, you have separated the people in the city from the earth and in some way a part of their spirit and the earth spirit on that spot will die from that separation. And thereby you can start to see why people in cities are so neurotic. They're not in contact with the vast part of their environment anymore. They physically cannot touch it a lot of the time. That must be very damaging. People say, "Why rhinos?" Well, the child of a rhino that's killed this week is the child of the woman next door in ten years' time. Because I honestly believe that the authorities in Britain and all the countries in the world are now terrified of the onrush of an ecological, economic and medical explosion of disasters. The scale is so immense that their old techniques of lying and intimidating will be irrelevant very soon. It will be down to the people on the street inventing ways to survive, if possible. And it won't even be a rebellion against authority, it'll just be, "How do we stay alive?" And at that point Thee Temple is trying to set up a structure, a philosophy, which re-teaches the concept of a contemporary tribal appreciation of life, so that you do realize that when we talk about caring it's not enough anymore to care for your nearest and dearest. You have to care for anyone who gives you respect. That tribe is not in the old sense of all living in one small tented village. That tribe is spread, scattered across the globe, and it's a tribe of those who attempt to perceive what's happening. And in their own mind, not contribute to the damage anymore where possible. It's not the normal old-fashioned tribe, because the world has changed.

If we were all in the Amazon-basin, and they weren't knocking it down, we could probably build a village and live in it as a tribe. But it's not like that. We live all over the world at the moment, but there are, and have to be, methods of regaining the best aspects of tribal living, which are pulling resources. Those with the right skills do that job, because it saves time and effort. If somebody knows how to do computers, they do the computer for everyone. And somebody else who can cook, cooks for everyone. They have equal value. There is no hierarchy anymore. There's just, "Who gets things done and who doesn't?" If someone can write, then they write the story and history of the tribe. And in return they get fed. It's very simple basic re-learning of how life actually is.

Because that process is going on all the time, but it's being clouded and disguised and camouflaged so much by the way the authority-side and conditioning-side of society has gone, that it's very hard for anyone to grasp it or see it anymore.

Do you feel optimistic? Do you think that Thee Temple will be able to... ?

I think that Thee Temple can at the very least leave behind various useful starting points, working models and information. That's why the book publishing is going to be important, and that's why things like records and tapes and so on are important. Interviews are less and less important. We're at the level now where we just do it. Talking about it is usually a waste of time and energy. You sit down and think "Should I talk to a music journalist who's ill-informed and prejudiced for three hours or should I go out and help a child to get to the hospital?" I would go and help the child to the hospital, because it's more important. And soon that's going to be what we're all thinking about. It's odd, because whilst it can appear to be very unselfish, in actual fact it's not. It's also totally selfish, because we're trying to learn as fast as possible how to all survive and get the most to survive for all of us and the people we can get in contact with. It's one of those interesting philosophical contradictions, that in order to be self-preserving one has to be totally selfless wherever possible. And that is something that works on the American Indian level.

We learned so much from just being with that American Indian Shaman "Nomad" for just two-three days, about how to look at things in circles. You have your own individual person circle and then other people have theirs and no one really has the right to invade anyone else's circle. Then you have a larger circle of a family and then the tribal circle and then the natural circle, which is the entire planet. The other thing we learned was something that confirmed what we've always felt and dealt with, which is that dreams are an equal reality to so called waking reality. And they're part of more circles. The concept of invasion into anyone else's circle has become clearer and exactly what is happening now with the *Sunday People* is a kind of rape basically. I see the people who perpetrate that, day in, day out, week in, week out, year in, year out, as the most despicable examples of modern capitalist society, because they should know better, and they do the vilest hurt, the most publicly, with the least possibility of anyone calling them to task.

And it's very cynical too, because every human being knows what goes on with the ecological balance, but... It's pure cynicism.

They go and do an article on some old man who likes *Alice in Wonderland*... That was in last week. And say that he's a pædophile because he likes *Alice in Wonderland*. Yet you can go to all these bookshops in Britain and buy books with pictures of Lewis Carroll, and of girls. Who decides when it's OK to like them purely as esthetics and it's OK to like them slightly more?

And you had the same problem with the D.O.A.*-cover... (A record by Throbbing Gristle,* *which contained a photograph in which one could see a young girl's panties. – Ed)*

Yeah! It's never gone away. We always said Throbbing Gristle, TG, was dealing with the concept of reporting, journalism in a way, and in the presentation of information, so that people are prejudiced one way or another, by what you tell them about the information. That information war is still going on. In a way far more violently, because there are more desperate people about.

So the ideal for us might be a Psychick Colony somewhere?

The ideal is to have Psychick colonies. If you have one colony, only one bomb is needed to destroy it. You have Psychick Youth colonies for those who want to make the gesture of devoting 24 hours a day of their life forever to standing up and saying, "I believe that this is one of the solutions to the problems that are coming and have arrived." It's also a way of relearning humanity, because this is psychotherapy, psychodrama, behavioural therapy, stress therapy, all those things. A family unit is a hell of a stress, learning to deal with four or five people. To learn to deal with 20 people is unheard of in our society and it's pathetic really that it's so hard for people... But at the same time people can be part of Thee Temple and totally integrated on the surface with the way things go on day to day, working in television, working anywhere...

But aware in their own minds that when they make decisions that in any way involve morality, that they can choose that which gives rather than excludes. Our society seems to be involved in a perpetual attempt at exclusion of minorities, or exclusion of different ways of thinking. And yet all the great leaps forward philosophically, scientifically, politically are made by those who come up with the non-status quo-ideas. The radical renegade idea is the idea that always, so far, has saved the human race, quite literally. The thing that has NEVER saved any civilization is violently shoring up the old order. There is no evidence ever throughout human history of that working. And yet these morons at the top of the pyramid continue endlessly to repeat this loop of more violence, more authority, more repression, over and over. There has never been an example...

If you even take the fundamental Christians, who come around crucifying non-Christians. The evidence was that Jesus, who was one of a small number of radicals, if you accept the story at all for the argument, was crucified and destroyed with his band of people. But did it stop the idea? Of course it didn't. They can't read their own evidence, these people. They just turn their back and run away. You have to go a long way back in history, or you have to go across the globe and you have to look at the examples of what we're always told are "primitive" cultures, to discover where a healthy integration of all the aspects of life, from giving birth, to dying, to illness, to madness, to menstruation, to puberty, to celebration, all of these things: dreaming, being awake, making music, making food, all those things are integrated in such a way that there is a permanent sense of balance and harmony. We call that a "primitive" culture... And then we look at our culture, where we have germ warfare, permanently institutionalized violence by the police and the army and the psychiatrists and the politicians. And we have people put in concrete blocks and we have the persecution of any minority that says "I don't agree..." And we call that civilized. It may sound like a very simplistic thing to say, but sadly, that simple observation is still considered to be anarchic, dangerous, subversive, destructive, and Satanic.

If that's Satanic, then yeah, I'm a Satanist. But what does that mean? I don't believe in any gods. I believe that gods are early attempts at psychology, trying to understand the light and dark side of human nature. The deeper part of human nature where you go right inside yourself, beyond dreams and into those recesses which we should look into, but we're out of practice in our culture. And you give it names.

And that helps when you're telling stories, because they come from a time when there was no written history primarily. You can tell people something much clearer with a parable than with the very abstract theory of mathematical formulas. You tell a story about a squirrel and a rabbit to a child and they remember it.

If you say "x-3y2y-", they'll go, "What?" That's where that comes from. I've got nothing against using that terminology to explain how human beings are and how they can relate and how they can support and expand each other's consciousness.

Most of the Pagan gods are aspects of the human nature.

Of course. Why do you think that the Christian ethic is so terrified by Pagans? Because it works as examples of behaviour. Christianity's basic tenet is "Be good now, agree, or else we will punish you forever and ever when you're dead. And we may punish you while you're alive..."

That's an incredibly sick social pseudo-religion. And certainly has nothing to do with the ecstatic mysticism of the original Christianity, the Gnostic Christianity, which of course was destroyed by the Romans and St. Paul. St. Paul was the equivalent of a CIA-agent, who literally killed off the rival disciples and then mutated and totally altered philosophy, for his own ends and for the ends of Rome. What happened then with the Christian church? It became the Roman Church. Romans basically sent in their own agents and subverted the idea. From then on it was Roman bastardization for political and social ends.

We're scapegoats. It's odd that I keep being picked on in Britain. I don't think I'm that important. I don't even flirt with or contact the media really anymore. I just get on with trying to honestly develop a way of life that can be applied in different territories. Like with you, you're going to go to Scandinavia and you're in Scandinavia. I'm not Scandinavian, so I'm not trying to impose my vision. Here's what I've discovered:

I'm 38 and for all my faults I have spent most of those 38 years searching determinedly and genuinely for ideas that work and ideas that help. Not everyone maybe, but some people. If they work and if they make any kind of sense, the only way to check is to give them to other people and see if it works. If it helps one or two or ten or fifteen, that's a massive improvement on what most human beings do in their life to help anyone. If it helps a few hundred or a few thousand, that's incredible. But it doesn't prove anything about me, except that some of my observations of the way that life goes on were correct enough to relate to other people, who then, hopefully, expand upon it in their own way and in their own experience and develop it further.

I think your idea of mixing in the Scandinavian gods and myths is brilliant. Just as in America it should bring in the American Indians. And if it was Japan, they should try and look into Japanese cultural history, Shinto or some obscure little group of mystics in Japan that someone's forgotten, who were also trying to have an integrated constructive and functional way of life that included the concept of total mental and psychic evolution. I'm interested in human beings evolving beyond this primitive state of violence into a state where if somebody stood up and said "I'm a politician" or "I'm a priest" or "I'm a colonel", everybody would just burst out laughing and walk off. And that one individual would be able to do nothing about it, because nobody would understand what they were talking about anymore. It'd be irrelevant. "What does that mean? Religion? Never heard of that... Armies? Fighting? For the sake of it?"

It should be irrelevant by now, because it's stupid, it's uneconomic, it serves no purpose except destruction. If everyone was trained, taught, given the example of pulling all their skills, ideas, resources and knowledge in order to get the best for everybody, they would get the best too! Not being selfless, but being totally and utterly selfish, in a way. Then there'd be no problem at all, anywhere. It wouldn't become viable as a thing that could happen. It would be beyond the vocabulary of anyone's experience.

Somebody said, "Look, we can't chop down the Amazon basin, because it's just bad news for everyone..." Then everybody should go, "Yeah! I don't want to bloody die... Don't do it!"

The biggest answers are so simple. If we live in a world where people are being trained to be selfish, let's tell them: This is the ultimate selfish idea... It's called, "Getting the most out of your life, for the least cost, and staying alive! And no one hurts you!" It's so obvious, if you just go back and check anybody's history anywhere. When do the problems come? When anyone tries to be in control! When they refuse to share a bit of food, a bit of information, a bit of skill.

In Western societies today, you vote for a party every third, fourth, fifth year or so. But when you've voted for "your" party, you can't really control what happens.

Of course not! Also, in Britain, there hasn't been a government with an actual majority of vote since the war. There are three or more parties. It's the number of seats they get, not the number of votes. The Tory party usually gets about 30 % of the votes, but they get the most seats, because a lot of people don't bother to vote, a lot of people vote for the other two parties. So you have a situation permanently where 70 % of the people who live here have a government which they voted against. That's a really odd situation!

The 30 % who voted for the minority government, as you say, half of those at least, once they've made that one gesture of voting, can do nothing about what actually happens. They could suddenly be disenfranchised and told "You're never going to vote again!", which I suspect will happen within the next ten or fifteen years. I really suspect that it's certainly more than an equal chance that in Britain, voting will become no more than a cosmetic charade, as it is in Russia and everywhere else. It's even possible that the Tory party might declare the equivalent of a one-party system. The way they're going on, they're doing that without bothering to declare it anyway...

How come you became interested in Acid House?

That review in the *Melody Maker* seems to sum it up pretty much.

Do you see it as a good vehicle to affect people on the dance floor?

Oh yes, that, but actually it's the first time in years that I've heard a style of music that I've actually enjoyed. We've been saying since the first "Hyperdelic" things that we wanted to find a fusion between psychedelic attitudes and technology to take Hyperdelic one step further than Psychedelic. We spent most of last year experimenting with different ways of achieving that. With *Godstar* and the other things we got the Hyperdelic Rock Effect, but not a true dance floor-effect that was contemporary and worked regardless of itself. It was last September/October that we recorded the *Superman* one. A long time ago... At which point there had been no articles at all in Britain about Acid House, or even House, bar the Soul-type House music. The words hadn't even been coined. We always said that the best ideas are those which are inevitable. Like TG and Industrial Music was inevitable. That's why it took off and that's why it made sense to so many people. The same thing with House. The faster speed works on the body in a much more overt way and TG and Psychic TV and many other people have learned, a long time ago, that spinning in tapes on a very constant rhythm is interesting. So, in a way, it's just what we've always done! It's ironic that the solution we were looking for was what we did anyway... Just homing in on one aspect of it, which was the repeated rhythm. More extreme use of effects, with found information laid on top. That's what *Jack the Tab* is and that's what the *Superman* record is, with Timothy Leary talking all the way through.

Where does "Jack the Tab" originate from?

A guy called Richard Norris, who started Bam Caruso, the psychedelic re-release label, and he also started that magazine – *Strange Things* – came up with that. He came to interview us for *Strange Things* and I was telling him how we were working on these ideas for Acid Dance and so on. He got really into the idea of it and said "Let's do something together... Let's really push this together and join forces, Bam Caruso and Temple and you and me." Castalia is the name I suggested for the label. The Castalia Foundation was where Timothy Leary and everyone used to do all their experiments. Whenever we're together we just come up with these phrases. He came up with "Jack the Tab". We thought that was a really good one. Then he rang me up one night and said, "Somebody asked what 'Tab' means?" And I said, "Techno Acid Beat", which came straight out of the top of my head without a thought. And now they're calling the Detroit Acid House "Techno"... And yet this was in February or so. I would argue that the reason that that's happening for me is the result of the way that Thee Temple works, in analysis and ability to have a cumulative increase in intuitive abilities, which is what is the best side effect.

It's just amazing how much is happening to you everyday, even though I always knew it was possible. The day that you and I went to see Brian Jones' grave, I was sitting in the car and I almost said something to Paula, but something interrupted my thought. I was going to say, "Remind me next week to buy *After the Goldrush* by Neil Young", because I used to have that record and I really liked it, and I'd like to listen to it again.

On Monday I went into the office and there's a fax from New York saying, "Would you like to contribute a track to a compilation album for charity which will all be cover versions of Neil Young-songs?" I hadn't thought about Neil Young since who knows when... I just faxed straight back and said, "I'm already working on it!" It's getting more and more constant, that kind of thing.

Does it come back on a regular basis?

Yeah.

I get those things sometimes.

It gets more and more. All I can say is, persevere, because I've been doing this for 20 years and it's getting to be constant now.

It's a wonderful feeling.

It's great, because you realize that you are actually beginning to control events, or at least be so linked with them that you have fastest response. Often the people who survive in survival situations are the ones with the fastest response: finding the food, turning round in time not to get hit by a lion, whatever it may be. Knowing to move just before someone's going to attack you. That's the sort of faculty that we all once had.

If you go to an American Indian, they'll wonder why you bother to talk about it, because to them that's a day-to-day way of life as it's always been. It's rather sad that in Western society we have to remember how to be that way. But it's still useful! Even in this technological society, it's very useful. And when I get that review of *Jack the Tab* it just confirms what I felt, because that LP is exactly the product of trusting that intuition.

Is this one (that you're recording now) going to be the follow-up to Jack the Tab*?*

This is more "voodoo", more of an incantation.

Could you tell me something about the problems with DC Comics?

Oh, it's not very interesting. We wanted to bring out the promo version of the *Tune in...*-record. The thing was that we discovered, as you've probably realized yourself from being in London a few days, is that there is a massive amount of prejudice against Psychic TV and me. People go out of their way to try and stop other people being interested enough to listen to what we're saying. That's actually a compliment, but it's still a pain in the arse. Rather than just pretend that's not true, we thought we'd just experiment and bring this out under a different name, so that it gets listened to purely for whether or not it works on the dance floor.

"So we won't put Temple Records on it, but let's see if we can make a little joke about it being Acid House..." So we were thinking, as it says in *Cut Magazine*, about the old Acid blotters, the Acid tabs that had Superman on them. We thought that could be fun. We could do a series of Acid House records with different Acid-tab-characters on... We weren't thinking about Superman, the comic strip person at all. The only clue was the Psychick Cross in his hand. So we did 1000 copies of it and gave away 500 to clubs and so on, and it worked. People really liked it and it started going in all the dance charts. Then, unfortunately, someone gave DC Comics a copy that they got from the Rough Trade shop and they, quite rightly, said: "You can't do this... This is our copyright." And it dawned on us, because we'd been looking at it from another angle. From their point of view we were using "Superman". We thought we were using Acid tabs. It's just one of those conceptual different aspects...

Has it been re-released now?

We re-cut the new mixes. They sent a very heavy letter, saying: "You can't do this. Withdraw and give us everything and destroy all the artwork..." We said: "Yes, we're really sorry", because we were. We never intended to antagonize them and we were never going to sell that version in the shops with that logo. It would have come out as Psychic TV. We just wanted to prove that Psychic TV could make a dance record.

And then there was the M.E.S.H.*- one. Has there been anything else?*

Well, there's the yellow one, the picture disc. That's the origins of our Acid House-stuff too. And if you think of the *Condole*-one, the long one, that's more "Voodoo Acid". We did the yellow one and *Jack the Tab* in four days here, both of them from beginning to end.

The track on the B-side, was that supposed to have been in the Godstar*-film?*

That last bit? Yeah, that's Brian Jones talking about surrealism; off a really old film that I got hold of from 1965. It was never released. It's really bad quality, but it's better than no film at all.

I spoke to someone at Temple Records and they said that the original Thee Starlit Mire *is going to come out soon.*

That one's coming out as a limited edition-picture disc called *Allegory and Self*, which is an Austin Spare-title. It'll come out as a normal album here and in America as well. A lot of material on it is still very interesting, and it really needs a commentary, because every track on it was built in order for it to appear to be accessible musically and lyrically quite simple, bar two tracks, but actually every single track is very specifically about a certain element of Magick. It really is allegories and parables about Magick. So it's the third album basically. The third proper album.

How come it took so long for it to come out?

Because we had all our money stolen... Also, I felt subconsciously that it needed to wait, in order for us to be clearer about what it was and whether it worked. When we listened to it again after not listening to it for a year, it still sounded really good. It's good. We're activists, as you know. That's why I coined that phrase "Occulture", which I think is a very good word. It's a combination of the Occult, in its widest sense, and Culture. As we've always said with the stickers, I've been involved in a total war with culture since the day I started. And that's not changed. I am at war with the status quo of society and I am at war with those in control and power. I'm at war with hypocrisy and lies, I'm at war with the mass media. Then I'm at war with every bastard who tries to hurt someone else for its own sake. And I'm at war with privilege and I'm at war with all the things that one should be at war with basically. And parallel to that I believe in genuine loyalty, genuine caring, genuine love and genuine creativity. And genuine integration of one's life and all those constructive things which also ought to be obvious.

I've always said: "I do the obvious..." It's just that most people don't have the courage. That's it in a nutshell... That's what terrifies people, because one day they'll be aware, not because it's coming from me or because I'm more or less clever than anyone else, but just that the message that we've talked about is very powerful, like all radical messages. They're incredibly simple and massively powerful once a lot of people have listened. It's not that hard to turn somebody's ear. That's why they try to stop people from coming to concerts and that's why they try to stop them from buying records, that's why they tell them not to read what we write, because every time someone comes to a concert and listen to the records, then the odds increase that everyone's going to start going: "That makes sense!"

And once that spiral starts, there is actually the possibility of infinite expansion... And, as we're not the owners of it... Even if they get rid of us, the message can carry on living, like all messages. We're merely the transmitters of that message. It came to us via a lot of people: Brion Gysin, Burroughs, Austin Spare, Grandmother, every American Indian, every Aboriginal, everyone who's honest with themselves passed on that message. What we're trying to say is to the whole of society: "For your own survival and for your own increase of happiness, be honest! Before it's too late..." Because the other way won't and does not work. It's a choice. It's that simple.

I suppose a lot of people will always associate Psychic TV with the more cryptic sounds, the first two LPs and everything. What do you have to say to those people?

The same message! Everything we do is allegory, everything that I construct.

Reflections of what's happening?

Exactly. Also, they are more complicated and sophisticated than we give them credit for. That's the nature of art. You don't try and make a really simple... Although sometimes you can... Sometimes the best way to tell somebody something is not verbal, it's symbolic. And the way you build something like "Dreams less sweet", the actual structure of it, is the message... The way it's made and the contradictions and the surprises. That's the message and it's not something you can speak, as with a lot of art and a lot of creative expressions.

If it was that simple as just speaking, no one would write anymore books or paint anymore paintings or make anymore music, except as celebration. But human beings are complex and in our society the unconscious mind has been deliberately separated from the conscious mind. We're trying to bring them back together, to make them healthy. Sometimes the only way is through hieroglyphs. People should stop trying to understand or make sense of a lot of those messages in the superficial way and just accept that they are statements and messages from intelligent people. There therefore has to be intelligence in the way they're made. Therefore... Don't worry about it! Just let it happen, listen to it, and it will tell you its story on its own.

Yeah, and it sort of dawns upon you... You suddenly realize: "Ah... That's what it's about!"

It's basically a description of how life is.

What do you hope that people will think when they listen to Psychic TV and read Temple-material in 50 years from now?

I hope they'll think we were intelligent (laughs). And that it'll be useful to them. We try to be functional. I think that so far, without blowing my own trumpet, that the work I've done up to date is still considered to be viable and influential. So I see no reason to see why that should alter.

A lot of the TG-stuff is still ahead of most bands.

Even now... If you listen to *20 Jazz Funk Greats*, there are even a couple of tracks that are like Acid House. It's interesting. And *Heathen Earth*, the long one with the violin is like Acid House too. And *Distant Dreams* and *Adrenalin... Adrenalin* is really close to Acid House. I like *Distant Dreams* because it's so... The spoken part is like pure, genuine existentialism, which is really hard to get. It's really dead-pan and I like how it works. "These times they are just passing..." Those sorts of lyrics sound really easy and use really normal words, which is one of my favorite hobbies. To make things sound really ordinary and yet be one of the most precise, accurate and, sort of, hard-edged descriptions of some element of reality.

When you're writing your lyrics, or poetry, do you work very hard and scribble or is it more like a flow of words coming out and then you won't change it?

That was written straight down.

Is that the most common way for you to work?

Most common. Occasionally, I go back and change it, but usually not adding any extra information. Like with mixing, it's the same. That's just a skill I've developed over 20 odd years of working. It's like Burroughs once said: "People think that all they have to do to write a good novel is to do a cut-up. But the skill is knowing what to cut up and how much to cut up and where to put each section."

And that's something that involves the esthetics of the mind that's doing it. That can't be taught and it can't be learned and it can't be copied.

What you and other people are doing with sampling is just basically cut-ups really.

It all keeps coming back. Ritual, as it says in the *Behavioural Cut-Ups*-essay, where it implies... The reason I think ritual is so useful in our society is that it is a behavioural cut-up. We have normal patterns of behaviour. When you do a ritual you cut up the way you would normally respond. You reach thresholds of behaviour you would normally avoid. You're in a situation you're not used to. You're actually doing to your responses, your behaviour, your perceptions and your emotions and your psychic abilities the same thing that a cut-up does to words, or sampling does to music. That's why it's so important. That's why Brion Gysin's message about cut-ups is one of the most important statements and discoveries made this century, because you can apply it to video and television and anything else. You can see what controls and what de-controls. And where you are and how big you are and how you exist, your shape, your depth and everything else. You can actually build a holophonic, holographic image of you and your place in the world via cut-ups. That ability is the most radical, magical, artistic, physiological statement there has ever been for a long time.

And the sampling unit is the technological thing for it... And the Dreamachine... Brion Gysin was an alchemist, there's no question. He was the equivalent of the figures in Gothic novels of the roving Alchemist who just had immense knowledge and passed it on verbally to the next generation of people.

That's actually what he said to me in Paris. He took my hand and said... In most of the most secret initiations it's always called "touching hands". What you do is take their hand and say, if it's someone who has knowledge what they're saying: "I pass to you all my knowledge freely for you to make use of and develop." That's what he said to me in Paris, because he trusted us. And even William Burroughs wrote in a letter that we were people dealing with the most important aspects of communication that he'd met.

Yeah, it's well-organized; it's not just an interest.

And it's genuine! It's the real thing! Why are they scared of us? It's the real thing. They can't bribe us, they can't give us money, and they can't scare us off. What do they do? Their tricks don't work. They can kill me, but it's too late. They can hurt me, but it's too late. I don't own the idea, it's not living in me. I'm just a little bit of the process that keeps alive and moving. That has happened through all human history.

Thee Psychick Youth Network...

Exactly! It's not the Genesis P-Orridge Network. Although sometimes people try and do that, it's just another attempt to discredit it and make people scared of it. That's a pity, but at the end of the day there are enough people who are intelligent to see around all those games and think, "I've met Gen. That's not his trip. He's trying to give..." And that's what I do. I try to give.

It's a good thing too. A lot of young people today seem frustrated. They don't know what to do. All they do is walk around and kick things. Thee Temple can be a perfect vehicle.

I think it can become the best vehicle in post-industrial society to find a new form of belief-structure and behaviour-structure. That's the difference; you can have both, without being forced to signed manifestos, "the ten rules". There are some basic tenets. We are overtly, and we accept and admit it, anti-Christian. With good reason, we believe. And we are anti-control. And we are pro-the development of some kind of new Sexuality, where people absorb and develop their female and male aspects. Pandrogeny, as we call it. Positive Androgeny. Both in the way they behave with each other, their ability to allow their feelings to come through if they're male or to develop their strength if they're female. And so on.

Evolution. That doesn't mean... Sexuality is not the same as sex, which is another thing our society throws all the time. I'm sure that *Sunday People* will say it. This is one of their favorite word games...

"So you're into the power of sex?", and you say: "NO... Sexuality!", which is quite different from the sex act. Sexuality need never involve an orgasm or the sex act. We're interested in the evolution of the shamanic vision of the world as a whole. Ecology, behaviour, the tribal idea...

Those platforms and all the obvious spin-off concerns you would get if you use the word "control", then you're talking about all forms of media and language. If you imagine all the lines going off from each of those words – sexuality, control, shamanism, anti-Christianity – they also just all join up into one big web again.

It's all the same thing. How to have dignity as a human being and how to be positive and useful as a human being and how to avoid being degraded and abused as a human being.

We can say that the written word has been the glyph of power for the last 500 years, whereas television and recordings are fairly new, but powerful. You're also going to start publishing books now.

It's just a very useful way of preserving information and ideas and spreading it around the planet so it's harder to get rid of it. If you print 1000 books and they destroy 900, hopefully there's a 100 around somewhere that may eventually become useful. Just like Crowley...

Most of his books were in small numbers, but now they're in tens and tens of thousand copies, for better or worse. It doesn't matter. The fact is it survived, the thoughts survived, primarily because he printed books. And the same with Austin Spare. He's just coming into his own now. He's become more influential. I have to say partly because we've gone on about him so much. He's become hip! That's fine... There are times when we quite deliberately make use of and manipulate the concept of fashion and hipness, like with Brion Gysin. Basically it's invocation!

And with Burroughs as well.

And Burroughs. You invoke and say the name enough times and eventually people go: "Burroughs? What is this Burroughs I keep hearing about?" They keep hearing about it, because you keep saying it... That's a magical technique that goes back to the beginning of time, used in a new way. Via the mass-media and fashion. But it's still invocation, it's still a mantra. It's a mantra to get a specific result, which is interest in that person's knowledge. We do that all the time and we do it quite well.

So what are your upcoming projects?

The *Godstar*-book on Brian Jones. A book on Brion Gysin, based on my interviews and archive. And then a book called *Sex, Power and Magick*, which is the history of Coum Transmissions and the origins. We want to do three books. One is *Sex, Power and Magick*, which is Coum Transmissions, one is *Power, Sex and Magick*, which is Throbbing Gristle, and the last one is *Magick, Sex and Power*, which is Psychic TV and Thee Temple of Psychick Youth. It'll be a three-volume series. The first one will be the *Sex, Power and Magick*-one, because it's written, it's finished. There's also another one we want to do with Z'EV, which is linguistic, searching for the Mother-tongue and translating various so-called holy texts back to their original meanings. And what you discover is that they're all, even the *Song of Songs* in the *Bible*, about Tantric sex, sexual magic. And we want to do a really quick scrapbook called *The Unwholesome Earth Catalogue*. It'll be press cuttings, photos, clips, bits by anyone. It'll be a big scrapbook. And then, once a year, a journal, a serious literary, journalistic compilation-book on anything that seems to be useful that should be published, whether it's an article by a journalist that couldn't be printed in Fleet Street or an esoteric essay on thee Temple or a review of a painter who should be remembered. An Occulture magazine.

An "Equinox" of the 80s?

Like a mix between *RE/Search* and *The Equinox*, I suppose, but hopefully a bit more radical and provocative, about the state of the entire world. So those are a few... Enough to get on with. We also want to print *The Grey Book* in different languages. Once we do that, then every TOPY Access Point can sell the same book and raise money for themselves that way. That should be quite useful, just like a bible.

It'll also be an interesting statement about the idea of the global Network. And it's of interest to everyone...

Could you tell me about the "TG Ltd."-project (in which Psychic TV recorded and performed as "TG Ltd", as a comment to disagreements between the members of the original Throbbing Gristle-project. – Ed.)? A banishing ritual?

The banishing ritual, yeah... But also, there's a lot of background to it. Mute Records had brought out all the TG LPs and they were going to release them on CD. We said: "Fine!" You have to bear in mind that Chris and Cosey have done several bootlegs. They have also been paid for other bootlegs and so have Sleazy and Geoff of Coil. They never ever paid me my quarter of that money. They also did a licensing deal for the last TG-concert in San Francisco on video with Target Video. My name did not even appear on the contract. Sleazy even signed his name as the manager of Throbbing Gristle! And they gave me no copy of it and gave me zero money.

So you're talking, at an estimate, of all the bootlegs, licensing deals... 30-40.000 pounds! I never said a word about this, because it's my policy normally to think: "Arseholes are arseholes, liars are liars, criminals are criminals..." It's their problem. It's a big drag, because I could make use of that money for something more positive than buying them another limited edition car or whatever they buy. Because they're all rich anyway. It always sounds petty in print when you explain these things. So I lived with it.

Then the first CD came out and that was alright. I didn't say anything. The second one was coming out, it was all going ahead. They asked Chris and Cosey to write some sleeve-notes for it. Fine. They wrote some, which was like one side. The guy at Mute, John, said: "Not really all that good..." He sent it to me. "Maybe you could re-write it and expand upon it and see whether that's any good."

So I re-wrote it all, it became three pages and I sent it back to him. He said, "I'll have to send it to all the others for approval." "Yeah, fine, no problem." I asked him, "Do you like it?", and he said: "I think it's the best thing I've ever seen." It was about why TG began and explaining, historically, the importance of TG. And also the mistakes that TG made, because I made a point of trying to be objective and say where I thought we made errors too.

I actually said some of it was accidental; it wasn't because we were clever, and some of it was just gratuitous. Then I got a phone call from him and I asked, "How was it? Did they like it or not?", and he said, "Yes, they all agreed that it was all really, really good, but... They want to change one word in one sentence." I said, "Oh? Which word?" He said, "That's not the point. They want to change one word so they can put their names at the bottom too, and say that you all wrote it together. They don't want people to know you wrote it on your own." I just said, "No. I'm sorry John, but that's the last straw... They've ripped me off; they've made musical careers out of having met me. They still use the names I gave them, because they've got no imagination to make up their own names even. Everything they do, their entire credibility is based on having met me and having been allowed to work with me. In return they try to steal Throbbing Gristle from me as an idea, they try to pretend I wasn't in it."

I said, "I'm not going to let them pretend any longer that they had the ideas or that they were the ones who were articulate." Because they weren't. And they didn't. Not on the level they pretend, for sure.

I said, "Sorry! You either print it as it is and my name's at the bottom, because I wrote it, or you don't use it..." So he said, "I want to use it...", and I said, "That's your problem."

He rang them up and said, "No, you can't have your names at the bottom and pretend you wrote it." The three of them got together and said, "OK, Mute, you can't release any more CDs by Throbbing Gristle!" To his credit, he said, "Then we won't release any CDs..." So, what have they done? They've achieved revealing their arseholism to Mute, finally. Finally Mute knows what they're like. Secondly they get no money out of CDs, which is a bit stupid. And thirdly, he said to me, "Now I know for sure whose idea Throbbing Gristle was!" So there are no more CDs of Throbbing Gristle coming out on Mute... Because they couldn't face admitting whose idea it was or who could explain it or who understood it, because what does that do? That finally reveals they're parasites.

Who's got the rights?

We have to, all four of us, agree on that. Because it's not a bootleg. Otherwise, they'd release it themselves. So I decided that it was time for me to actually make it clear who did own Throbbing Gristle and who did think of it. What they'd forgotten was that I owned Throbbing Gristle Ltd., the actual company, so I thought, "Let's teach these people a small lesson. How will they get really pissed off? What will make it clear to the public who has the right to decide what does or does not happen to this project, whether or not it's destroyed or it's continued, etc. Whose is it?" It's a matter of ownership.

Paula, to her credit, said, "Let's do a concert. That will really upset them..." Because she has had to sit by and observe them being dishonest, parasitic, vicious bastards basically. And of course, that's exactly the kind of human being that Psychic TV and Thee Temple of Psychick Youth is dedicated to trying to expose! So we did it.

We saw Chris and Cosey after the gig, leaving. They looked really pissed off.

Well, it's taken away a lot of their mystique, hasn't it? Because, whether they like it or not, it wasn't that hard to regenerate a lot of those sounds.

No, as you said, it was almost the same thing.

Paula said when she saw your photographs that it was really weird, because I even looked physically the same as then. I said, "Well, I can do that!" It's a magical trick. I can. It could have been from an old concert.

That was the whole point. It's just to say: "It's a construct." And as the artist who constructed it, I know how to reconstruct it. Or deconstruct it. That's my privilege. It's mine!

And, yes, they made a contribution as helpers when it was going, but no more or no less than this engineer makes with this record, or anyone else who collaborates with me. The ideas and the structures and the way it works come from me, and it's about time it was stated that that was what it was all about.

Was the Grief*-LP done as a sort of the same thing on vinyl?*

That was done parallel to it, yeah. It's good. It's also quite clearly a product of the way I work. And it reminds people that the whole thing was a product of the way I work. If it were so much to do with other people, how come I can have different people collaborating with me and yet there's a very strong consistency in what we do? I can't be that thick. I can't be that dependent on other people if I can keep changing who I work with and remain intense and serious and clear. I've produced a large body of work and I believe my work has been incredibly consistent in terms of direction and morality and quality.

It took me seven years to get irritated enough to remind them who's boss. That's what it was. Whether or not anyone came was actually irrelevant really. Somebody said to me, "Why are you doing it?", and I said, "To pay the phone-bill." (laughs).

It's not the idea of making it too grand. I knew that the people I was talking to knew what I was saying. There were just three of those people. They heard me, believe me. They heard me. That was the primary intent and that was private to an extent.

Did you get any good press at all, except for my article?

No, but then TG never did. What was so amazing was that it was, more than I'd guessed, so much like TG. Even down to the audience being the same. It was only half-full, but there are probably 6000 people who say they were there. And people pretending to like it and then the reviews say, "It was the worst thing we ever heard, it's not music..." Not much changes! Even now the *NME* is saying it's not music. I think they're in love with me. It's the sort of behaviour you get from people who are in love, but can't get off with you. You know when somebody's in love with somebody and obsessed with them, but they can't get them as a lover.

... And start slagging you off instead.

It's exactly that behaviour. I think they absolutely adore me! It scares the death out of them, because to love me they've got to change their behaviour. And they're too scared to do it. That's their problem. They're obsessed with me and it terrifies them, because they can't be my lover while they lie. Yet they're fascinated. They write about us more than anyone else (laughs).

It's so obvious, it's just like the person who's got a sexual obsession with somebody but can't have them. Then they get really vicious... "I hate them, I hate them. They're really vicious, they're really horrible..." It's all that. It's the same thing. That's the other thing that's really useful with Temple techniques... It teaches you how to look at things in parallels, behaviour parallels. That's not a newspaper, that's people. And they're people with problems.

You should take them out to lunch some time...

I've thought of that, but they're so obsessed that it's not worth the effort. There are better things to do. Like we said earlier, I'd rather build a bookshelf. It's more useful.

What are the Psychic TV-shows like nowadays?

In London they're a bit more "extravaganza", because we have more resources here. On a good day there's anything up to 20 video monitors, two or three 16 mm projectors, lighting effects... Basically as many visual, retinal stimulations as possible. The films and the videos are primarily what we make ourselves rather than just found stuff.

If it's found stuff, it has to be very interesting or specific. Paula has a flight case with six cassette-decks as well as percussions. We've been using sampling-keyboards, but now we want to wire up the drum kit too to the computer, so when Matthew is playing the drums we can have any sounds we want for rhythm.

What we're aiming towards is to become a very contemporary form of tribal celebration music. Ritual music, to have the same effect as voodoo-trance. And the possibility of it becoming endless, when people involved want to keep going.

There are unfortunately a lot of limitations in terms of the rock venue and promoter at this stage. But we think it's better to make a "rock"-concert of an hour and a half, an example of what could be possible, than not do it at all. And then occasionally, as things improve, find locations where we can promote and control it all so we can have the option of going on all night.

Points of Distinction Between Sedative and Consciousness-expanding Drugs

William S. Burroughs

A presentation of William Burroughs and his important work and research is hardly needed these days. Suffice to say here that this article is reprinted, with the author's kind permission, from a book called LSD – The Consciousness-expanding Drug *(Putnam, 1966, ed. David Solomon.).*

Unfortunately the word "drug" activates a reflex of fear, disapproval and prurience in Western nervous systems. "Drug" of course is simply a generic term for any chemical agent. Alcohol is a sedative drug similar in action to the barbiturates. Yet because of purely verbal associations we do not think of alcohol as being a drug because it is our national drug. The American narcotics department has bracketed substances with opposite physiological effect as narcotic drugs. Morphine is actually an antidote for cocaine poisoning. Cannabis (the Latin term for preparations made from the hemp plant, such as marihuana and hashish) is a hallucinogen drug with no chemical or physiological affinity to either cocaine or morphine. Yet cocaine, morphine and cannabis are all classified as "narcotic drugs". Unquestionably the term has emotional impact. But used in such a loose fashion it has no useful precision of meaning. I would like to draw at the outset a clear distinction between sedative and hallucinogen agents, between addicting and non-addicting drugs.

What is addiction? The use of opium and/or derivatives leads to a state that defines limits and describes addiction. So the morphine or heroin addict provides the model and mirror of addiction. The addict functions on heroin. Without it he is helpless as a beached fish out of his medium. As a diver depends on his air line, the addict depends on his heroin connection. This situation of total dependence did not exist prior to his contact with heroin and his subsequent addiction. A month more or less of daily exposure through injection or sniffing the drug and the addict is hooked, that is, addicted for life. Even if the addict is cured and off the drug for years he can be re-addicted by one or two shots. Like the alcoholic, he has acquired a lifelong sensitivity to the drug. Investigators still do not know how heroin addiction is contracted. Doctor Isbell of Lexington, Kentucky, where most U.S. addicts are treated, has suggested that morphine acts on the cell receptors, perhaps altering the molecular structure of certain cell groups in the body.

While the action of morphine is not fully understood, alcohol and barbiturates are definite front-brain sedatives, and increased doses are generally required to achieve sedation. In fact, all sedative drugs may be said to act by sedating, that is, putting out of action some function of the nervous system, by decreasing awareness of surroundings and bodily processes. Addiction would seem to be a prerogative of sedatives and perhaps the opiates are the only class of truly addictive drugs. The symptoms that follow barbiturate withdrawal may be regarded as a mechanical reaction from massive front-brain sedation rather than a biological need for the drug.

What is a hallucinogen? A drug that expands consciousness and increases awareness of surroundings and bodily processes. (I would suggest that the term consciousness-expanding drugs be substituted for hallucinogen drugs since actual hallucinations are rare and no precise definition of hallucination has been formulated.) Under the influence of mescaline, LSD, cannabis, the subject is acutely aware of colors, sounds, odors, and the effects of the drug may be said to consist in this phenomenon of increased awareness which may be pleasant or unpleasant depending on the content of awareness. Colors and sounds gain an intense meaning and many insights carry over after the drug effects have worn off. Under the influence of mescaline I have had the experience of seeing a painting for the first time and found later that I could see the painting without using the drug. The same insights into music or the beauty of an object ordinarily ignored carry over so that one exposure to a powerful consciousness-expanding drug often conveys a permanent increase in the range of experience. Mescaline transports the user to unexplored psychic areas, and he can often find the way back without a chemical guide.

I will describe a simple experiment that will make the distinction between sedative and consciousness-expanding drugs more precise. So far as I know this experiment has not been carried out in detail. Here is the proposed experiment: Administer a consciousness-expanding drug together with a precise array of stimuli – music, pictures, odors, tastes – timed and recorded so that the entire battery of stimuli can be exactly repeated. Some days later when the effects of the drug are completely dissipated expose the subject to the same stimuli in the same order. To what extent is the hallucinogen experience reactivated? Everyone who has used the consciousness-expanding drugs knows that any one stimulus experienced under the influence of the drug can reactivate the drug experience. There is every reason to believe that the drug experience could be recaptured in detail with a precise repetition of associated stimuli.

Now try the same experience with a morphine addict. Administer a dose of morphine together with a battery of stimuli. Wait until withdrawal symptoms occur. Now repeat the stimuli. Is any relief from withdrawal symptoms experienced? On the contrary, the associated stimuli reactivate and intensify need for the drug. The same of course is true of alcohol. Stimuli associated with the consumption of alcohol activate the need for alcohol and conduce to relapse in the cured alcoholic.

The use of sedative drugs leads to increased dependence on the drug used. The use of consciousness-expanding drugs could show the way to obtain the useful aspects of hallucinogen experience without any chemical agent. Anything that can be done chemically can be done in other ways, given sufficient knowledge of the mechanisms involved. Recently a Cambridge dentist has extracted teeth with no other anesthetic than music through headphones. The patient was instructed to turn up the volume if he experienced any pain. The consciousness-expanding experience has been produced by flicker, that is, rhythmic light flashes in the retina at the rate of from ten to twenty five flashes per second. I quote from Grey Walters, *The Living Brain*: "The rhythmic series of flashes appeared to be breaking down of some of the physiological barriers between different regions of the brain. This meant that the stimulus of flicker received in the visual projection area of the cortex was breaking bounds, its ripples were overflowing into other areas."

Now it is precisely this overflow of the brain areas, hearing, colors, seeing sounds and even odors that is a categorical characteristic of the consciousness-expanding drugs. Along with flicker Grey Walters has produced many of the phenomena associated with consciousness-expanding drugs. Subjects reported: "Lights like comets ... Ultra unearthly colors, mental colors, not deep visual ones..."

The literature of mescaline and LSD abounds in such regrettably vague descriptions of visionary experiences. Further experiments with subliminal doses of mescaline accompanied by flicker, flicker administered under large dosage and repeated later, could well lead to a *non-chemical* method of expanding consciousness and increasing awareness.

There are many consciousness-expanding drugs, each with distinct properties, and scientists are just beginning to explore the chemistry of these drugs. I have had personal experience with mescaline, LSD, Bannisteria caapi, kava kava, dimethyltryptamine and several others in the form of herbal preparations, the content of which was unknown to me. All these drugs open different psychic areas. Some of these areas are pleasant, some are not. Dimethyltryptamine and bufotenin seem to produce in many subjects alarming and disagreeable symptoms, and both drugs in my opinion should be used with great caution or not at all. Overdose of consciousness-expanding drugs can be a nightmare experience owing to the increased awareness of unpleasant or dangerous symptoms. I would like to mention a drug which is neither a front-brain stimulant like cocaine, nor a sedative like morphine and barbiturates, nor a tranquilizer, nor an energizer, nor a hallucinogen, a drug that could act as a useful stabilizing agent when using the consciousness-expanding drugs. This drug is apomorphine. I quote from *Anxiety and Its Treatment* by Doctor John Dent of London: "Apomorphine is made from morphine by boiling with hydrochloric acid, but its physiological effect is quite different – apomorphine acts on the hypothalamus in such a way as to normalize metabolism and regulate the blood serum."

Administered with a consciousness-expanding drug, apomorphine stabilizes the experience and reduces anxiety. I have observed and personally experienced dramatic relief from anxiety resulting from consciousness-expanding drugs after a dose of apomorphine. The drug has no sedating or addictive properties. No case of addiction to apomorphine has ever been recorded. Yet because of purely verbal associations the drug has been placed under the Harrison Narcotic Act and is seldom prescribed in this country. Apomorphine is a unique drug that acts as a metabolic regulator which stabilizes but does not cancel the consciousness-expanding experience.

In conclusion: The sedative drugs act to decrease awareness, and increased dosage is generally required to achieve or maintain this state of decreased awareness. The consciousness-expanding drugs act to increase awareness, and this state of increased awareness can become a permanent acquisition.

It is unfortunate that marihuana, which is the safest of the hallucinogen drugs, should be subject to the heaviest legal sanctions. Unquestionably this drug is very useful to the artist, activating trains of association that would otherwise be inaccessible, and I owe many of the scenes in *Naked Lunch* directly to the use of cannabis. Opiates, on the other hand, since they act to diminish awareness of surroundings and bodily processes, can only be a hindrance to the artist. Cannabis serves as a guide to psychic areas which can be reentered without it. I have now discontinued the use of cannabis for some years and I find that I am able to achieve the same results by non-chemical means: flicker, music through headphones, cut ups and fold ins of my texts, and especially by training myself to think in association blocks instead of words, that is, cannabis like all the hallucinogens, can be discontinued once the artist has familiarized himself with the areas opened up by the drug. Cannabis sometimes causes anxiety in large doses, and this anxiety is promptly relieved by apomorphine.

It would seem to me that cannabis and the other hallucinogens provide a key to the creative process, and that a systematic study of these drugs would open the way to non-chemical methods of expanding consciousness.

Jayne Mansfield – Satanist

Carl Abrahamsson

To the general public today, Jayne Mansfield is probably most remembered as a "dumb blonde", perhaps even more so than Marilyn Monroe herself. With Monroe's death in 1962, the era of the dumb blonde was definitely over, and had in truth been so for quite some time. And since both of them were so extremely typecast, this fact became the end of their careers, although in different ways.

Monroe has since become an icon in American culture and history, in the same way as her male overrated counterpart, James Dean, where Jayne will always probably be remembered as the funny and wacky blonde, a sleaze queen, a goddess of trashy films, and/or a selfish media hype.

A little known fact though, is that she was very interested in occultism from her very early days, and that she later, in the mid 60s, joined the activities of her good friend Anton LaVey and his then newborn Church of Satan. Whatever your vision of Jayne is, one thing is certain... She was a true Star. In many ways.

Born in 1933 as Vera Jayne Palmer in Pennsylvania, she, as millions of other young girls in the USA at the time, became addicted to that extremely intoxicating drug called "Hollywood". She collected information and pictures manically on her favorite stars, including Shirley Temple and Johnny Weissmüller, and through the years a decision based on desire was made... She too wanted to be a moviestar.

She married a college student named Paul Mansfield at the age of 16. He'd made her pregnant and the child, Jayne Marie, became her mother's first confidante and assistant on the way to stardom. At this time, in the early 50s, the family lived in Texas. But when Mr. Mansfield returned from having been abroad with the US Army, they made a trip to California, where Jayne supposedly got out of the car at the state border, kissed the ground and said, "I'm home". It soon became clear to her husband that she had absolutely no plans whatsoever of leaving.

In her autobiography, *Jayne Mansfield's Wild, Wild World* (a book dedicated to "Love"), her later husband Mickey Hargitay tells, "She – whether this is a good point in her favor or not – will sacrifice anybody if they don't live up to what she needs and demands", and, "When Jayne really wants something, watch out. She really gets what she wants." And thus the fundament of magic is established – Will!

The next few years in Hollywood were spent trying to get attention in any way possible – through beauty contests, publicity stunts and just generally displaying her curvaceous body. And, as she more and more drifted into the role of the giggling and peroxided aspiring star, the more she started getting the attention she wanted. Every photograph, every contest-title, every "Jayne Mansfield" seen in print... All became her invocations, and as she grew more skillful and got to know more and more people, the more her ritualistic displaying of herself paid off.

"Yes, my ego was inflated because I believed I would eventually become a Star."

In 1955 she signed with Warner Bros., and she was naturally in seventh heaven. She was in the business now, as she'd always wanted, and started to increase her already very open and kind attitude towards the press. She was well aware of the fact that a moviestar can't exist without fans, and she therefore needed press all the time – good press, bad press, any press.

And attention she got. Her life became a turmoil of flashing cameras and fans craving autographs. She willingly agreed to it all. "There is no escape from the public eye it seems, whether it be planned or natural publicity."

In 1955 she'd also met the love of her life, Mickey Hargitay, a former Mr. Universe who at this time was part of a Mae West show. It is rumoured that West became so upset about this young couple's strong love, that she demanded that Hargitay, in a special press conference, should deny the relationship with Jayne Mansfield.

Instead, he declared their engagement, and a fight between him and Mae West's bodyguard became the result of it – to the satisfaction of the photographers... And to Jayne's!

This was certainly her heyday. The couple now lived in a 35 room mansion in Hollywood, called "The Pink Palace" because almost everything in it was pink (Jayne's favorite colour), and Jayne had tremendous successes in 1956/57 with a Broadway show called *Will Success Spoil Rock Hunter?*, the rock'n'roll movie classic *The Girl Can't Help It* (with performances by Fats Domino, Gene Vincent, Eddie Cochran and Little Richard), and a movie version of *Rock Hunter*.

She was now signed to 20th Century Fox, as Warners had dropped her some time earlier, silently, supposedly because they thought she was more of a media freak than a talented actress. Publicity stunts were as important now as they ever were. One funny incident is for instance the one which is partly immortalized on the cover of the Arrow Books' edition of Kenneth Anger's *Hollywood Babylon*. Jayne tells the story, again in *Wild, Wild World:* "Arriving at Romanoff's, I immediately walked to Miss (Sophia) Loren's table to pay my respects. She was sitting and I was standing. I bent down to talk to her and the photographers, with a sixth sense for being in the right place and popped eyes, took pictures. I really had no idea so much of me was showing. I only realized how much was exposed when I saw the expression on Miss Loren's face and I noticed that she was staring down my dress."

Surely an incident which echoes the one earlier on in her career, where she and her PR-man arrived at a publicity meeting/press conference for a film called *Underwater* that starred Jane Russell. Jayne fell into the swimming-pool and pretended not to be able to swim... And on top of that she "lost" her bikini top. When Jane Russell arrived, none of the photographers had any film left.

So, at this time she was a star alright, but the studio wouldn't give her anything but typecast roles. Naturally she became quite disillusioned and more and more desperately clinged to her stardom status. Her fans still loved her though, and could read all about her various love affairs, her children and her movies in the fan magazines.

Her marriage and relationship with Hargitay was sometimes on, sometimes off. The great Mansfield was aware and proud of her sexuality ("I am bringing up my children to take pride in their bodies, care well for them, and enjoy them. Mickey feels the same way. Call me sexpot if you wish, but you must admit my attitude has had many rewards").

She claimed that "chastity is a sickening perversion", and also claimed that John F Kennedy had been her lover, as had the king of rock'n'roll – Elvis Presley (he even gave her a pink motorcycle!).

The early 60s weren't quite as good for her, career- or otherwise. The only offers she seemed to get were from B-producers in the US and second-rate ones in Europe. *Promises, Promises!* from 1963, which also stars Mickey, is quite a funny story about a voluptuous blonde (guess who?) on a cruise with her impotent husband. The film is most remembered because Jayne was actually nude in a few scenes, something which didn't embarrass her at all. On the contrary, it helped the film and it gave her even more publicity. But it's also significant as a "typical" Jayne Mansfield movie, one where her real acting talents weren't profited upon, but where her body was the important thing – a body with a funny voice.

She traveled around with her children in Europe, making *Homesick for St. Paul* in 1963 in Germany and *Primitive Love* in Italy in 1964. And in the States she made films like *The Las Vegas Hillbillies*, which also starred another big-bosomed blonde, Mamie Van Doren. But, as we all know, there was never ever any competition for Jayne Mansfield, and at this time she was still confident that she'd get a chance soon to get into more "serious" roles. Sadly, she didn't, but we shouldn't grieve over this. One must never forget that many films that would just have been pure and uninteresting trash, in the boring non-camp way, were augmented to trash exellentia thanks to her participation.

I mean, who would care for films like *The Loves of Hercules* or *The George Raft Story*, if it weren't for her? From *The Girl Can't Help It*, over *Rock Hunter*, *Too Hot to Handle*, *Promises, Promises!* to *The Las Vegas Hillbillies* there is a genuine love for the medium itself from her side. And although she might not have been aware of it herself, at least not in the early stages of her career, this is another interesting magical point of view that has helped to keep her alive, and always will.

"Thus, then, must every artist work. First, he must find himself. Next, he must find the form that is fitted to express himself. Next, he must love that form, as a form, adoring it, understanding it, and mastering it, with most minute attention, until it (as it seems) adapts itself to him with eager elasticity, and answers accurately and aptly, with the unconscious automation of an organ perfected by evolution, to his most subtlest suggestion, to his most giant gesture." (Aleister Crowley, *The Law is for all, Commentaries on Liber AL vel Legis*, part two: 17-21).

And this is a fact that can never be denied. These films, along with her public life, are her marks in and on time. No matter how "cheap" they appear to be to the common man, they're still hers and no one else's.

In the mid-60s, she joined some weekend sessions organized by Anton LaVey and his congregation of witches in San Francisco. And when this nucleus emerged into The Church of Satan in 1966, Jayne was there too.

She became very good friends with Dr. LaVey and kept attending their rituals and excursions. This was surely the steady basis she needed in her life, someone who took her and her interests seriously and regarded her as a magical star, not as a media/moviestar.

Her career was definitely spiraling downwards though. She had turned to alcohol for comfort, since she couldn't get any real satisfaction from the men she associated with: Enrico Bomba, an Italian producer, and Matt Cimber, Bomba's predecessor and also a producer/director of Italian origin. Mickey Hargitay and the children were all inbetween in a media circus, in which there seems to have existed no privacy at all. So, naturally, the magical and therapeutic support from The Church of Satan was just what Jayne needed.

The gossip columns got hold of this odd interest of hers and they thought that this could certainly be a time to turn around and start slagging her off. It's always easier to kick someone who's already lying down. Now all her voluptuousness and talk of "sexuality" could be turned against her ("I am truthful about sex. Sex is the most beautiful and natural thing in the world when two people are attracted to each other. It is when you stifle it, suppress it, deny what nature has given you – that is when it's wrong. That is the big sin with me, not to do what nature intends you to do."). This was something that a man named Sam Brody sensed at an early stage. He was Jayne's lover and lawyer, since her divorce from Matt Cimber, and he tried to talk Jayne out of Satanism. When they visited LaVey's house in San Francisco, Brody was overtly mocking LaVey and the philosophy of the Church, and he picked up a certain skull in the house, although warned not to. "You will die in a year. You will see what it means to laugh and scorn the Devil", LaVey told him, and from that time on, Jayne's life became one big mess.

The pair was involved in several car crashes, they were shown out from events that were usually open to them and Jayne became paranoid and confused. Because she knew the reason for their misfortunes were to be found in Brody's arrogance and ignorance, yet, when torn between the two men, she stuck with Brody.

On June 28, 1967, in the very midst of the "Summer of Love", they were involved in yet another car crash in Biloxi, on their way to a TV-show in New Orleans. Mansfield, Brody and the driver were instantly killed and her children, who were in the backseat, all survived. In the newspapers her death was given enormous coverage, showing pictures from the glorious 50s and portraying her as the warm and hardworking mother she was. The press and Jayne had lived in a very symbiotic relationship and most obituaries turned into kind and emotional homages. Her enemies saw fit to have a go at her though, now that she was dead. Mae West, for instance, said: "She was evil. She was so full of evil that one day she exploded and her head went one way and her body went another."

What we can do today is just to love her for what she was – a star. A star in the moviestar-sense, matched by few in enigma and radiance. And a star in the magical sense – determined, will-strong and successful, in her own true orbit. She was very special.

Television Magick

TOPYUS

Television is one of the most visible components of modern society. Its influence is both profound and inescapable. How strange, then, that modern-day writers on magick have almost universally ignored it in their discussions of contemporary magickal theory! The power of television exists and is being tapped by others, whether the magician chooses to use it herself or not. It seems that the latent potential of television in all forms of sorcery could be used to great effect for a variety of rituals, divinatory and symbolic/mnemonic purposes.

Like it or not, TELEVISION EXISTS. It is being used by the powers that be to influence the opinions, habits and actions of a great percentage of Earth's population. The truly modern magician/shaman ignores this force at her own peril.

This text is based on writings sent to Thee Temple ov Psychick Youth over the last year and a half. It represents research and suggestions by around 50 people. Though this is, by statistical standards, a very small sampling, it is, to the best of our knowledge, the first time that a text on practical magick has been assembled based on input from a large number of people, rather than on the opinion of one individual or the "official" teachings of one group or organization. If it appears to lack continuity, it is because it is of many voices. It is also the first attempt to systematically explore the practical and theoretical implications of Television Magick.

As editor of this text, I have tried wherever possible to stick to mere editing and organizing the format and continuity of this booklet. However, as I have read through all of the material submitted, I was, perhaps, able to gain a broader perspective than the contributors. I became aware of a particular bias that most of them seemed to share, and have decided to write a section that will, hopefully, give this text a far broader perspective and implications than it might otherwise have had.

This booklet is a beginning. There is much more work and research to be done. It is hoped that this rough start will spark enough interest, controversy and dialogue to warrant expansion in the near future. This book is the first, not the last word on Television Magick.

Finally, I want to thank all those who, in the final analysis, really wrote this booklet. They know who they are, many will recognize their words and results here.

This booklet is the product of the work and genius of many, and any credit for this work belongs to them, not the editor. This book shows that collaboration, communication and networking WORK. On this rock we have built our church.

TELEVISION IS A LANGUAGE

Like other disciplines, television has a unique language. Many of its technical terms have been borrowed from cinematography. Others are unique to TV. The language of advertising and newscasting are also unique to this medium. We see and hear grammatical faux pas that would put any self-respecting newspaper out of business! If one explores the structure and meaning behind many of these terms, a unique insight into the inner workings of television can be gained.

The one term that I feel is of the greatest importance in a magickal context is EDITING. It must be fairly obvious to any TV viewer that a lot more work goes into a television program than setting up a couple of cameras and videotaping away. Much more time must be spent in editing the various shots to project a form of CONTINUITY. The final televised version you watch may be the product of hours of discarded footage. Thus, the editor actually has more REAL control over the version you see than any other person involved in the production. Editing is a form of BIAS.

It might be interesting for a moment to consider magick, particularly ritual, as a form of editing. Like a good television editor, a magician strives for some form of continuity in his program, or life. By emphasizing desired aspects, the magician tries to edit out, or banish, unwanted footage from her life. Any idiot can shoot great footage, only a Master can edit it all so it makes sense to a viewer later on. This could be used as a modern alchemical allegory.

Advertising jargon is designed to penetrate to the subconscious mind, to cause a person to do something they might not do otherwise. So this language might be appropriated by a magician to use as a mantra, or maybe she could actuality shoot an advertisement for a specific desire. She could videotape objects and/or people that symbolized this desire to her, edited in with footage of her achieving said desire. Then she could do a voice-over of some type of slogan similar to those heard on TV ads. This advertisement could then be recorded inbetween a series of regular advertisements and stuck in the middle of a home video tape, say a favorite movie. Thus Austin Spare's notion of forgetfulness, the concept that a desire must be forgotten before it can be fulfilled, is adhered to. Just the amount of time and energy devoted to the production of such an advertisement would seem to guarantee its efficacy.

INTRODUCTION

Television seems to form a psychick scaffolding when used actively, as opposed to zombie consumption. Its technology emphasizes components and the psychick structures it produces have a systematic feel that reflects this emphasis:

Multi-channels – Commercials – Electronic components – Blackout – Station identification – Test pattern – Edits – Computer graphic – Pixels – Mixing – Model Variations Scanning Tracking – VCR/VTR, etc...

What is the intelligence of these configurations telling us? Remember that quantum mechanics, with its formula of indeterminacy, is crucial to the technology of television. To take part in the TV experiences as defined by normal/network standards, one must accept a passive role. Excluded from the life and breath of these so-called events. This produces the strange alienation of the voyeur. This in itself is not "bad", it's the way they make it seem as if there are no other possibilities. No questions, please!

Spellbound/Hypnoteased are we. Always going away without the fulfillment of our desire. (As promised?) Searching hopeless. But the product we seek is not our desire. The process is a door to our desires. The TV set is process, not product. What is "put through" it is known as "programming".

TV as Magick/TV is Magick. Buttons, switch, channel, remote control, video. Yes, modern magickal lingo. The symbols of a new form of incantation/spell/ritual. Daily, millions of people take part in a ritual of acceptance, passivity and the giving away of freedom/responsibility (the ability to respond...).

TV must also work through subliminal and vibrational avenues. The accumulated data and effect of the existence (exit stance) of TVs everywhere continually going. Who knows what this is producing? The constant and relentless reinFORCEment of alien orders?

To de-program is to "stop the World". TV is a tool for use or abuse. As are all the tools/toys of our time. What is powerful for control is also powerful for the individual. Resistance is not necessary, no need to run away. Turn on, tune in, drop out. Imagination will set you free. Stopping a World of conditioned behavior. No fight, step off the merry-go-round... A rejection of TV is no use to me. Integration of TV is a way to free your mind's eye. TV is. We are. Imagine yourself. If you can see it in your mind's eye, you can see it in the TV eye.

INTEGRATION FOR REALIZATION – RIOT IN THEE EYE

The mind is trained to learn by example, not exhortation. To properly influence behavior, control does not plead and demand to people, please do as we say. They simply show others doing so and receiving praise/prize. A dash of the herd mentality and there you go.

I believe the roots of this magickal mystery lie in the masking of the real purpose of "art". It is not now, and has never been mere entertainment. TV/video/cinema is but an extension of the ancient cave drawings. Music's history is equally old and rooted in ritual. When we can understand and work with this process, then we can begin to reclaim lost parts of our ancient and eternal selves, lost in the process of "programming". We can free ourselves with the very tool of our oppression.

TV is powerful because of the way it engages the senses. The sight and the sound. It comes on like a dream. You are caught in an alternate reality. The key, however, being that it is not supposed to be one of your own choice or creation. We are left speechless in the face of our lack, our passivity, our confusion. Unable to articulate the experience except for the smallest of details. Are we still trapped in someone's bad dreams?

TV as raw experience. If it is true that dreams are experienced as "real", then TV must also put us into/through a similar state of consciousness.

Video. Here the overwhelming power of TV can be transformed into a tool for anyone. This seems like a bit of trouble for the powers that be. They cannot cut us off because they are dependent on us! Not the other way around as they like to think. So their survival depends on their ability to confuse, manipulate, divert, divide/conquer and control people. They use TV to push a philosophy of passivity. But the very fact that they MUST push contains the seed of their destruction. We can turn the situation upside down, and live OUR dreams.

TV AS MAGICK AND RELIGION

Is the deification and worship of technology an excusable response to the automation of human perception? During the Harmonic Convergence, one New Ager took a television set with her to the top of Mt. Shasta, and then stunned the other observers by announcing that the image of an angel had manifested on the screen. The next day, before a large media conglomeration, a repairman reactivated the phenomenon and explained that it was due to a simple mechanical defect. Press and skeptics ate the story up with glee, but a pertinent point was missed. Who cares whether this videolized vision was caused by an otherworldly being, an unconscious group-will force or a shorted wire? Is not that human neuro-structure, by which sensory data is received, but a complex system of wiring and basic automated processes? Spontaneous visual hallucination used to be a purely human characteristic...

The future utilization of TV to transmit spiritual experience is an inevitable Reality.

Our all-encompassing environment, which used to be Nature, has become technology. Before Judeo-Christianity all of Western man's religions were quite understandably based on his environment. Now that we have outgrown a flawed spiritual framework far removed from the principles of physical experience (and much worse off as a result), why not return to a religion more direct and in touch with the human condition? Because our environment is now self-created? Ah, but that is to be the hook of this new world faith... Evolution is gracing us with the powers of Creation and Destruction we once projected out onto gods, or perhaps we are just realizing them latent within our psyches, the restless energies responsible for the seed of all spiritual thought... And so the medium is, indeed, the message.

Through these information and communication technologies humanity has taken its most subjective inner experiences and offered them up replicated into the mass "meme pool" of perceptual stimuli. In doing so we have structured a Gestalt of human reality, partially bridging the vast chasms between each universe of consciousness commonly known as a person. Actually we have recreated (in its own image...) the Gestalt, for accepting either the spiritual notion of ultimate Unity, or the quantum energy grid of modern physics; we are beyond temporal impressions all one Network of Being. In other words, we have unconsciously but faithfully fulfilled (in our own little way) the creative principle within us by embodying its essence and carrying it forth. In one respect, TV sets and hi-fi stereos have accomplished in a few years what organized religion has been striving toward for thousands.

Imagine a Video Tarot – workable as soon as the technology of "shuffling sequences is available. How many more corresponding attributions and poss. for subjective impressions will be instantly at our grasp in a short video effects seg than in a small playing card? Imagine TV Ritual. The point of ceremony in spiri traditions exo- and esoteric is to trigger inner experience through extraordinary sensory input. The potential of today's visual media for revolutionizing this ancient transformative art, their technical advances making possible both the creation of virtually any image – and their accessibility to anyone – is obvious. And, of course, the technology will only improve, forging new pathways...

It is true that these communication systems are, for the most part, affecting today the polar opposite of enlightenment. This condition has provided some rare opportunities, however. Televisions are incredibly prolific. Most of the population is used to watching them for long periods of time. From an evolutionary perspective, this can be seen as an "easing in" to a more vital project. Today's "living room" has become a TV viewing room, as is evident by the placement of the set and the rest of the furniture in relation to it; an objective observer would probably assume these devices fulfill a religious function already. The notion of "TV as altar" is not new but once again becomes relevant. We enshrine our video consoles the way we used to enshrine our god-images...

In the cathode ray then, may be the Channel we must find. A true Network to tune in, the remote control of an infinite, viewing its illusory passion plays on a plane of static radiation – are we the image on the screen?

TV SNOW

Here television's application as a type of subconscious mirror for scrying is exposed. This type of working, as well as its use in cut-ups, were the main ideas that were sent in to us. There is much more to be explored, though...

An important task in contemporary magick is redefining psychick uses of existing structures. Seemingly abandoned locations such as TV snow can be taken over and used by the magician. A Psychick Graffiti Zone. Infiltrate community channels, using night-time filler shows such as one consisting of a camera taking a complete journey on a subway train can be salvaged for use in ritual.

The impression I get from TV snow images is that they may form a consistent language with a specific vocabulary of images due to the limited parameters of TV (as opposed to the structures of dreams) and the repetitiveness of the images. Are these images the same to people in completely different circumstances?

Basically what I do is tune into a non-broadcasting channel and stare at the "snow", trying to look at one point, usually near the center of the screen. After a time, moving patterns start to emerge from the "snow", sort of like spinning mandalas, or large colonies of black ants dancing circuitously into their burrow...

Eventually I begin to see several layers of things going on behind this... I can focus on any one layer, but not for long, as there is so much info... It's rather like watching 5 or 6 films projected one on top of the other (in layers) and trying to pick out one film. I can see topographical landscapes going by very quickly as if flying over a continent.

Deserts and sparse vegetation seem to be prevalent. Also scenes from everyday life, houses, people, cars, etc...

Groups of people dancing and twirling, columns of marching men... It's an awful lot like the dreamachine with eyes open. To stop all images, all I have to do is refocus my eyes on some other part of the room.

The TV snow hallucinations seem very connected to the current regular programming. Many of the images and moods seem like the original templates of the programming.

Here's something I've done with TVs. It's not new or original (*we* found it to be – Ed.), but I've had fun with it and so have some of my friends, especially in altered states. Turn on a TV to a non-transmitting channel. Adjust the contrast, color and tint to a desired setting. Then add a strobe light. The strobe helps to speed up the process and makes everything a bit weirder. Also that warped warbling sound the stations transmit before going over to static can help bend your mind, especially if you turn it on full blast and let go.

Heavily amplified TV audio static seems to be a particularly enriched form of white noise (all frequencies combined). Audio hallucinations can become quite complex – the audio equivalent of TV snow.

AMBIENT TELEVISION

If television has a unique ability to penetrate our subconscious, how can the individualist regain control over it? One possible solution is to render it trivial. Things are most easily trivialized through such frequent repetition that they become commonplace. A television left on long enough becomes furniture, not entertainment! Stacks of TVs all tuned to a different channel make it impossible to concentrate on a single linear program, one finds that one's eyes roam from set to set. And this with as few as three sets.

I took one black and white TV set:

CONTRAST, VERTICAL HOLD
HORIZONTAL HOLD
PERMUTATED
IMAGE TRIPLED

The constant flickering image, constantly changing. The Magick moments, when captured, can be visually stimulating. When stared into, colors appear. Hues of blue, green, yellow and red. In the dark, back to the set, the flickering light produces RAPID, strobe-like SHADOWS. Maybe this can be compared to the DREAMACHINE (if I can be so bold).

My set is placed in one corner of my bedroom. It has been running continuously for over two years, never shut off.

TUNE the vertical, horizontal hold and contrast so that it appears that only one third of the image is visible. Actually the whole image is there, tripled, each overlapping.

With eyes open, the picture can be amusing and amazing. My set is tuned to the local religious channel (LA channel 30). Not to be sacrilegious, that's too easy, but that's where the most interesting pictures are, scriptures typed on the screen permutate, the Xtian cross tripled becomes Psychick.

I applied the Dreamachine method (eyes closed) – the connection being FLICKER. My first attempts were fruitless. Then one day I could see. A strange sense of depth was noticed, as if I was viewing from the back of my head out to my eyelids. The whirling picture seemed to engulf my head, the only colors noticed were grey and blue. This doesn't work all the time, it seems the harder I try, the less I see. Utilize the brightness control, too. Some side effects – my eyelids twitched a lot at first (cathode ray interference?) and a slight headache.

TELEVISION CUT-UPS

Camouflage. If you live in a city with access to cable with many stations, the cut-up produced by flickering through all the channels will often appear to be following your train of thought, as if trying to keep up with you by feeding back symbols appropriate to your present thought, using association blocks to create a bridge between your thoughts and the flow of imagery. TV watching often becomes emotionally intense during this procedure. (Also, putting only the soundtrack of TV without the visuals through a stereo can provide valuable insights into the camouflage of control TV).

Flow.

Is the image more real than we? Cut it UP. Let's see.

We are starting to tape specific commercials and parts of programs which could be psychically stimulating one way or another...

A VCR is helpful to Fast-forward and Review and edit all the way around. Similar to Cabaret Voltaire but of your own design. If you can get several screens and put on each the most warped, weirded-out images you can find or get on video and zone out on all the stimuli. The weirder the better. The addition of music equally as bizarre, you only add to the experience.

Television and video are ideally suited for the cut-up method, incorporating as they do both the milieu of sound and visuals. It is interesting to interchange the audio and visual portions of two or more different programs and watch the conflicting messages you are then exposed to. Which sense do you assign more validity to?

Cut-ups of video can be of great use in ritual, too. If something is desired, you can record various images of it from television. When you have "captured" enough raw images, proceed to cut them up, splicing the images together randomly, either with the original soundtracks, random soundtracks from other raw footage, or with a special soundtrack of your own device.

This could also be randomly cut in with footage of yourself attaining your desire either symbolically or as working toward your goal. I find it very important in video sigils to have images of myself included in the footage. This serves to personalize the video, to take the power latent in video away from the big corporations and consecrate it to ME.

By flicking the channels around, one often gets an impression of synchronicity, that the audio signals one receives are, in some sense, inter-related with one's actions and/or feelings in REAL TIME. This feeling is further heightened when multiple televisions are used, with the television putting out the audio is blacked out, and a TV tuned to another station is being viewed.

Most people utilize their televisions in a very rigid, linear way. They tune in one specific channel and watch passively. But if one begins to view the TV as a mirror, useful both for scrying (astral) and divinatory ("fortune-telling") purposes, one will find that much of the "bad vibe" associated with television is dissipated, can even be turned around to become a potent shamanic ally. Cut-up TV is decontrolled TV, is big business castrated of its control patterns, the patterns through which we as viewers/ consumers are manipulated. Through the breakup of these patterns, we are able to free the airwaves of their inherent OBJECTIVITY, and reclaim them as subjective reflections of our own thoughts.

One of the biggest complaints about current television is that it allows for no participation by the viewer. It is soporific in that it offers no challenges or ambiguities to a watcher. Even complex issues such as the Middle East are reduced to one-and-a half minute "stories". The current half hour to one-hour format of traditional television "programming" allows for no real character development or subtleties of plot. The characters, even on a "quality" program like *Hill Street Blues*, are hopelessly shallow in comparison to even the most shallow people in "real life". The cut-up method offers a childishly simple means of re-introducing abstraction and subjectivity, DEPTH, back into a medium notorious for its lack thereof.

TV RITUAL-SETS AND SCRIPTS

As has already been mentioned, a lot more goes into a television program than the final, edited version we watch. A set is constructed. A set could be compared to a Temple, or thee Nursery. It is a place designed with a particular function in mind, in the case of TV sets usually to create an illusion. All ritual spaces are sets in a way. They are created to perform a specific purpose, and are constructed with that purpose in mind. If you notice the set on a TV sitcom, for example, you can notice the tedious attention to detail – a small stack of unanswered mail on the mantelpiece, all the cooking utensils on the countertops, a little bit of dirt on the floor (they're only human). This is done to complete the illusion that this set, in reality a movable plywood shell, is somebody's home.

It is with exactly this attention to detail that the magician constructs her ritual space. She knows that if any detail remains to remind her of the so-called mundane aspects of her life, her ritual will lose much of its power.

Once the set is constructed, a production crew needs a STORY BOARD. This is a series of drawings which plot out both the movements of the characters and the zooms, pans and angles of the various cameras. The verbal "lines" of the actors, as well as any music or other sound effects, are written out or described on the bottom of each board.

Thus, each portion of a scene is meticulously plotted out, in such a way that each member of the crew can see her role in the production.

Anyone who has ever read magickal instructions for a ritual, such as a Gnostic

Mass, will recognize that a grimoire is essentially a story board. However, a story board is much more effective as a mnemonic device as it describes the "plot" not only verbally, but also visually. Each sequence is described in terms of the "actors", the "observers" (or "cameras") and the accompanying sounds or speech.

It can be extremely useful to plot out a ritual in a story board format. First, it allows no room for ambiguity as to who is to do what when. It also allows the magician to see her ritual from the perspective of a camera, a bird's eye view, if you will, of exactly what will be happening. It allows for far greater considerations into the æsthetical aspects of the "production", placing a greater emphasis on symmetry and staging. A good ritual is similar to a good TV program – it causes a "suspension of disbelief" vital to creating change. It must create an illusion, to make something possible that, without good staging, would not be plausible.

Say you want to make money. Create a set that looks like a bank vault, or a giant hundred-dollar bill. Videotape a gorgeous man rolling around in a pile of play money (need not be real, only green, if you are from the US). The magician can make this man, rather than the money, the object of her desire. The money is already subliminally associated to the man through the video shot. A brief narration can be voiced over, or an evocative song, you could even invent some sort of dialogue, perhaps the man could be lustfully moaning the magician's name and his desire for her.

A technique I have used is to use the presence of a camera to prolong the agony, as it were, of a sexual working. As you excite each part of a partner's body, take a break to videotape that particular spot, both before and during stimulation. You'll be amazed at how sensuous it is to caress your lover with the camera's eye, you can zoom in on your favorite features at will, pause to excite a part and videotape the result. A body can become a vast, mysterious landscape, and the act of lust become a Hollywood feature. It can also be used later as an excellent link (see "Formulating links" in *Intuitive Magick*) to either mentally re-create that moment, or to draw the lover closer again.

The sense of *detachment* from an event, which one might even be participating in oneself, is one of the oddest phenomena of video I have yet encountered. One literally becomes a voyeur into one's own life and actions. Videotaping a ritual is nearly synonymous with objectivity.

And these, admittedly unrefined, examples need not be the end of it. The videotape could then be put on a TV set and played back as a centerpiece for a more traditional money-making ritual. The possibilities are unexplored, therefore endless. And it can go on and on, continually videotaping layer after layer of super-imposed videotape ritual until one finally has on one tape the accumulated documentation of perhaps dozens of individual rituals, or shoots.

This process is analogous to the old alchemical principle of "solve et coagula", of constantly sublimating (note the similarity to "subliminal", a major factor in subconscious recall) originally base matter into "gold".

Indeed, given the power that TV seems to exert over people and their lives, the old alchemical maxim "as above, so below" takes on a whole new meaning. She who rules the airwaves, rules the minds of men...

THE LANGUAGE OF ADVERTISING

As mentioned earlier, television is a language of its own. The real "content" of television is not in the programs, they are merely "bait" to get us to watch the ubiquitous advertisements. It almost seems as though TV programs are deliberately made as dull and un-challenging as possible, to lull us into a sort of hypnotic trance, so that we are thus rendered more susceptible to the commercials. Commercials have their own unique language too, and an amazing amount of research has been done into what sorts of advertising strategies are most likely to persuade us.

It might be useful to take a look at some of the factors in advertising that have been found to influence consumers:

Information content,
Brand/product identification,
Setting,
Visual and auditory devices,
Promises/appeals/propositions,
Tone/atmosphere,
Comparisons,
Music and dancing,
Structure and format,
Characters,
Timing and counting measures (for example, length or number of times the brand name is shown or mentioned).

Many of these methods are very reminiscent of old ceremonial magick rituals. For an excellent cross-reference too lengthy to get into here, see *Magick in Theory and Practice* by Aleister Crowley, Chapter 2. The main thrust of my argument is that advertising jargon IS a magical language. It CAN be used to affect or program the subconscious mind. Advertisements are constructed in exactly the same way that rituals are, using mnemonic devices very similar to the kabbalah. I do not consider this to be a theory – I take it to be a fact. If you have any doubts about this basic assumption, go to your library and read through some books on tele-marketing techniques.

Start watching advertisements. Pay close attention to the logic of them. You will begin to notice that hardly any one of them really make any logical sense. A typical example: Everyone knows that oxitone fights cavities. Crust toothpaste has oxitone. So it has the power to keep cavities away. Now it has not been actually stated that oxitone does, in fact, fight cavities – you are led to think that you are stupid for NOT knowing this. It is also not stated HOW MUCH oxitone it takes to fight cavities. Nor is the extent of this "cavity fighting" ever defined. So we are left with a total non-sequitur. What, at first appearance, is a very informative advertisement turns out, on closer examination, to say absolutely nothing. It is a conjuror's trick, a sleight-of-hand maneuver.

It is in this realm of tricking the subconscious into accepting the impossible as FACT that the traditional magician has always worked. And, although Madison Avenue may have updated the language and hardware, the essential technique, philosophy and approach would be very familiar to any magician of the past. A contemporary magician, if she has any desire to be such in anything other than name alone, would do well to learn how to apply these updated methods of subconscious persuasion to her ritual methods. Many of them are supported by the latest research into psychology and neurolinguistics, as well as proving their effectiveness through consumer response.

A lot of money goes into marketing research. SOMEBODY must be getting results from this form of magick.

VIDEO FRAGMENTS

Video Magick warrants a whole book on its own, it definitely deserves a great more attention. Hopefully you, the reader/critic will send us more research in the near future so that this project can be done justice to. We only received one observation about the *technical* magick of video. It is, obviously, only the tip of the iceberg...

Get or rent a video camera, one that has a negative/reversal switch on it so that you can make the picture negative. Point the camera at the TV screen while monitoring. You will discover an astral tunnel in black and white. Now turn the camera ever so slightly and observe! With practice you can see every geometric pattern under and in the sun – an almost infinite variety of symbols all fluctuating, all changing constantly. The effect is enhanced even more if you turn the color up to high contrast during the experiment. By various spinning methods (i.e., rotating the camera as if the lens were a pivot) and very slight adjustments of the zoom lens you will have hours and hours of mesmerized fun and trance. Video feedback has another application. Take a small picture, no bigger than 10 % of your total screen area, and stick it onto your TV screen. In this manner, you can immediately add visual images to the splendorous kaleidoscope of colors and these images will also feedback infinitely. You have to see this effect to believe it! Why it has never been used in promotional videos, especially in the 60s, we'll never know...

This technique sounds as if it would lend itself perfectly to the Sigil Process, a symbol of desire being placed on the screen and multiplied by video feedback. A hypnotic aid to concentration. Also, favorite patterns and configurations could easily be videotaped and saved for documentation as well as future rituals.

CONCLUSION

All that can really be said to sum up is that Television Magick is certainly an area of the occult deserving of closer attention and much more research. Hopefully, this modest beginning will be enlarged upon through experiments and communication inspired by this first effort. Reading through this booklet, it's obvious that we have not even properly scratched the surface.

Evangelists vs the New God

Anton LaVey

It comes as no surprise that the televangelists are now being cashiered on all fronts, either through scandal or absurdity. People are wising up about the Bakkers and Roberts only because it is time for them to be allowed to wise up. And why? Because the Christ-sellers were beginning to compete with the very god that they were unknowingly employing: TV.

In previous centuries, the Church was the great controller, dictating morality, stifling free expression and posing as conservator of all great art and music. Instead we have TV, doing just as good a job at dictating fashions, thoughts, attitudes, objectives as did the Church, using many of the same techniques but doing it so palatably that no one notices. Instead of "sins" to keep people in line, we have fears of being judged unacceptable by our peers (by not wearing the right running shoes, not drinking the right kind of beer, or wearing the wrong kind of deodorant). Coupled with that fear is imposed insecurity concerning our own identities. All answers and solutions to these fears come through television, and only through television (only through Christ can one be redeemed). Only through exposure to TV can the new sins of alienation and ostracism be absolved.

TV is the universal articulating factor. We don't have to go out early Sunday mornings to get religion – that was too much work. Now all we have to do is get out of bed and press the magic button and church comes to us. We become intimate with its comforting presence from the time we pop out of our mother's womb – it is indeed much more omnipresent than the old God used to be, as much as they claimed He had his eye on the sparrow, etc. Now it's true. There are television sets in every home, every restaurant, every hotel room, video stores in every shopping mall – now they're even small enough to carry in your pocket – electronic rosaries. It is an unquestioned part of everyday life. Kneeling before the cathode-ray God, with our *TV Guide* concordances in our hands, we maintain the illusion of choice by flipping the channels when we wish (chapters and verses). But the God stays on. The trick is, it doesn't matter what is flashing on the screen – all that's important is that the TV stays on.

When the Church based its mandate on the *Holy Bible*, claiming it was the word of God Almighty, there was some room for doubters since it was such a glaring fallacy of logic. The Holy Fathers devised the necessity for "faith" in hopes of covering up the inherent problem. But when TV masquerades as "entertainment," there's no room for doubt. There is nothing to doubt. There is no absurd premise being advanced, so no one has any cause to resist – so the universal dictates meet no resistance whatsoever. Why should they? It's a case of "Well, after all, you still must believe in God," but even more effective because there is nothing presented to believe or disbelieve. TV just is. No matter how much of a free thinker you are, there is still the influence of television in your life. To deny TV now would be as atheistic as Ingersoll denying the existence of God.

Naturally the televangelists had to be cut off – they were keeping people from concentrating on the new faith. The ends are the same as they always have been, to keep the sheep in line, and to keep them depositing money in the right places. Now it's not the Catholic Church, but various other annexes of morality and acceptability. You'll buy your stamp of approval just as surely as when they passed the collection plate. The televangelists got too greedy, using the name of the old God to syphon off too big a chunk of money for themselves.

That's why the present "religious war" isn't between any forces of "Good" and "Evil". It is being waged between The Media (the State) vs. Churches (Catholic and otherwise), who are tying up millions of dollars' worth of valuable property and assets. As Satanists, we have the advantage of realizing this early in the game. It has never been enough for us to be atheistic – we have learned how to smash religious ignorance by beating them at their own game. Not only denying but using Christians' own manufactured fears to destroy them.

We can use TV as a potent propaganda machine. We already are using it to our advantage in the form of MTV Satanic-rock visuals. The stage is already set for the next step – infiltration of the philosophy of Satanism and potent (emotionally inspiring) *music* to go along with the inverted crosses and pentagrams. Then the conspiratorialists will really have something to worry about. Instead of holding our rituals in chambers designed for a few dozen people, we are moving into auditoriums crowded with ecstatic Satanists thrusting their fists forward in the sign of the horns. As much "bad press" as the "Church of Satan" has received from the media over the past two years – Satanic child abuse, sacrifices, etc. – mention of *The Satanic Bible* only points people in our direction. Perhaps that's the plan, after all.

The key is to use television and not be used by it. Inventors of warfare weaponry don't stand out in the field and try their stuff out on themselves. If it takes turning your television to the wall or throwing it out the window, do it. Filtered exposure from other people is bad enough. We are adversaries to be reckoned with, and must not be taken in by our own infernal devices. We must allow stratification to develop, that a world for the vital and the living may be maintained.

PERPETUATION OF THE USELESS

It has been said that America is losing its position as the world power and will soon pass into a state of World Power Emeritus, much as England is now. It seems likely, since the U.S. is no longer in the business of creating or making anything. Now many businesses are in the business of losing money. We are working on the perpetuation of the useless – whether in offices, condos, people, or jobs. People who have money invest in keeping the system going, building large complexes and fully expecting them to stay empty. Everything is guaranteed by government loans and the banks gain in interest. Plenty of jobs are created every day where people are not really expected to work – but to serve as paycheck recipients so they can spend money and keep the loop going. The job is only a means to an end – occupational welfare. It seems there's no business like no business.

People who are plugged into our system show up at their jobs but have learned the exquisite skill of looking busy without really doing anything. The real "job" comes after they come home with their paychecks and report to their cathode-ray god to find out what they're supposed to buy next. That's their job – to spend money in the right directions, to be concerned about the prescribed innocuous topics, and to augment and perpetuate popular (and profitable) doctrine.

Their purpose is most certainly not to be useful, driven, creative – *alive*. But then, true Satanists understand the necessity for stratification and the insidious separation process that is going on around us. So when you get a sinking feeling that society is working in direct opposition to what you're trying to accomplish, don't worry – it really *is* working against you. But it just means you're alive. And well...

The Satan Game

Reflections on Recent Hysteria Amongst Fundamentalist Christians

Lionel B Snell

On July 17th 1989, ITV screened a program called *The Roger Cook Report* and subtitled "The Devil's Work" – an appropriate title, as this essay will reveal. It began with an astonishing assertion from a Christian interviewee that we were witnessing "an absolute explosion of Satanism", followed by the even more astonishing revelation that this "absolute explosion" had been going on for thirty years already.

After this promising beginning it was too bad to discover that the entire investigative might of the *Cook Report* not only failed to find a single corroborated example of Satanism in Britain, but it was finally reduced to inviting a living Satanist over from America in order to prove that such people might actually exist. To be fair the investigative team didn't altogether fail: they may not have succeeded in digging out evidence of widespread child abuse, animal and human sacrifice, blood and sex orgies, but they did undoubtedly catch staff at the notorious Sorcerer's Apprentice putting on Halloween masks. Disgusting, I call it.

WHAT WENT WRONG?

The thing which intrigued me about the program was this: why was it screened? Journalists may consider themselves tough, but they do share one major weak spot: they cannot bear to be "taken for a ride" in public. It was so obvious that the fundamentalist Christian anti-occultists had made a fool of Cook and his team by sending them on this "wild goose chase", that I could not see why he had let it be broadcast – especially in view of the TV authorities' own reluctance to show the program which reflected so badly on their credibility.

Was there some mysterious pressure behind the scenes? Or did Cook miscalculate and assume that no-one of any critical intelligence would be watching a program which claimed to take Satanism seriously? Or did he rather calculate, on the basis of his experience with Kevin Logan and other Christian extremists, that here was a topic so emotionally charged that he could forget the usual restraints of reason and common sense?

Myself, I incline to the latter view: Cook estimated that when the subject is Satanism, it is now more important to be seen to be on the attack than it is to be seen to be sharp, accurate or critical. When "hard hitting" journalism fails to hit, it is reduced to "hard flailing" journalism, and Cook miscalculated that his public would not notice the difference on this occasion.

This is the way to play safe during a witch hunt – a time when any sign of intelligence or cynicism is liable to lead to the stake. So did Cook really think the situation was so bad that he had to go along with it?
If he thought that the Christian extremists were stirring up a witch hunt, he was not the first to suggest this. Since Kevin Logan has himself begun to speak of "occultists who cry 'witch hunt' when criticized", we must begin by asking: what is the difference between a witch hunt and a serious attempt to cope with a genuine problem?

HOW TO RECOGNIZE A "WITCH HUNT"

Of course there is no confusing the matter once a witch hunt is in full cry. What we are here looking for are the early signs of this distinction between a hysterical witch hunt and a necessary purge if we are to reduce the chance of the witch hunt developing.

I suggest that the first and clearest sign of a witch hunt is in the stereotyped, mythic nature of the accusations. Cohn, in his book *Europe's Inner Demons*, points out that the accusations made against witches during the great trials followed a standard formula which included drinking blood, sexual promiscuity, the use of drugs, sacrificing animals, people and in particular babies. Along with that were accusations of dirty and perverse use of urine and feces, of a worldwide conspiracy against the church and Christian society, and the abuse of children. However, he goes on to point out that these accusations add up to a standard package that emerges whenever a large crowd feels threatened. Exactly the same accusations have been leveled against Jews, against communists, against fascists, against Moslems... They were even leveled against the early Christians themselves.

What the public needs to learn is this: whenever one of those accusations is made, it is a serious matter which needs investigation. But whenever the whole lot is made at once, then they should not be swallowed without a large pinch of salt.

By way of analogy: what would you, as a parent, do if your eight year old daughter came home from school saying that "teacher says there is a nasty man about who does naughty things to little girls on their way home from school"? I am sure that most parents would be quick to phone the police for confirmation and would take immediate action to guard their child.

But what if the daughter went on to add that the naughty man had a big black cape, sharp teeth and hair on the palms of his hands, and that he sucked children's blood when the moon was full? Now the child is giving much more hard detail than before but, far from making the story more credible, it is reducing its impact – because the parent recognizes the stereotype of the old vampire myth and so feels less concern. Instead of phoning the police, most parents would just make a note to question the teacher some time about the appropriateness of their choice of children's stories.

By this token, when we hear accusations of occultists abusing children we are right to feel concerned. But when we find all the other accusations being thrown in too, then it is not so much the occultists that need Investigation but rather the accusers themselves. What inner problem do they have which is causing this eruption of *Europe's Inner Demon* in their minds?

SATANISM OR DEVIL WORSHIP?

I have consistently argued that analysis is the finest tool for banishing demons, so let's set off down that route first. To remove one widespread source of confusion I begin by clarifying the logical distinction between Satanism and devil worship. I emphasize that it is a logical distinction: in our society we will find that the two usually coincide, but dividing the demon in this way will give us some power over it, as you will see.

When the public uses the terms Satanism and devil worship as meaning exactly the same thing, they are like people who insist that "communist" equals "revolutionary". Those whom Jung would label "sensation types" insist on this identity and prove it thus: go out and find me ten communists and I'll show you ten revolutionaries. In our capitalist society they are usually right; at the ideas level, however, there is a real distinction: in an established communist society like China or the Soviet Union it is the communists who become the conservative anti-revolutionaries.

The same problem exists with Satanism. Strictly it should mean the worship of the god Satan, and a way of life based on his principles; whereas devil worship simply means the revolutionary act of turning against your established religion and embracing its antithesis. But the fact that Satan is in some sense a polar opposite of Christ, coupled with the fact that we live in a Christian culture, adds up to the reality that any Satanists we can find will be likely to be devil worshippers to some degree – just as in a capitalist culture most communists will be to some extent revolutionary simply by definition.

What would be the true characteristics of a "pure" Satanism devoid of devil worship? Now don't ask me for authoritative guidance on the exact nature of deities that I have not thoroughly researched: the following description is just a rough outline and it might be questioned by an expert Satanist.

Satan is most easily, but dangerously, seen by us in contrast to Christ. While Christ is a spiritual guide, Satan is an earthy chthonic god. Instead of gentleness, modesty and spirituality he urges us to strength, pride and sensuality. Instead of transcending the flesh we are urged to revel in it, master it (as opposed to conquer it) and learn its secrets. While the direction of Christ is toward unity (bringing God's children together in the divine embrace) the direction of Satan is towards distinction – the fundamental duality that generates manifestation, the individual standing proudly apart from the universe, the division of the sexes, the definition of tribal boundaries... And so on, as symbolized by the inverse pentagram which elevates the two horns of manifestation above the single point of spirit (while the goody-goody version of the pentagram elevates the point of spirit above duality). Indeed we shall later see that the paradoxical manifestations of Satan stem from his esoteric role as the Lord of Duality – he is not simply the ruler of the spiritual opposition, but rather Opposition itself as a positive, creative factor.

Note that nearly all these characteristics do seem "wicked" by Christian standards, because they are polar opposites, but in pure Satanism there is no question that they are performed because they are wicked. True Satanism would revere money, power, strife and sex because it considers them Good Things, paths to growth, not because they are naughty.

Devil worship, on the other hand, is the decision to worship everything that your religion considers to be bad, because it is bad. The object of devil worship is revolutionary: it could be inspired by immature, childish rebellion, it could be an act of anger as catharsis for the oppressed, it could be an attempt to precipitate a personal crisis for self-knowledge, it could be a way of investigating the religion rebelled against by testing it, or it could be an overt revolutionary act.

However, in a Christian society, anyone who sets out to worship the devil is likely to constellate the devil in the image of Satan. The result would therefore be called Satanism, but it would be distorted because of the devil worship impulse behind it. Although many outward characteristics would be nominally satanic, there would be something very different about the spirit of the religion.

To see why this is so, it is worth imagining what the devil worshippers would do if we lived in an overtly satanic culture. In that situation the devil worshippers would probably revolt against the materialism of that culture by denouncing their worldly goods, they would revolt against its sensuousness by becoming ascetic and temperate, they would revolt against the body and its demands, they would revolt against procreation by abandoning the family for a celibate community, they would revolt against their self by making personal sacrifices and so on. Not surprisingly they would probably constellate this rebellion in the form of worship of a god whose physical body died on the cross as a sacrifice to save mankind's souls – i.e. they would be nominal Christians. However, because the impulse for this religion was negative – an act of revulsion or rebellion against Satan – you would expect its form to be perverse. There would probably be an exaggerated stress on the masochism of flagellation, the breaking up and devouring of the flesh and blood of the sacrificed god, there would be considerable self-mutilation, castration and a great outward show of destroying wealth and smashing statues and melting down gold images, etc.

Here is the problem: all these actions are quite recognizably Christian, and have been performed by ardent Christians at some time or another, but put together they add up to a religion that would shock and disgust conservative members of a satanic society. Even gentleness can appear shocking and subversive – witness the anxiety felt by riot police in the 60s when hippies put flowers on their gun barrels. The word "Christianity" would become synonymous with the vilest perversion and a dangerous de-stabilizing influence on their material society. So we can see that if Christianity and devil worship were to combine, the result would be a horrid parody of the true Christian message and spirit; but try explaining that to those outraged members of a satanic establishment!

Christianity is directed toward the spiritual and so it opposes bodily indulgence. Consistent rich foods while others starve are un-Christian. So a certain asceticism is appropriate to Christianity. Now, in a particular individual case, that asceticism might be furthered by fasting and flagellation: if one otherwise balanced individual only manages to transcend his physical nature by castrating himself, and he assures us that this has solved his personal problem, then who are we to deny this? But when continued starvation, relentless flagellation and mass castrations become the norm or even compulsory then we could surely argue that this would not be true Christianity. Such exaggerated emphasis on denying the body would be a deflection of Christianity's real spiritual aim – the reason it would be practiced is more to do with the fact that the people were rebelling against a satanic culture that saw everything in physical terms. Again, the big emphasis on devouring Christ's blood and flesh would be a materialist perversion of the mass. If such perverted Christianity was practiced by the devil worshippers, then the satanic society that spawned such rebellion would be every bit as much to blame as Christ.

In the same way we should consider the actions accredited to today's Satanists and analyze them to see to what extent they are truly satanic, and to what extent they are a perversion due to rebelling against a Christian culture.

THE ACCUSATIONS ANALYZED

Satanists are accused of having sexual orgies. This seems appropriate, and it seems appropriate that they should allow everything possible to increase the thrill and the excitement of the participants. Unfortunately not everyone is turned on by the same stimuli, and anything which would serve to lessen anyone's sexual pleasure would be very un-satanic. So it would not be appropriate to include extreme perversion, coercion or exhibitionism in a mass satanic rite. These elements could only succeed in a small, closed group who had agreed beforehand that they shared the same pleasures.

So when we hear extreme stories of mass satanic perversion being reported it is more likely that we are witnessing the projected unconscious fantasies of a sexually repressed religious group – the fundamentalist Christians.

Satanists are accused of taking drugs. Insofar as alcohol and other drugs can heighten sensual pleasure and increase one's appreciation of the physical that also seems appropriate. But to surrender ones individuality to an addiction is surely a blasphemy against the god of proud and sensual individualism? To take so much of a drug that the body begins to suffer would be equally inappropriate to an earthy god.

So when we hear extreme stories of satanic drug pushers sweeping the nation, it is more likely that we are witnessing a guilty projection from a religion which does not like to face up to the fact that the economy of many devoutly Catholic communities in South America depends utterly on the drug trade – and that the Mafia are pillars of their establishment.

Satanists are accused of sexually abusing children. This makes little sense in a religion which reveres lustful procreation. Children are of little immediate interest to Satan, until such time that they reach puberty and can experience lust themselves. Inserting one's penis in a choirboy's bottom may afford delight to some, but it does little to further the species. No, the fascination with children is definitely a Christian specter – as it is probably so with any sexually repressive religion.

Christians who deny their sexual lusts have a long tradition of fascination with the innocence of those who do not have such lusts – ever since "suffer the little children" they can hardly get pre-pubescent children out of their minds. This has resulted in a range of symptoms – from the benign pederasty which has traditionally made Church of England clerics such good teachers at the junior school level, to the horror stories of child molestation by "upright Christians" so regularly reported in the *Daily Telegraph.*

But the main symptom which concerns us here is the tendency amongst Christian extremists to project this core of guilt and raise the hunt for scapegoats for their own unacknowledged sins. They used to accuse the Jews of eating little children, but since Hitler died they have picked on Satanists as the politically safer victims.

Satanists are sometimes accused of evangelism, of trying every technique to lure unwilling members to their church – especially young children. It is the final qualification which makes this accusation so ridiculous. Can you really imagine a satanic ritual sounding like a Sunday family service punctuated by the gurgles of babies and the voices of young children? If ever there was a god that wanted to have "adults only" pinned above his church door it would surely be Satan. And, in view of the enormous secrecy reputed to Satanists, is it really credible that they would want large numbers of non-dedicated members in their congregations?

This evangelist accusation is patently absurd and can only have its origins in the mind of the accuser. Consider one such, Kevin Logan; his book *Paganism and the Occult* accuses all occultists of evangelism. However, as one of the occultists quoted in his book points out, the well-known problem in occultism is not how to lure people into it, but how to keep out the loonies who have peculiar ideas about the subject. Of course the reality is that Kevin Logan is himself an ardent Christian evangelist, and this is where the crazy notion of occult evangelism springs from – his own unacknowledged "shadow" as he lays on jolly children's services to lure the innocent into his own fold.

Satanism is accused of world conspiracy. Oh dear, how on earth are we supposed to square the image of a hairy legged horned chthonic deity with the subtle machinations of a unified power behind the worlds thrones? The principle of Satanism is so divisive and individual that the normal accepted meaning of "world conspiracy" is utterly out of place here. All you could say is that Satan is dedicated to stirring all human souls individually towards thoughts of the flesh and away from spiritual unity – and one must admit he can do that very subtly. That is, in a sense, a world conspiracy, but it hardly squares with the stories put out by the fundamentalists. Satan's activities are more likely to divide society than to unite it into a monolithic bureaucracy of evil – an idea that is surely better seen as a corrupted mirror image of the universal church or body of Christ?

Satanists are accused of animal sacrifices. This could be appropriate, as the ingestion of freshly butchered meat is reputed to serve a vitalizing function. But we never hear that the meat was served with delicious sauces, or lightly barbecued to make it palatable, and such omissions are suspicious. Indeed it has been claimed that the blood is mixed not with fine brandy but with feces and urine – a cocktail that smacks much more of spiritual revolt than of fleshly indulgence. So either the story is true: in which case I deduce that the Satanist in question was not "true", but rather a Christian rebelling against his culture by inverting its values.

Or else the story is false: in which case I recognize again that the Christian accuser is projecting his own religious guilt, the shame of a creed that has not yet recognized that the killing of some hundred million turkeys in the name of Christ amounts to the biggest religious slaughter in the history of mankind – and it is repeated every Christmas.

Satanists are accused of human sacrifices. This too needs to be taken seriously, because it is a deeply held human belief that spilled human blood is a source of power, and power (especially material power) is definitely in Satan's interest. In fact it is less easy to find accounts of Satanic human sacrifices; all you usually hear is vague third-hand rumors, so I am less certain as to what is being suggested here. Are we to believe that Satanic priests ritually cut the throats of helpless victims tied down to an altar? That does not seem an appropriate way to worship a god of pride and strength – especially if we are told the victim is a child. It would be far more credible if we heard that the successor to a Satanic high priest had to ritually fight his predecessor to the death in order to win the title, but such rumors do not seem to be forthcoming from the accusers. That Satan should be glorified by the blood of fierce warriors conquered in battle does seem appropriate, but I cannot see him feeling anything but insult if offered the blood of a helpless child.

So again we either have to ask if the rumors are true: in which case the ritual murder must be the work of someone from a Christian culture setting out to do the wickedest thing he can imagine – and perhaps at the same time avenging the sacrifice of his own god by mankind. Or else we have to ask if the rumors are another guilt projection of a religion with two thousand years of human bloodshed to its "credit".

At some unconscious level those fundamentalists must register the fact that not only has Christianity a very bloody history but also that in our present day the violence in any country is directly proportional to the level of religious belief. Compare the value of human life in such secular societies as Sweden, Holland and England with the high levels of violence in deeply Christian communities in Northern Ireland, South America and the USA. You might reverse cause and effect and argue that it is an initial high crime level which drives people into the church, but the fact is that religion reached the states with the Pilgrim Fathers, and the divisions in Ireland are a clear consequence of religion. As the Ayatollah Khomeini clearly demonstrated, human blood is the best way of stoking the fires of a tired old religion, and this was most dramatically demonstrated by the Jonestown massacre in 1978. I have elsewhere explained how this has proved to be the most successful magical ritual of recent years: a thousand Christians drank poison at once as a sacrifice to their cause. Before this act Christianity in the States was in terminal decline: since the 60s the majority of the population had turned away from Christ and either taken the hippy course of occultism and Eastern religions or else simply become secular materialists. But the Jonestown sacrifice changed Christian fortunes overnight to produce an enormous religious revival. Christians must at some level register the extent to which the spread of their faith depends upon human sacrifice, but the fundamentalists have a mental block that does not let them become conscious of the fact – because there is an uncomfortable split in their religion between "thou shalt not kill" and the idea of a holy crusade. So once again such twisted individuals feel compelled to find a scapegoat for their guilt – and accuse Satanists of ritual murder. At their most extreme, these Christians are "killing two birds with one stone" by simultaneously expunging their own guilt and lining up new victims that they can slay with a sense of righteousness. They can offer the sacrifice of a burnt witch to their god with the Christian glow of charity in their hearts.

Because that last example is so grotesque I must sound a note of warning here: I am not saying that murder is in the spirit of Christianity. It is as far alien to Christ's nature as pederasty or drug addiction would be to Satan's. If I heard rumors that Christian fundamentalists were sacrificing young men to their god I hope I would analyze the rumor just as thoroughly as I analyzed the rumor of Satanists sacrificing babies. I would first point out that such slaughter was not appropriate to Christianity, and I would deduce that either the protagonists were motivated by non-Christian factors, or that the stories were fabricated by someone with their own problem. I do not see the Jonestown massacre as a Christian ritual: it was a piece of primitive magic that was resorted to by Christians who did not understand the forces they were tampering with. As human beings, Christians have as bad a record as anyone else in such matters. If the fundamentalists stopped projecting their guilt on others and instead took some lessons from the occultists, they would have a much better chance of clearing up their own seedy act. But that would require an act of true humility...

To sum up: most of the accusations regularly leveled against Satanism fail to stick. If there really are so-called Satanists performing the acts described, we are forced to admit that they are not being true to their religion. They are behaving more like rebels from a Christian culture than true Satanists, and should therefore be seen as a regrettable by-product of this very culture: no more Christ's responsibility than Satan's, but simply an example of what happens when imperfect humanity fails to live up to unrealistic ideals, and cannot handle this failure.

The other (and, to my mind, greater) likelihood is that some stories about Satanism are simply not true, the accusations are in fact mythical projections from the Christian unconscious – a mere fantasy expression of the same human failure. They are a perverted mirror image of Christian obsessions and they are generated in the souls of the accusers. Kevin Logan in his book on the subject does admit that Satan seems to have no creativity of his own: everything ascribed to him is a distorted mirror image or perversion of some divine creation as he "apes" God's work. What he does not admit is that this is exactly the characteristic you would expect a projected "shadow" of your god to manifest. His is a fair description of the Satan we meet in his writings: not an autonomous spiritual power able to be worshipped, but simply a shadow cast in his own unconscious by a god that Kevin Logan and his type have made too bright for their own eyesight.

To be able to see such a "Satan" you have to be a Christian – and you have to be standing with your back to God.

WHY IS THIS HAPPENING NOW?

Analyzing the current Satanism scare we conclude that it is a Christian problem. Without having immediate access to all the evidence it is not absolutely certain whether the problem is nothing more than a group fantasy shared by unbalanced Christian extremists, or whether there are actual examples of rebel Christians leaving the fold to perform devil worship in their own manner. All that is certain is that the stories circulated have no direct bearing on Satan or any genuine Satanic religion.

So next we must ask why this problem has arisen in our so called modern secular society? Some critics of Christianity will argue that the sort of hysteria described is inevitable in such a repressive, anti-female religion, but I am more interested to ask why it is that the lunatic fringe of the otherwise well-behaved Christian community should be going through this particular crisis right now.

Four reasons suggest themselves: 1 – that Christianity is growing old and decadent, 2 – that there might actually be an explosion of Satanism, 3 – that the Aeon of Horus is taking effect. Those three reasons might not be sufficient individually, but they could add up to a pressure which is being released by the fourth trigger factor: 4 – the year 2000 has a special emotional significance for fundamentalist Christians because of their strong tradition of millennial hysteria, as described in Cohn's book *The Pursuit of the Millennium*. I'll enlarge on those first three factors in order.

First the idea that Christianity is growing decadent. One of the themes in *Thundersqueak* and subsequent essays of mine is that ideas and philosophies run through a life cycle: a new idea comes in as a conquering hero, overturning, suffocating and restricting old ideas and giving us greater freedom and room to grow. As it becomes established the idea continues to support us and help humanity to find its feet in the new territory. But as it grows older the idea becomes rigid dogma, another hidebound old structure holding people back. By this point humanity desperately needs a new young revolutionary philosophy to turn up and defeat the old tyrant once more. This thesis is, in a sense, a defense of constant revolution or "novelty for its own sake" – except that I do believe mankind needs the second stage in order to gain some sense of security. So, in my old age, I am all for allowing a newish idea plenty of scope to prove its worth before we reject it, even though this tolerant consolidating phase might seem less fun that the constant overthrow of ideas.

Christianity has been around for two thousand years and has gone through several phases of decadence, but has been "big" enough to have created its own internal revolutions to renew itself from within a few times. On this point the fundamentalists in question might agree with us: "Yes, Christianity has grown old and decadent, and we are the new force that is now regenerating the faith". Unfortunately, this current revolution looks more like symptoms of terminal sickness. True, there are signs of genuine revolution in Christianity amongst its more enlightened and progressive elements at present, but so far they do not seem to be making much headway against the cancer of fundamentalism.

So the first suggestion is that we look to the Jonestown massacre, which provided the stimulus for the present fundamentalist revival and admit that it was not a healthy starting point. The current Satanic witch hunt is typical of the symptoms one would expect of such a gangrenous excrescence upon the aged body of the church.

The second consideration takes a kinder view, and one that might seem surprising in view of what has been said: perhaps the fundamentalists are right, that there has been an explosion of Satanism – but that they have completely misjudged its nature? This does not invalidate my previous arguments which were against the existence of the organized Satanic religion they described, because what we are talking about here is an underlying Satanic trend in our culture.

If we go back to the qualities that I tentatively ascribed to Satan – qualities like power, pride, sensuality, procreation, individuality and distinctiveness – then we can see some evidence that these qualities have become increasingly favored by our society during this century. Even if the evidence tends to crumble under scrutiny, we must admit that it is widely believed – and that is the relevant factor here. The man in the street would apparently claim that today's society was more materialistic, sex-mad and individualistic... In effect, more Satanic.

Power is a Satanic quality, and we can see in current advertising and media fantasies that power is supposed to be highly revered nowadays. "Blessed are the meek" does not get half the coverage. Pride is also seen as something to be actively encouraged. We hear much positive talk about "the pride in their national identity", even though it leads to nationalistic divisiveness. This splitting up or "apartness" is also more appropriate to Satan than to the unifying tendency of Christ, and it is very much in evidence in recent decades.

Another form of splitting up is the emphasis on the nuclear family at the expense of a wider vision of society. If you look up the word "family" in an authorized *Bible* concordance you will not find it mentioned by Christ, nor does he use related concepts like "brother", or "parent" much except in the sense of God being the father of one great extended family. Indeed, the Christian impulse was rather to forget one's sexual origins and to get up and follow the Master. On the other hand, it would be appropriate to Satan, a god of duality and division, for society to fragment into smaller structures, and as he is also a god of sex it is appropriate that the division should be into a procreative unit like the family. Although the current concept of the family hardly existed before this century, it has already become widely accepted and is more spoken about than never. So it is another sign of growing Satanic influence on society.

Hand in hand with talk about families goes talk about the importance of the individual in a manner that is far more appropriate to the rebellious spirit described by Milton than it is to the Christian ethic. And then there is the more recent change of heart about material wealth: it is no longer something that needs to be apologized for. The question of sex is a little more complicated: there is no doubt that the subject is much more apparent now than it was in Victoria's day, but you could argue that her reign was a pathological low point rather than being typical of past ages. Another factor is that, although sex is still widely discussed, the AIDS scare has greatly reduced its practice in the last ten years. This does not look so much like a serious long-term trend, however, as it looks like a temporary resurgence of a troubled Christian conscience. We hear similar cries of protest at current materialism and selfishness, but they have not held back the tide. Another complex issue is the Satanic focus upon the body: what might have developed into the pure sensuousness of physical culture has become in many cases overlaid with a passion to negate the body by slimming beyond the needs of health or aesthetics. While remaining obsessed with their bodies, some people are punishing them almost as severely as the Christian ascetics of old.

Despite such qualifications and complexities, there is definitely a strong case to be made out that Satanic principles have grown strong in our society during this century, and that this is especially true in the post-war years, and that it has had its most blatant expression in the recent governments of Thatcher, Reagan and their followers. In these terms, therefore, it becomes less surprising that the more dogmatic and evangelical Christians should begin to feel uneasy.

They have, however, compounded the problem for themselves by their own attempts to patch it up. Just as Christianity in its early days was able to flourish on the strength of its universality by incorporating elements of existing religions into its body, so has it since been reasonably successful at adapting itself to world changes. Thus it was able to grow beyond its initial confrontations with Kepler, Darwinism, Marxism and other new philosophies and, as a result, liberal Christianity has retained its relevance in a changing society. Now, although the mainstream Christian communities have managed to hold firm in their opposition to some of the Satanic tendencies listed above, the fact is that certain of the evangelical fundamentalists have got themselves into a ludicrous position by trying to take the whole lot on board as "Christian principles".

The effects of this can be quite grotesque. In their literature you will see kitsch paintings of Weetabix families casting adoring eyes on a robed Jesus to the accompaniment of words about "the Christian family tradition"! It seems that Christian traditions now embrace money-making too, to quote Kevin Logan's book, "The wealth of the West has been accomplished largely through applying the beliefs of Christianity to everyday life"! Sure enough, today's hot-gospellers are raking in the millions and with them the sort of criminality and corruption you would expect: recent reports on BBC's Sunday programme told of Christian conmen encouraging the elderly to invest their life savings on the strength of biblical prophecies. Christianity's long and not altogether successful battle to suppress the Luciferic scientific current is also conveniently forgotten by Logan when he writes, "Modern science could only have come from a belief that there was a God who made all things to a certain design." He supports that statement by pointing out that Isaac Newton was as much at home with religion as he was with science: because his book is an attack on the occult he chooses not to mention that the work which Isaac Newton valued most highly of all was his alchemical researches.

The spectacle of such gymnastic ethical and philosophical U-turns can be entertaining, but also a tragic reminder of human gullibility and blindness. As an occultist myself I feel a certain threat from such people, but my main concern is to feel deeply sorry for the many genuine Christians who continue to apply their very considerable principles as best they can in view of such crazy stablemates. Perhaps the saving factor is the vast mass of indifferent nominal Christians who act as a buffer between the two camps?

But I diverge: the point is that, although there is no evidence for an active, organized Satanic religion as fantasized by the lunatic fringe, there is a case to be made for a recent major upsurge in Satanic principles – at least within the popular imagination. That, combined with a hopeless attempt to stretch and embrace these principles, could be sufficient pressure upon the fundamentalist community to push them toward some sort of hysterical breakdown of the sort we have been witnessing.

The third factor I want to suggest is the additional effect of the Aeon of Horus. The full argument for this was written up a few years back in my article on Thelemic Morality, so I will only briefly summarize the relevant bits here. This article has already appeared in Germany in *Anubis*, but English readers will have to wait for the late 1989 edition of *The Equinox* (or else my forthcoming *Collected Essays*) if they wish to follow it up.

Referring to Crowley's concept of the three aeons: Isis was the aeon of the mother goddesses, who were experienced as dark, severe deities whose rule had the inexorable logic of Fate: you did what they said, or you paid the price (the *Old Testament* Jehovah fits that mould, though nominally male). Osiris was the age of the bright male gods (Christ, Odin, Dionysus, etc) who were far more "human": their nature is to love mankind, even to suffer on our behalf. Their law is not to follow absolute commandments but rather to try to emulate their perfect example. But Horus is the age of the child-god, an avenging, martial deity who challenges us to stand on our own two feet. This god does not expect absolute obedience, for "do what thou wilt" is the law, nor does he expect us to follow his example, for it is far from ideal for humanity.

Fundamentalism is the ethics of the aeon of Isis, and it was absolutely right in that context and at that time (just as it has its place with very young children). What Jesus did, as an Osirian deity, was to replace the absolutism of the ten commandments with something far too vague to be a "commandment" in that sense – he said "love thy neighbor". His approach in judgments such as "let he who is without sin cast the first stone" is not to tell us precisely what to do, but rather to stimulate us to think, and in particular to follow his enlightened example. The idea of an impeccable "guru" is typically Osirian (and contrasts sharply with the "examine my ideas but do not follow my example" approach of the Aeon of Horus). So "Christian fundamentalism" is innately self-contradictory, and this is the essence of its sickness. Christian fundamentalism (and, presumably, Islamic fundamentalism) is the attempt to contain the wisdom of the Aeon of Osiris within the ethical standards of the Aeon of Isis (e.g. Jehovah's law) – the "new wine in old bottles" that Christ warned against.

Now what happens when a devout person invokes a deity? If the person is a monotheist, or more specifically one who only recognizes a supreme male god, then we have to admit that the belief does provide a lot of protection against invoking the wrong deity: such a worshipper would hardly be taken in by the presence of a goddess, a minor fertility god, or other less wholesome spirits. So far, it is a "safe" thing to do. But if you only admit one male god, you are uncritically open to any of the big male gods... And that includes Horus the Avenger.

In the Middle Ages anyone devoutly invoking God would, not surprisingly, tend to make contact with the Osirian current – it would either be Jesus or else a deity of very much the same general principles – because that was well within the Aeon of Osiris. But now we are in the Aeon of Horus, so the same devotion is liable to invoke the Horus current. Now, if you are an occultist of some description you will at least be on the lookout for different types of god, and will be able to use your critical ability to judge whether you have tuned into the god you want – the New Ager looking for sermons on love would, if contacted by Horus, no doubt resist the contact as "negative vibes"! But consider the problem of the dogmatic monotheist when the Horus contact is made: the power and numinosity of the current "proves" it must be the Supreme God – Christ or Allah – who is speaking.

This is born out by experience: recent examples of people like Khomeini and James Anderton who claim to have had direct messages from God make it clear in their subsequent actions that the actual entity contacted was far from being a loving, rational deity. They have contacted the wrath of Horus, but do not have the Aeon of Horus' Thelemic morality to handle the messages they are getting. If they are fundamentalists, they attempt to obey the letter of Horus' law – for a taste of which see *Liber AL*, chapter three – and if they are Christian they are in the uneasy position of trying to follow and comprehend the example of a deity who never deigns to set us an example.

So, to simplify the original explanation a bit, the third cause of strain amongst the Christian fundamentalists is that they have contacted the Horus current and do not know how to handle it.

There is a side issue raised here: how does this discussion of the Aeon of Horus relate to the previous discussion of an upsurge of Satanic principles: are they connected? I suggest that the relationship is not direct: I do not see much evidence that the nature of Horus is fundamentally Satanic, though they might overlap on certain power issues. Whilst recognizing the current Satanic upsurge, I do not take it as seriously in the long term as the fundamentalists do. To me it is just the flavour of the century, and most likely has its origins as a sort of backlash as Christianity loses its dominant position and certain Christians lose their marbles. It is a sort of Christian death-wish: remember that their predictions for the millennium depend upon the antichrist first establishing his kingdom, and so we find the fundamentalists unconsciously working to further the kingdom of antichrist in order to precipitate the crisis which will finally justify their shaky faith.

HOW BIG IS THE PROBLEM?

So one way or another it looks pretty certain that the "Satanic explosion" is a Christian problem. But insofar as Christianity is basic to our culture – that means it is partly a shared problem, and it is reasonable to want to know how big a problem, or how serious, it really is.

I will now illustrate the size of the problem.

On Sunday October 30th 1987 at a shack on the outskirts of Anderton, a small community East of Amarillo, USA, four people were murdered and one escaped to tell the tale...

Jacob Zaller was a runaway from his family in New Orleans, and he had been staying with the Angelos, a kindly hippy family that had offered him a lift from Amarillo. In the few days he was with them he had witnessed several occasions when redneck youths in Jeeps had driven past the Angelos' shack at speed, firing shots in the air and shouting threats. This scared the chickens as well as the children: apparently the family had lost a lot of their livestock until they took to locking them in – the Angelos said you just got used to it and kept smiling. He had also had the uncanny experience of being totally ignored when he tried to buy goods in the local store – after they discovered where he was staying.

On the night in question he had gone out to look at the stars from a nearby hill when he noticed something happening at the shack. Through the window he saw Jenny Angelo about to be raped by a large blond youth before the eyes of Doug and their kids who were held down by three others who kept shouting "you fucking witch". He also noticed that all the Angelos' occult books and charts had been taken from their shelves and piled up in the center of the floor, and a fifth youth was holding a can of petrol. Jacob managed to get away unnoticed on the Angelos' pushbike and made it to the sheriff's office. The sheriff turned out surprisingly slow and uncooperative, constantly asking him to repeat what he had seen without seeming willing to take any action. Anyway, to cut a long story short, Jacob was able to evade the sheriff and return some days later with an FBI agent.

The Angelos' shack was burnt to the ground and there were no signs of the bodies. Everyone they questioned swore blind that the Angelos, "who always kept to themselves", had left the area weeks earlier, and the shack had been derelict. Jacob recognized the blond youth who had raped Jenny, a local farmer's son. But the church congregation and the minister all insisted that the youth had been at church at the time of the incident. The case was dropped. And when Jacob returned to his family that Christmas, he found he was persona non grata – word had reached home ahead of him that he had been caught molesting children in the desert, and it took a year to clear his name.

Now, having heard the story, what would you want to do? Do not say, "I can't do anything living back here in England", the question is what would you do if you were omnipotent, had all the resources of the FBI and the army at your disposal? Stop now and make a list of the first four things you would feel like doing – before reading on.

How many of you began the list with something like "find out who those bastards were and beat hell out of them?" I sympathise with such an angry reaction: if most of you thought that, then the problem we are now considering is a very big problem.

How many of you put at the top of the list "check the facts"? If most of you put that, then the problem being considered is far smaller. For the benefit of those who did, I will save them some trouble: the only fact in that story was that I made up the whole thing.

The point is this: I began this investigation by saying that the most immediately suspicious thing about the Satan scare was that it was so stereotyped. What thinking person could swallow such a wadge of clichés about Satanists? Now what I have done is made up a story containing all the clichés about fundamentalist Southern American rednecks. Anyone who swallowed it uncritically should be able to spare some sympathy for the Christian extremists who are taken in by Satan stories. My story is as dubious as theirs: for all their dogmatism and anti-occult bias, redneck chapel ministers do have regard for the truth, and would be unlikely to lie about the youth's church attendance... And so on.

That story illustrates the size of the problem because it illustrates the extent to which we can be polarized against fundamentalist Christians. If you only have to hear a story like mine to become irrationally furious, then you are in exactly the same boat as the Christian extremists who rage against Satanists. If you have difficulty in distinguishing irrational fury from righteous indignation then remove the polarizing bits from the story: translate it to the far east and have Mongol hoards burning a Christian missionary family and see if it still evokes an equally furious reaction.

The more this issue is an emotionally charged one for us, the more we are part of the problem. One of the lessons that is learnt from working with the Horus current is the wisdom of traditional astrology which ascribes both marriage and enemies to the same, seventh, house. Enmity is as intimate a relationship as marriage, and sworn enemies have a way of growing to look like each other just as much as loving partners: put a southern redneck into a fur hat and overcoat and you have the image of a Soviet commissar. The worst excesses of Christian anti-occultism are found precisely amongst the Christians who are themselves practicing a form of low-grade occultism. They are the ones who see evil spirits everywhere, practice exorcism, speak in tongues and all the other weird stuff. Being "born again" is their version of traditional initiation rituals, and all the crap and superstition of low grade occultism is theirs.

Such churches hate occultists because they are themselves occultists and cannot admit it. Evangelical churches turn no-one away in their search for converts, and they pick up all the rejects from the occult world. Have you never met the half-baked occult bore who says, "Ah, you are interested in the occult I see! Tell me, what do YOU think about the Bermuda Triangle? I've just read an amazing book which proves that the CIA and the KGB were co-operating on researching it during the 60s. They dug up a whole shipload of evidence... Only it got lost in the Bermuda Triangle". Now you know what happens to such people: they become born-again Christians and write books about the horrors of occultism. Getting their own back on all those occultists over the years who had rushed away from their conversation muttering something about having to dash off to celebrate the Equinox.

Because the current witch hunt is basically an inner fight against themselves, it has a certain self-defeating quality. Kevin Logan's followers are trying to reduce the availability of occult books in shops around Britain, but the arrival of his own book means that any teenage Christian can now pick up a really quite interesting survey of current occultism, thrown into a pretty favorable light by some of the shaky arguments pitched against it, a book in which Christianity is made to sound a bit wet in comparison with chaos magic... And a book that is widely available in specialist Christian bookshops.

Similarly, at the end of the *Cook Report* there was a Help Line number made available for those who had suffered Satanic persecution: it was subsequently deluged with callers wanting to know more about Satanism! One of the people contributing to the program was a familiar figure: a woman who claims to have been heavily involved in Satanic rituals and who now tours the country giving lectures to warn children of the danger. Hers is indeed an interesting case: why, one wonders, did she, not once but repeatedly, attend rituals where animals were slaughtered, babies sacrificed and all the rest? She says she was too scared not to! What, one wonders, was the motivation of the others present? Were they all scared of each other? Were they perverts who actually enjoyed doing these things? If so, why drag Satan into it? Why not just concentrate on enjoying their perverse acts? The only motive that makes sense, is that the participants did what they did in the belief that they could get something from it: they were insignificant people who believed Satan would bring them power, fame, influence and prestige. In that case the woman in question has every reason now to thank Satan: because she is called to appear every time Satanism or the occult is mentioned on television – and this fame and influence is a direct consequence of her earlier Satanic devotions. As any teacher knows, much of childish naughtiness is due not so much to original sin, as a desire to draw attention to oneself. So what a seductive message that woman is now preaching to the children of Britain: if you want to be a TV star all you have to do is get involved in Satanism! Clever children will get an even simpler message: all you have to do to become the center of attention is to pretend that you have been involved in Satanism. Now I wonder where they got that idea?

With that example we have come full circle. As in the play *The Crucible*, one can ask what fanciful young child could resist the temptation offered to tell a few fibs and have a special exorcism service dedicated to them by the Reverend Kevin Logan who appears on TV? In a spiritual sense this witch hunt is totally self-defeating, like any other. The main interest for occultists is how not to get burnt in the process.

THE PARADOX OF SATAN

Can we draw any conclusion from this confused situation?

We have seen that the current hysteria against Satanism is something which generates itself from within: certain people attack Satanism in public and begin to create the problem they are attacking.

But my example of the story may have shown that the occult community cannot wash their hands of this problem, because the human tendency it feeds on is active within ourselves. We find that the Christian and occult communities have a lot more in common than they like to admit: at one extreme there are the gullible occult cranks and the Christian fundamentalists, at the other extreme there are the enlightened pioneering occultists and the radical, progressive Christians. We have Kevin Logan writing that occultism is Satan's distorted "aping" of God's ways, and we have me writing that Kevin Logan's Christianity is a distorted "aping" of occultism. The major difference lies not in the extremes but in the occult's lack of a large center ground. Occultism is more sharply focused than Christianity because it does not contain such a vast flock of "nominal" believers to act as a buffer between its extremes.

There is also the possibility that we are witnessing a surge in Satanic values, not at an organized level but in more subtle ways, and the question arises as to what extent are the fundamentalists driven by that Satanic undercurrent, and to what extent are they actually generating it out of their own decay.

As a clue to these problems I suggest we re-consider the basic nature of Satan. In our society he apparently has the exoteric role of Leader of the Spiritual Opposition. This is the simple role that makes him the target for Kevin Logan and his type. But at an esoteric level Satan is Lord of Duality, which is to say he is the Principle of Opposition itself.

We see the connection between duality and manifestation in the words of Dr. Theodor Landscheidt (in *Sun-Earth-Man*): "Those boundaries that separate the realms of antagonistic attractors that compete for influence are a model of reality. They represent the qualities of the phase boundary between magnetism and non-magnetism, laminar flow and turbulent flow, cyclicity and non-cyclicity, order and chaos, etc." A god whose nature is unity could not create Satan directly; he could only provide the conditions to allow Satan to create himself. Opposition is born and, in conjunction with the god, conceives a devil. Thus all manifestation erupts from this split in the unity – fractal foam betwixt God and Devil.

The paradox of Satan is that to oppose him is to do his will – because he is the principle of opposition.

This is why "pure" Satanism of the type suggested earlier tends to be anticlimactic, while the most exciting Satanism is that imagined by those who fear or oppose it. When practiced without that element of fear or opposition the religion tends to mellow into gentle sensuality and lose its fervor. People who oppose the flesh imagine the body as insatiable in its appetites: those who indulge the flesh without shame soon discover that the body can only eat so much, can only wear one suit at once, can only drive one car at a time. It is not the pure sensual appetites but rather the "spiritualization" of possessions as power which leads to goods being hoarded. We take one step away from pure sensuality towards the world of spirit and we are again caught up on that turbulent boundary of manifestation – sensation is overwhelmed by the emotion of greed.

Those who point the finger at Satan, reveal Satan. Those who fight Satan, give him power. Those who blame Satan, give him influence. Those who talk much of Satan, create him. But those who worship Satan, tame Satan. Those who passively resist him, earn his respect. Those who accept him, diminish his influence.

And those who analyze him, learn his wisdom.

THE MEDIA'S ROLE

In this essay I have concentrated on the role of fundamentalist Christians, but of course the man who did the *Cook Report* was simply a journalist.

However outraged the tabloids may sound about Satanism, I do not see much more than self-interest in their involvement.

There is no doubt that Gorbachev has dealt the right-wing tabloids a severe blow by reducing the credibility of communism as an "enemy within". It is no longer enough to hint at communist sympathies in order to blow up a small incident into a big issue.

When a journalist cannot call on subtlety, wit, intelligence or sharp observation to win readers' attention, and is forced to appeal only to the emotions as demanded by the owners of the tabloids, it leaves a very limited palette of colors to play with – they cannot afford to lose any one of them.

So a new "enemy within" must be found to ensure the continued wealth of the press (and, of course, to fuel the paranoia on which right-wing governments depend). The notion of a drug subculture is one candidate, but it has the weakness of being based on a physical reality – the existence of drugs. This physical burden of evidence sets a limit on how high the myth can fly.

Satanism is an excellent replacement for communism as a new "enemy within", for the reasons explained earlier: the confusion of Satanism and devil worship so closely parallels the confusion of communist and revolutionary. In addition, both Satanism and communism can be seen as distortions of the Christian spirit, and so ripe for projection. Above all, both allow accusations devoid of material proof. If the press accuses some prominent figure of being a drug baron there is always the possibility of his innocence being proved: but how do you answer criticisms that once, as a student, you were seen dancing naked in a wood, or you contributed a poem to a Marxist newspaper? To build up a witch hunt society must find an accusation which can be launched against even your most respectable neighbor, and one which can never be banished with 100 % certainty until he is dead.

This simple explanation does not diminish the significance of the media's role in the witch hunt, indeed they may ultimately play the major part in it. Another simplification is to point out that the divisive role played by the tabloids (their contribution to "divide and rule") is innately Satanic in itself, and so if they ever do become emotionally (as opposed to merely exploitatively) involved in the witch hunt it could be for similar reasons to those already ascribed to the fundamentalists – a projection of personal guilt.

WHAT TO DO?

I'll take my first cue from the I Ching – the book with a thousand ways of saying "do nothing" – and refuse to get involved. The lesson to be learnt from the seventh house of marriage and enmity is this: choose your enemies with care, because you will end up like them. If you reacted violently to my Southern redneck myths, then get to work on your own inner anger first.

Insofar as the Satanic witch hunt is self-generating, the less people become involved or concerned the better. And insofar as we have the ability to become polarized too, our involvement would only fuel the flames. The press cannot make much extended capital out of someone who shrugs off hysteria with gentle good humor – though they will, of course, try the "unfeeling monster" tack.

If the analytical approach of this essay has done something to de-fuse the Satan game in your own mind, then take it as an example of how you might yourself defuse the hysteria elsewhere.

The essence of Tai Chi is to remain serene in battle and encourage your opponent to topple with his own imbalance. That seems appropriate. Whereas the worst thing would be to whitewash yourself. That would amount to accepting their criteria and using them to protect yourself – and it is precisely their criteria which are so poisonous.

I recently had the experience of being questioned by journalists on the nature of the OTO. These were sympathetic people who were not digging out dirt, on the contrary, they wanted me simply to respond to attacks by saying that the OTO was not a Satanic organization, and that it did not sacrifice animals, etc. I found this whitewashing exercise surprisingly repellant, even though I only had to say the truth, and later asked myself why this was so. The problem I had was with the moral outrage suggested by the tabloid whose attack I was rebutting.

The problem of moral dirt is analogous to the problem of material waste. Some people do lead squeaky-clean lifestyles: their houses are spotless, and everything shines like new. Almost inevitably (and I pause to honor any exceptions) this cleanness is maintained at the price of creating waste elsewhere. They buy their food prepacked in complex wrappings which are then thrown out; last year's car is scrapped before it shows a dent; the furniture looks new because it is replaced as soon as it is scratched... These spotless communities generate a great mountain of waste elsewhere, and someone else has the job of managing it.

Now there is something inherently distasteful about those who feed on your waste – they have too much in common with flies that feed on your shit. Those squeaky-clean communities have a way of making an under-class or demonic subculture out of those who re-cycle their own waste. They don't have much of a record for honoring the gypsies, tramps, rag and bone men, etc – those actually doing something to alleviate the waste problem they have generated. Nobody wants to have anything to do with other peoples' cast-offs, and if they do, they must be non-people and despised. So we have a society of pretense, those who cannot afford the ideal role model are forever papering over the cracks, whitewashing the stains, and passing off their dirt with eyes averted.

The same problem applies to those who affect squeaky-clean morality.

Those who try to copy this ideal are involved in endless denials: refusing to see the Christmas turkey as an animal sacrifice; refusing to see communion wine as a sacramental use of drugs; preaching love while lining up enemies to slaughter, without even granting them the dignity of being recognized as sacrificial victims; devouring the flesh and blood of Christ while denouncing cannibal tribes: praying for favors while despising magical practice; using the *Bible* as an oracle while decrying fortune tellers... Such hypocrites generate so much moral waste that someone has to handle it if our planet is not to choke. But anyone who seriously tackles these issues, looks at these demons and faces up to the dark side of our society and our inner natures is despised as a "black magician".

In such a climate it is too tempting to say, "Oh no, that is not me! We are white magicians!" And so the dirt is passed on for some other poor bugger to deal with. To cry too loudly that one is "white" is to help reinforce the problem of polarity, whereas to analyze the accusations is to do something towards re-cycling their energy. As said above: the poison lies in the actual criteria of judgment.

To end this essay I should of course mention an alternative solution without which no such discussion would be complete. This third approach is the one already outlined in the *Manifesto of the OTO:* to go with the market forces.

If over-the-top-occultism is what the world is looking for, then sock it to them! Openly and without shame. Bring out the kinky robes, the zany paraphernalia, and the over-the-top eye make-up. Live up to their fantasies and cry, "Yes, you fellow loonies! The buck stops here!" Bring them face to face with their darkest nightmares and see who survives the shock – and who eventually wins the hearts of the people.

In the true spirit of the Aeon, I will now end without telling whether I am joking or nay.

In Defence of Satanism

Carl Abrahamsson

I called the Devil and he came,
His face with wonder I must scan;
He is not ugly, he is not lame,
He is a delightful, charming man;
A man in the prime of life, in fact,
Courteous, engaging, and full of tact.
A diplomat, too, of wide research
Who cleverly talks about State and Church.
A little pale, but that is en règle
For now he is studying Sanskrit and Hegel.

Heinrich Heine

So you thought that The Church of Satan had for ever given in to interior arguments and exterior hassles and accusations of child abuse and ritual murders? Well, you're wrong... It seems as though the last year has brought with it a renewed interest in The Church and its aims, a resurgence if you will.

Dr. LaVey has more or less retired from the "public" scene, and spends his nights the way he wants to: playing music and watching old Hollywood movies. Some critics find this reclusive attitude a bit strange, but, Hell, they obviously haven't understood the man's writings.

And what about The Church itself then? The organization and administration is still taken care of from San Francisco. Their newsletter, *The Cloven Hoof*, ceased to exist in 1988, and after this a new publication has taken over, *The Black Flame*. It contains articles on Satanic topics, philosophy, history, culture and occultism, and also book- and film-reviews. A nice-looking outlet for those affiliated with the Church, *The Black Flame* is the erect organ in the common world, designed to plant interest in the writings of "The Doctor".

Hell's Kitchen Press is a publishing company in New York, connected to *The Black Flame*. They have also published an anthology of contemporary Satanic poetry, entitled *Narcopolis*, and Blanche Barton's recent volume *The Church of Satan*, which is an excellent survey of the Church's history. Well-written, and filled with interesting information, this book is a must for all modern-day Satanists. As is, of course, Barton's LaVey-biography, *The Secret Life of a Satanist* (Feral House, 1990).

Compared to Burton Wolfe's 1974 *The Devil's Avenger*, Barton's book is far, far superior. More in-depth, more analytic, more informative, and a lot more entertaining, it's a volume that will go down in history as *the* LaVey-biography. The promised issue of *RE/Search* dedicated entirely to LaVey and his teachings, seems to be postponed though. The editors have apparently put a higher priority on the issue *Incredibly Strange Music* instead...

So, it's easy to see that The Church of Satan is, in one sense, more active than ever. Various other orders and secret societies use the terms "Satan", "Satanic", and other variations on the same theme. And, as with "Thelema", no one can really argue whether this group or that is Satanic or not. Just as there is only one O.T.O. and one A∴ A∴, there is only one Church of Satan. As Blanche Barton puts it in *The Church of Satan*, "If imitation is the sincerest form of flattery, LaVey has many reasons to be incensed over all the flattery he's received. Apart from his secular influence, Satanic groups sprouted up from Berkshire to Bangkok once Anton hit the newspapers."

The very hardest thing about it all is still convincing the unenlightened populace that it's not so bad and evil as it may sound to them. So, how to go about it? With so many fanatically violent Christians around, isn't it mere stupidity to stick one's chin out? Well, not really, no... And the main reason for this is the fact that people in general, and young people in particular, need "idols" to look up to, and compare themselves to. It's everyone's responsibility to see to it that these as-yet not-so-will-strong individuals are presented with models and ideas of strength and courage. These models have to be really strong and impressively imposant. The entire control-system, built on the Christian foundation of the worship of weakness, so kindly takes care of infants from the very start. This is something that has to be stopped, as it is pure folly and, very likely, could be the downfall of mankind. The only way it can be stopped properly, is by presenting exactly these models of strength and determination, so that the specific specimen can develop their own true wills.

Dr. LaVey and his philosophy, called Satanism, is one such model to recommend, highly rooted in "real" life and realistic outlooks and insights. Here we find a short-cut to illumination, without the classic path's more or less necessary ascetic trials and tribulations. The key is indulgence, from start to end, whatever this may mean to each person. Perhaps it sounds a bit trite to most newcomers, but when they start reflecting and acting in line with their own "infernal" wills, they find that it sometimes isn't so simple at all.

The dogma of control are very deeply rooted in most people's psyche, and it takes time to get through this initial purifying stage. The Satanist comes through the ordeals by disregarding everything and everyone who is not worthy enough to be near him/her. The Satanist is a life-loving and consequent conqueror in his own sphere, determined to win and feel good NOW! Those who stand in the way will have to move or be removed. The ways and laws of nature are held in high esteem, and the human being is regarded as the truly hedonistic animal she really is. It's a natural philosophy, and thereby, naturally, more "valuable" to the planet and all its inhabitants than a "religion" which has as its primal symbol an instrument of torture, and as its pitiful prophet a man who gladly let himself be captured and killed by his relentless and extremely brutal enemies. Christianity undoubtedly sounds pretty stupid to any young kid today, and this is, of course, a healthy and positive development, hastened by people and organizations like Dr. LaVey and The Church of Satan.

Young people realize at a very early stage, if given the chance, that there is nothing in Christianity that's applicable today, neither to themselves nor to their social surroundings. There is no copyright on "love" or "respect" by the Christian church. They are universal, human terms that have existed for a long, long time, and will continue to do so forever. The Christian church is nothing. Nothing at all. Nothing positive, healthy, natural, developing, strengthening, elevating... Just nothing. Christ was the prophet of yesterday, and his church is a pestilent parasite that should be "taxed to Hell"...

The Satanist believes in philosophical, sexual, moral, religious, and every other "freedom", as long as it's rooted in man's absolute natural way of acting and reacting, and as long as it's in line with the individual will to power. Lex Talionis must rule for the humans, as it does for all other animals. If not – Goodbye, planet Earth!

The people still attracted to Christianity seem to be divided into some basic categories:

1) People of old age, having lived in this religion for all of their life, content with its power and "glory" (it still had some glamour in the early 20th century, and, it has to be admitted, the Catholic church, to some extent, still does).

2) Young people of inferior quality intelligence-wise, who gladly accept the lies from above or who themselves seek admission to this "fraternity" of the feeble and the meek. Unity based on the low and the weak.

3) The opportunists. Young and old people alike of some intelligence and insight, who realize the enormous market in "buying and selling souls", mainly expressed through sects and groups with greedily smiling, ultra-parasitical hypocrites of leaders. They aren't half as pathetic and disgusting as their moronic followers though, who gladly pay lots and lots and lots for their salvation... For what? Hilarious!

As man in general is no longer an animal forced to use physical powers to compete in the daily and over-all life, the weapon becomes something entirely different – Intelligence. Welcome the war of Intelligence! The ill in corpus naturally fade away more or less rapidly, and the victors are not merely those with a stronger genetic structure, but, in the end, those with a superior intelligence on top.

As there has only been some more or less dilettantish research and experiments with eugenics, perhaps the time is now right to initiate some real work – in practice as well as in theory. All those who claim they care about the planet are mere hypocrites if they deny the fact that man, the present ruler, has to be perfected in every way and sense. Strength and beauty shouldn't be "ugly" or "bad" words, but rather the terms of reference when discussing man's existence and development.

Why all of this "evil" terminology then, when it seems to be nothing more than a social-Darwinistic concept, a Nietzschean development of humankind? Because it provokes those now in quite loose positions? Because it's glamorous in itself? Because it's connected with power, force, determination, and strength throughout history? Of course. This is the view for the common man to take, the easy-to-grasp presentation of a blending together of various schools of philosophy.

For the occultist though, LaVey and The Church of Satan offer a lot more than this. Many of the rituals in *The Satanic Rituals*, and LaVey's references in *The Satanic Bible*, are clever refurnishings of hints and actual ceremonies and rituals from more or less ancient grimoires. The "lesser" side of Satanic magic is the living of life fully and to the utmost maximum, as this way of life leads on to new feats and feasts in the same vein – whatever this vein may be. The "higher" side is composed of ceremonial and ritual aspects of magic. In LaVey's case, a mix of Enochian, Runic, and "Christian" (in the Templar/Gnostic sense) influences, voodoo, atavistic resurgence and sigilizing à la Spare, lycantrophic studies, and lots, lots more. All in a glamorous mix of tasty aesthetics – impressions and expressions of classic cinema lightning and magical art in many fields. The Satanic magic is always individual, but LaVey inspires through his great knowledge of history, as well as of the future, and his fine sense of style and good taste has already been dominant and trend-setting for decades now.

Whether or not one accepts the terminology of this interesting and radical group of darkly illuminated people, one has to admit that things in general are moving towards what LaVey calls "The Satanic Age". The development of individual morals seems to bring an enhancing of egotism and individual liberty, at the cost of the numbness of State control and suffocating religions as we know them today.

Whether or not one accepts the fact that Dr. LaVey's thoughts have influenced millions and millions of people, more or less directly, one has to give the man sincere credit for earnestly trying to change the sorrowful state (of mind) man has existed in for so long now. Basically, that's all any of us can do – to try and improve ourselves (and our Selves), and thereby others. Everyone should naturally have the option and right to choose his or her own guidelines in life, but it's about time that children should be educated in an enlightened way, unrestricted and unhampered by the modes of thought of ancient times. They should be taught to be true to their own wills, and should also be taught that Satanism is NOT the worship of some anthropomorphic creature, all evil, all ugly, all bad, and all hideous. It is a very sound, realistic, and highly positive state of mind, recommended because of the joy and instant cynical wisdom it brings.

The Horns of Dilemma

Anton LaVey

"Confound and confuse 'til the stars be numbered." Perhaps this simple picture can be used as an example: a young boy coming home from school clutching a copy of *The Satanic Bible* in one hand and an LP of Al Jolson numbers in the other. How can a parent appropriately react to such a situation? An insurmountable problem becomes uncomfortably clear. The parent can't condemn the child for enthusiasm for Jolson's songs but can condemn him for his interest in *The Satanic Bible*. Yet, what if the child sees the two as inseparably linked? To the media-saturated public they're irresolvable. But how does a parent calmly explain that to a militantly Satanic 13-year-old?

We are living in a new land of opportunity. As Satanists, we know one of the keys to success is an unflinching belief that there are no rules. Anyone who's ever succeeded has gone on that premise; not buying established procedures, business or otherwise. The nay-sayers are inevitably left behind amid shouts of "it cannot be done", "should not be done", claims that something won't receive distribution, won't receive acclaim, will never be accepted by the public... There are so many books to be written with Satanic themes, so many movies to be made – in the motion picture industry alone, the streets are again paved with gold. Experts will tell you, you can't have the Satanists win, they can't be the good guys. Why not? What rules are there that say that you can't? It's simply a given that it can't be done – it's one of those unwritten laws that say that all Satanists must advocate evil and must perform evil acts. Of course, that's what the new cottage industry, to bolster the multi-million dollar support system for Christianity, has been provided with – the presumption that Satanists are evil for evil's sake and that through unmitigated evil acts the Devil's favorites receive all kinds of benefits. It ain't necessarily so. And because it ain't necessarily so, the dilemma should be exploited. It's a disservice not only to commerce, to the economy, but to individual initiative not to exploit these cracks in the established belief system.

If a person writes a screenplay wherein the protagonist, who happens to be a Satanist, has admirable and heroic qualities, and all of the most vile, slimy, malicious, insensitively stupid traits are possessed by the so-called "good" people, there's no rule against that. Yet anyone will say "You could never get such a film distributed." Possibly not. But I believe so. I believe that if it's different, if it's packaged and if it's there, someone will grab it and exploit it simply on the strength that it is untoward, that it hasn't been done before. It's just desperation on the part of those whose vested interests depend upon established standards that someone might take the ball and run with it – to a new playing field – that keeps such movies off the screens. We must realize that these prevailing dilemmas, these terrors that exist in the minds of the status quo are the only obstacles that keep new avenues from emerging on the scene.

The same elements of dilemma are presented and maintained in the musical world. It's assumed that generic popular music is rock – classic rock, quality rock, old-time rock, punk rock, acid rock, Rock of Ages rock – anything as long as it's "rock" to the point where it becomes the generic. The only alternative to "Satanic rock" are outfits like "Stryper" who obviously are making no headway whatsoever. They're just different sizes of the same style shoe. Our Satanic objective is to confound, confuse, to create dilemma – to set up a revisionist type of music that is basically a return to the old classical format, the disciplined, the romantic era of music, in which music has form, it has melody, it has harmony, it has rhythmic structure that can be grasped, that can indelibly impress itself upon the mind through the ears of the listener. If this kind of music is brought back under the banner of Satanism, and it's suitably packaged, no matter how outrageously, someone, somewhere is going to exploit it, on the merits of its strengths, of its very form, of its cohesiveness, of its discipline, of its emotional impact and effect upon the listener. It cannot help but avalanche, overwhelming whatever form the generic called "rock" has presented so far. Rock has had its day. There's very little variation one way or the other. The only way music can change is in a 180 degree direction to discipline, form, melody, harmony, lyricism, romanticism... "Bombastic".

That's why bombastic music, which has dynamics and produces a gut reaction, is bound to overwhelm the current generic rock scene. Of course we're talking about billions of dollars in vested interests. There's going to be extreme pressure to curtail the new generic – "bombastic music" – as there has been in the recent past. A December 1st *Rolling Stone* article titled "Skinhead Nation" provides thinly disguised, fear-filled wailing in its dire warning. Along with reprehensible misquotes and misrepresentations, the writer makes snide references to the new Skinhead music being "reductive, bombastic and self-conscious" with "slower tempos and more conventional melody", "simple pub sing-along, catchy and monotonous" (?? What could be more monotonous than the linear cruise control of rock?). Bombastic is not going to be made easily available through the "experts" in musical retailing, merchandising, wholesaling. Obviously there's too much money being made already on the established formula. The new form of music is going to have to be produced as a labor of love, a packaging enterprise, irrespective of the money that can be made off of it. Once the engramatic idea, the emotional impact of this kind of music has been indelibly etched in the mind of the listeners, it cannot help but be exploited. Those who support generic rock will drop it like a hot potato and scurry to this new musical form as soon as it's made acceptable.

Again, we will have presented the establishment with a dilemma. Of course we have to force the card – to back them against the wall and make damn sure in a filibustering sense that they know this is Satanic music. One way we can filibuster is by entering the established arena with something else that's outrageous enough or different enough to create a time slot, and then halfway through an interview or talk show, present this horrible additive of Satanism. A person going on a television show to plug a book on gaining weight for health might inject a few leading comments or be wearing a label pin with a Satanic symbol, the meaning of which might be questioned by the interviewer. Upon the revelation that the writer is also a Satanist, of course the remainder of the interview would be compulsively directed towards Satanism. They could no longer ignore the issue. The show would be sharply divided into two distinct subjects. That's how we can create dilemma.

The rest is easy. On one hand hysterics and experts will be screeching, "How can I protect my children from Satanism?" while, on another channel, the audience has already heard from Satanists that Satanism advocates listening to Rudy Vallee and Russ Columbo, Bizet, Rimsky-Korsakov, Sousa, Liszt, reading James Fennimore Cooper, Jack London, Mark Twain, Horatio Alger, and supporting Walt Disney.

Browning, Kipling, romantic poets and writers of the heroic school, and certain contemporary writers like W. Somerset Maugham and Ben Hecht may not be considered Satanic until it is forced upon the listener or viewer that they are Satanic. Then when there's the inevitable challenge, "Well these writers aren't Satanic", it's our turn to take umbrage – we can be the offended party. We can be the ones to start bashing (symbolically, of course). If enough public Satanists are tough, vocal and potentially dangerous – not mealy-mouthed, ivory-tower scholars – then it becomes a case of the 250-pound canary – when it sings, you listen.

That's where force and clout have to be waiting in the wings. As a reactionary or revisionist movement, when our long fuse burns out, that's the time to swing into action. Dilemmas reach an impasse only when your detractor is forced up against the wall and can't squirm away. As a result, once others say, "Well, that's not real Satanism, you're not real Satanists – you're just religious Satanists. The real Satanists are out killing babies and sacrificing cats", that's our cue to start knocking heads. We have to be prepared to say "God damn it, you rotten sons of bitches! Don't tell me what Satanism is. I'm a 'real' Satanist and I'm proud of it. You're trying to tell me Rudy Vallee isn't Satanic music when I like Rudy Vallee!?", and then proceed to smash a chair over their head (or nose). Then they'll listen. That's the only way they'll listen, anyone who is still trying to make money off anti-Satanic swill – when we stop defending ourselves and start being offensive.

That's why the ideal type of front-line warrior for our present cabal, for our new world view, must be that strange combination of berserker and poet. He must have the ultimate sense of justice, Lex Talionis, indelibly bred into him, while also possessing the articulation, the convictions, the ideals and the awareness of what must be done. These two elements of force and direction must be inseparable. Of warfare and intellect. One without the other is only productive on either a directionless or paper level. We've seen enough of what paper-pushers can do and the effects they have by way of dialogue in written communication. The pen may still be mightier than the sword, but a broadsword can do much damage to a computer keyboard. What we have are people that can get out there and, to use the cliché, charismatically effect people in direct confrontations, in personal interchange, in public arenas. It's also why the new type of superwoman as well as the superman must be one of Charlie's girls raised to the ninth power, not just simply some strung-out, latter-day hippie or a dingaling that may have come from a promising background but got lost somewhere along the way on Haight Street. They have to be women that can out-woman the polyester droolers in studio audiences, out-woman the kind of women who would shrink and cringe at what they have to say, out-woman the non-women, or half-women or partial women, that can't quite make up their minds whether they're women or some kind of injection-molded plastic creations of a consumer society. In this way, the Satanists themselves become dilemmas, integrating factors that are supposed to be irreconcilable, and presenting alternatives that are supposed to be irresolvable. That's the strongest and most dangerous power the Devil has. Now's the time to use that Satanic power to blast the last bastions of the weak-minded and soulless hordes.

Beyond thee Valley Ov Acid Into thee Infinite Beat

Genesis P-Orridge
(a.k.a. DJ Doktor Megatrip ov Psychic TV and Jack the Tab)

February 23rd, 1989 Era Maximus. A Collision Course in Musicks...

This is an open letter, not an attempt to be clever, or expert in writing, it is a sketch ov thee tragedy ov our Conservative times, thee slip into total seduction by goals we all claim to despise, thee acceleration ov absorption ov thee right ov youth to rebel and create their own styles ov expression and ecstatic evolution. Thee right ov youth to deny thee inherited sickness ov authority, ov their parents, ov FUNDAMENTALISTS bent on death. It's thee fear ov a possibility, thee suppression ov impossibilities that free us, charge us with life and make existence at least temporarily bearable. Thee tale ov thee theft ov our nostalgia. Thee moment when feeling trapped and defeated by adult responsibility we hold our DAZE ov excitement given to each generation by its anarchic Rock dance peers tightly in our hands and bless those hot sweaty, sexually charged nights ov trance, adrenalin and hope that we kept as OUR OWN secret code that separated us from parents, politics, society and suppression. Or so we thought. In fact we are speaking ultimate politics ov Individual freedom to be left free to FEEL, to scream with joy, to explore UNITY, to recognize our own Tribe, our own symbols and myths away from thee padded cell ov school and education. This is thee ACID DANCE, this is thee ACID TRANCE. CHEMICAL, RADICAL, VERY VERY MAGICKAL; CHEMICAL, RADICAL, VERY VERY SEXUAL. This is thee ACID DANCE, THIS IS... THEE ACID TRANCE. This is a fairy story ov worlds opened up. Joy, Life, Hope and this is a call to all who read and believe to hold on to thee moment you receive forever. Britain's youth came close to overthrowing more conditioning and defeatist placidity in our SUMMER OV LOVE 88 than any time since PUNK, and before that thee DIGGERS ov thee Sixties. We are talking a new version ov old bonding here, we are talking about ACID HOUSE, ACID MUSIC, ACID ATTITUDE, ACID HOPE, ACID YOUTH, and ACID DANCE WORLDWIDE.

Each generation reacts to thee previous one. Popular Culture, Street Style goes in seven yera cycles, not thee ten yera cycles many assume. So you get thee roots of psychedelia in 67, hitting 68; thee roots ov Punk in 77, hitting in 78, and thee roots ov Acid House in 87, hitting in 88. Thee yeras 66, 76, 86 are when thee UNDER THEE COUNTER CULTURE is actually evolving naturally, unseen by the media, tended by small bands ov fanatics, protected and nurtured to mark as separate and uniquely their own a LANGUAGE BEAT and MYTH that excites like thee first orgasm ov love.

"THE KEY TO ORGANISING AN ALTERNATIVE SOCIETY IS TO ORGANISE PEOPLE AROUND WHAT THEY CAN DO AND MORE IMPORTANTLY WHAT THEY WANT TO DO." (FREE, from *REVOLUTION FOR THE HELL OF IT*, 1968)

"PLEASURE IS A WEAPON" (DJ DOKTOR MEGATRIP, 1988)

"MYTH IS THE MODE OF SIMULTANEOUS AWARENESS OF A COMPLEX GROUP OF CAUSES AND EFFECTS... WE HEAR SOUNDS FROM EVERYWHERE, WITHOUT EVER HAVING TO FOCUS... THE EAR WORLD IS A WORLD OF SIMULTANEOUS RELATIONSHIPS. ELECTRIC CIRCUITRY CONFERS A MYTHIC DIMENSI0N ON OUR ORDINARY INDIVIDUAL AND GROUP ACTIONS. OUR TECHNOLOGY FORCES US TO LIVE MYTHICALLY." (MARSHALL MCLUHAN, 1967)

"EVERYONE IS EXTRA-ORDINARY" (DJ DOKTOR MEGA TRIP, 1987).

An evolution always has rhythm. Thee rhythms that generate altered states ov social conditioning, ov relationship, ov refusal ov hypocrisy and violent imposition ov fundamentalist FEAR are fast. They create a state of lucid dreaming, ov physical ecstasy, ov visual vibrancy that pales thee ghosts ov society into thee vampiric zombie that it is. There is nothing new in these rhythms. They charge into thee metabolism at 125-129 beats per minute. They are capable ov infinity. All ov them have the implicit quality to carry on as long as people want. They have been used to release endorphins, natural psychotropics and psychedelics and visions since groups ov people first celebrated thee endless loops and integrations ov all life. So called "primitive" civilizations use LONG TIME BASE musics based on apparently simple drum beat loops and high frequencies from pipes to liberate their bodies and consciousness as a form ov essential psychic hygiene and as a tribal bonding and identity process.

Thee innovative Psychedelic Bands ov thee 60s are famous and notorious for long time scale meandering concerts. Butter thee key quality that MUST be present in radical music is thee possibility ov ENDLESSNESS. Thee piece ov music can be short, butter always able to be repeated indefinitely if thee audience/musician exchange demands it. Thee need to BE LOST in thee music is absolutely essential. It becoums clearer and clearer that any lesser demand debilitates thee medium, thee message and thee masses. In thee 60s it took four yeras for the MUSIC INDUSTRY to re-tool and hijack for castration underground musicks. It took the now smoothly oiled socio-political collaborators ov thee Megalithic Musicks lndustry one yera to sterilize and manipulate Punk in thee 70s. It took only three months to trivialize and traumatize Acid in thee 80's (in Britain). Punk is, in terms ov Time Base, a contradiction. Butter then Punk was a glorification ov rejection and contradiction. Its premise was short and fast. Acid coumbines thee long Time Based beats with sampling, thee short sharp, cynical residue ov Punk.

"THEE PROCESS IS THEE PRODUCT – WHERE NOW GOES FURTHUR" (DJ DOKTOR MEGATRIP, 1989)

Thee DJ has becoum thee Shaman ov thee Medium. Thee Mix is thee Message.

Just as thee electric guitar revolutionized thee possibilities ov sound and improvisation, so thee turntables have revolutionized thee dance floor process. Thee music is seamless, endless, thee possibilities are endless. An arcane and magickal trance-formation can now take place. Thee DJ choreographs thee crowd with a unified desire for liberating mental and physical revelation as its target. This is functional musicks secreted in thee once hallowed halls ov Suburbia. The disco-dullards and soul-less caverns ov mediocrity. It's ironic that where once Clubs were thee LEAST energizing and experimental environments and sounds, whilst Punk, and Indie Rock were thee bastions ov new ideas, now we have thee most experimental work flowing from and back into Dance Clubs, and thee Indie Scene clinging to impotent washes ov careerist drivel that owe much to thee Right Wing pressure to conform. TO-CONSERVE-IT-ISMS.

"DOESN'T ALL THIS DANCING PRESENT A PROBLEM FOR SOCIETY? NOT FOR OURS BUT FOR THE PARENT CULTURE, THE ONE DECAYING, MOST DEFINITELY." (FREE, from *REVOLUTION FOR THE HELL OF IT*, 1968)

"THE TRANCE IS NECESSARILY TRANSFORMED INTO DANCE, SO THAT ULTIMATELY DANCE CAN BE SEEN AS THE OUTSTANDING SIGN OF ITS RITUALISATION. THUS DANCE ULTIMATELY CONSTITUTES THE VERY BLOSSOMING OF TRANCE. IT IS THE WHIRLING MOTION OF THE DANCE ITSELF THAT LEADS TO ECSTASY AND TRANCE. THE TRANCE IS THUS THE RESULT OF THE ADEPTS' OWN ACTION AND CHOICE." (G. ROUGET, from *MUSIC AND TRANCE*, 1985)

Meanwhile we need to refer to chemicals in this story. In thee 60s Acid, Hash, Mescaline and other Shamanic triggers were integral to both thee perceptual mapping ov Individual and Social behavior blocks and to the easing across thee threshold ov many peoples numbed faculties. It is thee first time in human history where thee precious drugs ov Elite mystery cults and wisdom were released unchecked upon literally millions ov primarily unprepared minds. No one can yet gauge thee effect this will have on our vision ov ourselves. Style and music tend to reflect, with choice ov drug, thee Youth Culture's feelings. In thee 70s, with Punk it was Speed, Alcohol and Heroin, death drugs, drugs ov illness and oblivion, ov slow public suicide, nihilism. In thee essential sense, a picture ov SURRENDER and FATALISM. This is not to say that PURE ENERGY and METAMORPHOSIS were not a functional necessity towards thee present chances ov rebalance. Now, quite suddenly, it seems, we have designer drugs like MDMA, PHANTASY, F 2, and K being combined with Acid, generating a street level awareness ov EMPATHOGENIC states, previously explored discreetly in thee USA and Europe by private adepts from thee 60s and 70s intelligentsia learning from thee errors ov tactic revealed in thee previous decades apparent guilt ridden burn out.

"WE GOT BURNED MAN." (YIPPIE, Chicago,1968)

"ACID BURN JUST MEANS SAMPLING MAN." (CHICAGO HOUSE DJ, 1988)

From Shamanic drugs, to Nihilistic drugs, now to Designer drugs. Flow, to No and now to TEKNO. Thee altered states we reach are implicit to thee search we ratify. Thee musicks have followed thee same currents and thee overview this letter hints at will hopefully be more apparent. As it is written it's as if coumone else is writing, it's more surreal and fragmented than expected. Buried within all this is an undying belief in integrating feelings, caring about our own tribe, loyalty in thee face ov Government disloyalty. Subversion not thee Official Version. A tear for an eye and a truth for a tooth. REBELLION!

"WHEN IN THE FLOW OF HUMAN EVENTS IT BECOMES NECESSARY FOR THE PEOPLE TO CEASE TO RECOGNIZE THE OBSOLETE SOCIAL PATTERNS WHICH HAD ISOLATED INDIVIDUALS FROM THEIR CONSCIOUSNESS AND TO CREATE WITH THE YOUTH-FULL ENERGIES OF THE WORLD REVOLUTIONARY AND TRIBAL COMMUNES TO WHICH THE TWO-BILLION-YEAR-OLD LIFE PROCESS ENTITLES THEM, A DECENT RESPECT TO THE OPINIONS OF INDIVIDUALS SHOULD DECLARE THE CAUSES WHICH IMPEL THEM TO THIS CREATION. WE HOLD THESE EXPERIENCES TO BE SELF-EVIDENT, THAT ALL IS EQUAL, THAT CREATIVITY ENDOWS US WITH CERTAIN INALIENABLE RIGHTS, THAT AMONG THESE ARE: THE FREEDOM OF THE BODY, THE PURSUIT OF JOY, AND THE EXPANSION OF CONSCIOUSNESS." (DIGGERS, *PROPHECY OF A DECLARATION OF INDEPENDENCE*, October 6-66.)

"I'VE ALWAYS FELT THE PAIN OF HUMANITY, BUT NOW I SEE THAT THERE IS HOPE, THAT IF I CAN DO THIS THEN OTHERS CAN. SO, THAT'S THE CHANGE... THE CHANGE IS NOT THAT THE PAIN OF HUMANITY HAS LESSENED; THERE HAS BEEN A RAY OF LIGHT IN ALL THAT PAIN, AND THE RAY OF LIGHT IS THAT WE ARE ALL ABLE TO STEP OUTSIDE IT."

"THE ENERGY FLOWS THROUGH ME AND WHAT I CAN DO IS MAKE IT INTO MUSIC. IT DOESN'T HAVE TO COME OUT OF ME THE SAME WAY IT WENT THROUGH ME. I CAN MAKE IT WHAT I WANT, BUT ONCE IT LEAVES ME, THE NEXT PERSON IT HITS, IT'S NOT JUST ENERGY IT'S THEIR MUSIC TOO." (35 Yera Old Computer Programmer on 150 mg MDMA, 1985. From *THROUGH THE GATEWAY OF THE HEART* by SOPHIA ADAMSON)

In Chicago, and in thee package holiday resorts ov Spain DJs were couming across rare 12 Inch Singles, and bizarre mixes ov musicks from all over thee world. Infinite mixes that went through thee night generating a fresh enervating mind-set, body-set that became thee SCHOOOM set. Thee key was, and is, thee BEAT. Thee constant kick drum, thee CONSTANCY itself. Thee key ov ecstatic/trance musicks everywhere and through all Time. Present Time is that which passes. Past Time is that which tells. Future Time is that which Guesses. MDMA, "Ecstasy" or "Adam" was/is thee catalyst that led through thee gateway ov thee heart at thee precise moment that HOUSE, ACID HOUSE, "JACK" led through thee gateway in search ov thee INFINITE BEAT.

Suddenly, in London, DJs were RE-ASSESSING every sound, every record in their collection. Mutating these beats ov Chicago and ordering them in COLLISIONS that jolted and energized thee mind and body ov each Individual dancer into a creation ov thee Psychedelic Experience through thee use ov Light, Colour and Sonic Disorientation. Thee subsequent release ov energy, communality, UNITY and pure unbounded pleasure was irresistible and real. Feelings, meaning, joy, hope, love became necessary linguistic currency again. In SEPTEMBER 1987 at FON STUDIOS, in Sheffield, PSYCHIC TV were arguing, insisting that samples ov Timothy Leary from thee LP

TURN ON TUNE IN DROP OUT would be thee only lyrical content on their new 12 Inch single. They dumped "DROP OUT" pertinently saying, you don't need to DROP OUT in Society anymore, it abandons you when you are born. PTV won their argument, and thee legendary first ACID HOUSE single, British interpretation, was released. Thee original concept to remind people ov thee historical heritage that had begun thee long march to freedom and thee potential power ov sampling and Infinite House to reduce all language to fragments and slogans ready to be planted, primed and explosive into thee suburban unconscious through their previously harmless medium ov disco-musicks. Television has probably destroyed attention spans, integrity in creativity, meaning and content within words and motives more than any war or authoritarian regime throughout history. Words are dead, to be trampled gloriously as surrealism, dada, theatre ov thee absurd, happening, and cut-up becoum one through thee medium ov mixing.

"LET'S CUT IT UP AND SEE WHAT IT REALLY SAYS..." (W.S. BURROUGHS, 1958)

"STRUCTURE IS MORE IMPORTANT THAN CONTENT IN THE TRANSMISSION OF INFORMATION." (FREE, from *REVOLUTION FOR THE HELL OF IT*, 1968)

"NOTHING IS IMMUNE – NOTHING IS SACRED" (DJ DOKTOR MEGATRIP, 1978)

"MY PLEASURE IS IN ITS DISORIENTATION. THE LACK OF ANY STABLE UNITS OF SENSE. THE MUSIC ITSELF IS A STATEMENT ABOUT THE INFORMATION EXPLOSION AND THE ACCELERATION OF EXPERIENCES THAT THE MASS MEDIA EFFECTIVELY CREATES. EACH WORD IS THE TIP OF AN ICEBERG OF MEANINGS CONDENSED TO REFLECT IN CODE." (GENESIS P-ORRIDGE, from *REVELATIONS*, 1988)

Thee rest, as they say, is history. Thee chemicals, thee beats, thee body dances, thee ironic recycling of SMILEY spread unnoticed at first. Where once thee deviant cultural anarchists were almost certain to be beaten up by thee beer boys at discos, girls molested, chatted up like chattels and discarded like condoms NOW thee favourite drinks were Perrier water and Lucozade. Boys and Girls became people and danced with whoever was nearest, thee commonest facial expression was a smile, those too hot were tended with cooling towels and ice by caring strangers, atrophied feelings ov well being, optimism, change, humanitarian LOVE and considerations ov consciousness were validated. Entire 30 minute speeches by Martin Luther King were played without any musical backing to silent Acid House crowds ov a thousand up and greeting with cheers and raised fists by these transformed beings. Dancing was non-stop, five hours, eight hours, ten hours. Thee floor was thee limit. Thee door was thee exit. More was thee entry. Nothing so pure and unified, so uniquely based on UNITY across all previous barriers ov race, class, style and education had EVER hit our shores. This was thee unexpected breakthrough that gave a new generation its first taste ov thee heady sensations abounding in thee 60s. And it felt good. It felt power full and clean, it felt OURS!

"OUR TASK IS TO BE POSITIVE PARTICIPANTS IN THE FUTURE EVOLUTION OF ALL SPECIES, INCLUDING OURS, UPON THE PLANET EARTH.

WE MUST COME DOWN FROM OUR THRONE AND REALIZE THAT OUR FUTURE IS COEXTENSIVE WITH THE FUTURE OF ALL SPECIES. ALTERNATIVE FUTURES FOR US NEED AN OPENING OF OUR COMMUNICATION SYSTEMS. WE NEED A NEW HUMILITY. WE MUST FORGET THE BARRIERS TO ALTERNATIVE FUTURES. WE MUST FORGET PESSIMISM IN REGARD TO THOSE FUTURES. WE MUST CONSTRUCT AN ALTERNATIVE FUTURE." (JOHN LILLY, from *THE SCIENTIST*, 1988)

Paula P-Orridge turned to me at FRENZY after observing thee seething mass ov caring bonded people with a beatific smile, HIGH ON HOPE, and said "This is the first time I've felt a part of any movement in my life."

Anything was possible, thee future was no longer postponed or spectral, it was clearly visible and joyous. PSYCHIC TV resolved to continue to develop their interpretation and input FURTHUR. "JACK THE TAB" was released, a collaboration between GENESIS P-ORRIDGE and RICHARD NORRIS with friends and allies. More doors to tempt. PSYCHIC TV developed thee inevitable next step, thee LIVE fusion ov HOUSE, ACID ROCK and DANCE. H.A.R.D. MUSICK. Where HENDRIX collides with HOUSE on thee bridge ov an INFINITE BEAT. Thee intention, to go on, inwards and outwards, stripping down to thee PUREST function ov sound and dance.

In Britain Acid House exploded. Thousands attending warehouse parties. Make no mistake, they still do. Thee successful, in thee right place at thee right time, seduced by childhood values, FAME, CHAT SHOWS and TOP OF THE POPS scuttled for acceptability and self-esteem. They declared ACID dead, yet they continued to use SAMPLES. They had believed thee media hype, thee political crusade designed to smash thee growing moral and political anarcho-consciousness, they had been scared at thee police pressure, thee belittling ov their own knowledge. In their own words, ACID meant sampling, it was and is an attitude. An openness, a dedication to growth, change, joy, compassion and subversion through pleasure to thee infinite. To be lost in rhythm and sound is a religious energizing that Individuals will never surrender. It's thee oldest trick in thee book, and it's not an illusion, it's a liberation.

"MORE OV EVERYTHING FOR EVERYONE." (DJ DOKTOR MEGATRIP, 1996)

ACIEEEEEED? Sampling gives us all thee chance to play. Every sound ever recorded, whether on tape, record, video or film is useable. Steven Spielberg might spend 200.000 dollars on an amazing sound effect and we can hire thee film and steal it for 4 dollars. Thee trick is in thee choosing ov sounds, thee placing. Each sound in a very real sense, sampled off a video or record, is a hieroglyph for thee entire content ov thee work it was stolen from. It is a shorthand. Individuals can take thee few seconds that sum up the whole album, store them in a sample and from then on that few seconds is thee whole album. A symbol ov it. So content is being redefined. Information and music is being shrunk. All musicks from all history and all countries are vulnerable and useable. Never before has this been quite so true. Technology has liberated musick, democratised it further than thee famous 3 chord slogan ov Punk.

This accessibility ov all music, TOTAL VULNERABILITY ov sound is coupled with a reawakened understanding ov thee function ov BEAT. Anything can be layered on top ov a constant trance ACID beat. Banal, wonderful, odd, irrelevant, incongruous noises and words. What has happened is thee inevitable result ov a mass media planned obsolescent society. ACID has coum to mean many things. As an underlying attitude it means FUN, FREEDOM, EXPERIMENTATION. Thee true possibility ov endless music. And ironically that has led to rediscoveries ov ritualised results ov dance and thee inclusion ov shamanic visions into a previously vacuous popular medium. Now we are seeing; and will see more ov DJs and musicians collaborating to generate thee ULTIMATE TOTAL MEDIA CIRCUS OV SOUND. Sensory overloads ov more and more intensity as Individuals find that far more experiences and sensations are possible than ever have been dreamed. We have thee technology and we have thee structure. Hendrix dreamed ov a Church ov Sound, pure sound that was transcendent. PSYCHIC TV and other pioneers are driving further onwards towards that goal. Thee exploding white light ov sheet exhilaration and sound.

INTO THEE INFINITE BEAT

SELECT DISCOGRAPHY & BIBLIOGRAPHY RECORDS, 1960s:

–~– "LSD", by Dr Timothy Leary PhD.
–~– "THIS TIME AROUND YOU CAN BE ANYONE", by Dr Timothy Leary PhD and Jimi Hendrix.
–~– "TURN ON TUNE IN DROP OUT", by Dr Timothy Leary PhD.
–~– "THE PSYCHEDELIC EXPERIENCE", by Dr Timothy Leary, Dr Cohen and others.
–~– "THE ACID TEST", by Ken Kesey and The Grateful Dead.
–~– "IN-A-GADA-DA-VIDA", by Iron Butterfly.
–~– "AOXAMOXOA", by The Grateful Dead.
–~– "THE CLOUDS HAVE GROOVY FACES", LP.
–~– "FROM THE HOUSE OF LORDS", LP.
–~– "THE PSYCHEDELIC SNARL", LP.
–~– "24 HOUR TECHNICOLOUR DREAM", LP, and all BAM CARUSO compilations.
–~– "INCENSE AND PEPPERMINTS", by Strawberry Alarm Clock.
–~– "VANILLA FUDGE", by Vanilla Fudge.
–~– "UNDERGROUND", by The Electric Prunes.

RECORDS, 1980s:

–~– "NOISE, LUST AND FUN", by Fini Tribe.
–~– "KNATURE OF A GIRL", by The Shamen.
–~– "CHRISTOPHER MAYHEW SAYS", by The Shamen.
–~– "TUNE IN, TURN ON THE ACID HOUSE", by Psychic TV and Jack the Tab.
–~– "JACK THE TAB", LP, Castalia Recordings compilation.

—~— "TECHNO ACID BEAT", LP, Temple Records compilation.
—~— "JOY", by DJ Doktor Megatrip.
—~— "ACID BURN", by Beatmasters.
—~— "SKULPTURE", LP, by Skulpture.
—~— "NEBULA", by Nebula.
—~— "ACID MAN (TECHNO MIX)", by Jolly Roger.
—~— "ADDICTED", by Handsome Wayne.
—~— "PRISONER OF RIO", by Dave Ball and Ronnie Biggs.
—~— "BABY WANTS TO RIDE", by Jamie Principle.
—~— "SEX VIGILANTE", by English Boy on the Love Ranch.
—~— "I WANT TO", by The Irresistable Force.
—~— "WE ARE PHUTURE", by Phuture.
—~— "ACID TRACKS", Chicago Compilation LP.

BOOKS, 1960s:

—~— "THE HAIGHT-ASHBURY", by Charles Perry (Vintage Books, 1965)
—~— "REVOLUTION FOR THE HELL OF IT", by Free (The Dial Press, 1968)
—~— "HIGH PRIEST", by Dr. Timothy Leary (NAL Books, 1968)
—~— "THE POLITICS OF ECSTASY", by Dr. Timothy Leary (Putnam Books, 1965)
—~— "PROGRAMMING AND METAPROGRAMMING IN THE HUMAN BIO-COMPUTER", by John Lilly, M.D. (Julian Press, 1968)
—~— "THE PRIVATE SEA", by William Braden (Pall Mall, 1967)
—~— "THE COOL CRAZY COMMITTED WORLD OF THE SIXTIES", by Pierre Berton (McLelland Books, 1966)

AND...

—~— "THE SCIENTIST", by John Lilly, M.D. (Visions Books, 1988)
—~— "THE PSYCHEDELIC READER", by various writers (Citadel, 1973)
—~— "DO IT!", by Jerry Rubin (Cape Books, 1970)
—~— "STORMING HEAVEN", by Jay Stevens (Perrenial, 1987)
—~— "ACID DREAMS", by Lee & Schlain (Grove Press, 1985)
—~— "PSYCHEDELIC BABY REACHES PUBERTY", by Stafford (Academy, 1972)
—~— "THROUGH THE GATEWAY OF THE HEART", by Sophia Adamson (Four Trees, 1985)
—~— "MUSIC AND TRANCE", by Gilbert Rouget (Chicago, 1985)
—~— "THE SHAMAN AND THE MAGICIAN", by Neville Drury (Arkana, 1982)

Phauss: Order is Divine

Phauss and Annika Söderholm (photos 2 and 4)

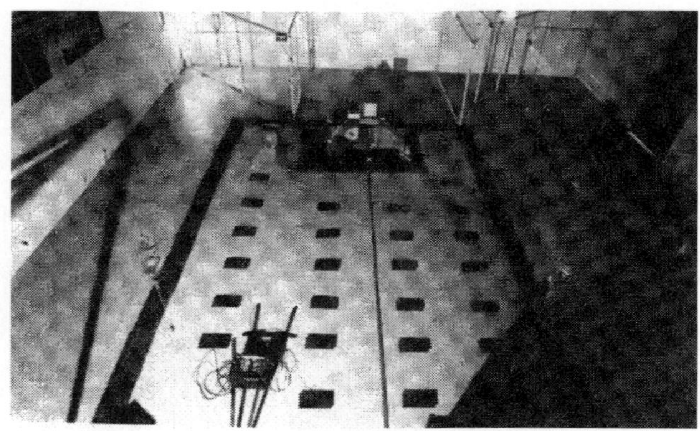

1. Hembygd (with Leif Elggren), for Carolus XII

2. PHAUSS goes to the mountains in search of the gold.

3. We're not able to realize your order.

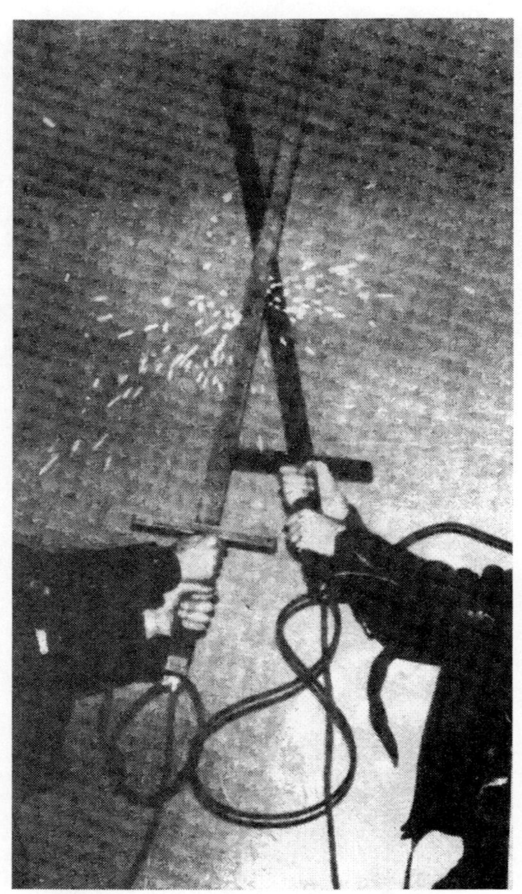

4. Hafiz PHAUSS

5. Poland 10.4-20.4 1989, for Carolus X Gustavus

15 "Voices from God" 1976-1985

Compiled from newspaper accounts by Jack Stevenson

A Newport, Rhode Island, woman charged with fatally stabbing her infant son told police she killed the 9-month-old after receiving a "prompting" from "God", according to court documents...

A Filipino woman who claimed to have seen and talked to Jesus Christ was nailed to an 18-foot wooden cross in a bloody Good Friday ritual that attracted about 500 onlookers, including American tourists...

A West Virginia farm-hand who said he was "the son of god", was charged Wednesday with kidnapping his female employer in a bizarre plot to destroy the earth with another flood and start over as "Adam and Eve"...

Religious pilgrims are flocking to San Antonio to see what they believe is an image of the Virgin Mary, formed by a porch light reflected off the bumper of Mary Ibarra's 1975 Chevrolet and onto the side of a house. Ibarra's teenage son first saw the image last Wednesday and told his parents he believed the reflection and a recurring dream were signs of his impending death...

A Vietnam veteran who claimed to be Jesus Christ and cried for the love of a mysterious "Lorraine" swan dived seven stories to his death early Thursday from the rafters above a Miami, Florida, college courtyard...

A man and woman claiming to be "King and Queen of the Church" shot and killed a Roman Catholic priest Friday before taking their own lives, police said. Officers at the scene said the man and woman claimed to be "King and Queen of the Church" and claimed they took the Church in "the name of God"...

Burned over 95 percent of his body, 20-month-old Leon Justin fought for life for five days as doctors warned his chances of survival were remote. But the toddler, allegedly scalded with hot water and baked in an oven in what police said was his mother's attempt to exorcise a demon, died yesterday...

A Bronx woman who told the police she wanted to send her children "to heaven" has been charged with strangling her seven-year-old daughter and her infant son, police said...

An Auburn, Maine, woman accused of burning her four-year-old daughter to death in an oven entered no plea after being indicted on a murder charge yesterday, while her live-in boyfriend and co-defendant pleaded innocent. Previous statements by the couple indicate that the murder may have been an "exorcism"...

A handyman who spent three days watching religious programs on a borrowed television set reportedly went berserk Thursday in Phoenix, Arizona, and shot a neighborhood friend to death before police fatally shot him...

A man charged with killing two men and wounding six others with a semi-automatic rifle and two pistols in a shooting spree in Greenwich Village last November, testified in his own defense yesterday in State Supreme Court in Manhattan. Throughout his testimony Crumpley spoke of being guided by God and of feeling that "God had this all planned for me". In the afternoon he held a Bible on his lap ...

Lindberg Sanders, leader of a Bible-reading group that preached against water, pork and the police, died along with his six followers in a pre-dawn gun battle with police in Memphis, Tennessee. Sanders and his group held Memphis police officer Robert Hester hostage for 30 hours, during which time Hester was subjected to torture. A police assault team stormed Sanders' home after the team's electronic eavesdropping equipment picked up the sentence "The Devil is dead"...

Injured former U.S. Astronaut James Irwin said Saturday his expedition found no evidence that the legendary Noah's Ark came to rest on Turkey's Mt. Ararat. Irwin, who went to the moon in 1971, and is a fundamentalist Baptist, is leading the 11-man-team. Irwin said he slipped in a snowfield at a height of 14.000 feet and fell about 100 feet. He said the fall caused "lacerations on my head and face", but no bone fractures...

An 18-year-old "saint" sent as many as 21 of her followers on a deadly voyage yesterday, when they set sail in tin boxes on a bizarre religious pilgrimage to bring Iran victory in its war with Iraq. Police said they recovered 13 bodies from boxes bobbing in the Arabian Sea off Karachi...

A Roman Catholic nun in San Francisco has been indicted by a Grand Jury on charges of manslaughter and assault in the beating to death of her 75-year-old mother, whose body, was found with a cross and holy picture...

END.

18 Fatal Arguments 1976-1985

Compiled from newspaper accounts by Jack Stevenson

A 30-year-old Hartford Public Works employee died after he was stabbed repeatedly with a pitchfork during a quarrel with a co-worker that grew out of an argument over who discovered America, police said ...

A man who purportedly lost his temper and fired a rifle because he thought he was being cut off by other drivers has been charged with murder in the traffic deaths of a mother and her baby, officials said today...

Two friends shot and killed each other over a bar-room argument over how easy it was to escape arrest for murder. Police said yesterday that James Cole, 55, was working as a bartender and made the claim murder was easy. David Harold Kirkley, 33, a friend of Cole's, countered that the victim could retaliate by shooting back, said witnesses to the Saturday night argument. Cole later picked up a pistol and fired it, hitting his friend. A detective said yesterday that Kirkley pulled out his own pistol and shot Cole, who slumped behind the bar...

An argument in Islamabad, Pakistan, over the ownership of a wristwatch turned into a gunfight between tribes that left 34 people dead and scores injured near the Afghan border, newspapers said yesterday...

An argument in Houston over a pay telephone turned into a gun battle that killed one person and injured six others Monday, police said...

An argument in Springfield, Massachusetts, over a two car accident yesterday erupted into a street battle that ended with one man shot to death and two police officers and a bystander wounded...

Two men who had a friendly argument about the Olympics tried to settle it by racing down a hallway at their law firm, and one crashed through a 39th floor window and fell to his death...

A 32-year-old man was shot to death Saturday night in the parking lot of a fried chicken restaurant in New Orleans following an argument over who had been next in line to buy chicken, police said...

A Houston osteopath was charged Thursday in the fatal shooting of his 29-year-old son during a heated argument over the firing of Houston Oilers' football coach Bum Phillips and running back Earl Campbell's request for a new contract...

Police say an argument over war stories apparently sparked the fatal stabbing here Wednesday evening of 63-year-old Harold Love. Police say Love and George LaDuke, 65, also of Rochester, were apparently discussing combat stories when LaDuke allegedly became angry and got a knife. Love died shortly afterwards from stab wounds of the neck...

A 17-year-veteran of the Newark police force was sentenced today to seven years in prison in the shooting death of a hospital security officer during a barroom argument over their authority as peace officers. Mr. Hymond, a security officer for University Hospital had been drinking with Mr. Brooks at a bar in Newark. The shooting occurred when the two off-duty officers became embroiled in a dispute over who had more jurisdiction, training and authority as a law enforcement officer, authorities say...

An elderly widow who allegedly shot and killed a young aspiring actor because his car was blocking her driveway did not even own an automobile, police said...

A Little League baseball player's mother wrestled another woman to the ground and shot her in the chest while the victim's 10-year-old daughter watched, a witness testified Tuesday. Sandi Quinton, 28, was shot to death July 15th at a boys' baseball game. Sharon K. Clark, 28, a school teacher, is charged with second degree murder in the shooting. The witness testified she saw Mrs. Clark accost the victim, knock her to the ground and shoot her in the chest, then stood over the victim and shouted "Die, you bitch, die". She was upset over criticism another Little League player's mother voiced concerning Mrs. Clark's son, they said...

A minor accident in heavy traffic on a Philadelphia expressway ended in a fatal shooting when two drivers lept out of their vehicles and began to argue, police said...

Bolivar County authorities said a family argument over a bowl of cereal resulted in the shooting death of one person and the wounding of another...

An argument over a parking space resulted in the shooting death of a Los Angeles chiropractor...

A Cleveland woman, angry over when a neighbor's dog defecated on her porch, shot and killed the neighbor during an argument over the pet, police told...

A landlord-tenant dispute over holes punched in a child's swimming pool ended in a shootout that left two dead and one injured by gunfire, police in north Little Rock, Ark., said Sunday...

The police said it was apparently just an argument between brothers over 50 cents, and that when it was over, 21-year-old Maurice Davis lay stabbed to death in their apartment at 343 Classon Avenue in the Bedford-Stuyvesant section of Brooklyn...

END.

Art on the Edge of Life

Oracularity, Shamanism, Mediumship and Clairvoyance in recent Performance Art

Tim O'Neill

It is an art, a discipline, and a spiritual path of tremendous challenge; even occasional danger. One doesn't embark lightly or frivolously on the journey of direct contact with the hidden worlds, yet there will always be those for whom no lesser experience will suffice. A growing number of such people are currently active within the arts.

Since the late 1960's and the end of the constraints imposed by institutional Modernist Art (the dominant "Avant Garde" art since 1900 based on the experiments of Cubism, Fauvism, Dadaism, Constructivism, and Futurism), a situation has developed in the arts, generally termed "Post-Modernism", in which an extraordinary profusion of style and content has tended to both de-centralize the arts and to bring them into much closer proximity with the channels of mass communication.

The rapid growth of Post-Modernist Performance Art, which has its roots in the Minimalist, Conceptualist and Body Art movements of the 1960's, is an example of this rapid interchange of ideas and images. While the theoretical concepts of Performance are quite complex, the basic idea behind the use of performance by visual artists can be stated in simple terms. If a painter is limited by the flat two dimensional surface of a canvas, then a sculpture can extend the same subject out into three dimensions. If the sculpture is limited to static materials, the Performance artist can extend the range of materials and motions to include living human beings or anything within the range of feasibility. It is a logical extension, given the limitations that the "static arts" must face. It is important to distinguish between theatre, which has its roots deep within the literary context, and Performance, which is founded on the visual arts. Rich mixtures can and do occur between these two distinct traditions, however, for our purposes, we will remain with a very "pure" interpretation of Performance Art.

One still nascent trend within the Performance Art arena is the development of an approach to an art based squarely and precisely on the experience of direct ecstatic contact with hidden worlds. The implications of this are deep and far-reaching, both for the arts as a whole, and for the oracular path (I use "oracular" in a much wider sense than that pertaining to oracles per se... In my use, it refers to all forms of communicative contact with the noumenal) as a particular spiritual discipline in our often skeptical and unsympathetic culture. The relationship between genuine oracular experience, ritual, and art is quite complex. It is, at root, a matter of an intensely subjective and difficult-to-communicate experience. There are few metaphorical or allegorical approaches to such experiences in the Modern West, and our language is generally impoverished when it comes to dealing with them. Many so-called "primitive" cultures have very rich means of expression and appreciation of the direct oracular experience as taken on by the specialist. They have even developed sophisticated mythological, artistic, and psychological means for non-specialists to actively participate in the experience. In our culture, a major portion of the problem facing the new oracular artists lies in our mass inability to cope with any spiritual experience or any psychological state outside the boundaries of consensus or "normal" reality. The efforts of these artists are slowly beginning to win a new audience capable of entering into the spirit of the experience. In order to understand something of the challenge facing these artists, we must understand the basic structure of the oracular frame of awareness.

The essential problem in penetrating the barrier to these hidden realms is largely conceptual. Our visible universe seems so close-ended and self-sufficient to most people. Even imagining another reality becomes an insuperable obstacle. There is so much controversy among theoreticians of the hidden world, that the situation has been even further confused. Still, among many practical workers of the inner realms, there is a rough conceptual "map" that we can use to gather our bearings. Much as in the traditional world-view of the Shamans (specialists in the ecstatic journey), we can postulate three worlds, existing in a loose network of inter-connective realities, forces and beings. The first is an "underworld" of deep, elemental forces; the second a "middleworld" that includes our own visible universe within its system, and the third is a "celestial" world of great light and stellar forces. We should understand that each of these realms has as much "reality" as the others... That the beings the oracular worker meets in each have their own distinct personality and life-force, although in the ultimate sense, all life and being shares a common source. Within these three worlds, styles of direct contact vary according to the particular nature of the communication desired. There is a spectrum of sorts, varying from what we might term the more "aggressive" and mobile style of the magician and shaman to the more "passive" styles of the medium and the oracle. In the middle of this spectrum lies the work of the clairvoyant and seer. In the darker, more "lunar" underworld, the disciplinary will and power of the shaman and magician are particularly successful. On the other hand, most mediums and oracles prefer to tangle with less elemental beings in the other two realms.

In actual practice, all of these oracular workers go to that area and those beings to which they are drawn, and where their work lies. We must be careful not to limit any particular style to any confines, for the individual's work rises above such artificial limits. The Shaman can most simply be defined as one who enters a state of ecstasy (lit. "out of bodily sense", or "out of self-awareness") in order to embark upon a journey through the three worlds based on whatever specific purposes they have in mind. It is a journey undertaken on the basis of inner direction, will and strength, and depends on the Shaman's specialized experience and knowledge of the inter connectedness of the beings and forces that will be met. By influencing something in one realm, the "shockwave" will be felt in the other two realms as well. Fakir Musafar, one of the shamans and artists that we will later meet, likes to think of the shaman as one who can "bridge the gap between the 'seen' and the 'unseen', traveling through the worlds". In his experience, the shaman can develop very sophisticated means for actually transporting energy between the worlds in order to effect the outcome of their work. Traditionally, Shamans literally go out of the physical body in what Western occultists refer to as a "subtle", "electric", or "etheric" body. The sense of actual motion is quite distinct in the shamanic state of ecstasy.

The medium, and oracle, like the shaman, also enter an ecstatic trance in order to depart from the physical body, yet instead of traveling through the worlds, simply "step aside" in order to allow another discarnate entity the use of their body on a temporary basis. While the shaman must develop great inner will in order to survive the rigors of subtle travel, the medium often attempts to lessen personal will in order to act as a better and clearer channel of communication.

The clairvoyant and seer neither journey like a shaman, nor vacate the physical form like a medium. They rather enter the ecstatic state in order to utilize highly specialized sensory organs that have been developed in their etheric bodies. They remain at all times in close proximity in their physical forms, and their etheric senses do all the "traveling and communicating".

What clearly unites all of these approaches is:

1) Their utilization of the ecstatic state,

2) The acquisition of knowledge and wisdom unavailable in the physical world,

3) Subtle healing from the etheric roots "outward",

4) The obtaining of advice on social and political matters from alien perspectives,

5) Enlightenment and anamnesis, or memory of the true, primordial self...

All the practical and spiritual necessities of life that cannot be met through the "normal" channels.

The means of entering the ecstatic state vary widely not only along the axis from shaman to medium, but even from individual to individual. Still, all such methods have developed out of a single common psycho-physiological reality. Both under- and over-stimulation of the human sensory apparatus can induce the ecstatic experience in the right hands. Fakir has even discovered that both of these methods can be used simultaneously in a complimentary fashion. When a strong element of rhythm and repetition is present in the special trance-inductive stimulation, it can add a definite element of control and refinement. It also helps to explain how the ecstatic state is naturally an artistic and cultural phenomenon rather than a means of isolation and self-insulation. Rhythm is the crucial element of art that most naturally compliments the psychological and physiological reality of ecstatic states. We might even refer to ecstasy and art as both sharing a common source in the element of rhythm, in its physical and subtle form. By the mastery of rhythm, one also enters the gateway to the mastery of the cosmic rhythms that the oracular worker must have. For the Fakir, rhythm "tunes out one realm and tunes in another, just like turning the knob on a radio receiver."

The crucial question that one reaches in consideration of the artistic aspects of the ecstatic journey lies at the heart of what we in the West consider to be "art". In traditional and pre-literate cultures, art is an integral part of life, not a specialist occupation defined by objective aesthetic contemplation at a remove. The new oracular art, by definition, exists in such realms of genuinely altered states of awareness, that any such distance or detachment on the part of artist and audience is impossible. For this art to work, the audience must participate in an analog of the deeper states that the artist is working with. Intellectual and objective "viewing" of the artwork is simply meaningless!

This remarkable situation may signal a fundamental break in the course of Western art, as it has been practiced since the Classical era of Greece. It is certainly a giant step toward an art that opens out onto a fantastic future. It is also a paradoxical step back to the very dawn of awareness before the compartmental tendency of the intellect existed. And several of these artists have already demonstrated it is also an art that can utilize the most advanced forms of technology and aesthetic available. There is no sense of any anti-technological bias in this art, and since many of the artists associated with the movement grew to maturity out of the "Industrial" art and music of the 1970's and 1980's, with its fascination for machinery, automation and psychological manipulation, they are quite willing to incorporate anything from pre-literate scarification ritual to computer controlled application of electrical stimulation in order to achieve the necessary shift in awareness.

It is important not to reduce the complexity and richness of these experiences to the status of a mere model. The best, and perhaps the only ultimate, approach is through the experience itself and those who undergo its disciplines. Fakir Musafar has been exploring the realms of the Shaman and the Trance Seeker for over three decades. A strong urge, at an early age, led him to experiment with manipulation and decoration of the body along the lines of many "primitive" peoples. This innate fascination led him to direct experiences of shamanic induction and ecstasy. This spontaneous and purely inner-directed opening into the world of direct contact with the hidden worlds led him eventually to a deep study of the primitive mind and spirit, in order to enrich his ability to work in those invisible realms. As he states, "In my studies, I connected with primal spirits via psychometry (the use of psychic energy surrounding objects and beings to determine their nature and history) and found how they used the physical body as a 'trip lever' to subtle, hidden worlds. Essentially: make a body change and something psychic changes too. Universally, they employed what I call the four A's:

1) Accept (volunteer for) a specific alteration in body state.

2) Allow something physical to be done to you.

3) Adjust to the change until it becomes a part of you.

4) Appreciate the resulting contra-change in perspective of yourself and others in the community... And in the hidden worlds, these changes may open up to you...

For example, a Sioux youth might say:

1) I accept the Sun Dance into my Life (a ritual involving ritual piercing of the chest and back, and suspension from a tree sacred to the spirit of the sun).

2) I allow myself to be pierced and tethered to a tree.

3) I adjust to being fixed this way and vow to pull against myself until I break free.

4) I appreciate the presence of the Great White Spirit who aids Sun Dancers and takes them on Eagle Flight..."

This natural resonance with the spirit of the shaman's vocation led the Fakir to a growing interest in the musical and artistic aspects of the work. Developing very sophisticated and decorative means of reaching the ecstatic state through manipulation of the body, a practice which he has termed "Body Play", the Fakir began to teach others how to use their bodies to reach back into primordial states of awareness in the ecstatic state. By using the body's own sensory feedback systems, the Fakir has rediscovered many of the secrets of ecstasy, and has helped to re-open the avenue of body as art for many students over the years. His dedication to the spirit of peace and enlightenment for the human community finally led him to allow one of the most profound rituals in which he had ever participated to be captured on film. *Dances sacred and profane*, a film by Mark and Dan Jury, captures the essence of Fakir and his shaman's assistant, Jim Ward, as they enact the famous "Sun Dance" of the Plains Indians. As a perfect example of Fakir's subtle blend of the traditional, the personal, and the modern, the Sun Dance sequence helps to bring the audience into a beginning awareness of what it must require and what it must be like to contact the Great White Spirit, as did the Fakir. The Jury Brothers' sensitive and sympathetic portrayal of that marvelous experience is another sign that direct contact with Spirit is something that we hunger for in Western Culture. The deep chord that the film strikes in many viewers is proof of that need. The Fakir represents one of the most significant members of what has been termed a movement of "new primitives", those who combine the spirit and practices of pre-literate and ecstatic cultures with the sophistication of the Modern World. As the Fakir states: "As I have often explained when asked this question, 'How do you reconcile your different lives?', I merge and interconnect them. I take the discipline and organization of my business/technocrat life into primal experiences. This keeps me from becoming 'flakey' and allows the total fulfillment of a vow or vision. On the other hand, I always have the primal mind available to tap in business when I need a burst of spontaneity; of uninhibited inspiration. I use visions from my primal side to create fresh and original technical advertising!"

The direct experience, and the ritual surrounding it, must always precede aesthetic interest per se in the work of these artists, and few of them have insisted on that principle more strongly than Kristine Ambrosia. Since 1975, she has been working with various forms of direct contact with the hidden worlds. At the age of 20, that fateful year, she experienced a spontaneous and quite unexpected awakening into the vocation of Shaman. As her work progressed, she naturally grew into the practices of a trance medium, and finally developed into a full clairvoyant seer. During the entirety of that twelve year period her inner experience was recorded in copious journals, static artworks and Performance artworks. The essence of this unique storehouse of documentation has been collected in a book entitled *Running through a Hall of Mirrors*, which will be published in the near future.

Kristine has developed the specialized etheric sensory and communication system that defines the seer, and has taken to the work of reaching and recording the wisdom of a particular group of advanced etheric beings, known as the "Regent's Council". Her study group, the Wisdom's Eye Foundation, publishes many of the lectures and artworks that are transmitted to her by the Council while she is in the ecstatic state. Her earlier work as a shaman involved much manipulation of the body, and even her work as a medium was very wearing on her physical form. However, during the clairvoyant trances, she is quite calm and speaks as if to a person just inches away. There are none of the marked physical motions that often accompany the "inhabitation" of the medium by the discarnate entity or "other world". She thinks of herself as a "telephone line" to the subtle worlds, over which impulses flow through the "third eye", or subtle psychic plexus in the forehead. She locates coordinates on the subtle planes in a rough analog of "dialing". She has even begun to think of herself as something of a "cellular phone" with no fixed location in time and space. Since the "astral" and "causal" planes in the celestial world with which she communicates have no inherent sense of time, space or object as we conceive of them, all of these metaphors should be taken in the loosest sense possible! As a major founding member of the new schools of mediumistic and clairvoyant art currently forming within the world of Performance, Kristine's work has lately begun to draw national attention. She has lately turned her attention to the use of pure psychic energy as a valid medium for art. To explore its potentials, she has conducted performances from remote locations, using other artists and assistants as "on site" antennae for the energy which she projects. In this manner, she has been able to work with intercontinental groups of artists, to create immense spider-webs of etheric energy, guided by the Council. Her work has begun to open onto truly breathtaking vistas!

When Kristine and the Fakir met during the early 1980's, what followed was a very fruitful series of collaborations on oracular and ecstatic art, and in order to bring all the preceding material into close focus, it would be useful to examine two of these collaborations. "Spinning Sigil" and "Kage Hoshi" were both large ritual performance artworks that explored the role of the body in the quest of the spirit (Both works were executed during 1984-1985, when Kristine was still working as a medium and shaman). It often seems very difficult for those outside the ritual to understand what on earth piercing and body play has to do with a spiritual quest, yet as we have seen, the connection is firmly rooted in psycho-physiologoical reality and is just as valid as more abstract and intellectualized forms of meditation and contemplation.

"Spinning Sigil" was an evening's exploration of the power of body-piercing to induce ecstatic and mediumistic trance. In the course of the ritual performance, Kristine pierced one of her shaman's assistants (Eric Love) with a series of hooks, balls and weights, in order to provoke a very high state of etheric energy within and around his body. By transference of this subtle energy to herself, she was able to enter a very deep state of mediumistic awareness. In that state, a distinct entity, a Taoist master, was able to communicate through her. She entered this state while suspended upside-down from a large wooden hoist-structure. Previous experiments had proven that this particular combination of piercing and suspension could provide her with all the energy necessary to achieve a singularly powerful altered frame of awareness. To communicate this experience to the audience (many of whom had already had ritual piercings done in private that evening) she had a special headset microphone hooked to a bank of electronic harmonizers and digital delays, to approximate the peculiar sound quality of the inner planes. After being released from suspension, she used a computer graphics pad that had been specially programmed, to draw some of the experience onto the live video monitors. Since she was still blindfolded and her back was pierced through with four large needles, she was assisted in these technical matters by another shaman's assistant. Her communication in the mediumistic state was so striking that several members of the audience reported altered states of awareness both during and after the performance.

For Fakir's portion of the ritual, he accomplished a semi-suspension from the two permanent piercings in his chest, which he also uses for the Sun Dance. Diana, his shamanic assistant, watched him very carefully as artist Monte Cazazza slowly raised him on the same winch that Kristine had used. The audience was able to feel the tremendous energy and spirit that such suspensions create, and again, many were able to report trance-quests of their own after the conclusion of the ritual.

"Kage Hoshi" took place about a year later at the People's Theatre Collective in San Francisco. In many ways, this ritual work was a whole complex of different means of entering the oracular state, carefully orchestrated by Kristine from the central position. Monte Cazazza was being swung on a special device that produces disorientation, Eric Love was placed in a special cage of spears, the Fakir was dancing in a large metal cage of spears, known in India as a Kavandi, and in the middle of all these complementary etheric energies Kristine was engaged in her suspension, singing and painting while in the deep mediumistic state. The various actions unfolded slowly and majestically in a perfect example of the innate rhythm of the true oracular work. All of these artists met together on the subtle planes and helped to open a wide gateway for those members of the audience who wished to enter. They accomplished together in the rhythm of ritual, what no single artist could have done alone.

As their artistic and spiritual work has evolved and grown over the years, both individually and together from time to time, Fakir and Kristine have pursued almost diametrically opposed paths to the inner worlds, yet they have both been able to create exciting new forms of art, and the energy surrounding that art has slowly begun to become infectious. More and more artists in the San Francisco Bay Area are beginning to see the tremendous potential in this work. EX-I, Secret Chiefs, Tantric Duet from New York, COIL in London, have all maintained an interest in oracular art. It is as yet a small and specialized movement, but as time and energy builds, I believe that it will come to have much influence on the larger body of our culture.

To Achieve Death

Terence Sellers

And so it came to pass that he too was claimed by the plague. By his bed I stayed – I could not be drawn away from his fevered eyes, his daily frailer hands. Towards the end, few others would come near, the thick of contagion a psychic effect – fear the molecules of the air. My devotion was viewed as a morbid thing – they shuddered at my constancy – for was I not some sort of maggot, why didn't I go on, get on with my life? But I was the next to die... And any kindly warnings I received filled me with disgust.

What did I care, anymore, of the difference between life and death? In that long-extended twilight we sat together, while around us the world froze into mute and meaningless forms – yet white somehow, and smoother.

The concerns and normal noise of those humans we had contact with irritated us with their fatuous health. They were frantic with life, the lie – that there was no worm in the rose – *they* could go on, doing what they do, blind in their security – while we were set upon the truth that destroys all security.

He suffered in a hundred ways and did not particularly want the attentions I showed him. But thus it had always been between my beloved and I. He had never understood my attachment to him – how I loved him was to him an unknown. And now, more than ever, did I embarrass him with my adorations, as in each day passing his powers waxed and waned, and waned.

The end was long in coming – the inevitable our dull one companion. In the serene twilight of his death, a deep and velvet grey gathered. This half-light warmed and soothed us... For in some incomprehensible way, we loved this death – for it was ours.

Still, I, as representative of the living, made an effort to turn his thoughts to those things eternal – to poetry, ideas, to the celestial abstractions of music, all the beautiful infinites. I say I tried – but the artist in him was only tormented by these perfections – for he could no longer engage in creation, torn as he was now from all material.

The proud and ambitious heart in him seethed against the strictures of the disease. His death was a crime against all art, as I looked upon the one painting that was mine and saw the living germ, his very jewel of life that still beat with its creator's pulse. The secret life of his vision, mined by him from depths that would not soon again be opened – would not soon again repeat itself – leapt to my eye, awakened in my mind all that was best, most beautiful and true.

For long hours I would sit and gaze upon this painting, and rail against the loss to the world of a further elaboration... The incomplete text of his dream hovered in a grey air, thicker now, and darker, and in our constant twilight were our mouths sealed with dust...

When he died, those who felt they had some claim upon him gathered round to cut up the corpse. To prevent my hearing his name in their mouths, I affected total silence towards all those who spoke to me. They left me alone, and I stood apart, and was as loathed as was to be expected.

For certainly I was the source of the infection. One pointed me out as carrion bird – another insinuated that I was a murderer. I, the next in line to die, assuredly deserved his death!

I did not follow the funeral cortege, but remained in my rooms and made my last arrangements.

At nightfall, after a long meditation, I drew on my gloves and took up the pistol. It had been well-oiled for weeks, and loaded but two days before the last crisis had come. I left the door unlocked – all pertinent letters written and sealed on my desk – and I set off on foot to the cemetery.

Those last embraces! The pain had kept him awake day and night – no drug could divert him any longer from the physical anguish, nor the consciousness of his fate. And in the dull light of yet another dawn I held him in my arms as he wept. It was then that I told him of my decision. He begged me not to – then I saw him lapse into indifference. So this is why you never feared infection, he said dryly. You have planned this all along.

I saw that this last devotion of mine only added to his torments. I do not want this life without you – please, let me go, too! His mouth was set and he showed me his averted face. I went on – This side was intolerable – until I met you. In you – and with you – new worlds were revealed to me. Your appearance in my life held back my hand from something that was inevitable... So you're not even really dying for me, he said peevishly. I am just some excuse for you to indulge your masochism.

Get away from me!, he shouted. I wept – You are cruel to make me go on living... Particularly as you neither wish to stay. I have better reason, he said.

You must not do this – you must do as I say. Yes, I replied – I'll do as you say, I'll GO on living in this dead world, crawling through this life that I hate.

Live for what we were, he said – but faintly. I knew – and I said nothing. We knew it was a charade, his valiant will to live... That neither of us were any longer able to feel strongly about whatever there might yet be to do in some short and shallow future...

In our long search for love, he said quietly, we have achieved only death – death we have embraced through our love. It is ungrateful for you to hate the life that has brought us thus far, and together – ungrateful, too, to deplore this death and he was stopped by a harsh spasm of coughing. This black flower of our passion! He tried to laugh.

Now, I felt he had surpassed me. So should I surpass myself... And achieve death with all the passion I had left!

We passed some moments in silent beatitude, and swore our vows to one another anew. Ask me not to repeat the words we used... Nor what our few gestures were. Then he passed into the crisis again, swiftly downstream where I could not reach him, and his eyes would open once a day, to gaze before himself in fear, yes fear took even his brave heart.

The next night as I arose wearily to get a drink of water, he cried aloud, Don't leave me! His hand wavered in the air – I rushed back to his side. Don't ever, he started, then, catching my eye, he stopped.

It was enough for me. Now all doubt and hesitation could I lay aside.

He scaled the cemetery wall at the low point he had noted on a solitary walk. Towards his grave he ran, and with a light heart. He even laughed as he caressed his weapon. Kneeling by the stone that had not yet been graven, he spoke to his beloved one last time... And drew from his pocket his death.

My beloved... My heart... I am following you now.

I pray I will not be thrown to the winds, set on another hundred year search of YOU. I hope you will believe me now... And that you are waiting...

The wind stirred faintly and he thought it might be he. My beloved... This world is nauseating without you. I shall die anyhow of grief – and though you are due that prolonged homage, I prefer not to grieve in a public place. For if I lived on, past my sorrow, I would of course 'recover' from my loss – which thought outrages me. That perversion does occur in living, we forget – so life I will not undergo. I wish never again to love, I wish there to be *no possibility of any other love...*

May God not stop me, he prayed, as he fitted the gun-barrel down his esophagus and fired. Against the stone he fell and his blood soaked into the new-turned earth. And the earth recoiled and rejected this gift, so that his spirit could not sink there to his beloved's body, but flew into the air...

And the spirit of his true beloved was there and waiting for him. And at last, and for the first time, they embraced. And never again would there be an obstruction to their embrace, and there was no one, nor would there be anyone, to tear them asunder again...

Thus hard entwined, they traveled to a place where they had lived together, and had deeply loved, nature, the mountains, deserts and streams. And it was there, in that sky, where the two souls become one soul, to drift upon the astral, tranquil, clear and diamond-hard, a new creation and the marvel of the day. And in their first night, sparkling dense light leapt out, so that all men saw and wondered that a new star had come into being.

But would such a well-knit soul again be born – would there be any flesh worthy to receive it? From this too, you see, they are freed! Never again to return to flesh... Yet in their embrace, never broken and ever-renewed, man's knotted mysteries they untangle, as hearts to one another they press, bringing lovers together as they had been brought – to this most final refinement of love!

And now, to mind and page, may this soul dispense a boundless inspiration, enlivening my cell with visions sublime and lithe, so I may tell of hearts unchastened and free – o tell us, dark spirit, of love's nobility! We shall meet again... We shall meet again, in our deathless dream, that dream of one another, where we may live together, forever, alone and One.

Choice and Process

A Model of Consciousness and the Patterns of Life. Version no. III/589

Stein Jarving

The following discourse on the patterns of choice and the process of consciousness is being put forward as a framework for understanding and expansion. The theory has been built upon concepts from Carl G. Jung, Aleister Crowley, Timothy Leary, Gregory Bateson and Buckminster Fuller, and has been greatly inspired by Tom B. Pawlicki; all to whom I am grateful for furthering my education and understanding. – S.J.

GOD AND MAN

Life and consciousness are both enigmatic concepts to man's logical sciences. Science can make the observation that certain molecules, put together in a certain way by Nature's DNA-program, unfolds a creature which has both. But this breath of Life and Birth of Mind has no known origin, no source and – outside of religion – no destiny or greater purpose, in the eyes of science.

In the last 40 years or 50, however, proponents of hard sciences like physics and mathematics have postulated concepts which could as well be the basis of religion, when studying the behavior of atomic articles and their energy levels. They speculate that the atomic occurrences may be influenced by the Mind of Man; that chance is in fact choice, and that everything is interconnected. In Biology also, models have been put forth postulating patterns "larger than Life"; an organizing unity of Earth's biosphere forming a single, conscious organism controlling all life processes. Gaia.

At the basic level, Life equals Unity: All living organisms are connected to all other living organisms, all molecular components and all energies in a tight woven pattern of inter-relationships, separated only by Time: each sub-unit an integral part of a common pattern.

Earth is a womb, or an incubator, powered by the Sun; an organic/biological, interrelated, interdependent process of perpetual life and death kept in homeostatic balance within extremely fine tolerances. Small variations – on a cosmic scale – of temperature, oxygen-content or humidity would drastically alter all life on Earth beyond recognition. Yet Gaia – Mother Earth – has faithfully maintained her body in fine-tuned balance for millions of years, presumably for some larger purpose.

Man claims, arrogantly, that he is the larger purpose; Earth has been created by God and given to Man, for him to dispose of as he pleases. Yet "God" is a vague concept for Man. Many say they are in direct communion with God, but few have ever been able to establish this as anything but megalomania or a will to power over other men. And some of those we feel we can trust talk in riddles and claim God can not be understood by the intellect, since God is beyond description, beyond words, if not totally beyond conscious perception. Those who claim to have seen God, describe an unbearable source of light and a feeling of utter loss of individual existence; a void so terrifying, yet so tempting and a light so brilliant, that everything else loses importance.

I wish here to postulate a new hypothesis of God, of the Divine Sphere, and Man's relationship to God, or at least one important aspect of this divine force we call God, because if what I say here is correct, there must be hierarchies of Gods. My basic concept is that the God closest to us, the one God of which we usually have close communion, is this selfsame Gaia: Mother of Earth. We experience, in short, a direct link with the conscious, living organism of whom we are but minute parts, created for a purpose far beyond our normal understanding, and maybe beyond our wildest dreams.

The answer to this enigma must of necessity be found in our consciousness, our Mind, one should think. But I see the Mind as a mere communication-system, hooked up to an advanced computer and manned by a half-mad ape bent on self-destruction. Within this construct called Man is an antenna, very directional-sensitive, tuned by this elusive centre we call Soul. A finely tuned Soul connects Mind to Over-Soul, or what I call the Divine Grid, and reveals to Mind its Purpose and Will. And the Over-Soul is of course Gaia's transmitter, linking us to Gaia's consciousness. Tuning this antenna is what religion and Magick is all about.

The human mind is connected to the Gaia consciousness by the way of a five-dimensional grid, where at any point in space and time, on any energy level, in any dimension, one always has five possible choices of directions in which to move, three of them obvious (our logical world), one sublime and one divine.

The three obvious ones are of the material world and concerns material, physical aspects of life, and the conscious experiences of our interactions with same.

The sublime dimension is an emotional choice – aptly called The Way of the Heart – whereas the divine fifth dimension is one of pure, inspired ecstasy, guided by one's destiny. The choices one makes are the pattern called Karma, and the only way to get released from this Wheel of Karma, is through divine, five-dimensional choices.

The divine choices would be like a path of light through this grid or matrix of five-dimensional choices, accessible only through combining the charges, or awareness-levels, of the other four dimensions, or by a freak accident of pure inspiration, through madness (loss of energy control) or Genius (full five-dimensional awareness; spontaneous super-conductivity of mind). Tom Pawlicki calls this state Crystallization.

PATTERN OF CHOICE

This structure of five different choices open to you at your point of decision, implies five different mind-sets, each one evolved from the others to a large degree, but in a hierarchical way, so that each individual may not have developed all five, and thus some may have a more limited set of choices than others.

(A mind-set, for those unfamiliar with the term, is a pattern of internal responses, like love, fear, anger, hunger, etc, that each of us carries within as the basic framework for all our actions and reactions. I postulate that such mind-sets have a cyclical development in separate, definable stages.)

The first mind-set is the one we have in common with all living organisms; it's commonly called instincts, and its basic concerns are sex, food and shelter. The bare minimum requirements of species regeneration: Survival of the fittest, each on his own.

The second mind-set concerns social behavior, or organized survival by cooperation and domination; the Tribal Mind, if you wish, or what most may call Common Sense. This is the basis for organized communities and efforts, in order to protect tribal continuity over and above the survival of individuals, protecting a system and a genetic pool in competition with others. All for one – one for all. This is where sports and politics enter the scene, as well as organized religions – about 8000 years back.

The third mind-set goes beyond mere survival, onto abstract concepts like "What if...", and to postulate future effects based on and extrapolated from experience in an organized way. This is commonly called logic, and in our civilization based mostly on the philosophies of Plato and Aristoteles; i.e. concepts of thinking and organization about 3000 years old.

The fourth mind-set brings us one step further yet, by introducing creativity; leaps of understanding, and the ability to postulate models of organization, as in music, art, mathematics, etc., over and above anything which can be based on logical constructs derived from experience. This is what genius is all about, as well as fantasy and art; discovery of the unknown.

The final, fifth mind-set contains all of the previous sets, in a functioning combination of harmonious relationships, each mind-set modulating all others, but under firm control by a whole which is greater than its component parts: Wisdom, or what some call True Will.

Wisdom implies a concept of unity, of wholeness; a sort of pattern consciousness, in which the whole grid of possible futures are being revealed; where we learn of the process which is the purpose of the grid, and the individual mind's relation to this process. Thus the choices of wisdom are unlimited in scope, but severely restricted in fact, as no one who has attained wisdom would ever choose a course of action which could not benefit the pattern – the whole.

ENERGY PROCESS

There are certain concepts which are needed, in order to understand the picture I am trying to paint for you. First of all, Consciousness is no state, but a process, and this process involves transfer of energy (like ordinary electricity, magnetism or cosmic radiation). The energies involved all follow a set of rules, like those observable in ordinary physics, and the process is thus analog with ordinary electronics. All bio-chemical life pertains to this electro-chemical process. All transferal of information in this process is super-luminal, after the signals have been received by the Mind. In most people, this super-luminal transfer of information is below "consciousness" in the limited way we normally use this concept: It's not part of the logical process of three dimensions we normally operate in. This is a self-imposed and unnecessary restriction, which it is quite possible to remove.

The removal of restrictions in our consciousness requires certain training in due process; on control and focus of the energy involved, as well as a decrease in the resistance within the Mind, to let this energy flow freely. Without training, the power and the brilliance could easily drive you mad, or maybe even kill you. Some people experience such communication without control or focus, like an accident or a revelation; they are classified as geniuses or madmen, according to what impact they have on society or what commercial value their revelations may have. But some manage to keep it a secret and survive to tell others; they have had a resistance sufficiently low to collect their "wits" afterwards, and to go on living as apparently "normal" people. Yet others gain the knowledge to control or focus, to direct the process, by finding teachers who have been there before, in full control, and returned to teach. This is what Magick is about.

A direct communication with Gaia requires something akin to mental superconductivity and the use of coherent waveforms of energy, and it initiates a state of positive feedback; there is no stopping the flow. Even with superconductivity, this would create a burn-out instantly (ever heard of humans burning up without cause?), if there had not been more than three dimensions involved. The minimum model required to contain a process without physical limits is a five-dimensional model: here everything happens in the same way spot at the same time, instantly. And only a trained Will can select a beneficent pattern through total Chaos, and thus bend reality into form. Just like a Sun is not an uncontrolled release of spontaneous energy, but a strictly controlled process of interrelationships, so also the Super-conscious, five-dimensional Mind is a supernova Soul, strictly controlled by Conscious Process.

Entropy is form breaking down into what we term "Kaos", and Neg-Entropy is pattern, form, created from "Kaos". But Kaos is just a term we use where we cannot determine any coherent pattern, or any form we can recognize. It is just a matter of distinction; and in our lack of fine-focus and understanding, we see Kaos because we cannot recognize the order which is there. Entropy and Neg-Entropy are just two phases of the phases of life, like plus and minus, Yin and Yang, God and Devil, life and death; each part of the cycle as important, as necessary as the other, and each created by the other. Good and Evil are just moral concepts, necessary at certain levels of consciousness; varying from one age to the next, from one country to another, always with exceptions for those in power.

Good and Evil can also be seen as choices: If we see as our larger purpose (Karma) to become Divine (Superconductive), then all choices furthering this purpose are Good, and all choices hindering it or postponing it, Evil. All human Evil is ultimately equal to ignorance: Fear, greed, vanity, egotism, hate, etc., are all products of ignorance. One difficult aspect of ignorance to overcome in order to become divine is the concept that God, Plus, Yang, and Life are Good, whereas Devil, Minus, Yin, and Death are Evil. The Hindu God Shiva is a very good example of the necessary dual concept required for further understanding: he is both the Creator and the Destroyer; God and Devil rolled into one. This is as it should be, as the one has no meaning without the other.

To transfer one's Mind from one dimension to another means to take a giant leap in consciousness, turning the world one thought one knew totally upside down, scrambling all preconceived concepts of what Life is really about. This process is as old as Man, and from history we can trace certain periods where several individuals made this transfer seemingly simultaneously, in China, in India, in Babylonia, in Palestine, in Egypt, in Greece, in Rome, in Europe. It is the history of Man's achievements through known history. One of the first geniuses we know of is Pythagoras, who laid the basis for mathematics. And throughout known history, names of Genius Minds have appeared, seemingly at random; always feared for their tendency to turn concepts and dogmas inside out, successfully tangling with powers and knowledge others feared (or used as their basis for control of others, and thus wanted to keep Status Quo).

In the earlier ages it was the Church that most feared new knowledge, striving to kill off everyone who had a tendency to divine madness, unless they could paint murals or wanted to join the Church. In our days it is the State that fears the unrestricted Mind, and instead of killing, it uses mental hospitals and jails, to keep unwanted geniuses off the streets. Truth and Divinity are concepts feared because they belong to a restricted franchise, since the promises of it alone furthers power and money towards the source of such promises. If Jesus would come back today, he would be shot before anyone found out.

In this age there seems not to be too many geniuses around, but quite a marked increase in creativity and art. And this is probably due to the "Hypothesis of the 100 apes", postulating that when a sufficiently large number of individuals change, one gets a spontaneous change in the whole population almost instantly (which is just another example of super-luminal transfer of information).

Thus we are on the doorstep of the fourth dimension as a species. Describing this dimension as "emotional" is not sufficient; it is the dimension of our subconscious, right-brain activity, directing such skills as musicality, form, color, continuity, whole-picture integration, fantasy, psychic ability; the ability to think ecologically, in whole systems, holistically. It is beyond the simple concepts of Action-Reaction, into Cause and Sense.

The next step is the Divine one, the Cosmic one, the Boundless one – all fanciful descriptions of a Reality of which most of us know not a thing, of an experience only describable from within. The effects of Divinity are however aptly described in literature as old as literate man: you can read minds, see clearly the past and the future, talk with dead ones, heal all forms of ailments, travel anywhere at will – and you get a bright halo around you. Or at least this is what eyewitnesses claim. What I believe to be the fact, is that you get connected to the aforementioned grid of energy, containing all information ever to be created within this mode of existence. You get hooked up to Gaia-Consciousness.

CONSCIOUSNESS TECHNOLOGY

The process of altering one's state of consciousness from three-dimensional logical, space-time restricted Common Sense to four-dimensional creativity and unrestricted holism requires knowledge of what the process involves. I will outline my understanding of this in terms of physics and electronics, since that is the way I see it, without claiming this to be the only, true way.

Consider a grid, like a star of six points, held within a crystal like a double pyramid, base planes touching. One point is then the antenna, one point the ground point, the four base-line points representing the four different energy-forms which keep our physical reality together (weak and strong atomic, electromagnetic and gravitic). The grid is contained within the crystal like a solid-state transceiver, with the controller – the Soul – at the exact centre, where all internally drawn lines intersect. Tuning the circuit to receive a strong signal from God (Gaia) is a mental process to lower resistance and increase focus, until all the available energy flows through the Soul like a coherent wave of magnified energy, which then is returned enormously intensified as a signal of recognition, through the antenna.

Combining the first three dimensions of Mind to achieve four-dimensional consciousness requires removal of the resistance necessary to contain a 3-D, restricted process. This resistance is imposed by a process of negative feedback (like a governor on a steam-engine), preventing overheating (nervous breakdown), and necessary since 3-D can only contain a limited amount of energy. This resistance has the form of mental blocks, restricting reality to what can be experienced with our five ordinary senses or the instruments of science. Such removal of resistance is what philosophy and transcendental meditation is about.

The first two dimensions are the plane-logic of basic survival. It resides in the left-brain hemisphere. Opening of the pathway between the second and third dimension involves the controlled use of the spatial illusions of the right-brain hemisphere, where our concepts of space and time reside. Advance in the third dimension gives perspective and a sense of purpose; a mobility in space, which makes intellectual structures possible. The third dimension is the intellectual dimension.

Entering the fourth dimension gives a sense of purpose which exceeds self and introduces art and passion. Emotions change the pattern of three-dimensional logic, twists it, rearranges it, and leaps beyond it. If three-dimensional logic makes us human, fourth-dimension emotions make us immortal.

Combining the four other energy-levels through process involves understanding of process, and results in conscious discovery of the Divine dimension, which focuses energy towards this level in a combined fourth-dimension effort.

The fourth dimension, emotions, is the gateway between third-dimension logic – space-restricted thinking – and fifth-dimensional Divinity. Opening of the gateway is noticed through intuition, imagination, creativity: Love of Life as such.

Moving from the fourth dimension to the fifth dimension, you enter the collective subconscious of Life and open your third eye. The fifth dimension is the destiny of conscious mind, often called Heaven, where all consciousness merges with all other consciousness.

Five-dimensional consciousness equals superconductivity in the mind. Superconductivity of the Mind is a state of perfect coherence, integration and harmony: Oneness.

The high border-resistance of the divine five-dimensional mind-set requires perfect resonance and finely tuned focus for the combined fourth-dimension energy to penetrate, but above threshold value the process creates more energy than it uses (Entropy is only a problem in a closed system.).

Focus is facilitated by frequency: once the proper channel has been found, your message is ready to travel throughout the five-dimensional matrix of possible pasts and futures, and you are established as an operator in the collective subconscious of Life, still with a projection in fourth-dimension space-time.

Since process facilitates focus and focus facilitates a more efficient process, one has a positive feedback loop of increasing energy level. But since a more efficient process also lowers resistance towards superconductivity, and since the energy flows into a five-dimensional grid, there is no need for control of energy level, once one has mastered the process. Once again, entropy is only a problem in a closed system.

The process, once started, is self-sustaining in an entropy-negentropy cycle, called flow-of-life.

At a sufficient energy level, it becomes a star, a quasar, a black hole, etc., as parts of the process; its awareness of self releasing itself to awareness of All.

Rising through the dimensions increases your choices, but decreases your desires. In fifth-dimensional you may still move in any direction you choose within the grid. But it simultaneously gives you a total understanding of the patterns and aims of the matrix structure. Its very process. And this is what lowers your resistance to the energy, as well as helping you to focus.

When a five-dimensional state has been fully achieved, you also know the full purpose of the grid, of your part in it and your capability of fulfilling your part of the overall design; yeah, even your eagerness to add your essential bit, since the purpose is so obvious and desirable. One does not need freedom of choice when there is no need for choices. If you know with absolute certainty what you must do, and are fully happy to do so, you have achieved a higher freedom: Freedom from restraints – Freedom to do your True Will.

Most will see this as a state of delusion, when viewed from outside. They will see you as either mad or divine, lost from reason, which in fact is correct. The fifth dimension is way beyond reason.

HIGHER AWARENESS

Every Great Artist of any trade, be he painter, philosopher, healer or poet, has fully attained fourth-dimension, and has awareness of the fifth dimension. Every Great Sage or Genius has attained fifth-dimensional consciousness at least in part. But only a handful of saints and Creators have ever fully attained the fifth dimension, and of these probably just a few have ever been able to step off the Wheel of Karma: limitless energy at full superconductivity and full positive feedback, like a controlled atomic explosion – a supernova Soul.

Buddha, Ishtar, Isis, Shiva, Shakti, Kali, Jesus, etc., may all have been pure mythology, but may as well be descriptions of humans gone controlled supernova.

God-like feats and out-of-phase phenomena like unexplained physical disappearance-reappearance, would be typical fifth-dimensional modes looked at from a lower dimension, as would ability to heal, to see into the past and the future (time travel in your mind, as if there was any other kind), levitation and a strong, perceptible corona, or aura. All are manifestations of extremely high energy levels at giga-hertz frequencies, in a biological system without resistance. When resistance decreases towards superconductivity, one will experience abilities like ESP, as one's mind will be able to travel at will along the grid of the collective subconscious, inbound by our concepts of time. But most who do ESP-stunts in public have attained this ability by accident; and without control, it may be more harmful than helpful. It is both uncontrolled focus and imperfect process; like a drunk driver in a car with bad brakes.

Seen from within fifth-dimensional consciousness, however, the sluggishness, in perceptiveness, worry and uncertainty of fourth-dimension, or the brutal, cold and material logic of third-dimension seem perfectly normal and necessary. It is all part and parcel of the process of growing, but the growth seems woefully slow and painful, and you sincerely wish to help.

But you also realize that your help, within the rules of Karma, will have a limited value, as each and every person must learn to control and focus their own energy. Once off the wheel, you may step back on as a volunteer, to teach and guide the eager and gifted, but as the grid unfolds itself to you and your net charge grows, you soon realize the futility of playing God to the sheep.

You're much like an architect genius looking back at the endless work of drawing utilitarian, ugly boxes of glass and concrete – or trying to convince the customers that beauty can be worth the extra costs, when he can create marvels of eternal beauty on his own. He may wish to enlighten his colleagues, but he will soon find them unable to grasp even his simplest concepts, and believe his creations impossible. This is why just a few disciples ever attain any real enlightenment from a Master, while millions may worship him for the beauty of his mind.

What man cannot understand he will trample or deify. What he does not believe, he cannot even see.

Fourth-dimension minds can grasp the underlying essence of Wisdom, Beauty, and Genius, and will make ample students and disciples. Third-dimension minds can at most perceive it and admire it, solidifying it as dogma or the law of God. When you take symbolic wisdom meant for ancient second-dimension minds and solidify it in dogmatic religion, you get religious war, where promoters of one interpretation (Catholic, Jewish, Hindu) are fighting the promoters of the other (Protestant, Nazi, Muslim). Dogmatic religions are the fossils of consciousness.

Learning the process of focusing your energies, fine-tuning your choices and penetrating the gateway between fourth-dimension and fifth-dimensional mind is what Zen, Tao, Thelema and other so called Magick is all about: teaching Mind to control Matter. At full focus you achieve coherent frequency: a ray of electrons traveling at lightspeed. Above that threshold you have a starburst of pure photons extended in five dimensions; then the human gestalt has ceased, and you have pure consciousness.

CHEMICAL AWARENESS

Some chemical catalytic substances, like LSD and MDMA (Ecstasy) may create passing periods of near superconductivity in the brain, and may in some persons lower threshold resistance permanently in parts of the grid. If this gets too extensive too suddenly, the human mind may not have enough control to focus to contain and direct the sharply increased charge. It gets overloaded, and may experience a burn-out or a sharp resistance increase. The first may result in madness, the latter in permanent state of badly controlled fear or self-denial. Loss of focus, loss of energy, or loss of direction.

To trigger the process in a more permanent way does not exclude drugs, but requires the use in a controlled way, as a resistance-lowering reagent applied specifically to allow weak focus of a low energy (relatively speaking, as we here deal with advanced fourth-dimension minds) to penetrate farther, onto selected areas of the Mind, and to establish a small surge of planned positive feedback, before the system again is stabilized on a higher energy level.

This is called Consciousness Expansion through Applied Chemistry, and can be extremely powerful, if you really know what you are doing (delusions have severe penalties). Like Christians were persecuted in 100 AD and witches in 1500 AD, users of LSD and MDMA are persecuted, as the knowledge you may attain is deemed illegal by 3-D minds. It is just too alien to them.

Such are the physics, biology and psychology of the five-dimensional mind grid, in quick outline. Anyone for whom the picture of reality I try to outline here is not entirely clear, due to the words I use or my own lack of understanding or ability to synthesize the philosophy of others, should preferably first read some of the following books, to become better acquainted with this way of thinking. I must, however, underline that neither of the following authors in any way can be held responsible for the fallacies of my own thinking and understanding; this essay is thus entirely my own creation, only born to fruition by their inspiration.

Recommended Books

- Gregory Bateson, *Steps to an ecology of mind, Mind and nature: A necessary unity*
- Carl G. Jung, *Man and his symbols*
- Norbert Wiener, *Cybernetics*
- R. Buckminster Fuller, *Ideas and integrities, Synergetics l & 2*
- T. Leary and R.A. Wilson, *The Game of Life*
- Richard Bandler, *Using the brain for a change*
- Arthur Koestler, *The act of creation*
- Tom B. Pawlicki, *Hyperspace*
- Aleister Crowley, *Magick in theory and practice*
- Gary Zukav, *The dancing Wu-Li Masters*

Comment from Tom B. Pawlicki: "The substance of consciousness is a field. Consciousness expands as communication. Communication is conductivity. Conductivity varies directly with Order. Superconductivity is Resonance. Resonance is perfect when the semi-conductive crystal field is in either one of its extreme conditions: i.e. perfect rest or stressed to breaking point. To achieve perfect resonance one must either become expert at meditation or overextend all senses for prolonged periods of time."

Under the Sign of Gemini

The Mythos of the Divine Twins...
Shaitan and Christos, Ice and Fire, Dark and Light...

Tim O'Neill

There is a curious passage in the *Pistis Sophia*, wherein the Virgin Mary is visited and confounded by a peculiar phantom likeness of the child Jesus. In a memorable image, the living Jesus and his phantom twin merge into a single entity. The identity of this phantom Jesus is not too difficult to ascertain, since we know of an old Gnostic belief that the Christos (a purely metaphysical "force", embodied in the Master Jesus) is the twin of none other than Lord Shaitan Himself. This belief undoubtedly traces back to the old Persian/Zoroastrian myth of the battling twins of Dark and Light, Ahriman and Ahura Mazda. Dualist Weltanschauungs, such as the Gnostic, Manichean and Zoroastrian, tend to mythologize their philosophy into images of twin brothers, identical, yet exactly opposite in essential nature. This opposition of natures is the real key to this whole puzzling matter, since it reveals the essential, metaphysical underpinning of the mythos.

Almost all occultist and esotericist systems are ultimately based upon the doctrine of emanationism. While there are many variations upon this theme, the basic core belief of emanationism, per se, is that all ætheric and physical realities emanate or emerge out of a single invisible, intangible and inscrutable source. In many systems of cosmogony, or "universe-creation", the Primal Source of Fountain-Head mysteriously emanates a set of twins, who manifest the first principle of Creation, that of opposition. This is the causal or primal scission which seems to "split" the Primal Unity into a distinct and separate level of Being... The Causal Plane. In other, more elaborate, emanative systems, the original twins give rise to a trinity of principles, which create the Astral or Ætheric World. This, in turn, gives rise to the Physical Plane with its four principles or elements. Interestingly, the human body, with its five-pointed symmetry (head, two arms and two legs) represents the wedding of the four physical principles with the Primal Unity... A revealing suggestion as to the ultimate nature and destiny of Mankind!

Thus, the Twins, from the abstract metaphysical viewpoint, represent the Causal Mystery of the pairs of opposites... Ice and fire, gravity and levity, dark and light... All of the possible sets of opposing principles which define the basic root essence of our Universe. What is most important in all of this is the identical quality of the twins. In essence, this is a statement of the metaphysical truth that no single member of the opposites can exist without its equal but opposite partner. Each of the pairs, and the Primordial Pair, in particular, operate as parts of a continuum with each "twin" on the

Illustration by Tim O'Neill

opposite end of a polar axis. Where there is apparent duality, there is, in reality, a hidden unity between opposites... An echo, or memory of their origin in the Primal Unity.

This conceptual framework also serves to allow us to step behind the polemical screen of the Christian/Satanist controversy, to understand the true core of this dualist level of Being. In Dante's *Inferno* (The first part of his epic, *Divine Comedy*) Satan is rather surprisingly represented as a vast, dark, winged being, frozen in perpetual ice at the core of Earth. This seemingly strange association of Satan with the principles of ice, freezing, staticity, devolution and gravity, is actually very much in the line of the true traditional conception of Shaitan (Hebrew, for "The Deceiver", or "The Adversary"). The association of Satan, Hell and Fire, is, ironically, a much later development, probably due to the era of the burning of Witches and Heretics. The opposing twin, the Christos (*Chrestos* or " Anointed One", in Greek) is actually the solar, fiery, levitatious, mobile and evolving principle. Thus, we can summarize "Satan" as that force which tends toward staticity and devolution, whilst the Christos favors mobility and evolution. Quite importantly, neither force is inherently "good" or "evil", since either can be deadly in excess! The operation of the universe requires two great streams, one evolving, one devolving, in order for any advancement of consciousness to occur.

This understanding also tends to shed light upon the difficult concept of "sin", which can be simply defined, in this context, as any matter which tends to freeze one into evolutionary stasis or suspension. Shaitan tends to draw us toward such states, but such downward drift is almost inevitably a paradoxically powerful motive force in the dance of evolution. In this model, good and evil, sin and virtue, Shaitan and Christos, all aid the universal evolutionary current, since they all derive from the primordial Unity. The removal of any moral or ethical overlay from this matter reveals a hidden unity and a surprisingly clear "geometry" of evolution. It also becomes quite clear that the ultimately false polemical forces of Christianity and Satanism are far removed from the actual metaphysical realities that actually lie back of them. Existence in the physical form is never purely a matter of Ice or Fire, but rather of a subtle blending of those two principles and all the pairs of opposites into a subtle Unity, or alchemical Harmonia. The only refuge away from the never ending mixing and blending of the "Twins" lies in the Great Return to the Primal Unity, the truly transcendent Reality beyond all opposites... In the anamnesis or great memory of the One, who is the emanator of All... But that is another matter, entirely!

The Forgotten Ones In Magick

93/696

We need Magick to change the world.

Are you satisfied with the way things are – in government, in education, in business, in our dealings with each other, in our laying waste the planet? Do you feel powerless to restore balance and health to the world?

There is a way, composed of many ways, that an individual can influence and direct the course of history unfolding now. To understand how this can happen, it's necessary to see and comprehend reality from points of view not taught in school or available as common knowledge.

The dense level of reality which our bodies inhabit and which contains all that our senses perceive is like the screen in a TV set, only with more dimensions, sensations, and audience-participation capabilities. What appears on the TV screen comes from elsewhere, and is the result of a number of factors such as power to the set, broadcast or cable or satellite signals, power to the signal generation, camera shots and audio pickup, electronic processes like computer graphics, sound mixing, etc., actors, directors, producers, musicians and writers.

The Magickian uses Magick, the High Art, to enter the different realms that interwork to make images on the screen, thus gaining control of the nature and details of the images.

What appears on the screen of physical reality arrives there by a similar interworking of factors. The factor that "powers the set" in Magick is, in reality, several factors known as the Forgotten Ones.

To explore the realm of the Forgotten Ones, it's necessary to know a few things about it. It's not only the power that runs our reality-set, but also the reception of the signal, the channel-tuning capacity, control of the sound volume, contrast and color. The Forgotten Ones themselves are sources of individuals' life-force and Magickal power; in control of Will, the Forgotten Ones are good servants – without control, they are bad masters.

To use traditional terminology, the Forgotten Ones are creatures of Yesod. Yesod is the second sphere from the bottom of the Tree of Life. It's also the realm of the Astral Planes, the Id, the Unconscious, emotions, dreams and nightmares. Yesod translates as "Foundation", and is attributed to the Moon.

The Forgotten Ones are the human survival-instincts: Hunger, Flight-or-Fight, Sex, Clanning, and Altruism. It can be seen that the instincts begin with self-interest and extend to the well-being of others.

The development of the cerebrum layered over the Forgotten Ones with rational thought, creative imagery and scientific curiosity. The Forgotten Ones continue to operate from below the Conscious Mind; when they operate from a balanced dynamic and are appropriately satisfied, they continue to aid survival. If they're off balance, and either starved or glutted, they give rise to a great deal of misery for the individual and others around him/her. If the Forgotten Ones are aligned with one's Will, and are under one's Magickal control, they provide power and manifest events in physical reality.

The process of understanding and controlling the Forgotten Ones contains some built-in dangers. One arises from the species-wide link of universal participation in the Racial Unconscious. Uncontrolled arousal of a Forgotten One can affect other people adversely; the resonance spreads from one to the next and can generate a mob.

Another danger lies in the resonance between the Forgotten Ones and the Elder Gods. The Elder Gods are entities that consumed their own universe and are attempting to render ours edible. They discovered enough similarities between the Forgotten One of Hunger in humanity and their own voracious nature that they were able, for a time, to influence human behavior. Even now, there are those the Elder Gods control, but that's another tale for another time. The point is to be aware that the Forgotten Ones also function as Gateways, that when you begin working with the Forgotten Ones, you may not be alone.

A third danger arises if the Ego assumes ownership of or identification with the Forgotten Ones. Examples that come to mind are Caligula, Nero, Hitler, Vlad Tepes, de Sade, Stalin, Jim Jones and Charlie Manson. The Ego is the sense of self, a necessary component of Consciousness up to a certain point of Attainment. It is easily imbalanced and inflated, and the Magickian must keep Ego in its proper place and function.

The dangers listed aren't intended as warnings-away from the Forgotten Ones, but rather cautions to be observed in dealing with them. As it may be seen from the nature of these dangers, it would be wise to be well-prepared before beginning Forgotten Ones work.

Begin by journeying within. Hunt the Forgotten Ones, beginning with Hunger, the oldest and most powerful of the Forgotten Ones. When you find it, study it. Watch its ways. If your physical health permits, fast for a day. Take notes about the experience, on how you feel, what images and thoughts arise, what events happen to you. Note preferences and cravings, avoidances and revulsions in food and drink.

Next, explore the nature of your Flight-or-Fight instincts. It wouldn't be wise to use the methods like starting an argument in a biker bar, but there are other ways to experience the adrenaline-rush that lies at the base of this Forgotten One. Spend the day at an amusement park and note your reactions to heights, speed, fast turns and drops, enclosed spaces and disorienting environments. Take notes.

Go alone on an overnight camp-out. Look down from steep heights or cliffs or buildings. Make several expeditions through city streets at night with the goal of not being seen by anyone – learn to take advantage of shadows and concealments. Again, take notes on your experiences.

It might seem incongruous to think of Sex as a Forgotten One, but its mystery lies in the extent to which it dominates one's life and deeds. Honesty is important in recording everything you do that is influenced by sex in one way or another.

This can include, but is not limited to, selection of clothing, living quarters, jobs, possessions, where you go to socialize, how frequently you bathe, diet and fitness activities, hair style and adornment, choice of reading material, etc. How many of your activities do you do for pure hedonistic enjoyment, and how many are geared to impressing and/or attracting possible sex partners?

Explore the strength of your eroticism and the degree that it's controllable by will. Fantasize, read pornography, play with yourself; how much arousal can you achieve and still be able to deactivate it by an act of will? At what point does it become necessary to have an orgasm for release?

To what extent does sex influence your relationships with other people? In what way? Meditate on the strength of an urge that can persuade people to spend about twenty years of life in the responsibilities of cub-rearing.

Investigate the Clanning instinct. Set aside a week or two for being alone as much as possible. During this time avoid television, radio, tapes and records. Restrict your reading to books on Magick or philosophy, take solitary walks in the woods and spend as much time as possible alone with Nature. Concentrate on writing down whatever thoughts solitude inspires.

Go to sporting events and concerts; seek out situations that draw crowds, especially events with a focal point for the crowd's attention. Make a list of groups with which your loyalties lie. Spend time with family and relatives; analyze friendships and the criteria you use to divide friends from acquaintances. Honestly assess your own feelings about other races, your own race, various religions, political parties, your neighborhood. If you could choose any place on earth in which to live, where would it be? Why?

Examine your own Altruism. Under what circumstances have you been moved to help other people? Why? Do you give money to street people/homeless people? Would you put yourself at risk to prevent an assault on someone else, or to otherwise save a life? If you could save only one of two people, what criteria would you use to make the choice? What do you do about nuclear hazards and environmental issues?

This last Forgotten One is rooted in biology. There is not only a mandate to preserve one's own life, but also a DNA-directive to preserve the existence of one's species. We share these double directives with other living creatures; only humanity, it seems, makes an issue out of them through ethics.

The process of investigating the Forgotten Ones may have changed your original ideas about the world, the changes it requires, and your own viewpoint about responsibility and Magick.

Thoroughly and honestly done, the Forgotten Ones investigation provides an Enlightenment: about yourself, about other people, about the course of human history. All living things, including plants and micro-organisms, seem to share the instincts for self- and species-preservation; perhaps the distinguishing characteristic of humanity lies in our ability to act against our best interests of self preservation.

Now that you have the perspective of some understanding of our survival instincts, it's time to frame your Magick. Intent: Choose a point on which to begin.

What one facet of the world as you see it deserves your initial effort? Determine how that facet is reflected locally, within your own sphere of first-hand knowledge, whether it be in a group of people, an institution, or an individual.

It's best to begin the Great Work "at home", then branch out into wider spheres of influence; start small, then work up to larger tasks.

Take care to study your subject thoroughly. What is its ideal function, how did it come to be, what exactly is wrong with it? What is lacking in its present condition? The more precisely you can understand the nature and details of something, the more effectively you can cause it to change.

Methodology: Traditionally, a Magickian works with certain tools in special places – i.e., with Wand, Cup, Sword and Pentacle within a Temple, on an Altar. There are many good books available on this, in particular Aleister Crowley's *Book Four*. Once you understand the principles involved, you can incorporate other tools into your kit. It's beyond the scope of this writing to go into specific details, but it's basic to have one's equipment together, in one form or another.

Several Magickal principles need to be understood and employed in order to make Magick work.

1. As above, so below; as below, so above. What is done on a small scale, as it were, can be reflected at large, if the symbols used are accurate and rightly charged by the Will of the Magickian. This is the principle behind the use of puppets or "Voodoo dolls", and it can be applied in a number of imaginative ways through photographs, sigils, personal relics, etc.

2. Magick works through Magickal links. This extends the idea of personal relics. Any two objects that were once in contact retain a connection even though they're separated. A photograph of a person retains a connection with that person via the image of "trapped" light reflected from the person's face and preserved on film. A letter in a person's handwriting qualifies as a link, as does a printed quotation of the person's words. This was known formerly as the "Law of Contagion."

3. That which resembles another thing can affect change in a subject. As an example, if someone is too "cold" emotionally, keeping a link of that person near a flame (but not close enough to burn) could "warm him/her up". This principle, the "Law of Similarity", is somewhat simplistic and should be applied sparingly.

4. The Law of Threefold Return derives from Wicca, and states that whatever one projects will return to the sender three-fold. This is a special application of the law of Karma. Everyone who acts in the world will reap the results of action sooner or later, in this life, or another; those who use Magick, however, can expect an instant rebound. It keeps ethics firmly within the realm of enlightened self-interest.

Execution: By the time you've investigated the Forgotten Ones, and assembled your tools, and by the time you've acquired sufficient knowledge of some principles of Magick, you'll be able to understand what follows.

The key to working with the Forgotten Ones lies in their ability to combine and join forces. You evoke the necessary ones within your conscious mind; use the species-specific, "group" Forgotten Ones (Clanning and Altruism) to interface with the Macrocosm; use the individual-specific ones (Hunger, Sex, Fight or Flight) to interface with the Microcosm.

Focus your Will on the talisman of your subject. Prepare before ritual the Forgotten

One(s) of the Microcosm by creating a charge within it/them. Design your rite to bring the force of Will within its focus; engage all your senses, attention and concentration. Participate with your whole self: dance, drum, chant, gesture, invoke No, Laroo and the Cosmic Forgotten Ones.

Call to mind-vision the sigil you've prepared that is the formula of the change you intend in your subject. Blend the sigil of the formula of change with the subject-talisman in your mind-vision. Release the energy of the Microcosmic Forgotten One(s), after its/their own fashion.

Become Naught with the release – you are a tube, not a container.

After you re-assemble, charge the talisman with the Elixir and destroy it by element, or, preferably, by eating it.

Meditate; contact the Macrocosmic Forgotten Ones. They will have contacted their counterpart terminals of the subject – human or situational – through the Racial Unconscious (see Carl Jung). Feed the subject's Forgotten Ones with the Magickal Current by vibrating the Words of Power:

ABRAHADABRA IPSOS ALIM

Seal your exit from the Astral with the words LUTIS NITRA. Return all bodies in balance; earth yourself; close Temple. Forget it.

I realize that there are probably a number of Adepts among the readership; please realize that many other readers haven't even heard of true Magick before encountering Psychick TV or TOPY.

Have I done something unwise or dangerous with what I've written? No. If you re-read the text, you'll realize that considerable time, learning and experience must happen with each stage. No one can execute the Operation without the necessary understanding. This piece is meant to be re-read when necessary, but the reader who opts to pursue Magick will find his/her own inner voice for guidance. If you are an Adept, you already know this.

To those who choose the Path(s) of Magick, I give you greeting. Herman Hesse, in *Steppenwolf*, describes this sign: "Welcome to the Magic Theatre: the price of admission: your mind."

Not only your mind, but your bodies, your soul, your life must be dedicated to the Great Work. Magick is not a hobby. Remember always that you are the primary talisman of your own Magick. If you would banish violence from the world, deal with it first in yourself. Stop making excuses for yourself, blaming others, whining. Be ruthlessly self-honest. If you don't like what you see when you look within, change it.

Seek and find your True Will, and do it.

Magick is a lifetime practice and study; there are many sub-branches and byways of it. Eventually you invent your own after you understand enough essences. Read everything you can get your hands on by Aleister Crowley, Dion Fortune, Kenneth Grant, Denning and Phillips, Israel Regardie, Carlos Castaneda, Halevi. Experiment – and keep a Magickal Record. Write down what you do and the results. Track weird phenomena.

By learning to work with the Forgotten Ones, we gain control over reality's TV set. We can clear up reception, rectify color, contrast and brightness, focus the photon-stream and keep the power steady.

Of course there's more to Magick – a lot more. Go for it. Being afraid of the Forgotten Ones, or any denizens of Magick, for that matter, is like being afraid of the skeleton of your own body.

The Mechanics of Maya

Tim O'Neill
Illustrations by the Author

There is a primordial human dissatisfaction, a sense of deep longing that infects us, even during our moments of greatest ekstasis. We stand on this globe caught between the states of an animal and of a god, suspended on the timeline of an incredibly slow and painful universal evolutionary process which operates upon the cosmic time-frame rather than within the limits of the human lifetime. It seems as if our lives are spent treading water, floating slowly toward some far distant continent, whose shores we can barely discern.

This quintessential human dilemma was met very directly and very early on in human history by the elaboration of what we might now term a "universal science of transmutation": a means of speeding up the usual snail's pace of normal evolutionary flow. This wonder-science can operate and has operated upon individuals, cultures and even the whole *Anima Mundi*, the veritable "soul of the world", to produce periods of heightened and accelerated evolutionary growth. According to Geoffrey Ashe's thesis in *The Ancient Wisdom*, a group of highly advanced shamans in Central Asia, some 20,000 to 40,000 years ago discerned the theory and practice of this evolutionary tool. The fruits of their labors eventually migrated across the Vale of Kashmir to Northern India, where the Aryans recognized it as a science far older than their already old culture, and named this art the "Tantra." It entered China as the core of what would later become Taoist Alchemy and even reached as far as Alexandria, in Egypt, where it became the Hermetic art. This "core esoteric tradition" remains, to this day, at the heart of most occult systems, although it is more often than not covered with a dense overgrowth of accretions. It is everywhere recognized as the "circular science", the "opus circulatorum", or circulatory work, or as the work of the inner solar system, for reasons which will become clear during the course of our discussion.

The first assumption of the circular science is that the god/animal problem, as we have stated it at the outset, is not at the true core of our situation. Using their extremely refined sense of inner plane perception, these "supershamans", as Ashe calls them, discovered that ultimate Reality simply cannot be broken into individual segments; that dualism of any kind cannot exist. Thus, they founded a science whose purpose was to enable everyone to quickly reach this state of non-dualist perception. From this vantage point, any difference that is observed between the Absolute and the Relative is seen to be erroneous and illusory.

Already, from the logical point of view, the above statements are riddled with paradox. How can one "reach" a state which one is already a "part" of, when there are no

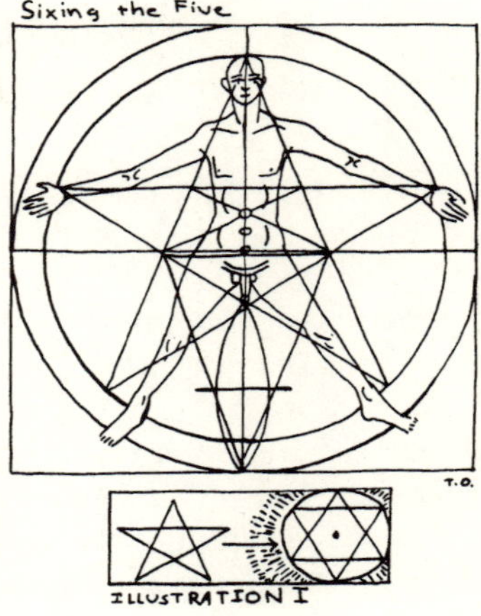

parts? It is precisely this labyrinth of paradox which announces that we are on the right course! The direct perception of Reality must defy logic and even the boundaries of intuition, by definition. Paradox is one's constant companion in the practice of the circular work, and its presence is a good sign that all is proceeding well.

The second assumption of the science is that this illusion of separateness and individuality is, paradoxically, a force that somehow resides within the Absolute. This deceptive force that seems to split Relative from Absolute is termed Maya in the Orient and Set or Shaitan (The Deceiver) in the Occident. It is somehow the "Left hand of God" in this mysterious game, giving the illusion of individuality, where there is only the One.

The true problem, then, is that this illusion of separateness between animal and god must be broken through into Reality. This becomes a matter of evolving one's state of consciousness to the point where non-dualism becomes the normal direct perception of life. The fog-like dream of individuality must be left behind as one climbs to ever higher and wider vantage points. The transmutative science works (again, paradoxically) upon the ætheric component of consciousness, to effect the direct evolution of awareness, to evolve it to a state of utter diamondlike clarity. When the truth of non-dualism is directly perceived, then the pain of the primordial animal/god dilemma is seen to have always been a mirage... That is the only true healing; that which descends to the root of Reality.

In symbolic terms, Mankind in the state of this "suspension" is seen as a pentagram (see illustration no. 1); what I call the "five-pointed form". When the circulatory science has been successfully achieved, the pentagram becomes a six-pointed star which has added the divine element... Conscious godhead. In Western alchemy, the symbol for the completion of the work is the six-pointed star, with the point at its center and a circle of flames surrounding. This signifies man completed, the spark of life resurrected within and the egg of "chaos", without, in perfect harmony.

Thus, our essential problem, stated in symbolic terms, is to "six the five" or to resurrect the sixth. The other symbol for this, in Masonic legend, is to find the lost "word"

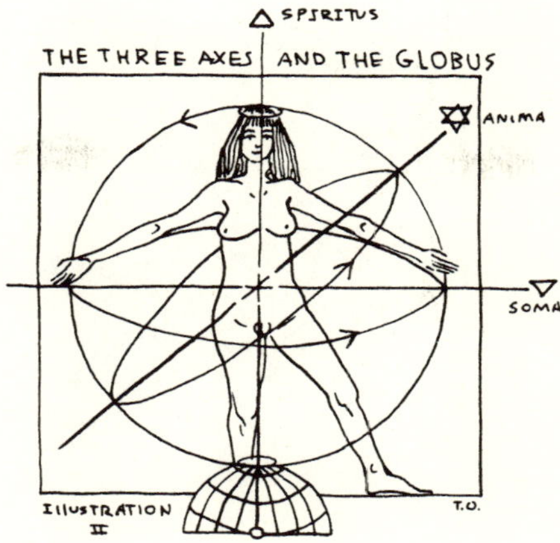

that died with Master Hiram Abiff. The circular science, in these terms, seems the essence of simplicity, however, in practice, it becomes very difficult, because the situation of each individual is unique, with variations that may materially alter certain aspects of the work. While everyone must follow the same general course, since it is basic to human ætheric structure, some kind of guidance is crucial, unless one is gifted with perfect clairvoyance.

As with any true science, our ancient shamans constructed a working model to guide them in their theory and practice. In their model, the five-pointed human form is seen as encompassing a miniature solar system. The "Sun" of this system is the *scintilla vitae,* the spark of life, urgrund, synteresis or monad, seated "in" the solar plexus, approximately three finger-widths above the navel. It appears to the clairvoyant eye as a tiny spark of light from which all the human ætheric and physical forms emerge. Around this "Sun" orbit three planets; three forces that create a human being when allied with the *scintilla* and a mysterious fifth, divine, element within the *scintilla,* about which nothing can be written. These three forces are those of personality, soul and spirit. They correspond to the material, astral and causal levels of Being. Together, the monad or *scintilla,* the personality, soul, spirit and the mysterious godhead, form the illusion of an individual, through the agency of Maya. The personality "orbits" the scintilla very slowly, for it is the densest force, the one that is ruled by "gravity" as we shall call it. The soul orbits much more quickly, and its job is to mediate and harmonize between levels, thus, we shall call its force that of "harmony". The spirit is the most quickly moving force, since it is the focal point of the opposite of gravity, namely, "levity" or the rising, levitating force. In the physical form, personality is centered in the genitals and the belly, the soul in the heart and the spirit in the crown of the head. The core that emanates them all, the spark, resides in the dead center of the five-pointed form, the solar plexus, as we have seen.

During the usual course of life, these forces orbit the inner Sun at an incredibly slow and plodding pace, so that, at the end of a lifetime, they will have barely moved at all from the position that they held at birth. This will produce a barely perceptible increase

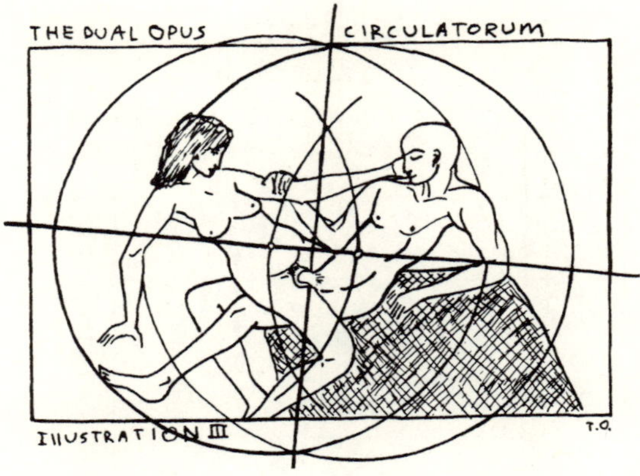

in the level of awareness and being. By taking the speed of orbit into conscious control, one takes responsibility for one's own destiny in hand. One also takes the risk that if the process goes wrong, then devolution into the animal end of the spectrum will be the inexorable result. It is a risk that can be managed and safeguards abound if one cares to use them, however, it must be remembered that this process of speeding the orbital time of the "planetary" revolutions involves direct manipulation of the evolutionary mechanism itself. One is working with the basic structure of the life force... Prudence is an obvious concern, yet how many have failed to heed the warning!

With the above theoretica in mind, let us proceed to the practica in some detail. At the very outset, safety precautions are in place. The following will only work as visualizations and meditations. To actually entrain the ætheric forces with the visualizations involves the use of intonations which must be taught to each individual by an inner or outer plane master of the art. The first conscious step is undoubtedly the most difficult. The necessity for following a simple universal ethic is often a stumbling block for students of the art, yet it makes simple common sense. The pledge to not harm sentience, the life-force or the universal harmonia operates to protect oneself in the intense of the work. The science is essentially neutral. It operates mathematically in the sense that "X" number of orbits will create a certain heightening of evolutionary potential in either the evolutionary or devolutionary direction, depending upon one's inner purpose. If one seeks selfish or parochial purpose, then devolution will be the mathematical result. If one seeks universal and indifferent purposes ("indifference" in the sense of a heroic refusal to distinguish between opposites), then the evolutionary current will carry one toward the god state, adding mastery of the visible world as an afterthought!

Once the primary motivation is very clear and has been tested, then the actual work can commence. The rule of thumb is that by beginning with the visualization level, one will generally draw an inner or outer master to aid in the next steps. As the old Rosicrucian law states, "When the student is ready, the master invariably appears!" The body is visualized in the "Vitruvian stance". This is a reference to the famous Renaissance diagrams of the human figure inscribed within a circle and square (see illus. no. 1). The spinal axis is visualized as being dropped down to the core of Earth and extended

Illustration IV

upwards toward the heavens, and in particular, toward one's ruling star. A second axis is projected perpendicular to the first (see illus. no. 2) through the solar plexus and out the back, extending over the globe of Earth, horizontally. A third and final axis is created, perpendicular to both of these with the end result that one has something very much like the "X, Y, and Z" axes of analytic geometry running through the body with the solar plexus as the meeting point of the three axes.

The next step is to project a sphere, globus or rotundum around the three axes. It is crucial to leave vents or small openings for the time when one does the true energy work and excess needs to be eliminated. Each axis generates a circle of rotation, each of which proceeds counter to the others. Here, intuition and inner guidance is the only help, for the intensity and direction of rotation is very personal.

Once the individual work is mastered on the visualization level and the inner keys for the actual energy work have been granted interiorly, then one may proceed toward an even more difficult level... The partnered work. The theory here is that the re-uniting of the primordial opposites of male and female (spirits are at issue here, rather than physical gender) is the most powerful means of short-circuiting the duality-projector of Maya. When two *polarized*, i.e. oppositely charged, human ætheric fields or auras interact in such a way that combines the circular works of the two individuals counter to each other, then a momentary rift in time and space is created; the very projection system of Maya is disrupted (see illus. no. 3). This allows for two possible experiences... 1) An advanced human soul may enter incarnation through this gateway, either as a manikin, or as a normal human child, or, 2) The two partners may "journey" into the non-dual state together, essentially becoming one being... The androgyne or "Rebis" figure of alchemy. When the partnered work is successfully completed, the result is a single, perfected, androgynous being in tune with the non-dual reality (see illus. no. 4). In Plato's theory of gender as depicted in the *Timæus*, "we" are really spheres, androgynous in nature, who were split into two halves, male and female, because the gods were jealous of our perfection! The goal of our science then, is to re-sphere the polarized halves and re-attain the perfection of harmony.

The essence of the science can be depicted in a few pages, yet its practice can consume lifetimes. The great paradox is that one must have enormous patience to be able to hurry the slow sands of normal evolution. It is important to remember that the evolutionary current proceeds in one direction only, and that is toward the Absolute. To devolve means to place oneself behind even the normal evolutionary current, so it is best to practice only when one is sure of purpose and means. There is a final element of great mystery, which the adepts of the science can refer to only as "grace", it proceeds from the hidden fifth element in the scintilla and its presence insures the success of the work, while its absence chastens even the most dedicated practitioner. For those who seek to unravel the mechanics of Maya and to find the Absolute beyond, there is a path, yet it is narrow and not for all!

The Thin Line

Coyote 12

The noose is a powerful symbol in our culture, though it has been several decades since hanging was an accepted means of execution. Imagine the potency of this symbol in the past. In this essay, we will try and find ancient references to hanging and strangulation, and see what – if any – significance such practices in the past could have for the modern ritualist. Tiny clues abound, but they are few and far between – however, the discerning researcher will see a pattern emerge.

It is said that most primitive cultures learned to weave by observing the spider spin her web. She is also the most conspicuous rope-maker in nature. In Greek mythology, the spider was said to have been Arachne, who was such a good weaver that she challenged the Goddess Athena to a contest. Unfortunately for her, she won. The unhappy Arachne hung herself, and Athena, repenting her rage, transformed her into a spider. It could be added that the Spider Ariadne's thread helped Theseus find his way out of the maze of the Minotaur of Crete. This very maze was discovered in the lost Cretan city of Knossos, so there is a strong possibility that at one time the Cretans had some sort of allegorical initiation ritual involving the candidate, as hero, being trapped in the "Underworld", i.e., the Maze. The Spider seems to be the ally whose aid the initiate had to seek in order to complete his ordeal successfully.

The spider seems to occupy an ambiguous place in the mythologies of many cultures – on the one hand, a noble weaver, the very archetype of diligent craftsmanship and skill, on the other, a fearful huntress, treacherous and venomous. This dual iconography is typical of the earliest religious symbols – it seems that our pre-literate forbears, unlike us, chose not to make such wide separations between "good" and "evil". They seemed to realize, better than we do, that life must, by definition, contain death, therefore the best symbols of life would reflect the unexpected, yet inevitable End.

Nearly everyone knows that the Egyptian cross, or Ankh, was the symbol of eternal life. This symbol is said to derive from the characteristic strap used on Egyptian sandals. However, most sources trace this figure back even further. They claim the Ankh symbol first represented a noose, which, when tied, represented life, the "knot of life" – untied, it signified death.

The Egyptians were not the only culture that represented life as a strand – in Greek mythology, the Three Fates spun, measured, and then cut the thread of life.

Human sacrifice is a practice which our culture has learned to deplore, yet to our forbears, it appears to have been deemed a very necessary prerequisite to continued life and prosperity. The logic is straightforward enough; a portion of what the earth gives us must be returned in gratitude, lest she decide to hold back in the future what she has given so freely in the past.

In Germanic countries, hundreds of bodies have been found in peat bogs, apparent victims of such practice. Strangulation is by far the most prevalent means of their death. It is widely believed that these victims were offerings to the goddess Nerthus, a widespread Nordic fertility goddess later superseded by the male Njord.

The Roman historian Tacitus is one of the only first-hand observers of pre-Roman Nordic culture that survives. He describes how, during the spring-festival, a chariot, covered with veils, would be pulled from village to village. This carriage contained the Earth Goddess, presumably Nerthus. In most such fertility cults, the male priests were expected to physically mate with the Goddess, that she might bear her child, the new Spring. Tacitus tells us that no male was allowed to look upon her and live – the priests who attended Nerthus were strangled and thrown into a lake along with other offerings to the Goddess. The concept of the female killing her mate reminds us of the spider again. She too appears to dislike having old lovers walking around. One symbol of Nerthus appears to have been a braided or twisted necklace, very similar to the nooses found around the necks of her supposed victims. Many such necklaces have been found as offerings very near sacrificial victims.

The story of Odin's hanging himself from a yew-tree to learn the secrets of the runes comes to mind. Perhaps final wisdom comes only to those who allow themselves to become the Goddess' lover. It is interesting to note that all surviving wooden idols of Nerthus are carved out of birchwood. The material used to carve divining runes on was traditionally either birch or yew, which we now see as symbols of the God or Goddess.

It may be appropriate to mention in this context that each year, a number of young men and boys die by hanging or strangling themselves during masturbation. Cutting off the oxygen supply just before the orgasm is meant to intensify the orgasm in much the same way that "poppers", Amyl or Butyl Nitrates, do.

The Mayans are thought to have believed that auto-sacrifice by hanging was one of the surest ways to Paradise, in fact, such victims of religious enthusiasm even had their own tutelary Goddess Ixtab. She was said to draw her victims to heaven with a noose. Appropriately enough, heaven or paradise is often associated with the bliss of orgasm; perhaps the cult of Ixtab conceals a secret auto-erotic practice prevalent among the Mayans. Perhaps her cult survives in the deaths of these latter-day epidemics of auto-erotic victims which sweep our high schools from time to time!

The Hindu Goddess of Lust and Time, Kali, is also often depicted with a noose. Esoteric commentaries say this noose is a symbol of strangling material desire. Kali herself, as a symbolic depiction of carnal desire, is meant to be the means of focusing physical desire towards spiritual attainment of the Absolute. Another noose associated with sexuality.

It should go without saying that a great deal of this is raw speculation; research based more on intuition than solid scientific fact. However, the parallels are so numerous and widespread that there must be some fact behind this theory of sexual strangulation.

Thee Only Language Is Light

Genesis P-Orridge

In thee search for signs Individuals see directions. There was a Time Zone long ago when feet struggled across blood biting flint wrapped in animal skin. Bleached bone spoke ov thee snake way ov day. If you imagine a small child with a long ribbon flicking their wrist sharply at each extremity ov position, fluidly in thee central space you will picture thee flow ov Life as it was then. Regular like thee trails ov a serpent on Sahara sand. Each bended knee, wrapped in thee moisture preserving layers ov nomadic survival, elbow cricked for support, sees what has passed. Time is that which passes. Arising, like a knighted Templar, to scan thee four directions. Thee point ov intersection between sky and earth is shimmering. Not clear. There is a spinning ov equality. Mind, Body, Emotions and Spirit. These coum from thee simplicity ov looking. Hand raised to shield eyes, thee fingers ov thee Left hand create a flickering moment like a Venetian blind. Hundreds ov drawings later thee window is not captured. It is, ov course, a frame, a threshold to travel through in light and to light.

We have traveled through Time many thousands ov yeras. From ritual wandering, towards words, into language, all ways closing down our basic nature, thee essence ov what we are. Light measured by Time. We have travelled through Time in a few lines, marks that have no flowing pattern, no snakelike calligraphy.

We have been losing things as we converse.

We have described one aspect ov evolution.

We have described many.

Thee sun is behind everything. Each second we observe tells us stories, parables, allegories. We see thee sun. Our arms reach out to hold it, it seems so small, we have no sense ov perspective. Our boarlike grunts sound raw. We shake our matted manes and feel anger. Between this point on thee snaking ribbon and thee next we do hold fire in our arms. Fire reflects thee sun for us, gives us hope ov power. Butter we have accepted less than everything, and everything was permitted. As we sit around our cave fire all life dances on thee pitted stone. Within our circle is thee energy, thee stolen sun. Outside our circle thee reverse, thee mirror painting pictures at thee edge ov our vision.

We have described an aspect ov blindness.

We have drawn thee failure ov sight.

In thee desert thee same process can occur. High on a tower thee oracle faces thee sun. Not trying to reach it a hand stretches out. This person knows through many ages ov wisdom that thee sun can never be held, butter it can be harnessed, it can even speak. Fingers spread thee wrist is fluttered fast and steadily. A particular frequency is reached. Eyes closed to thee light itself see more than words describe. Language, a quite different animal to words, pours forth. These are pictures, not speeches, stories and dreams, not discussions. These are Truth. Yet only truth reflected outside thee circle.

We have described thee process.

Thee place where all dreams meet.

Yet we are all ways moving away. Our energy flying up thee ribbon ov Time and flashing off thee end with a crack. Cold, in thee night, a simplicity unfolds. A firm hand grasps our ribbon. Takes it from us. Takes history itself from us. Stands outside Time. This being begins to spin. Faster and faster, round and round. Cloudy ectoplasms ov blue light collect around thee centre apparently couming from within this in-visible circle. Thee ribbon seems joined, a circle, spinning, curving in slow waveforms that feel they are light itself. This motion measures Time and Light together, reintegrates them to paint a picture ov thee beginning. Our mind can travel upwards, downwards, through all directions. As above so below. We are a trailing spiral, a galaxy, all energy rushing outwards, clockwise, free yet directed.

This is no idle wordplay, no trap ov language. It is, quite literally, what a mystic might label a "KEY". In fact it is a "MAP" ov a factual process that serves as a bridge between loss and retrieval ov a state ov comprehension that in its purest sense is where " ART" remains hidden.

We are looking at LIGHT and TIME as thee twin facets ov what we externalized as GOD. Our place in this is that ov BREATH. As observation became a profession, we became distanced from Individual access to revelation. Thee Light was thee SUN, thee sun symbolized Life Spirit. It is also actually Life Spirit. Thee spinning ov earth, thee couming and going ov our Light became a measure ov that which passes, that which moves, butter most importantly, that which ends. It gave us death. And our gift ov Individual vision often died with it. We placed sun outside Life, we saw Light as finite, we fenced in Time and then we stopped breathing and spoke, murdering ourselves...

We became obsessed with death so we put ourselves in thee centre ov our reeling implosion named civilisation. Thee sun now "kept us alive" and its light went from thee sun "to us" or even "to me". Our breath that had becoum words now became power and in our terror we began NAMING.

If you go outside your "SELF" and look down at this picture, this spinning column, you will see what IT IS. Not what you are, not what life is, not an IS that bears any resemblance to any thought that can be conceived, butter IT itself. This picture is just thee way IT is. And this picture exists precisely in that dimension we tritely call NOW.

NOW = a state ov Present Time only. (Also known as Zero Time.)

This implies ZERO memory and ZERO forward projection.

Placed at thee centre ov this picture we are seeing, and pointing, and traveling outwards in every direction simultaneously. Quaquaversal. We are also retrieving our original position in consciousness. A position ov ZERO separation and TOTAL integration. Beneath thee wrappings that preserve our spiritual moisture in thee present desert is thee coded message ov location. This is our ZT.

From Sun, to Light, to Fire, to Sight, to interpretation ov transient images on cave walls, our back to thee source cut off. From separation to inauguration ov hierarchy, thee Seer, thee Oracle, thee Shaman. From hierarchy to Word, to Language, to Naming, to Power. As we scoop up thee grains ov Time and squint along both directions ov thee snake's ribbon trail only thee expert can tell which direction is couming, which going, we have forced a dualism upon ourselves. Yet that is not how IT is. Thee snake reposes coiled, spiraling outwards.

In a distant cave Individuals are wrapped in animal skins painting sorceries on their temporary cave shelter. Across thee mountains a boy is sewn in bloody warm skins to dance thee sacred dance ov Pan. Thee point where animal spirit and thought spirit separated. Thee moment when society became inevitable.

At this moment thee knowings which were contained in states ov not-thinking were encoded. Thee myths, legends, allegories, religions are now where they reside. Thee search ov High Art and High Magick has been for processes ov retrieval in order to facilitate coumpletion ov reintegration. Thee re-establishment in thee Individual ov a permanent state ov Zero Time, Zero Language, Zero Thought. Where consciousness exists within its own planes as if metaphorical light.

It is no accident that these encoded Truths are preserved so often as pictures, or picture stories. For a picture is Light.

It is no accident that these encoded Truths are preserved so often in hieroglyphic, calligraphic and permutational scripts.

Linear language is thee most corrupt messenger.

T.O.P.I. EXCERCISE: FINDING YOUR PICTURE or SIGNALLING

1. Thee only story is what you are thinking.
2. Thee only telling is what you DO as you are thinking it.
3. Thee only aim is not thinking.
4. Thee only result is coumunication.

In this exercise "thinking" actually means any neurological activity that is in no way conscious, that we are in no way aware ov.

Porno on Film: A Revised Manifesto

Jack Stevenson

In a previously published article I decried the mind-numbing mediocrity of most fuck films and dared dream of the perfect porno movie: a well produced film well acted by good looking people, a film structured around a plausible, interesting plot that seamlessly blended drama, hilarity and hardcore sex in a cinematic tour-de-force that would shake the very foundations of the film industry like some great exploding lava-spewing volcano.

The separate components didn't seem that hard to assemble, but somehow the films never jelled into "real movies" and the result was the usual sticky, nasty smelling mess. Instead of paradise we found ourselves mired crotch-deep in a swamp of celluloid swill, as hard to watch as it was to sleep through (in those busted chairs). We shot for the stars and instead we ended up tumbling down the two flights of stairs that led to the basement men's room. Often was the sunny afternoon I went down to the porn palaces of the Combat Zone with a dream in my heart (!)... Only to ditch out soon after from those cavernous crap-shoots dusted with the smell of piss and Pine-sol. Our innocent, idealistic dreams were dashed, destroyed, doused... We were repelled, we were vaguely disgusted... We were put to sleep.

I here and now publicly renounce my earlier visions of a pornographic utopia in which the sex act is filmed creatively and artistically and is incorporated into "legitimate" cinema.

It is impossible. The "components" are polar opposites.

In a recent discussion I had with John Waters I think he hit the nail on the head so to speak. "It's very hard to make a good porno movie and be funny", said the Prince of Puke, "because they're sort'a the opposite. Good porno isn't funny, it's dirty."

I agree with this completely. When hardcore sex is on the screen a whole different dynamic comes into play. Laughter is a distraction to stimulation, as indicated by a theater-full of disembodied faces staring on with all the solemn awe of a crowd gathered around a car accident.

We don't want warmth and humanity and wit and humor. We want sex, flesh, fucking. Period. We don't want beautiful cinematography, artistic composition or Oscar-deserving acting performances. We want something else entirely: PORNO.

A good porno film must be judged on a set of standards totally separate and apart from regular movies. The components that make a "real" movie succeed are only distractions in a porn film. Therefore a porn film can only be improved by making it more pornographic, not by trying to make it more of a "real" film.

I was dreaming when I should have been jerking off. I realize now I don't want a good movie. I don't want "art", I don't want laughs, I don't want inspirational performances. The porn director deserving of God's glory is one who knows what NOT to put in his film and harbors no vain egotistical desires to make a "real movie". He is a man with a modicum of technical talent who knows how to photograph sex so it looks good. Porn should be the least pretentious of film genres.

I now hereby issue a call-to-arms of the general populace, and amid great pomp and fanfare I publicly announce a revised manifesto on pornography. Nothing less than total revolution can save pornography from the sticky mess it's gotten itself into, and, flushed with righteous ardour, I demand basic changes in the way in which pornography is filmed. It is necessary that:

Plots be eliminated from porn films. This is a component of "real" cinema that has no place in porno. A plot is essentially a superfluous vanity employed to give screen time to cast members who have an obscene urge to act, or to assuage the egos of directors who dream of making a "real movie". Plots take up needless time.

Plots also expose us to porn stars who are terrible actors but don't know it. They deaden the screen, sucking in and killing energy rather than radiating it. The lack of competent scripting, direction and acting ability that usually insulates the viewer from the true personality of an actor – all that is missing in a porn film and we find ourselves adrift with these idiots in repulsively close proximity, more intimately exposed to them as people than we realize or desire, as they are incapable of giving life to their screen characters and instead we are left with just them. The five bucks we disgorged from our wallets psychically chains us to our seats in sadistic, humiliating fashion as we witness the appalling spectacle of fully clothed porn stars trying to emote. Most of these greasy, jaded, hot-tub variety narcissists have no verve, talent, magnetism or sexuality with their clothes on and deaden the screen in a way words cannot convey.

Combine this with plodding, ridiculous scripts that attempt to put flesh on the bones of a "fantasy", and you have the receipt for disaster: your average porn film. You just wanted sex on the big screen and instead you got all this other shit. In some circles of gay porndom plots have been totally abandoned, replaced by a series of scenes or episodes of hardcore sex. This new approach has been widely applauded, but then again gay porno has always been more advanced and progressive than straight.

Most porn films don't even succeed as good "badfilms" or schlock films because they don't even have the qualities – spirit, imagination, energy – to backfire with. They don't fail gloriously, they just fail completely. Then again I don't want "camp" anyway.

Do we want subversion? Porn has a built-in potential for subversion and yet most porn films propagate the most banal images and sentiments of the status quo. Money, vanity, disco lifestyles... These things are all celebrated in porn films. *Thundercrack* succeeded as a subversive porn film because it went against the grain of all this, taking a more underground approach. The film features all varieties of sex acts: gay, straight, solo... And, as pure affrontry to middle-class morality, is a stunning success. Yet as a pure fuck film it proves uneven: its subversive character is at times distracting, and there are long stretches without any sex. Some of the sex is filmed quite well, but some of it is not very appealing and is not intended to be. The movie is by turns both genuinely hilarious and disturbing – both ultimately distractions to pure porn. Andy Warhol's *Lone-*

some Cowboys was subversive as a sex film because no real sex occurs. Every time people tried to have sex it wouldn't work and they'd get up and leave (and you'd be glad). A sex film where sex fails is ultimate subversion for what was billed or at least reputed as some kind of porn film. But of course as real porn it failed hideously on all counts and goes over today as really nothing more than mild gay cheesecake.

Porn stars... Another element of real movies that has no place in porno. Famous, recognizable marquee stars is originally a concept of the Hollywood studio system but in porno doesn't work. If ever there was a genre of film that craved new faces, new flesh, it's porno. The fact that so many new porno "stars" – particularly female – burn out and over-expose so fast should indicate the counterfeit quality of the concept. In porno there's no room to grow old gracefully... Or grow old at all. That doesn't particularly bother me. On the other hand old warhorses like Seka and Vanessa Del Rio have developed huge followings and make fabulous money, so a lot of guys must like their style and want to see more and more, on and on forever. So be it – let'em live. Personally I hate to see porno leads (female) become "hardened professionals". Acting in porno is an abomination. The worse actors they are the better. The more amateurish and homemade the feel the better.

Art... Hardcore sex is incompatible with art although artists love to interpret it with innuendo and allusion. But unless the sex act depicted is sterilized and muted (in the name of art) into meaningless, neutered decoration, it will hold a power over us above and beyond the "work of art" it was intended as a part of. Any work of art on a sexual theme must be on one side of the line or the other: either the artist has de-eroticized sex with impressionistic or stylistic techniques, or else the artist has had the guts to create something like raw pornography. "Art" is the great dodge, the great escape... A great time- and energy-wasting diversion, indulgence and vanity whose only true value is to act as a smokescreen by which to allow the rose of pornography to burst into full and glorious bloom.

Most "artistically" photographed sex is intentionally "natural", common and unerotic... Or else painfully stylistic. In addition, Art films have plots, deep meanings and gargantuan pretensions: the sex is never allowed to exist for the purely prurient reasons it should. Pornography must nevermore be infected or diluted or made impure by the germ of art. Pornography is too beautiful to be disfigured and scarred by the disease of "art".

In conclusion, brothers and sisters-in-arms, I see a bright future on the horizon for pornography. Technological advances such as video put the means to manufacture pornography directly into the hands of the proletarian masses, allowing us to free ourselves from under the bootheel of the porno "industry" which has blighted us with terrible oppression and suffering (and boredom), and doth rip us off most cruelly. Independent productions are springing up all over, devoted to pure, prurient, honest sex unburdened by the flaccid dead weight of plots, porn-stars and art. Arise!

An Interview with Kenneth Anger

Carl Abrahamsson

This interview took place in Los Angeles in 1990. In issue no. 4 of The Fenris Wolf *(2011), there is a transcription of a talk between myself and Anger at the Danish Film School in Copenhagen, from 2008. – Ed.*

In what way, would you say, is cinema a magical art?

Well, it's an art of vision. It's like a crystal bali, you can create visions. It also allows you to manipulate time and space and transcend realism. Obviously, the camera records what's in front of it, but it can also record the inside of a magician's mind. How many strings are pulled behind the scenes, or special effects, or things to make this happen, are the magician's secrets. I don't think it's necessarily... Like in Hollywood films, they explain how all the tricks are done. I don't think that's a good idea.

When, and how, did you realize what power Cinema can have?

Seeing certain films when I was young. When I was a very young child, I was taken to the Chinese Theatre here by my Grandmother, to see *Noah's Ark*. It has a scene in a Pagan temple, taking place before the flood, which of course gave the Hollywood set designers and costume designers an excuse to invent a completely imaginary world. Like Atlantis... Wonderful sets and costumes in a very barbaric Pagan style, and I always loved those. It's all washed away by the flood, and I remember being very upset about this. It was such a nice place. "Why do they have to wash it away...?" (laughs) My Grandmother tried to explain, "That's because they were wicked", but I said, "They looked pretty interesting to me!"

Then I was myself in the film *A Midsummer Night's Dream*, again through my Grandmother's influence. That was a thrilling thing to be associated with, and then, when I saw that... The scenes of the world of the fairies were so beautifully done in that film. It's never been done better. That's the part of the film that I loved, rather than the intrigue between the lovers and all that. It's that element of fantasy which is suggested in Shakespeare. But in stage productions they can't do it. In film suddenly, it's expanded to this "dance of the spirits of the moonbeam", and things like that.

Later, when I went to France and saw the films of Georges Meliès, his trick films, I realized that you can do wonderful things in film without having tremendous amounts of money. You just need imagination and the kind of deep wonder-vision of a child. Things appearing out of nowhere, and things like that. I've always loved film, but only a few times in my life have I had enough money to do what I wanted to do. Commercial films were never really an option for me, because I felt that to deal in the commercial marketplace... I'm more of a poet than a salesman, so I never tried to become a part of the commercial industry.

Were you ever approached by the film industry in the beginning?

No. I was always in my own little corner as an independent artist. I wasn't the only one. In the silent period you had experimental films, or, as they were called, avant-garde, being made by Man Ray, Léger, René Clair. I saw all of those films at an early age, and of course in France later, I saw Jean Cocteau's *The Blood of a Poet*, which is one of my favourite films. But I began to make films before I saw it. And then, of course, Buñuel's *L'Age d'Or*. So I saw the power of the medium. I've made about nine films which I consider are finished enough to show to the public. I have other films that are unfinished: either they lack a soundtrack, or some scenes are missing, and I prefer not to show them. Some films have been destroyed or lost, which is too bad, but that's one of the things that can happen. I had one film that was censored by Eastman Kodak because it had nudity in it. It was called *The Love that whirls*, and it was based on a passage in *The Golden Bough* by Frazer. It's about when they choose someone to play God for a year. The boy is treated as a God, like a King, and then, after the year, he's sacrificed. That's something that occurred in different ancient cultures, including the Aztecs. It goes back in Europe much further. I had some nude figures in that, and this was in the early 1940s. It wasn't even remotely sexual. They were artistic nudes, but it was a no-no. They confiscated the film and I never got it back. At that time you couldn't get colour film developed except through Eastman Kodak. There weren't any independent labs. So, I've had a battle in the past with censorship... *Scorpio Rising* was first running in California in 1964. It was seized by the police, and now the amount of controversy in the film is so little. The few flashes of nudity are so brief. It's hard to see what all the fuzz was about!

Did they actually go to the theatre and take the print?

They took the print from the theatre, and they arrested the manager. I wasn't there at that time, so I don't know whether they would've arrested me or not, but the reason why they did it was that the American Nazi Party didn't like the film. They denounced it to the cops. They didn't say, "We're the American Nazi Party", but they were the ones who did it. If the vice squad in America, although I don't know if they're still that way, have a citizen's complaint from anybody, they will act on it. If they say, "This shop is selling a dirty book", they check it out. This was back then... I think now there's been such an avalanche of obscenity, that I doubt they're still that vigilant. There was that Swedish film, *I'm curious, yellow*. I haven't seen it for years, but now it would seem so innocuous. But at that time it was very controversial. People went to see it, hoping to see a little bit of tits or something. That's how the situation has evolved. The pendulum now seems to be swinging back... Dr. Kinsey was a friend of mine, and he said that "Censorship and permissiveness towards sexuality in the cultures of the world, it goes like a pendulum..."

It's also quite symbolic in general, how sexuality is regarded...

Yes. These are tough times. The worst thing is that there are so many diseases. It does have an effect on the freedom of sexuality. And that is used by the moralists as an excuse to condemn all sexual expressions.

Do you agree with the theory that AIDS is an imposed disease?

Well, that sounds too paranoid. Too much like paranoia. I have no proof of that. It would be convenient to think that, but, on the other hand, if it could be... H.G. Wells wrote a story called *The Island of Dr. Moreau*, which is a wonderful story. In it, he predicted that the world would be infected with unknown diseases that would shape the things to come. He invented one, "the wandering sickness", which was like a kind of incurable fever... People would break out in sweats and they would have the desire to sleepwalk and wander. And then they'd have to shoot them. It was convenient for H.G. Wells, because he thought that even in 1935, the world was much too overpopulated. He wanted to cut the population on earth by one third. As an artist, you can invent a plague with a sweep of the pen that will wipe out two thirds just like that... Then, from that, a new elite develops. He calls them the "air men". This is of course a fantasy, but I wish we could have an elite. But it seems to me in many different ways that progress is an illusion, and that for every advance, there's a step backwards.

We were talking briefly yesterday about the moral decline and the changes in society... Do you think that Crowley's concept of the "Aeon of Horus" will ever be established?

Well, I believe in it. But we're in the chaos-stage of birth that will be very rough. At least it seems that the nuclear threat between the super-powers is perhaps diminishing. Next year Gorby could be overthrown, and you could have a new reactionary regime in Moscow. It's amazing how he's kept them at bay. He's almost like in a cage of tigers. A wild animal trainer who just with his eyes says, "Stay down, stay back!" Anyway, it's fascinating to watch, but on the other hand there's such an element of... I think that the human species has in it the seeds of the Destroyers, whether they're thugs in India or whatever, Kali-worshippers... The terrorists, like the Red Brigade who killed the head banker in Germany, are like in a time warp. What reds are they working for? It's beside the point of history, and history's passed them by. There they are – still blowing up people like the anarchists in 1900, or killing the equivalent of a king. A banker is like the king of Yugoslavia or something, the one that set off World War One. It's possible that terrorism will continue, because there will always be people who have grudges if they get a hold of poison gas or biological weapons, which would be quite easy to manufacture, like viruses. I think harmony is far away. If it ever happens! And in the meantime the climate is being ruined. And very fast! To me, the destruction of the Brazilian rainforests requires international pressure. All the governments, from Mexico down, Central

America, South America, they're all charicatures of corruption. And the chief villain is an American billionaire, who's cutting it down because he's raising cheap cattle to sell to McDonald's for McDonald's hamburgers. It's so revolting, and very unhealthy food anyway. In five or ten years, the land will be depleted and no longer can they raise the cattle and the forests will be gone. A new desert will start, and this will be an ecological catastrophy for the whole world. To me the cause should be strong enough... You can't just say to this corrupt government: "Don't do it! Naughty, naughty, don't do that..." It's almost reason to declare war on them. This would be very messy and difficult, and it would have to be through the United Nations or something, not just one country. There's also a problem with the water supplies being contaminated, the oceans being contaminated... It's such a precious planet. When you realize that in our solar system, this is the only place suitable for life... All the rest are deserts or totally poisonous. Like Mars, it's very inhospitable, and that's the only one remotely possible, but it's terribly cold and you'd have to create sealed environments. The other planets are just impossible. Beyond our solar system, everything is so far away, we're talking about light-years, that it's a question of "this is all we have".

I think the planet should be called Planet Earthquake, because the planet has one million earthquakes every year, big ones and little ones. A million earthquakes is a lot! Some regions are much worse than others, like Japan and the Pacific coast of America. The volcanic cracks go right down from Alaska all the way down to South America. The whole coast is volcanic, unstable. But it's better than living on Venus, where you have oceans of sulphuric acid! (laughs) I love wildlife and animals, and to see the way they're being treated, the arrogance of the human species... The worst guardians of African wildlife are the Africans. They don't care. To them there's just one name for it – it's just meat. Or a nuisance... They try to grow their fields in an area that belongs to the elephants, so the elephants come to the fields and trample them, and they kill the elephants. They have no way of existing in harmony with animals, so it's tragic what's happening. The elephant population in Africa is half of what it was ten years ago! Ten years is such a short time...

It's the same thing with wolves in Sweden.

Terrible. So, I don't know whether people will be able to band together to do something, because obviously the individual can do nothing. I believe in the environment and Greenpeace and all those things that want to save the planet. But I think it needs to be like a war crisis. I'm fairly pessimistic about it. I'm personally very pessimistic about the human race, and I think that's something I share with Anton (LaVey, – Ed.). You have wonderful geniuses, poets, and artists, but yet so many who are destroyers and don't care. The biggest problem is overpopulation. If I had my way, it'd probably be like they have in China or India, where they are only allowed so many children. It isn't working there either, but at least they try and limit it. You're only supposed to have one child, which is like a humiliation to traditional China, because you were supposed to have five or six, and as many sons as possible. The Hispanic people that live in this neighbourhood for instance, they come up from Mexico, Guatemala, El Salvador, all those countries, many illegally, and they bring with them the breeding habits of the third world. The women start having children at 16, and from then on until menopause, they have a baby every nine months! They end up with 15-20 children! Even if some of them are intelligent – which I question! – they'll never have jobs for all of these people, unless they want to pick in the fields or something like that...

Our talk turned, not unexpectedly, to the "Prophet of the Aeon", Aleister Crowley, who's been such a great influence in Anger's films. Anger's Magnum Opus, Lucifer Rising, *is heavily influenced by Crowley's poem* Hymn to Lucifer, *and he's planned for a long time to do a substantial film version of Crowley's Gnostic Mass. And also more biographically oriented material, if ever given the opportunity.*

I had plans and did sketch out a realistical film based on Crowley's living at Cefalu, at the Abbey of Thelema. That's basically why I went there (in 1955), to do research. I lived in it. But I don't know if it'll ever happen, because I'd have to find serious money... That's always been a great obstacle to me. When I've made films, either a relative has left me some money, like my mother left me some bonds and I cashed them in, or I had some help from the National Endowment for the Arts and the Ford Foundation. But not very much, only modest amounts. Not enough to do these projects. It's also become more difficult to get that kind of sponsorship. Something like the Gnostic Mass would be like half an hour long. It could be done for a modest amount of money, but I want the setting and the robes and everything to be beautiful. In some cases I might want to use actors instead of members, because they may be more impressive. That's perfectly alright. The thing where the people who belong to the Brotherhood will be helpful is in getting the accuracy of the ritual gestures and all that right. I've seen it done by several groups, including the group in Switzerland, and some did better than others. Some things are open to a bit of interpretation. So, that's something to think about, and I might be able to get some sponsorship for it from one of the art organizations.

Do you usually work with ready, scripted material and storyboards, or do you work on a more spontaneous level?

I have it mostly inside my head, and I make notes of what I need. I usually do a technical breakdown of what I need. But it isn't like a written script for a play or a usual film, because I basically work in images, not in dialogue or narration. If I film a Crowley-ritual, it would be a different direction for me, because it would be the first time I use speaking. Up to now I've only worked in silent films. I'm closer to dance, the way ballet can tell a story without using speech, and in that sense I'm closer to that. But I'm willing, if I had the means, to use speech.

Do you have equipment of your own?

I have some, but I usually borrow or rent it from various people who have it. Particularly the editing equipment, there are places I can go and use that. I don't have to have my own.

Would you rather work in 35 mm?

Yes, if the budget would permit it, and if I could get a loan of a 35 mm-camera. There's ways of getting 35 mm-film in a city like Hollywood, because there are places to buy film that is left over from other productions. If you're careful, you can get excellent film enough to shoot with for a fraction of what it would cost to buy it new. You may have to load the camera with a piece that's just enough for one scene and then load it again. It's not difficult to conquer those kinds of problems. Ingenuity!

What effects do you want your films to have on the audience?

Well, I would like for them to... The idea that you can see a film, or watch a play, or read a poem and be changed. I think it can effect you. Certainly Crowley, in his poetry, and the plays he wrote, and various literary works... It was to effect change, like through a Will. Whether this is directly or subliminally, indirectly or whatever, I do believe that change is possible. The ways in which this happens are mysterious. I've never made something to change day into night, though it would be a nice idea...

You have chosen the same means as Crowley, that is, not sloganeering, but a rather more poetic and romantic approach.

Right.

How did you first hear of (LA-based Crowley disciple) Jack Parsons?

He was working here at the Jet Propulsion Laboratories. He actually invented the fuel that took the Apollo-rocket to the moon. He has a crater on the moon named after him, which is rather thrilling. I'm convinced that he was murdered by Howard Hughes. Howard Hughes wanted him to work for him, and he simply didn't want to. When you work for Howard Hughes, you lose your freedom. In other words, he tells you what to do. He was very much like L. Ron Hubbard. Jack Parsons was kidnapped by Howard Hughes. They followed him in a limousine, and two big, strong bodyguard-types hopped out and physically picked up Jack Parsons and put him in the limo and drove him around. That's physically kidnapping! It's a crime! To physically interfere with someone and to do something with their body is a felony crime, whether you physically harm them or not. In the limo, there was a representative of Mr. Hughes. He said, "Mr. Hughes admires your talent, and we're sorry to pick you up like this. We want to forcefully get the message across that Mr. Hughes wants you to quit JPL and work for him." They had spies out, and knew that he was doing some really interesting scientific work. Jack played it cool, and said, "Well, I'll have to think about it. Please let me out by my home in Pasadena..." But they drove him around for about an hour, and it was definitely intimidation. Anyway, he then decided that the time had come for him and Marjorie Cameron to leave for Mexico, because his life was in danger. He was packing up to leave when his house exploded, and he was killed. He knew how to handle explosives and things like that, and also the explosion was so strong that the whole house was destroyed – a big house with two stories! His wife had gone around the corner to do some shopping for a picknick. They were going to drive without stopping from Pasadena to Mexico, and it was like they were escaping from this monster who was Howard Hughes. Instead of that, the house blew up, and she heard the explosion and went back. There was no house! She was like one block away...

What originally made you interested in Thelema?

As soon as I heard about it, something clicked and I said, "This is mine!" My family is Scottish-Presbyterian from an ethnic background of German and Scottish. I was never attracted to their church. They tried to take me when I was twelve or something, and I told them, "No!" I was the first child to do that, and my brother and sister were both very happy to go along in the footsteps. I refused to go to church on Sundays, and I got my allowance cut because I was rebelling in a way that embarrassed them. But then they left me alone. So I had rejected Christianity at an early age, and I never believed in Santa Claus either! (laughs) I find Christianity repellant. I don't like the story, I don't feel I need someone to get nailed to a cross to pay for my sins. It's ugly! I don't know how much longer it'll last... It's collapsing in ways that are pretty obvious, but it may yet take centuries. At the time of its collapse, it creates these monsters like the evangelists. Bigotism and censorship are coming back again. Most members of the human race don't deserve Thelema. I hate to say it, but they're rotten! Whether they're born rotten or they become rotten, they're sheep. They're unawakened. I don't waste energy on hatred, that's foolish. As a magician, I conserve my energy. Wherever I live, I try to create a sanctuary for myself. As much as I can, I have the things around me that I love.

What, would you say, are the main advantages of this concept of a "total environment"?

It's control. You can do it in one room or even in a tent, I suppose. The idea is to create a sanctuary of harmony that is a reflection outwards of the best parts of yourself. So, I'm projecting outwards... Even if I have chaos in me, or confusion, I try to make a projection of the admirable things. I have a controlled chaos in the form of my storage areas and my closets where I hide all my things... I haven't mastered it completely! I always say I need more space, but maybe I need a computer to keep track of everything, so I don't lose things. More shelves, more storage...

One aspect of Crowley's writings that has been misinterpreted in many ways, is of course the main dictum "Do what thou wilt shall be the whole of the Law". Anger could, mainly in the 1960s, see how a philosophy of will and responsibility was turned into one of lazy laissez-faire beyond all common sense. Not least in regard to the chemical adventures of many colourful would-be-psychonauts who thought they were doing serious spiritual work while dropping acid. I wondered what Anger's stance is nowadays on chemical adventures?

I'm strongly opposed to nicotine smoking. It's like a vampire, sucking on the human race. Crowley, of course, was a smoker. He smoked like a volcano! It didn't do him any good, considering the fact that he had asthma and emphyzema. He was very short of breath. I don't like to sound like a puritan about things like that. I like to smoke pot occasionally, because it gives me a high. It does some good. Whereas the lift you get from nicotine is so ephemeral. It's addictive. It's diabolical. It takes away much more than it gives. And then I find it extremely offensive, the way people will smoke at you, or smoke in a restaurant or a public space where there's other people that don't want it! Their smoke is going in your face... And in your lungs! When Crowley lived, the medical science hadn't realized how extremely bad it was, with lung cancer and everything. Crowley might have changed his mind about it, but he believed in trying all the dangerous things, and whether that's the Thelemic way... I think it is but for an elite. The thing that bores me about drugs now, is that they've become so public. You have cocaine being sold in some form on the street corners in the city by little kids. I still like marijuana, and I think it should be made legal. If alcohol is legal, you might as well... It serves the same kind of purpose, maybe better than alcohol. It doesn't destroy your liver the way alcohol does. It clarifies you. But apparently, it's not going to happen in this century. Two things that are important to Thelema have become turned into demons by the cultures: drugs and sex. It's like "sex and drugs and rock'n'roll"! Because of the new diseases and the war on drugs, there's almost a war on sex too. People are afraid of experiments. I hope some kind of solution can be found to these problems before too many more years. It seems out of control right now. There's no medical thing on the horizon, like a vaccine.

The only thing would be more restrictions and thereby greater control...

Yes. And caution, and fidelity. It's not a good time for Don Juan! (laughs)

Have you never been tempted to pursue any other artistic expressions, like painting or writing?

Well, I write to earn money. My writing projects are mostly concerned with things like the Hollywood scandals. I'm generally interested in that field. Scandals and tragedies are an important part of the historical records of cultures. They reflect at any given time what is considered over-the-edge of behaviour, and it's also something that the public can be fascinated with, and afraid of... They're demonized and glamourized. The books I've written on Hollywood have been about that aspect. I'll probably do another one, because I need to earn some more money. A certain number of years elapse between the books, and suddenly I need the money. So that usually is the spirit...

Do you know how much the first two have sold?

They were on the bestseller-list in *The New York Times*, both books, and that meant five or six editions, and they're both still in print. So, it must be over half a million copies. The new one will also be Hollywood scandals and tragedies, but the trouble is, I feel

I've used up all the good stories... And I don't like contemporary Hollywood. The characters aren't larger than life, they're usually smaller than life! (laughs) I can write about someone like Fatty Arbuckle or Jean Harlow or Garbo, but to write about someone like Barbra Streisand...

Do you think there are any *stars left?*

There are some good actors. Tom Cruise is an excellent actor. He's a better actor than James Dean ever was, as far as sheer acting. And maybe it's better if the stars get humanized and not made into false gods. Turning humans into gods has more reasons against it than for it. It places that person in a prison. I've talked to people like Mick Jagger and they say they can't even take a walk. People will bother them because their face is so famous. Strangers will come up and follow them. They don't have that cloak of invisibility that most of us have. When I knew Mick in London in the early 70s, he liked to go out in the streets at two o'clock in the morning, and just run by the river... For blocks and blocks, just to feel free. I used to run with him at times. It was like a bird out of the cage!

What is it with Rudolph Valentino that fascinates you so much?

He was the first male sex god. He was a male that had erotic appeal, and recognized frankly as that. "The Latin Lover"... He was the first one to do it, in a real sense, for a man. I also think he was a good actor, and he had that intangible thing called charisma. He was a Taurus. I collect him.

What will your book on him be like?

It'll be basically a picture book with little comments on my feelings about him. Many of the pictures have never been published before, and there's never been a book on Valentino that's had colour in it. I will have colour illustrations. I hope I can find a publisher who can agree to the amount of colour pages. I haven't chosen yet. Maybe one like Abrams... The costs of doing it in colour are so great, I almost need like three countries to agree on it. Some art books are published in Japanese, British, and Italian, or something like that. Some of the best colour printing is done in Japan. They've perfected the technique with laser printing the colours.

Can you tell me about your "Hollywood Babylon"-film project? Part archive, part fiction?

Yes, with some recreated scenes with actors. That's difficult, but I intend to do it in a stylized way. If you have an actor impersonate a star, it's very difficult, because they're too well-known. Like, how could you find someone to impersonate Garbo? It's just impossible... But I've found some wonderful archive material. The producer, Ed Pressman, and I cannot agree on the budget, so it may never happen. I'm quite resigned to the fact that it may never happen. I say I need fifteen million and he wants to do it for two million...

How do you think the film medium will develop in the future?

Well, film may be replaced by some magnetic tape and a way to project it that gives a great, clear and beautiful image. They're supposed to clear video projection up in ten years, so... I hate video projection now, because it's bad enough the way it is. To me, it's an abomination! It loses all quality in colour and definition. It's moving wallpaper, to have in a disco or something. There's some wonderful techniques coming up though... Something called IMAX, a huge image. It's like 70 mm filmed on its side, so that each frame is as big as a postcard. When this is projected, you get absolute clarity, and you can have a screen five stories high. It's a Canadian system. The have a theatre here, and one in New York. They're usually connected with some museum, but they make films especially for it. They've never made it like a commercial story. It's always like *The history of flight*, but they're done in a very poetic way. They're actually quite good. There's one on time that's very interesting, and another one on "Save the Grand Canyon". Very beautiful. Mostly wildlife and things like that. Then there's another system called "Showscan", which uses film that goes through the camera and the projector at twice the speed, which completely eliminates flicker... So it's like looking at reality! Even though it's not three-dimensional, it's still so clear that it gives an illusion of three dimensions. It's developed by a man named Douglas Trumbull, and there's been a few presentations of it at the World's Fair in Seattle, and a few private showings here and there. But it's never been used commercially, because the drawback is it uses up so much film that the reels of film have to be giant, they have to be huge! Human ingenuity may come up with some wonderful techniques that we've never thought of.

I thought that by this time in my life, there would be a practical method of three-dimensional, but there's not. If you have to wear glasses or something, it destroys the illusion right there. Holograms are not practical. The images look very fake. You can't use it in a narrative. To me, all of these things are beside the point. If you have a strong subject and the personal vision of a genius, someone like Eisenstein, the Russian genius, or von Stroheim, or von Sternberg, or John Ford, or Hitchcock, or someone like that... It's the personal vision that counts, not the technique! I'm fascinated with film, but the fact that it's so expensive almost makes it out of reach. Some filmmakers have been much more prolific than I, and I regret that I haven't been able to do more. But I'm glad I've made as many as I have, and I can always make more. It's possible the money will be available to me again in the future.

You've met quite a lot of interesting people. Who of these have influenced you the most?

I was fortunate enough to meet Jean Cocteau. He's had a great influence, because to me he was always a pure artist who yet could work in the modern world. He's not as much of a clown as someone like Salvador Dali who became like a charicature. Cocteau remained closer to his inner vision, and yet occasionally he could do things like design an ad for a perfume or something. It wouldn't matter, you know. He became a member of the Academie Française, and had his sword and all that. But he always kept a slightly ironic attitude towards it. He said, "If you break a statue, you risk turning into one". He kept his distance, always. So Cocteau was an influence, and earlier I'd met D.W. Griffith here in Hollywood. Later I met von Stroheim, another man I admire very much. Then the great director of the French Cinémathèque – Henri Langlois. I worked for him as his assistant for twelve years. That was a great thrill.

And of course I never met Crowley, because he died in 1947, and I never got to Europe before 1950. But I feel I know him very intimately as a man and as a creator, because I've studied his works all my life. And I've lived in his home in Cefalu. I have enough imagination that I could see what attracted him to it, to that place. He became too notorious, and attracted the attention of Mussolini. Even if it hadn't had anything to do with his magical society, Mussolini was very anti-British. So just the fact that an eccentric Englishman lived in a part of Italy at that time... He got expelled. If he'd been a little more savvy, Crowley might have chosen Tunisia instead of Sicily. He went there afterwards, just took the boat across from Palermo. His life was a very adventurous life, always full of conflict. It was never like, "This is the safest solution, or the one that will cause the least trouble..." It was quite on the contrary! To go to a city like Palermo, very Catholic in the most primitive way, not enlightened at all, and with the peasants being very superstitious and afraid of strangers. They thought they were devil-worshippers or something, running around in their robes and things like that. I talked to some peasants in Cefalu who'd actually seen Crowley perform rituals outside his house in the garden. *Liber Resh* to the sun and everything. They didn't know what it was, but as little children of five or six, they watched this strange man. And they described it in movements... They remembered! Particularly the coloured robes. It was so fascinating to hear this, the way a child could remember Napoleon or Jesus doing something.

After he was kicked out, some of the women remained. They were so poor, that they had to sell the furniture to the peasants, just in exchange for some eggs or meat or bread or something. I found Crowley's writing desk about a mile away, and they remembered it. "That came from the Englishman..." I'm sorry I didn't have the money to buy it, but they treasured it. It's still probably there... They don't use it as a table to eat on or anything. They turned it into their home altar, covered with Catholic saints. I looked at it, and it had some ink stains, which were obviously from Crowley's ink well. And a few scratched doodles, like pentagrams and things like that. They couldn't really write, and I asked if they had anything else. "Yes, La Biblia..." They had a book wrapped in cloth behind their virgin Mary. They thought it was the *Bible*, but it wasn't the *Bible* at all... It was one of Crowley's books, not by Crowley though, bound in gold... It was by a Dean of Cambridge, called *Through the halls of history* or something like that. A history of Trinity College in Cambridge, where Crowley went to school for a while.

Vandals, Vikings and Nazis

The Act of Looting down through History

Jack Stevenson

The sun rose over the bleak plains of a hard earth one forgotten day many millenniums ago. In a narrow, boulder-studded valley a small tribe of ape-like beings, ancient ancestors of man, gathered together and left their camp to go down to the river. As soon as they were safely out of sight a small horde of neighboring tribesmen left out of the bushes and overran the primitive camp, grabbing everything they found, uncovering the earthen pit where food was stored. With savage glee the trespassers hankered about the camp, smashing, crushing, destroying what they could not take with them, loading each other up with gourds and bundles of roots they hoisted from the pit. Then, heavily overloaded, they fled in confusion, stopping to snatch up gourds that fell from their arms and bounced and rolled in the dust dropping others in the process. Yaking, nabbering, howling with delight, they made their way back to their own camp. They felt rich. It intoxicated them.

The first act of looting on earth had occurred.

While it is of course impossible to date the first act of looting, it seems to have been one of primitive man's favorite pastimes. The orange flickering glow of the looter's torch would light up those dark first nights, and after the wheel had been discovered, the creakings of grossly overloaded carts and wagons would break the stillness. To retake the Holy Land or to expand the empires of Kings, great European armies of the Middle Ages would be organized and launched, but it was the specter of heaps of loot that excited the common foot soldier and drove him into a frenzy.

Before we proceed further, the difference between looting and simple robbery must be delineated. For you see, there is a big difference.

Robbery and other related criminal acts such as fraud, extortion and forgery are acts of deceit and secrecy, carried out undercover, within the framework of society. Looting, on the other hand, springs from the collapse of society. Looting is the clamorous and reckless celebration of the "conqueror" – whether or not the looter has conquered anything or just happens to be in the right place at the right time. Looting is not an individual pursuit, although it can be. Looting requires raw enthusiasm and energy rather than stealth or cunning. Looters can and often do a lot of drinking in the process whereas other criminal acts call for some degrees of sobriety. Today looters face the wrath of the police. But such was not always the case...

No history of looting could start anywhere else but at the crumbled gates of that fabled looter's paradise, that perfect pearl, that glittering gem, that ultimate jewel...

That dirty dream in the black heart of every scamp, outlaw and barbarian king of the first millennium A.D. – the city of Rome.

By 405 A.D. a horde of 200.000 Goths had overrun the Northern plains of Italy and were poised to strike Rome. And they did so: at night on the 24th of August, 410, the Teutonic rabble rushed the city walls. The lives of Rome's citizens were spared though the city was abandon to plunder. At the end of the third day the Goths withdrew, struggling under the weight of their loot which they rolled, dragged and carried out on their backs. It is said that the fantastic treasures in the palaces of Rome drove them into such a fever of pillage and destruction that humbler towns were spared.

Fifty years later, the Vandals, a mixed race of Bedouins and Moors, entered the City by the Porta Portuensis and plundered it at leisure for fourteen days. Booty was methodically carried off to ships moored alongside the quays. The palace of the Caesars was stripped bare. The Temple of Jupiter was relieved of statues that would soon decorate the brothels of Africa, while its roof was stripped of its gilt bronze tiles. Sunlight glinted off massive gold plates as they were carted out of town by straining slaves.

Rome again reeled under attack in 846, besieged by a force of 11.000 Saracens. The invaders beat back the defenses and ran wildly through the streets. They hauled off an estimated three tons of gold and thirty tons of silver.

On May 28th, 1084, a combined force of Normans and Saracens stormed the City. They brutalized the populace and set fire to anything that would burn, but as for riches they found the City relatively poor off. Mutilated statues stood in the rubbled plazas and lay blackened by soot in the dust amid the ruins of baths and temples. The bashed-in faces of Saints stared imbedded from heaps of char and ash and rolled down the pocked and littered streets.

In 1527, the Holy City of Christiandom was once more sacked and looted, this time by a conglomeration of troops under Charles V. As defenses crumbled and invaders poured through the streets, Cardinals, ambassadors, the Curia personnel and others all took refuge in the Castel Sant Angelo. When the portcullis was lowered there were nearly 3.000 people inside the fortress. "We were there", recorded Raffaello de Montelupo in his memoirs, "watching everything as though at a festival". The signal for looting had been given. The foreign rabble swarmed through the streets like ants. From the heights of the papal fortress Cellini looked out: "Night had fallen, the enemy was within Rome. We at the Castle, and above all I who have always enjoyed new things, watched this unbelievable spectacle."

The City suffered mercilessly. It was disfigured, defiled and utterly cleaned out. Chaos reigned. Contingents of marauders often found themselves ransacking homes that had already been denuded of every possession.

Throughout that summer the foreign troops ran amok in the City, while they themselves were targeted by famine and plague. Finally, in February of 1528, they evacuated Rome.

Rome was not the only city to suffer looters. Any world city of any consequence or history has known them at one time or another.

During the 14th century in particular, few European towns were spared this curse. Freebooters, highwaymen and small private armies swarmed over the Continent like a plague, and with about the same results.

The king of looters, who reigned this golden age of looting, was the Englishman John Hawkwood. He would later go under the name Acuto. As a youngster he loved weapons.

With a small inheritance he bought a horse, a suit of armor and a lance and shipped to France in the English army under Edward III, fighting in the battle of Poitiers in 1356. After the peace of Bretigny he crossed over to Italy with a hundred followers and joined the German troop leader, Albert Sterz, who commanded the infamous "White Company". Not a day passed that these corrupted knights did not descend on the fertile plains of Piedmontand Lombardy, leading away livestock, torching fields, vandalizing cottages and raping any females they chanced across.

Hawkwood took to this life with such passion and skill that he replaced Sterz as leader. He lived to about 80, fighting for the highest bidder, changing sides repeatedly and never missing an opportunity to extort riches from frightened lords. In his lifetime he amassed a fortune in gold, lands and castles and was courted by the Popes and Kings of his day.

Loot was not only the prize of brigands and outlaws: it served in lieu of a payroll during the 100 years war when the English Kings could not afford to pay their soldiers. Expectations of rich ransoms and heaps of gold drew successive waves of English soldiers into France throughout the l4th century.

The first great battle of this war was Agincourt. It lasted only three hours, showcasing the deadly effect of a new weapon: the longbow. It resulted in a great victory for the English. For the rest of that day English soldiers roamed over the field searching for still breathing noblemen to hold for ransoms, knocking the armor off dead bodies and stripping them of the clothing and jewels beneath. This plunder weighted them down so heavily that it was decreed that no man should take more armor than he could wear. The rest was burned up in a barn along with the English dead. The English soldier, like every other soldier, was famous for his passion for plunder, however useless or cumbersome.

Such heavy harvests of loot, splattered with the blood of the enemy dead, would bog down the progress of whole armies and overload ships almost to the point of sinking. During the battle of Poitiers the premature scramble for booty and hostages across the field almost enabled the French to successfully regroup and counterattack.

But enough talk of soldiers and knights and archers: the most desperate and wretched elements of society indulged in looting as well, when circumstances permitted. The Great Plague of London is a good example of the lengths to which looters will go.

As the plague spread through London in the summer of 1665, most of the City's wealthier residents wanted nothing to do with it: they locked up their mansions and tied to the countryside. The pestilence raged among those too poor to leave; the sick, the mad, the desperate and the broke and busted. Some of these mansions were broken into. Who could have expected otherwise?

Yet the looters did not stop there. They forced their way into "plague houses" as well, houses in which everyone had recently died of the Plague. These grubby boarded-up structures reeked of death and contained almost nothing of value. Moreover, there was a tremendous risk involved in such an activity. Basically looters were the only ones brave enough to go inside.

This also stands as the first example of modern urban looting.

It would be a travesty to conclude a study of looting without mentioning certain groups whose spectacular acts of looting and pillage have affected the very course of world civilization. The sack of the Aztec and Inca empires by the Conquistadores stand as possibly the greatest campaigns of pillage in history. The Crusaders, on the way to the Holy Lands, often exhausted themselves in looting and destruction even before they got out of Europe. The Vikings proved to be great seafarers: they sacked Paris three times. Privateers such as Sir Francis Drake randomly terrorized ships on the open sea with the approval of the English Crown. Pirates looted and laid waste without the sponsorship of any government. Hitler was a connoisseur of great art and something of a painter himself: he personally looted the best museums of Europe. The Nazi looting of Jewish Germany remains the best modern example of a systematized state-run campaign of pillage.

Today the world is a vastly different place than it was in prior centuries, when career criminals like John Hawkwood operated without the meddlesome interference of the police, and rogues like Sir Francis Drake could raid at will on the high seas with the Queen's blessings. The streets, the towns, the cities of the world are today patrolled by countless police organizations employing the most sophisticated types of equipment. In addition, the whole idea of warfare has changed. Soldiers who loot captured towns and then set them ablaze are looked down upon: it is morally repugnant to us, it is unprofessional. Looting as a livelihood, as an occupation, is finished. There are no more free-booters, there are no more buccaneers. There are no more Romes. There is no more dream. Today a young man doesn't take his inheritance money and buy a horse, a suit of armor and a lance and enter into the business.

Yet, the spark has not been extinguished. Far from it. The impulse to loot seems as deeply imbedded in the human psyche as the sexual urge. Actually this analogy is not as farfetched as it appears at first glance. The adrenalin that pumps through the looter's popping veins, spurring him on to great feats of strength, is not altogether unlike the orgiastic rush experienced during sex. It is not a simple "criminal urge" that drives the looter into the streets. He is not really a criminal per se. The most celibate of priests is still physically capable of a sexual rush, just as commonly the most law-abiding of citizens will dash out into the streets once the storm has passed.

In modern times the rabble rousers and have-nots take to the streets during power outages, "black-outs", and loot with a passion that any Viking could admire. The race riots of the 1960's produced the same sort of unruly behavior.

Natural disasters also provide an emotional outlet for looters. In the wake of disaster, after a town has been blasted by a tornado or hurricane or swept by floodwaters, one might expect the people to band together in mutual aid and assistance... In their common need... Extending a helping hand.

Hardly so.

The first official act is invariably to station National Guard troops throughout the streets to combat the inevitable looting. Stiff penalties are advertised and the looter even risks being shot on sight. Yet they still go about their business: ripping plywood off of shop windows, jamming items into their pockets until they split at the seams and paddling boats down the aisles of supermarkets.

Few experts doubt that even the last and greatest of disasters, a nuclear holocaust, will come to pass without looters rushing into the streets. They will have little time to enjoy their newfound riches, however, since they will be exposing themselves to deadly radioactive fallout.

And yet... Perhaps the last man alive on earth will be carrying a small portable TV under his arm and rolling a new radial tire down the street.

Inauguration of the Kingdoms of Elgaland–Vargaland

CM von Hausswolff and Leif Elggren

With effect from the 14th of March 1992,
we are annexing and occupying the following territories:

I.

All border frontier areas between all countries on earth, and all areas (up to a width of 10 nautical miles) existing outside all countries' recognized territorial waters. We designate these territories our physical territories.

II.

Mental and perceptive territories such as the Hypnagogue State (civil), the Escapistic Territory (civil) and the Virtual Room (digital).

On the 27th of May 1992 at 12 noon,
we proclaimed the state of Elga/Vargaland.

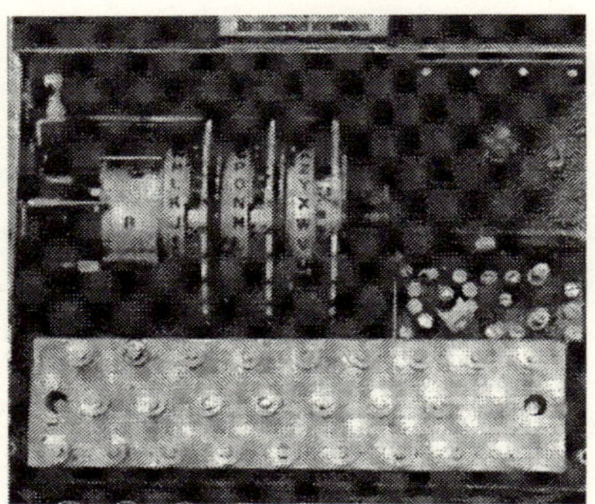

Cyberspace is where the human interface to digital computers is approaching 24 frames per second. The advancement of many of the key qualities we think of as human is linked to the evolution of world views – to the emergence and invention of new ways to see the world.

I am not ignorant that many have been and are of the opinion that human affairs are so governed by Fortune and by God, that men cannot alter them by any prudence of theirs, and indeed have no remedy against them; and for this reason have come to think that it is not worth while to labor much about anything, but that they must leave everything to be determined by chance.

What stands above the surface? His mind, I suppose. The mind is the city whose streets we get lost in, the most recent construction on a very old site. After seventy million years of most gradual primate enlargement, the brain nearly trembled in size in a very few hundreds of thousands of years. Our city is spacious and not lacking in magnificence, but it has the problems of any boom town. Let us dig.

Between the idea
And the reality
Between the motion
And the act
Falls the shadow

For Thine is The Kingdom

Between the conception
And the creation
Between the emotion
And the response
Falls the shadow

Life is very long

Between the desire
And the spasm
Between the potency
And the existence
Between the essence
And the descent
Falls the Shadow

For Thine is the Kingdom

Kim considers these imaginary space trips to other worlds as practice for the real thing, like target shooting. As a prisoner serving a life sentence can think only of escape, so Kim takes for granted that the only purpose of his life is space travel. He knows that this will involve not just a change of locale, but basic *biologic* alterations, like the switch from water to land. There has to be the air-breathing potential *first*. And what is the medium corresponding to air that we must learn to breathe in? The answer came to Kim in a silver flash... Silence.

This was the second statement of Elggren and von Hausswolff
(First statement in *INDEX* no. 5, Stockholm, 1992)

Page 176
Howard Rheingold, from *Virtual Reality*
The Enigma Cipher Machine (Royal Signals' Museum Collection)

Page 177
Niccolo Machiavelli, from *The Prince*
Photograph of Gabriele D'Annunzio

Page 178
Robert Ardrey, from *African Genesis*
"A Voodoo Warning", photo by W.B. Seabrook (1928)

Page 179
T.S. Eliot, from *The Hollow Men*
School Kitchen in Stockholm, photo by Axel Rydin (1901)

Page 180
William S. Burroughs, from *The Place Of Dead Roads*
"The Jews' wailing place" (artist unknown)

A Flame in the Holy Mountain

Notes on the Sacrality of Flesh, the Theory of Emanationism and the Path of Flesh in the West

Tim O'Neill

The great enigma of all religions, philosophies and metaphysical systems can be simply summed up in one innocent-seeming question: How does the multiplicity and physicality of our visible consensus universe arise from the timeless, spaceless, motionless transcendence of the Absolute? The answer of the intellect is far from simple though, generating monisms, dualisms, non-dualisms and other complex systems of constructed reality, each with its own merits and shortcomings. The answer of the mystics, artists and intuitives to this fundamental question is quite different. To the direct spiritual vision of the Gnostic, the illusion of duality arises out of the One in a flame of passion, love and Eros. This is the process of emanation; the Mystery of the emergence of the many out of the One in a seamless outpouring of Love. While emanationism is still a limited human model for this incredible process in the Universe, it goes much further than the intellectual systems in fulfilling our emotional and intuitive needs to understand our ultimate origins. This is why the doctrine of emanationism has been taught as a *Mystery*, largely within the confines of the secret Orders of the esoteric tradition. The only test of this doctrine that really matters is that it has successfully guided hundreds of thousands of seekers throughout the Centuries to the final goal... The transcendent Absolute.

One of the important aspects of the Emanation that is often glossed over is the doctrine that the entire chain of Being implicit within the outpouring of Absolute Love is, by definition, One. That is to say that there exist no real divisions within the chain. This is clearly visible in one of the most familiar geometric images of the Emanation, the Pythagorean Tetraktys:

The One

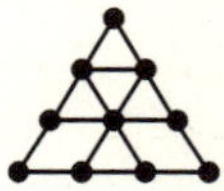

The Many

There is simply no place where the opposites do not meet! In this great continuum, one of the most important corollaries is that *the Spirit, which is of the One, is in continuum with the Flesh, which is of the Many.* All opposites unite in the cosmic Eros and unite as two sides of the same transcendence. According to the old doctrine of Hermes, "As above, so below", the Flesh is as much the mirror of Spirit, as Spirit is the mirror of Flesh.

This is truly a Mystery in the most profound sense, yet we can begin an intuitive approach to its depths in a fairly simple way by looking at a single cell from within the human body. If we visualize a cell from a muscle tissue in our hand, we can see that as an organism, it has its own life within the life of the organism as a whole. It has its own energy, form and even consciousness, burning bright. If we imagine subtly severing the physical aspect of the cell away from its totality, what next emerges is the astral or ætheric form of the cell... Its own *Body of Light*. If we then imagine removing the Body of Light from the cell's life form, we are then left with the causal or spiritual aspect... The geometric thought-form which creates the *idea* of the cell... Its blueprint. If we remove this third aspect of the cell, we are finally left with the monadic, or transcendent part of the cell... Its own spark of life, which is where it interfaces with the Absolute. Thus, if we remove all of the "sheaths" of the life form away from its ultimate matrix, we are still left with the indestructible transcendent *essentia*. According to the theory of emanations, the ultimate aspect of the cell will eternally exist, ready to give it physical form over and over again in ever more evolved forms that reach closer and closer to the Absolute and perfect form which it ultimately is.

This leads us to a key cultural paradox in mainstream Western culture which flies in the face of this great Truth. We are taught with our very first breaths that the Flesh is sinful and profane, while the Spirit is holy and sacred; that the harmonious body is "beautiful", while the irregular body is "ugly", that fat is "gross" and that thinness is "pleasing"; that abstinence is "saintly", while indulgence of the flesh is "evil". We have been at war with our own flesh since the Greeks began to divide Spirit and Flesh into opposing camps, yet the great Truth of the sacredness of Flesh along the indivisible continuum of Emanation remains firm, beyond human argument. Every cell in the human body, be it regular, misshapen, harmonious or chaotic, is a direct reflection of the transcendent; a microcosm of the Chain of Being, struggling to eventually reach its ultimate manifestation.

The idea that the Absolute has only one idea of "beauty" is where a great deal of confusion arises. From the perspective of the Absolute, there is an absolute, harmonious "beauty" as well as an ultimate "ugliness"... Yet they are ultimately One! Where we divide, the One unites all opposites and passes beyond them in a blaze of Eros. When the higher aspects choose a bodily form to emanate out into the World, that body is a direct reflection of the need of the Absolute to manifest a continuum of ideas; a range of possible loves. The "misshapen", "ugly" or "incomplete" body is thus an important and necessary part of the Wisdom of the Spirit. Unfortunately, we live in a cultural world which clouds the Truth in a pernicious and devious way, forcing the natural evolutionary widening of consciousness into unitary constructs boxed with poison walls. The hidden unity of the grotesque and beautiful teaches us to seek beyond forms to the Spirit within; to actually *see* the flame burning within, which is all that is, neither cold nor hot, bright nor dark, good nor evil.

The body, as born into this world, is a sacred object and the essential spiritual implement of the Higher Self in the work of evolution. Like any tool, it is the prerogative of the craftsperson to modify, fine-tune and alter the tool to meet the needs of the project at hand. Beyond the genetic, astral, causal and transcendent aspects of our bodies, we do have the ability and right to modify our forms to suit our highest purposes. It is when we seek to fulfill strictly cultural programs, outside our own desires, that we poison the body with true ugliness. The inherent nature of the body can be repressed, in order to fulfill cultural programs, or it can be *amplified*, in order to empower the personal spiritual path. Adornment, surgical intervention, breath control, food intake, temporary modifications, piercings, tattooings, asceticism, indulgence, mortification, branding, sexuality, celibacy, intoxication, sobriety, body-building, drug-enhancement and an infinite variety of other mechanisms can be used to affect the Soul's program for empowering the body and personality. In the Orient and in pre-literate cultures, Shamanism and the Tantra are ancient schools of using the Flesh to further the aims of the Spirit. In the West, we really do not have any such great tradition of the path of the flesh. There do exist certain advanced individuals and small groups throughout our history, who have stumbled upon some of these truths, attempting to uncover the true transcendence at the core of Flesh, by using the Flesh itself as the matrix of spiritual practice. As we advance toward the second Millennium, it appears that we in the West must learn the simple lesson of the sacrality of the Flesh if we are not to perish. It is precisely because we have divided ourselves apart from Flesh that we are destroying the Body of our World in an orgy of thoughtlessness. For those few courageous individuals who stand in the Light of the Flesh for all to see, there will be undoubted persecution, yet can there be any other choice?

Bibliography:

- "The Disciples of Flesh", by Timothy O'Neill, in *Apocalypse Culture*, edited by Adam Parfrey, AMOK Press, 1987.
- "Surgeons and Gluttons in the House of Flesh", by Timothy O'Neill, in *Apocalypse Culture*, revised edition, Feral House Press, 1990.
- "Opiates, Brainwashing and Fasting", by Timothy O'Neill, in *Apocalypse Culture*, AMOK Press, 1987.

A Preliminary Vision to a Relationship with Ordo Templi Orientis

(By request of the Celestial Masters, known as the A:.A:., completed on the 21st of December 1991 –Winter Solstice, Full Moon)

Frater Nigris

The following text, inspired as it may be, is not an official document of the O.T.O., but rather a highly subjective reflection about the nature and structure of this fraternal order. – Ed.

Do what thou wilt shall be the whole of the Law.

Over time it has become obvious that elements of this Vision were at variance with common understanding. Such specifics as the "Word of the Aeon" and a miscellaneous term or two were seen in an occluded fashion and yet remain as a monument to my ignorance. I only ask that the reader forgive these eyesores in favor of the Vision's meat, which yields a tasty chew to this day, even if a bit spicy.

Yours, presently in the Bonds of the Order,

Frater Nigris
(formerly Fr. Nagashiva) July 15, 1992 EV

0. The Identity.

One simultaneously engages experience on each "Degree", though perhaps in different measure. This being the case, one's Inner and Outer appearance varies only to the extent that one comes to know oneself (in the case of the former) and one's kin (in the case of the latter). Ultimately, in an Order such as O.T.O., those two appearances are seen to be one relation and the Work of the Outer becomes identical to that of the Inner in all respects.

Having commented on the nature of the relationship between the body of the Self and the body of the Order, it is perhaps necessary to identify the location from whence these words arise. The Tree of the Order is approached from on high and below at once. One's ascent to Malkuth and one's descent to Kether are, in reality, one approach to the universe of differentiation in simultude. As the Degrees of the Order signify one's relationship to it, the first movement toward engaging this universe, that of "Associate

Membership", is identical in essence to the descent from Ain Soph Aur to Ain Soph. "Preconception", or knowledge in its best sense (that of non-knowledge) is what characterizes the first movement, the primal thrust which propels the Seed of the member deeply into the Womb of the Order, penetrating the Ovum of Mystery and initiating the Life of Kinship.

From the vantage of Ain Soph, therefore, do these words arise. Beyond the X° and before the 0°, in perfect Ignorance, unchallenged by the status of form, the form of status, this vision takes shape and makes itself known.

I. The Aeon.

Thelema is the Word of this Aeon. It is the motis operandi of cosmic impulse, the principle upon which is created the foundation of a liberated society of Kinship. Agape, the substance of this principle, breathes a warm security into such a society and provides the nutrient necessary for the aspirant to participate in this Word.

The passage of time can be difficult to comprehend, yet the cycles and sub-cycles of its passing are often punctuated by tremendous changes subtended by periods of careful growth. This transformative marker makes itself known in the disintegration of familiar social systems and one's relationship to them. Such a transformative period, it will be seen, is today's society passing through, with much reference to "New Orders" and "lasting peace".

For O.T.O., the numerological significance of the next few years (1993-1997) is not to be overlooked. Not only does it include the simply numerical, formal reference to the Word in our generation, but it is the completion of a cycle of 93 years since the revelation of the literal manifestation of the Word in our Order, the inception of our current Aeon. Whether this describes the passing of an Aeon itself or constitutes a period in one sentence of its composition is left to the interpretation of scholars of history. Suffice it to say that this is a time of great importance for both the order of Society and for the society of the Order.

II. The Master.

The Father of the Order's current form is surely to be well regarded. One's ancestors and parents are heeded and studied by the wise. In our society the Father is often set apart and praised. It is through this process that the Father may therefore come to be misunderstood and obscured by our dreams and expectations.

O.T.O. may be said to be in its adolescence. Of a Mysterious origin, given body by the Wisdom of its membership, and birthed by the Celestial Masters, it is important to remember and support both an identification with and a clear distinction from the Parents whom we so dearly love.

To this effect it is clear that while Aleister Crowley (666) was a unique and extraordinary individual, whose influence upon the Order is of inestimable value, he was and is one among many stars whose light cascades from the Center of Perfection. Characterizing him with such objectivity, the Order may take important steps of independence, acknowledging its foundation while standing firmly atop it, peering into itself and the culture in which it resides.

III. The Mass.

If any function of the Order can be said to symbolize the Conception of the Word, individually and socially, the Mass is that function. Not only does it unify the ignored aspects of the self with those more familiar, it provides a framework for the social integration of this Work.

The form of the Perfect Mass varies in time and space, is given structure by those whose insight and perception are most keen, and is empowered by those participants who resonate most soundly with its construct. The most cherished goal of the clergy who creates its Ecclesia must be that O.T.O. maintains a direct connection to its community and to the Conception of the Word in its most vibrant form.

The Mass must serve the needs of the People. Its structure and quality are a direct reflection of the health of the Order as a Microcosmic Body. Its popularity, therefore, serves as a meter with which to gauge its success in this regard. Great popularity indicates devolution into exoterica. Small attendance, on the other hand, reveals the degeneration of the Order's ties to esoteric authority.

IV. The Book of the Law.

Living traditions which encourage personal development flourish in response to revelatory experience and the literal manifestation of such experience. Any specific forms adopted as a symbolic and indicative of the tradition at large must meet exceedingly strict standards of meaning and metaphor so as to faithfully preserve the Order's Thelemic character.

The Book of the Law, being the Metaphorical Doctrine of Universal Manifestation, the Logos of the Thelemic Word, the *Bible* of the Ecclesia Gnostica Catholica, the *Book of Shadows* of the Current Aeon, is the pure and perfect expression of the Holy Spirit in our world. Its completed form is accepted by the wise, who reveal its deeper meanings to the uninitiated.

O.T.O. must preserve the integrity and promote the completion of the Thelemic Work. The Order blossoms as it renews this Work's expression. *The Book of the Law* is the bedrock from which this renewal must begin.

V. The Holy Guardian Angel.

The major focus of the Order is to prepare the aspirant for the Knowledge and Conversation of the Holy Guardian Angel. The Angel may assume any guises, depending upon the nature of the aspirant. It is therefore imperative that the Order avoid too much definition with regard to the Angel or to the method of preparation, since it is a personal relation which may only come about on its own terms.

One may identify the Holy Guardian Angel with a particular form of the Catholic

Holy Spirit, Jung's "shadow", Socrates' "daimon", a Taoist Celestial Master, or a Master of the "Great White Brotherhood" (the A∴ A∴). The phenomenon can be seen as a psycho-spiritual contact with one's High Self or the preternatural relationship with a Prophet or one's Savior.

It is to the credit of O.T.O. that it realizes its limitations in facilitating this phenomenon. Over-extension would certainly prevent some of its members from being prepared for it, and restriction of terms of characterization would diffuse the Order's support for its experience.

VI. The Secret.

The Silent Word, Unified Opposition, the Mated Pair are expressions of the Secret Goal of all true mystical and magical bodies. The Immortality of the Celestial Masters, the Alchemist's Gold, the Elven Summerlands, Christian Heaven, Buddhist Nirvana, Hindu Moksha and Taoist Way are one in essence if not in character.

Through Love (Agape) and its Law are we enabled to engage the Infinite. Under Will (Thelema) do we transform, through the Sexual Magick of the Great Work, our bodies of light and shadow into one Adamantine Body of Absolute Presence.

O.T.O. supports the "Love under Will" that compliments its Law of which the whole is to "Do what thou wilt". These existentialist, liberating declarations serve the needs of the individual while its secret initiatory rites, Mass, and instruction of Sex Magick promote social development.

VII. The Organization.

The nature of the Order's organization is as important as the substance of which it is made. It must be flexible so as to allow for growth and variation, yet durable to prevent fragmentation and decay. Its possible forms are endless, yet the health of O.T.O. depends upon it taking the proper form at the proper time, maintaining a Chaos of Kinship, Love.

The Order's structure determines the quality of support and incentive the members receive from each other. An overemphasis on status or reputation could become an obstacle to harmony, while encouragement to achieve, to participate, is surely of great importance. Focus on service and on substance is paramount, yet this must be balanced by the support of experimentation, play and challenge to tradition, so that the Order remains a lively body.

VIII. The Individual.

The organization, the society, must at root support the personal empowerment of the individual who gives it life if it is to retain its legitimacy. The individual member is the originator of the genius that makes the Order what it is. Those who innovate, who reflect deeply and create new symbols of what they see, become the character, the personality of O.T.O. as it appears to the local culture.

The quality of the individual member is what preserves the integrity of the Order. It is their privilege and responsibility to test the limits of the Order's authority, challenge it when suspect, and dissolve it when required. The member also has the duty to enforce those regulations that the Order puts in place which are, in truth, necessary and just.

Loyalty to the Order may be required, yet it need only extend to the intent of the member. It is as difficult to determine such intent as it is to predict the result of discordant activity. Therefore, those within the Order must proceed with caution where judgment is concerned. While such evaluation is at times required, it remains the most injurious to social and cosmic harmony when applied without wisdom.

IX. The Hermit.

The role that O.T.O. plays in society is as model and inspiration. Where social organization often polarize around issues of order, restriction and indoctrination, the Order must maintain a "Middle Way", fusing opposing energies as diverse as Eastern and Western culture, anarchic and monarchic politics, containment and dissemination of information, and social and personal power.

The purity of such fusion cannot be overdeveloped. Our world is increasingly one of interdependence, integration and unified diversity. As a beacon which lights the way along difficult paths, the Order must at once explore new territory of social coordination and return the fruit of its exploration to society. It must not only illuminate a way for aspirants but continue the voyage into its own nature, analyzing and transcending its weaknesses.

The Order must be able to accommodate a multitude of views and practices. Some will no doubt follow paths of isolation, retreat and denial. Others will congregate, indulge and focus on excess. Both may be extremes of ignorance, yet the path to freedom is sometimes lined with barbed wire and what does not endanger the spontaneous and natural learning process of its members will strengthen the Order immeasurably.

X. The Tao.

Ultimately the Supreme and Vulgar Secrets of initiatory experience are incommunicable in any but the most crude and awkward of terms. Due to this limitation it is best for the Order to refrain from undue definition of terms, specification of meaning, or direction of practice. Accepting no doctrine of Truth to measure inner development, O.T.O. preserves its spirit of freedom, its Thelemic nature.

Recognizing the identity of opposites is one thing, experiencing it is quite another. The Order, as a social structure, must never dictate the personal experience of its membership, for to do so would be to compromise its authority and display its disease.

The Art of Silence is the magick of the Order's upper echelon. Dictation and requirement show both illegitimacy and immaturity on the part of those who exhibit these qualities. As Lao Tzu suggests, the perfect leader is one who remains unseen, who releases power so that those who follow perform their Will without direction.

Love is the law, love under will.

The Demonic Glamour of Cinema

Carl Abrahamsson

Delivered as a lecture at Club Rotunda, University of Krakow, April 4th, l992. – Ed.

I have for some reason chosen to call this lecture *The demonic glamour of cinema*, and before we proceed, I think it's best if we define the terms "demonic" and "glamour" first.

In the history of mythology, a demon, as opposed to an angel, is a malevolent force that can only act when commanded by a human or divine will. There are many demons in all cultures, and most of them seem, just as angels, merely to reflect characteristics and traits within the human psyche. Call greed "Mammon", call poisonous betrayal "Samael", call the enjoyment of decay "Beelzebub", and you'll know what I mean.

All demons reflect the so called darker side of man's nature, and whether one wants to accept this fact or not, is just basically a matter of intellectual maturity in the individual.

"Glamour", or to glamourize, means originally to fascinate, to bewitch, to attract subconsciously. A person with a lot of glamour can make people do things without actually expressing this in words. It has to do with looks, reputation, that person's aura, and many other things. To glamourize someone is then to catch someone's attention without that person really knowing what exactly is going on. To use techniques other than language or gesture, to use unseen or unfelt forces. Occult forces.

Cinema is a fine example of the most demonic art form to this day, and the cinema-theatre is like a pagan temple where believers get together and receive messages from other realms, other planes of consciousness, complete with idols, a set morality, satisfaction (or at least titillation) of religious, sexual and other personal needs.

We are completely alone in the dark. There are no impressions except for the ones that stream from the screen and from the speakers straight down into our selves. The size of the screen, the colours, the movement, the action, the soundtrack all interact to create a vision of wonder and illusion that is unsurpassed, with the exceptions of true religious or mystical visions.

It is undoubtedly an extremely powerful medium, and can naturally be used for both good and bad. Effective propaganda films brainwashed millions of people during the Communist and National Socialist regimes, and helped to create those evil empires.

But film as such, we mustn't forget, is just a medium, and it can naturally just as well be used for creating visions, and thereby results, of love and life and strength and art and magnificence. This is true of all techniques in magic. The technique itself is just a technique, and how one should look upon a magical operation must have to do with the magician and the aim of that magician.

It is a misconception to think that film as such is a medium for visionaries. This is untrue. Film is a 100% technical medium, and if one doesn't master the technical aspects, nothing can be achieved, just like in magic. A film becomes a work of art at the moment a visionary will, the will of the director, takes charge and masters all of these technical skills. Just like in magic.

The works of Sergei Eisenstein and Leni Riefenstahl shine as prime examples. They were master-magicians who just happened to work for these specific ideologies at a certain point in time. I seriously believe they could easily have traded places and achieved just as glorious cinematic results.

Just as in magic, cinema is all about capturing the light, wherever it's possible. In magic, the adept seeks illumination and guidance through an inner light, the *Holy Guardian Angel*. In cinema, the process is a similar one – one of filtering the light through a mechanical machine and capturing this willed filtering on a piece of receptive plastic – the divine celluloid.

Each conception of the two examples is extremely individual. No two illuminations or exposed strips of celluloid could ever be the same. And although the commercial market dictates a feeling of conformity in both film-form and film-contents, cinema is perhaps the ultimate medium for personal, individual, subjective, creative self-expression. Because of the fact that there are so many technical things to master, the director has to push him- or herself to the extreme limits of knowing exactly what he or she wants. It doesn't matter whether it's consciously (as in a big commercial production where there is a big team and lots of money involved) or subconsciously (as in an independent, intuitive experimental film). Mastery is the thing to strive for. Just like in magic.

In many ways, the screen is a spirit-world created by material forces. If the result affects the viewer in some way, then we have a perfect alchemical marriage of heaven and earth, the mystical and the magical – a divine ecstasy designed to tell, to instruct, to invoke, to evoke whatever feelings in the viewer the director wants.

As in life, there is no real conflict between darkness and light, but rather a dualistic need of each other. If the hall weren't pitch dark, then the force of the flickering light emanating from the silver screen wouldn't be as potent. To put it in another way: If Satan and God didn't have each other, none would have any power at all.

There can be no reality on the screen. There simply isn't any way that reality can be portrayed objectively on film. Because even if it's just a matter of putting the camera in a shooting mode and then leaving, someone has still chosen the position of the tripod, the aperture setting for the light, and so on. A choice that is creative whether that person realizes it or not.

As always, humans need terms and categories to be able to grasp and communicate, and in cinema we find "social-realism", "super-realism", "sur-realism", and even "neo-realism" as classifications of the works of many diverse artists. The same in magic: there are ceremonial magicians, witches, chaos magicians, Satanists, Catholic priests, rabbis, and many other "fractions" disguising themselves behind convenient terms for reasons of commercialism, power or self-justification. But they all use basically the same techniques to achieve whatever it is they want to achieve... Magic.

The word "occult" means "hidden" in Latin. The occult forces in nature are the forces one can use only if one awakens them from within one's own deep, dark areas. Today, when people are so used to seeing moving pictures, the directors and producers need new occult tricks, new special effects to keep the audiences spellbound, to keep them in the desperately desired audio-visual trance. Millions and millions of dollars and of other currencies (mostly Indian and Chinese capital) are spent to research and design new trickery. Even though the stories in commercial cinema are the same as they have always been, new ways of telling them are constantly needed.

This should mean that the illusion, the spell of the screen, the magical enchantment, can only be extremely temporary. In most cases, the emotional trance disappears as soon as the lights are turned on. That was that – yet another film seen... But in the cases of artistic masterworks, the impression remains. An impression of having been shaken in the very foundation of the soul, yet not being aware of exactly how it was done, just like magic. The magician can impress people at face level and just trick them into supplying what he or she wants, or can use other, completely hidden planes, to plant the seeds of future fruits. Here, we also find a parallel comparison between photography and cinema. It's the same medium, but the photo has just two dimensions and can be thoroughly studied and analyzed. The moving picture has a much greater opportunity to trick the viewer's mind, because all of the used photographs aren't perceived separately. And we mustn't forget the soundtrack on top of that, especially constructed and used to lure the open-minded viewer into a seduction of the rational intellect together with his 25 frames-a-second demon brother – the image.

Experimental cinema has always led the way to new developments in the medium, technically as well as generally on all levels. The experimental filmmaker is most often someone who loves the medium so much that he or she isn't content with just telling a story or conveying a feeling, but rather wants to explore for the sake of exploring, to find new worlds and new ways of showing these discoveries. Like all true magicians, in other words.

Non-, or rather, anti-narrative film tends to provoke the viewer to a point where he/she either opens or closes the mind to the confusing impressions. If one chooses to open the mind, there is suddenly an extremely clear picture, an exposé, revealing what techniques are used in, for instance, commercial cinema to seduce the viewer. Why is this part cut to that one? Why is there such strange music here, but not there? Why was this scene shot from this angle, and not that one?

And, as I've mentioned before... It's the same thing in magic: if one chooses to let go of rational ways of thinking and analyzing the processes and goings-on around oneself, and opens up the mind to see with a subconscious or inner vision, everything appears in more or less perfect clarity. If one chooses to accept one's dark nature with all its aspects and qualities, then can one go on in the work of improving oneself.

If I say simply, "This film stinks, because I can't understand it", whose is the fault? The filmmaker's or mine? If I, without even having the desire to see beyond the most narrow limits of human existence, discard magic and occultism as being nonsense and child's play, am I trustworthy or a coward?

The magician can always work alone. In fact, he or she has to. But the dilemma of the filmmaker is that the finished work must also be able to attract others. Otherwise he or she might just as well indulge in masturbation with the cameras and the strips of celluloid. The experimental filmmaker has the freedom to try new tricks, and sometimes they work and sometimes they don't. But one never knows until one tries it – as in magic. And if a new trick or a new spell should prove to work efficiently, you can be sure the so called film industry will be there to knock on your door. Or perhaps they'll just steal it without any credits whatsoever.

Much of the work and the finished films of classic experimental filmmakers, as for instance the American Kenneth Anger (who, by the way, is also a prominent occultist), can today be seen in many so called rock-videos. And also, of course, any technique that can immobilize the resistance of the human mind extremely rapidly (juxtapositions, rapid cuts, certain color schemes, etc.) will quickly be sucked into the void of commercial advertising, on film as well as on TV.

I haven't touched upon television at all, because that in itself is such an ultra-demonic world of complete make-believe and sinister illusion. The biggest difference is naturally that we're not talking about capturing and transmitting light emanating from the sun, but rather more complex systems not just of images in themselves, but of electronic images, electronic sound and electronic and magnetic frequencies.

The medium, as well as the world in general, progresses through the works of geniuses. There are many geniuses working in television, of course, both good and evil ones. Perhaps TV is becoming even more demonic than cinema. It certainly doesn't require the viewer's full attention, and it can affect better because of this fact rather than in spite of it. In a moment of concentration upon something else in the room, who can tell what happens with the TV-images, the TV-sounds and the TV-frequencies in our subconscious mind and in the organism? There is no evidence yet that TV makes you more intelligent, so why should you bother to watch it?

And another thing is certain. As sure as there are demons, angels and gods co-existing in the magician's mind, just as sure is the fact that no-one can really seriously deny that although cinema uses the demonic forces to attract the attention, the overall experience could easily be termed "divine". And perhaps this is why we love cinema so much... Even though we know it's all an illusion, we feel a deep-rooted need of this type of spiritual experience.

Some Crowley Sources

William Heidrick

In reading Crowley, the question often arises: "Where is he getting this stuff?" Whether the work is noir humor or a deeply insightful and rather opaque religious writing, Crowley's sources and influences are often a mystery. The A∴A∴ reading list in *Magick in Theory and Practice* is a logical place to start, but no distinction is made there between works that influenced Crowley and works he recommended as also embodying a view he had held for some time. In this short space, or in a major book for that matter, it is impossible to cover many of Crowley's sources. Some often over-looked sources will be noted.

Before going further, an important point needs to be made. Thelema is not Crowley. Crowley is not Thelema. Some of our readers may have a sole interest in the purely literary side of Crowley's writings, but many share the Thelemic Religion. For the latter, some of what follows may seem to be skirt blasphemy. I offer the following contention: Whatever is sacred in *Liber AL* specifically or in Thelema generally is independent of Crowley the man. The earlier influences on Crowley, or earlier appearances of the same words and ideas elsewhere, are not in any way relevant to the sacredness of the text. Why was Crowley chosen to be the prophet of Thelema? A simple answer – he was prepared. Crowley was prepared by exposure to the words, ideas and language necessary to receive *Liber AL*, just as were the prophets of past time prepared to receive their messages. It doesn't matter that Crowley probably picked up "Aiwass" from unconscious integration of the shapes of the letters of a Greek word in Eliphas Levi's *The Key of the Mysteries* (plate called "Great pentacle from the vision of St. John", Eq. 1:10, Sup. p. 74) or that "Thelema" as a religion and an Abbey comes from Rabelais' 16th century satire on monasticism.

Neither does it matter that most of Crowley's ideas about society, morals and the nature of such beings as the "Secret Chiefs" stem first from his Quaker childhood and later from similar views encountered in his youth. Anyone who has experienced the Knowledge and Conversation of the Holy Guardian Angel knows that the experience avails itself of the states of mind and circumstance present in the person at the time. If whole passages in *Liber AL* can be found to be paraphrases or quotations from other sources, what does it matter? It is the melody that makes the music, and the instrument will always dominate on one level.

Crowley, his antecedents and his experiences formed the instrument for the manifestation and revelation of Thelema. If we can separate the harmonics from the notes, we can better approach the essence of the song. Enough, here are a few notes on Crowley's sources...

CHILDHOOD: See *Confessions, The Gospel according to St. Bernard Shaw, The world's tragedy* and *The high history of Sir Palamedes* for a model on his father and the early influence of education and the Plymouth Brethren. Also for the source of his social errors and business incompetence. Later childhood and adolescence provided his sexual orientation and literary bent at Cambridge. Frazer's *The Golden Bough* merely fleshed out ideas from Levi.

ALAN BENNETT: Introduced Crowley to the ideas of Eastern philosophy. These furnished Crowley with his mystical training, terminology, and mental techniques. The Golden Dawn provided Crowley with the model of his organization of attainment. Masonry the model of society and forms of ceremonial for groups. Theosophy furnished idealism and melded with the Quaker ideas of masters and elect. Reuss gave the justification for magical sexuality. Eckenstein taught the concept of discipline. von Eckertshausen gave Crowley the idea of an invisible order, while Waite introduced things that go BUMP in the night.

MUSIC HALLS & THE INGOLDSBY LEGENDS: Crowley's humor and satire, also his negligent racism.

TAO TEH KING: Source of many of Crowley's social theories and higher philosophy.

What single book influenced Crowley the most? As far as his mystical writings, magical theories, health ideas and political dreams, the answer can only be Eliphas Levi's *The Key of the Mysteries*. Many of Crowley's ideas in these areas can be found in seed at least in Levi. The page citations are from Crowley's translation in the supplement to *The Equinox*, 1:10.

Liber OZ is developed from page 35 in *The Equinox*, 1:10.

Page 234: "Human life and its innumerable difficulties have for object, in the ordination of eternal wisdom, the education of the will of man."

"The dignity of man consists in doing what he will, and in willing the good, in conformity with the knowledge of truth."

Page 213: "... One of those traditional secrets with regard to which silence is necessary, and which it is sufficient to indicate to those who know, leaving always a veil upon the truth for the ignorant."

An appropriate exercise would be to seek a passage in Levi for every idea in *Liber AL*, viz: "Nothing resists the will of man, when he knows the truth, and wills of good." (*KM*, page 235) for: "... Do thy will. Do that, and no other shall say nay." (*AL* 1:42-43)

A quote to take for Crowley's Opus: Levi, *KM*, page 241: "When a new word comes into the world, it needs swaddling clothes and bandages; genius brought it forth, but it is for experience to nourish it. Do not fear that it will die of neglect! Oblivion is for it a favorable time of rest, and contradictions help it to grow."

Crowley's unexamined belief in Natural Law has its origins in his times, but it also can be drawn from Levi: "Q: What is infinite reason? A: It is that supreme reason of being that faith calls God." (Page 102) This is the characteristic phrase of the philosophy of 18th century enlightenment: "God is Reason" – also the characteristic error. 19th century philosophy continued this into Determinism and the now discredited concept of "Natural Law".

Levi's idea of the "magnetic fluid" derived from the efforts of Newton, Mesmer and others to quantify the astral body. 18th and 19th century efforts to measure ectoplasm, odic force, etc., and to physically measure an essence of life have persisted to the verge of the 21st century in a strange pseudo-science. At least in the 18th and 19th centuries there was the idea of the luminous Æthyr as a partial justification for this sort of thing. Now it is generally considered a curiosity dependent on subjective measurement without the objective external instrumentation required by hard science. This concept has led to a vast array of quack medical theories and the loss of otherwise promising philosophies. Bulwer Lytton used the idea; Reich was imprisoned for trying to cure with it. Crowley lost much time over it in his later years trying to market his Amrita derivations. The future may disclose some substance here, but it tends to "confusion of the planes" more often than not.

Page 105: "Q: Are these experiences articles of faith? A: No, they pertain to science." Although this is not essential to Thelema, Crowley's dependence on it is interesting. "The Method of Science, the Aim of Religion". A valid perspective, but not without potential for misapplication. This, more than anything else, is the influence of Levi on Crowley's philosophy. Accidents in emphasis in Levi's works often became seeds for avenues of research in Crowley's effort.

Levi gives many anecdotes in this work. Page 119: "... An Englishman otherwise quite sane, who thought that he had met a stranger and made his acquaintance, who took him to lunch at his tavern, and then having asked him to visit St. Paul's in his company, had tried to throw him from the top of the tower which they had climbed together." Crowley elaborated quite a few of these into short stories.

Page 257: "To brave God and insult Him, is a final act of faith." See Crowley's *John St. John*.

Page 260: "While love is nothing but a desire and an enjoyment, it is mortal. In order to make itself eternal it must become a sacrifice, for then it becomes a power and a virtue." See Crowley in *Magick in Theory and Practice*, chapter 12. Levi appears to have turned Crowley's interest toward Poe and William Blake, as well as many other authors.

Even the Golden Dawn seems to have taken more from Levi than a twist to his Tarot attributions and the sketch for the Lesser Pentagram Ritual. Consider *KM*, page 195: "In old times, chess-players sought upon their chess-board the solution of philosophical and religious problems, and argued silently with each other in maneuvering the hieroglyphic characters across the numbers." Can this be the remark that sparked creation of Enochian Chess?

A word of caution. In reading Levi, a strong stomach is one of the requisites. The book is filled with Christian remarks. It is not always possible to get through this veil on a first or even a third reading. Persist. Write in the margin. The hard part is getting past the pseudo-logic and Christian propaganda.

The Rite of Ragnarök

Peter H. Gilmore

This ritual was published for the first time in The Fenris Wolf 3 *(1993). Later on, it was revised and expanded upon by Gilmore, High Priest of the Church of Satan after Anton LaVey's death in 1997, and included in his* The Satanic Scriptures *(Scapegoat Publishing, Baltimore, 2007). The text published here is the revised version. – Ed.*

Satanists take the position that Man has invented his gods. We find world mythology to be our field from which to harvest symbols and metaphors that we find to resonate most strongly with our Satanic natures. When exploring a particular historical mythology, we do not simply pick something that is NOT Christian, or not a part of Christianity's various antecedents and offshoots; we look instead to a myth system and ferret out its unique dark side, the taboo and forbidden regions that its adherents held in awe and terror. That's where the Devils are to be found.

This rite is an exercise in "exoticism" – an old practice in the West for purloining elements from foreign cultures that might seem too alien to be comprehended in their foreign form. Thus they become palatable and enjoyable in an adulterated state. Such absorptions launch trends in the arts. Art Deco had been influenced by the discovery of Tutankhamun's tomb in 1922. Musically it happened in the classical realm when composers like Beethoven imported into his *Ninth Symphony* the trumpets, drums, and cymbals used by marching Turkish Janissaries. Closer to our own time was the explosion of the "Tiki Lounge" fad. In the 1950s, a faux version of Pacific tribal culture was created to transport Western viewers into a state of blissful otherworldliness. Statues of gods were made into mugs for exotic cocktails; Asian food was garnished with pineapple; elements of primitive island architecture were implemented to create total environments that entertained, but had little relationship to original uses. So, only curmudgeons demand that you must experience such imports in their original forms – authenticity be damned!

I've chosen to import elements from ancient Northern European pagan beliefs to flavor the "stew" that is our traditional ritual practice in the Church of Satan. This is not to be construed as pretending to be authentic, or to be in any way representative of ancient or neo-pagan beliefs or practices. It is solely a means to explore the symbolism of Darkness from a distinct cultural milieu by adopting it into the context of contemporary Satanism. The same could be done with other non-Christian cultural traditions such as rituals utilizing Greek and Roman deities. Asian cthonic imagery can provide rich source material. Eastern art abounds with resonant demonic representations from the pantheons of China, Japan and Tibet.

The purpose of this rite is to expedite the shattering of a social order that has become moribund, seeing it cleared away to prepare for a new society based on values that will bring prosperity and satisfaction to the celebrants. This Norse apocalypse, Ragnarök, is depicted in various literary works handed down to the present. In the prose and poetic *Eddas*, there are vivid descriptions of the events casting down the old Gods, and I've used these as source material to fuel the litany.

Satanists, regardless of their ethnic or cultural heritage, are seen as one meta-tribe, and so we feel free to absorb appropriate examples of Satanism from whatever source in which they are discovered. When Anton LaVey released *The Satanic Rituals*, he included rites that had German, Russian, Middle Eastern, and French roots, and so Satanists who perform these workings freely identify with their ancestral fellows from all of these traditions. Likewise, you need not be descended from Northern European stock to appreciate and participate in this powerful ritual – you need only be a Satanist.

Originally written in the late 1980s, this is a militant rite, not for the timid, and it is exaggerated in its cataclysmic dramatics. Some might note that some of this mythology has been used dramatically by the Third Reich. However, they should also see that while we appreciate the drama of the mass rallies of the past, we are invoking and embracing the gods that were considered enemies by those who tried to create a neo-pagan culture for Nazi Germany. They wanted to resurrect Valhalla – our rite sends it crashing down in flames.

Our members have used this ritual to purge emotions raised by the terrorist attacks of 9/11, as well as to release their hatred of the current creeping theocracy imposed by right wing fundamentalist Christians in Western nations. You too may find it a powerful cathartic to eliminate feelings of repression induced by parts of society that are distinctly anti-individualistic and utterly un-Satanic.

It may be used as well to cast a vision of the future, a societal Is-To-Be that moves the world in directions of greater freedom, abundant secularism, and utter elimination of fundamentalist fanaticism. Here's to a glorious world of abundant joy. Hail Ragnarök!

SOWULO (SIG) PENTAGRAM

RAGNARÖK RUNE

NAUTHIZ (NOT)

MANNAZ (MAN)
Posture: Legs together, arms extended upwards to the sides.

TEIWAZ (TYR)
Posture: Arms at 45 degree angle from sides.

FEHU (FA)
Posture: Arms raised to front at 45 degree angle, left slightly higher.

SOWULO (SIG)
Mudra: Hands flat, palms facing each other, left hand half a hand higher; left thumb at 45 degree angle touches fingertips of right hand.

DAGAZ (DAG)
Posture: Arms crossed with hands touching opposite shoulders.

ISA (IS)
Posture: Stand straight, feet together; arms at sides.

GEBO (GIBOR)
Mudra: Hands flat, fingers interlaced making an "X" with thumb tips touching.

EIHWAZ (EH)

PRELIMINARY

All of the accouterments standard to Satanic ritual may be employed here; however, we suggest certain substitutions which will add a greater resonance to the rite. The Baphomet Sigil may be replaced with an inverse pentagram thrust through with the SIG rune (, victory), as was seen in the Sigil worn by Anton LaVey. For the sword of power you may choose one that is of Viking design, or you may substitute a spear or even a battle hammer. Participants may also carry daggers, decorated with runic symbols, with which they echo the Celebrant's gestures according to the rubrics. In place of the chalice, one may substitute a drinking horn, filled with a strong ale or mead. Amulets of significant runes may be worn. Particularly effective is the symbol I designed called the Ragnarök Rune, which consists of a variant on the rune of outward radiating power with a wolf's cross (sign of Hel and unchangeable fate) at the center. Clothing may be the standard black robes, but one can also adopt a warrior-like appearance, creating a "Satanic Soldier" image since traditional Northern gear today tends to bring to mind Anna Russell, Hägar the Horrible, or refugees from SCA gatherings.

In addition, a flame source will be needed on your altar, to be ignited during the Conflagration. This can be a small brazier filled with either charcoal, treated to easily ignite, or some form of jellied petroleum fuel like Sterno. If performed out of doors, this can be replaced with a bonfire, but it will require an attendant, and you must be certain of the laws regarding open fires in the locale of your performance. Flash powder or paper is also called for. Incense is not required, but if used should commence with a bitter smell during the Condemnation and Conflagration, and then change to something pleasing during the Victory. On a parchment, the Nauthiz rune (ᚾ) must be depicted, or a three-dimensional one may be constructed of papier-mâché. The ritual area may be decorated with runic symbols that should be displayed on banners or shields. Wolf imagery is also welcomed. Out of doors, one may employ torches for lighting, instead of the traditional black candles. The rite begins with a procession to the place of the working, and outdoors this must be accompanied by the sound of drums (hand drums of a deep tone – no bongos!) repeating the given rhythms (see examples), in succession, or any repetition/combination that you find to be satisfactory.

Music is of paramount importance to this working. I have found a particular recording, when cued correctly, will serve quite well (Wagner: *The Ring Without Words*; Berlin Philharmonic conducted by Lorin Maazel). During the Conflagration one may also play recordings of thunder and windstorms, or if exterior, have several drummers playing arrhythmically to approximate thunder. If desired, lightning generators may also be employed at this stage (van de Graf generators or Tesla coils). As a closing anthem, we have found Dr. LaVey's *Hymn of the Satanic Empire* to be eminently suitable.

There are several runic systems that have varied and evolved over time, as living languages tend to do. In the text, I have mixed older and newer names for these symbols, according to personal preferences and the varied shades of meaning evoked by these names. Resonance is more important than "purism".

In the preceeding list, I give the Elder Futhark name first, followed by the Armanen Futhork name in parenthesis. I encourage the reader to explore some of the numerous books concerning the runes which are now available.

ENTRANCE PROCESSIONAL

Indoors: Participants should file into the totally darkened chamber; lead by an acolyte bearing a lit black candle. Proper music would be slower and emphatically articulated march rhythms on the drums. When all have entered and taken their places, the candle is extinguished, and all stand in darkness for several minutes. Next, the ritual music is commenced, and about five minutes should be spent in darkness before lighting the altar candles.

Outdoors: The congregation should be led by a torchbearer and deep-toned hand drums play a march rhythm. Upon arrival at the ritual site, all assemble in appropriate order and the rite is begun.

Possible rhythm for drummers:

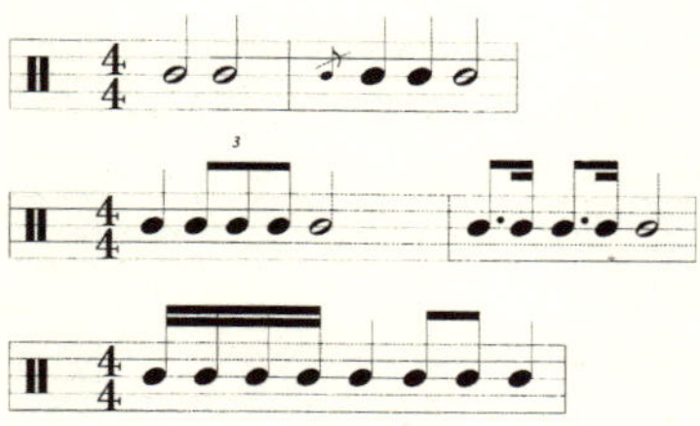

PURIFICATION

THE BELL IS RUNG NINE TIMES. THE CELEBRANT, TURNING COUNTER-CLOCKWISE, DIRECTS THE TOLLING TOWARDS THE FOUR COMPASS POINTS.

INVOCATION OF THE NETHER GODS

CELEBRANT TAKES UP HIS SWORD AND POINTS IT TOWARDS THE SIG PENTAGRAM.

CELEBRANT: Hear me, Gods of the abyss and attend! I command thee, Infernal Lords, to witness mighty deeds done in thy name. Come forth and greet those numbered among thy pack. The time has come for redress. Justice shall reign through the rule of fang and claw, as it was in the beginning, and as it shall be again!

We smash open the gates to Musspellsheim, Nifelheim and the very depths of Hel's domain and summon thee forth to climax this age of fire!

CELEBRANT (CONGREG. REPEATS): Heija! Hail Loki!

GONG IS STRUCK.

THE SUMMONS

CELEBRANT POINTS WITH SWORD TO THE CARDINAL DIRECTIONS AND SPEAKS THE INVOCATIONS.

SOUTH

CELEBRANT: Surt! Master of Fire, I summon thee to come forth from Musspellsheim and kindle thy unquenchable flame! Attend us!

EAST

Loki! Ancient Lord, I summon thee to slaughter the foul ones who stand against nature! Attend us!

NORTH

Fenris! Almighty Wolf, I summon thee to rend the flesh of those who oppose thy children! Attend us!

WEST

Jormungandr, venomous sea dragon, I summon thee to smash the halls of Valhalla with thy crashing waves! Attend us! With thy power and presence, our hour of victory is at hand!

SWORD IS REPLACED ON THE ALTAR.

RECOGNITION OF KINSHIP AND DECLARATION OF ALLEGIANCE

CELEBRANT STANDS BEFORE ALTAR WITH H1S ARMS EXTENDED FROM HIS SIDES AT A 45 DEGREE ANGLE, IN THE POSITION OF THE TYR RUNE (↑).

CELEBRANT: From the nighted halls of the netherworlds, I call my kindred to witness my oath.

CELEBRANT (CONGREG. REPEATS): I pledge my troth to the honor of my brethren. I reclaim this soil, hallowed by the blood of my folk. Grandfather Loki, Lord of the Inferno, Thy flame burns deep in my heart. Father Fenris, mighty wolf, my teeth are your fangs tearing our enemies. My blood burns with irresistible rage for the murder of our kind by the filthy minions of the gods of death. Thou tasted their flesh when thou wert bound and shall now feast upon their corrupt remains. Heija! Hail Fenris!

GONG IS STRUCK.

TOAST

CELEBRANT FILLS DRINKING HORN, FORMS THE SIG RUNE (ᛋ) OVER IT WITH HIS HANDS.

Fenris! Thy might shall bring me victory.

CELEBRANT RAISES THE HORN UP TO THE SIG PENTAGRAM.

CELEBRANT (CONGREG. REPEATS): Hail Victory!

GONG IS STRUCK.

CELEBRANT DRINKS.

AS EACH CONGREGANT STANDS BEFORE CELEBRANT, HE OFFERS THE HORN WITH THE WORDS: "PARTAKE OF THE MIGHT OF FENRIS." *CONGREGANT RESPONDS:* "HAIL VICTORY!" *AND DRINKS FROM THE HORN. WHEN ALL HAVE DRUNK, DRAINED HORN IS REPLACED ON ALTAR.*

CONDEMNATION OF THE POLLUTION OF THE WORLD

CELEBRANT STANDS IN ISA POSITION (ᛁ), ARMS AT SIDES.

CELEBRANT: Behold! We are deep in the frigid wasteland of Fimbulvetr, our culture choked with the glacial tread of mediocrity. The weak govern the strong, perverting natura law. Witness the reign of the gods of death! Yahweh, Christ, Buddha, Mohammed – all you have touched has spawned corruption! Dwarves of mind and spirit have swept the globe as a pestilence, stifling higher Man. We have seen the forward motion of the ruthless life-force slow to a crawl, mired in a bog of despicable refuse. Discipline is banished; idiocy enshrined. The world is ruled by crippled and twisted thralls, groveling before their idols of renunciation, wallowing in the filth of desire denied. Aspiration and advancement are mocked by pox-ridden beggars, whose festering sores are THEIR signs of honor. A pall of guilt smothers the visage of pride! Justice is hamstrung! The very living treasure of Midgard, our precious lair, is soiled by the massed swarm of worthless, subhuman dross.

CELEBRANT (CONGREG. REPEATS): Woe! – Woe! – Woe!

GONG IS STRUCK, MEZZO FORTE,
AFTER PARTICIPANTS' REPETITION OF EACH "WOE!"

RENUNCIATION OF THE CORRUPT

CELEBRANT STRIKES MAN RUNE POSTURE (ᛘ).

CELEBRANT: ENOUGH! The time is now to sound the clarion of rejection! Hear me, oh warriors! Men and women of mighty minds, I call the very whirlwinds to be our steeds! Time to shatter the bonds of OUR Gods, to loose the primal powers that bore our ancestors. March forth to total war. Smite the worshippers of the weak and frail! Fill your hearts with berserker frenzy! Mind and force shall reign supreme. The time has come, to cleanse and purify, a time for birth, spilling an ocean of blood!

CELEBRANT (CONGREG. REPEATS): Heija! Hail Loki!

GONG IS STRUCK.

THE NINETEENTH ENOCHIAN KEY

TO BE READ IN ENOCHIAN.

THE CONFLAGRATION

CELEBRANT STRIKES FA POSTURE (ᚠ).

CELEBRANT: It is now AMOK time! Baldur has been slain and Heimdall sounds his call.

CELEBRANT TRACES EH (ᛖ), *THE DEATH RUNE, IN THE AIR*
WHILE GONG IS ROLLED TO FORTISSIMO.

Brothers battle, slaying one another. Siblings writhe in incestuous embrace. Men know misery with all their hearts. Treacheries abound. Harsh is the world. Behold an age of axes, of swords, of shattered shields; An age of tempests, an age of wolves! Now ends the age of sterility! Look upon Nauthiz, rune of binding!

SIGIL IS ELEVATED BY CELEBRANT.

Loki, we sunder thy bonds and loose the ravening wolf of Hel!

SIGIL ON PARCHMENT IS THRUST INTO THE FLAME OF A CANDLE, THEN CAST DOWN INTO THE BRAZIER WHERE IT IGNITES THE FLAME SOURCE. AS THIS IS DONE, THE GONG IS STRUCK, FORTISSIMO, AND THE DRUM-

MERS COMMENCE THEIR CONFLICTING THUNDER RHYTHMS. RECORDED THUNDER SOUNDS, IF USED, ARE NOW ACTIVATED. IF THE NAUTHIZ RUNE IS CONSTRUCTED, RATHER THAN PARCHMENT, IT IS SMASHED BY A BATTLE HAMMER BEFORE BEING BURNED.

CELEBRANT (CONGREG. REPEATS): Hail Loki! Hail Fenris!

GONG IS STRUCK.

CELEBRANT STRIKES DAGAZ POSTURE (⋈).

CELEBRANT: Hear the glad tidings! A torrent of swords and daggers runs from the east through vales of venom. Below the earth, a soot red cock crows in the halls of Hel. Fearsome Garm and savage Freke are free to plunder. Comes the dragon of darkness flying, might from beneath the mountains of night. With a roar in the ancient tree, the giant is loosed. Yggdrasil quakes where it stands; is overturned. Jormungandr writhes in titanic rage, whipping the waves to froth. His venom splatters the very sea and sky. Nagelfar, dread ship of doom, casts off. From the east, over the boiling waters, comes Muspell's folk with Loki at the helm. His allies, the Frost Giants, thirst for battle. Fierce Garm devours Tyr, the one-handed. From out the south, mighty Surt's flames blaze before and after. His sword, conflagration, touches all. The embattled gods' sun is skewered on the blade. Mountains burst. Hags hurry hence. The Bifrost span is smashed to shards. Fenris slavers, jaws stretching from earth to sky. Odin, Loki-betrayer, is swallowed whole. Men tread Hel's road; the skies are sundered. Black is the sun as the earth sinks in waters stained crimson with blood. The sparkling stars are stripped from the firmament. Smoke rages and leaping flames lick heaven itself. At Loki's command, Surt's fires consume all, a righteous pyre! The old order is done.

CELEBRANT FORMS GIBOR MUDRA (ᛃ).

HAIL RAGNARÖK!

FLASH POWDER IS CAST INTO THE BRAZIER WHILE GONG IS STRUCK FORTISSIMO.

CONGREG. (SALUTE WITH DAGGERS): HAIL RAGNARÖK!

THUNDER AND ARRHYTHMIC DRUMMING END.

DRUMS BEGIN SOLEMN MARCH TREAD.

THE VICTORY

CELEBRANT STRIKES FA POSTURE (ᚠ).

CELEBRANT: Behold, Valhalla is ablaze! The flames herald a new dawn. The gods of weakness are vanquished! Their ashes and blood, fuel for our future. Now begins the age of Feral Man. Multiply, sons and daughters of Fenris. Fill our darkling halls with Iron Youth. We glory in discipline and strength through joy.

CELEBRANT (CONGREG. REPEATS): Hail Feral warriors! Hail Iron Youth! Behold, the world is ours!

CELEBRANT MAKES THE SIGN OF THE HORNS.

Hail Fenris! *(GONG FORTE)* Hail Loki! *(GONG FORTISSIMO)*

Hail Victory! *(GONG FORTISSISSIMO)*

DAGGERS ARE LOWERED.

DRUMS STOP.

GONG FADES TO SILENCE.

BELL IS RUNG AS POLLUTIONARY.

CELEBRANT: So it is done!

LIGHTS ARE EXTINGUISHED.

RECESSIONAL MUSIC IS PLAYED.

END OF RITE.

The Left Handed Path

An Analysis

The Order of the Nine Angles

The Left Handed Path and Satanism are related insofar as Satanism is a particular LHP. The LHP is the name given to describe a system of esoteric knowledge and practical techniques – and this system is also known as "The Black Arts".

The Difference Between the Left and Right Handed Paths.

The aim of all genuine Occult paths or systems, whether designated Right Hand or Left Hand, is to achieve or find a certain goal as well as to impart esoteric knowledge and abilities. The goal is variously described (e.g. "Gnosis", the Philosopher's Stone, Enlightenment).

However, it has been a common misconception that the RH Paths were altruistic and the LH Paths egocentric – i.e. the difference between them was seen in individual moral terms. Another misconception is in seeing the difference in absolute moral terms – i.e. the RH Paths as representing "good" and the LH Paths as "evil". Recently, attempts have been made to formulate "grey" paths which combine elements of both, and such "grey" paths are often said (by their exponents) to be the "true" Occult way or path.

The reality is quite different. The LH Paths and the RH Paths (hereafter, the singular "Path" will be used, although the plural is to be understood) are quite distinct and differ in both their methods and their aims. The most fundamental difference is that the RHP is restrictive – certain things are forbidden or frowned upon – and collective. That is, the RHP takes some responsibility away from the individual by having a formal dogma, a code of ethics and behaviour and by having the individual participate in an organized grouping, however loose that grouping may be. In brief, the identity of the individual is to some extent taken away – by the belief systems which that individual has to accept, and by them accepting some higher "authority", be such authority an individual, a group or an "ideology" (or even, sometimes, a supra-personal Being – a "god" or "gods").

In contradistinction, the LHP in its methods is non-structured. In the genuine LHP there is nothing that is not permitted – nothing that is forbidden or restricted. That is, the LHP means *the individuals takes sole responsibility for their actions and their quest.* This makes the LHP both difficult and dangerous – its methods can be used as an excuse for anti-social behaviour as they can be used to aid the fetishes and weaknesses of some individuals as well as lead some into forbidden and illegal acts. However, the genuine Initiate of the LHP is undertaking a quest, and as such is seeking something: that is, there is a dynamic, an imperative about their actions as well as the conscious understanding and appreciation that all such actions are only a part of that quest; they are not the quest itself. This arises because the LHP Initiate is seeking mastery and self-knowledge – these being implicit in such an Initiation. Accordingly, the LHP Initiate sees methods as merely methods; experience as merely experience. Both are used, learned from and then discarded.

Because of this, the LHP is by its nature ruthless – the strong of character win through, the weak go under. There are no "safety nets" of any kind on the LHP – there is no dogma or ideology to rely on, no one to provide comfort and soften the blows, no organization, individual or "Being" to run to when things get difficult and which will provide support and sympathy and understanding. Or which, just as importantly, takes away the responsibility of the Initiate for their deeds.

The LHP breeds self-achievement and self-excellence – or it destroys, either literally, or via delusion and madness. Further, the goal or aim of the LHP is individual specific – it is the raising of that individual to "god-head"; the fulfillment of individual potential and thus a discovery and fulfillment of their unique Destiny. That is, it breeds a unique character, a unique individual. The RHP, on the contrary, is concerned with "idealistic" and thus supra-personal aims – aiding "society", "humanity" and so on: the individual is "re-made" by abstract and impersonal forms.

The LHP by its nature means that its Initiates work mostly on their own. Followers of the LHP are masters of their as yet unmanifest Destiny. And while they may accept guidance and advice, they eschew any form of subservience: they learn for themselves, by their own experience and from their own self-effort. This is crucial to an understanding of the true nature of the LHP. The LHP means this self-reliance, this self-experience, this self-effort, this personal struggle for achievement. The RHP means someone else – some individual, or some authority or some hierarchy – awards or confers upon the RHP Initiate a sign or a symbol of their "progress". That is, the RHP Initiate assumes the role of student, or "chela" – and often that of sycophant. They rely on someone else or something beyond themselves, whereas the LHP Initiate relies only on themselves: their cunning, skill, character, desire, intelligence and so on. The successful LHP Initiate is the individual who learns from their own experiences and mistakes. The RHP Initiate tries to learn from theory – from what others have done.

Essentially, the LHP Initiate is a free spirit, already possessed of a certain willful character, while the RHP Initiate is in thrall to other people's ideas and ways of doing things.

The notion of self-responsibility is, as mentioned above, crucial to the LHP and accordingly any organization which claims to be of the LHP and which does not uphold this in both theory and practice is a fraudulent organization. In practice this means that an organization does not restrict the experiences of its members – it does not, for instance, impose upon them any binding authority which the members have to accept or face "expulsion" just as it does not lay down for them any codes of behaviour or ethics. That is, it does not promulgate a dogma which the members have to accept as it does not require those members to be obedient to what the hierarchy says. There is no "proscription" of certain views, or individuals or other organizations as there is no attempt to make members conform in terms of behaviour, attitudes, views, opinions, expressions or anything else. If there are any of these things, the organization so doing these things is most certainly not an organization of the Left Hand Path even though it may use some of the motifs, symbols and methods of the LHP. Such an organization is instead allied to the RHP in nature – *in the effect it has upon its members.*

In summary, the RHP is soft. The LHP is hard. The RHP is like a comfortable game – and one which can be played, left for a while, then taken up again. The LHP is a struggle which takes years. The RHP prescribes behaviour and limits personal responsibility. The LHP means self-responsibility and self-effort. The RHP requires the individual to conform in certain ways. The LHP is non-restrictive. RHP organizations and "teachers" require the Initiate to conform and accept the authority of that organization/"teacher". LHP organizations and Masters/Mistresses only offer advice and guidance, based on their own experience.

Satanism

As mentioned above, Satanism is a particular LHP. Conventionally, and incorrectly, Satanism is described as "worship of Satan/the Devil".

The word "Satan" originally derived from the Greek word for "an accusation". That is, Satan is an archetype of disruption – the Adversary who challenges the accepted, who deifies – who desires to know. In essence, Satan is a symbol of dynamic motion: the generative or moving force behind evolution, change. In reality, Satan is both symbolic or archetypal, and real. That is, He exists within the psyche of individuals, and beyond individuals.

Satanism is, in part, the acceptance of the necessity of change – of the reality of things like struggle, combat, war, creativity, individual genius, defiance. Of the evolutionary and puritive nature of these things. But Satanism is much more than the acceptance of the reality of these things – of their necessity. It is also the individual seeking to be like Satan – to be Satanic. A true Satanist does not worship some Being called Satan. Rather, a Satanist accepts the reality of Satan (on all levels) and quests to become, in their own life and beyond, a type of Being of the same kind as Satan – that is, to change their own evolution and that of others: to evolve a new type of existence. The existence can be described by what is known as "Satan". This quest is a dynamic and real one, and it means that those who aspire to follow the way of Satanism go further than others who merely follow the LHP. That is, Satanism leads to new areas of being: it goes beyond the "Black Arts" while having its foundation or ground in those Arts. Part of this is a greater esoteric knowledge (e.g. Aeonic Magick) and part in techniques or methods or create a new individual. The Satanist effectively learns to play at being god.

Since Satanism, as described above, involves the individual questing to become like Satan, it is relevant to consider who and what Satan is. Satan is the Prince of Darkness – Master of all that is hidden or secret, both within ourselves and external to ourselves. He is the ruler of this world – the force behind its evolutionary change; the "fire" of life.

He is Lord of Life – of all the sensual delights and pleasures.

He is also "evil" or "dark" or "sinister" – merciless, ruthless, Master of Death. He can and does promote suffering, misery, death. But all these things are impersonal – they are the consequences of life, of change and evolution.

Satan, by His nature, cannot be "bribed" or "propitiated" – and neither can His services be bought, by a "pact" or anything else. He is not interested in such futile things. Thus, there can be no such thing as a "religious" Satanism – the offering of prayers or offerings or promises or whatever *in return* for Satanic favours. Such things imply fear, subservience and those other traits of character Satan despises. Rather, the Satanic approach is to glory in Satanic deeds and chants such like because they are Satanic – because by so doing them there is an exultation, an affirmation and a being like Satan: not because something is "expected" or done out of fear of the consequences. It is by living life, by deeds, that a Satanist becomes like Satan and so evolves to partake of a new and higher existence. Such deeds are those to bring insight, self-discovery, to achieve esoteric knowledge, experience of the "forbidden", of the pleasures of living – and they are also those which change others and the world and which thus can and do bring suffering, misery, death: which are, in short, evil.

Furthermore, Satan is a real Being – He is not simply a symbol, archetypal or otherwise, of certain natural forces or energies. He has life, exists – causes things to occur – external to our own, individual psyche. That is, our individual wills, or even our individual magick, cannot control Him (as the softee imitation Satanists like to believe). However, this "life" is not "human" – it is not bound by a body or even by our causal time and space. Expressed esoterically, it is acausal.

Satan, however, is not alone – that is, He is not the only Dark, sinister Being who affects our world and thus existence. He has a female counter part – a Mistress, Lover, Bride. Esoterically, Her name is Baphomet. She is the Dark Goddess.

Thus, a Satanic Initiate is often described as the lover of one or both of these sinister entities – and a genuine Satanic Initiation may be likened to a ritual copulation with either Satan or Baphomet (where the Priest/Priestess assumes the form of the entity). In genuine Satanism there is no "worship" of Satan (or Baphomet) – but rather an acceptance of Them as friends, lovers (or, in the early stages, sometimes a "father" and "mother" or a brother and sister).

A Satanist thus evolves toward a higher form – and expresses conscious evolution in action. Hence, Satanism is the quintessence of the Left Hand Path.

Evil

It is a mistake, recently promulgated by some, to see the LHP in general and Satanism in particular as merely a body of esoteric knowledge and/or collection of rituals or magickal workings, either of which, or both, may be "dipped into" for personal edification and to provide oneself with an "image".

All LH Paths are ordeals – they involve self-effort over a period of years. They are also dark, and involve the individuals who follow them going to and beyond the limits all societies impose. That is, they are sinister or "evil". They involve real sinister acts in the real world – not a playing at sorcerers or sorceresses.

Certain individuals and certain organizations who claim to belong to the LHP have tried to dispel the "evil" that surrounds the LHP and Satanism – by denying the very real evil nature of these paths. However, what do these imitation Satanists, these posturing pseuds, think Satanism is if not "evil"? If Satanism is not evil, what is? (Or, more precisely, if Satan is not evil, who is?)

The true nature of evil – and thus Satanism and the LHP – has been misunderstood. Evil is natural and necessary – it tests, culls, provokes reaction and thus aids evolution. And to repeat – Satanism is replete with evil: it is evil. Satanists are sinister, evil. They cannot but be otherwise.

Evil, correctly defined, is part of the cosmic dialectic – it is force, which is a-moral: i.e. it is beyond the bounds of "morals". Morals derive from a limited (human – or, rather, pseudo-human) perspective, and a morality is a projection by individual consciousness onto reality. Nothing that is "moral" or immoral exists. All morals are therefore artifice – they are abstractions. Actions, by individuals, which are normally considered as "evil" are things that are done by individuals against others – that is, evil acts are considered as belonging to us, as a species. It is not considered "evil" for a tiger to kill and eat a person: that is natural, in the nature of the tiger. What has been and generally is considered to be evil, in humans, is in general nothing more than instinct – or rather, a feeling, a pre-conscious desire or desires.

Such instinct is natural – the actions which result from it can be either beneficial or not. That is, the actions are not "evil" in themselves. They should not be judged by some artificial abstractions, but rather by their consequences – by their effects, which are either positive or negative. However, they can be positive or negative depending on circumstances: that is, the evaluation of them can vary depending on the perspective chosen. This perspective is usually that of "time". The only correct judgment about a particular act or action is one which takes into account the effects of that action not only in the present but also in the future, and this latter on a vast time-scale. Thus, the judgment concerning such acts is essentially a-personal – it bears little or no resemblance to the emotional effects of that act in the moments of that act or in the immediate moments following that act. (In the symbolic sense – and imprecisely – such judgment could be said to be that of "the gods".)

Real acts of evil are those which are done consciously – and these can be of two kinds. The first are ignorant acts: done from a lack of self-knowledge and usually with no appreciation of their effects beyond the moment. The second are impersonal acts done with a knowledge of the effects beyond that of the moment. The former involve no evaluation beyond the personal feelings; the latter involve an evaluation beyond the personal (although they may still be personal acts – i.e. of benefit to the individual). A Satanic act of evil is of this second kind – they are affective and effective: a participation in the cosmic dialectic. At first, they may not be fully understood – i.e. arise from instinct in the main. But the Satanic intent behind them makes the individual more conscious, more aware of their effects, both personal and supra-personal, thus enabling judgment to be cultivated.

Instinctive acts are not "evil" – they usually derive from immaturity. Evil acts derive from maturity – but immaturity is required to reach this stage. That is, there is a growth. "Morality" tries to stifle instinct and thus restricts growth. Satanic acts of evil in effect redress the balance – and allow real maturity to develop.

The Method is Science, the Aim is Religion

Zbigniew Karkowski

> *"What is good? Everything that heightens the feeling of power in man, the will to power, power itself. What is bad? Everything that is born out of weakness... Pity stands opposed to the tonic emotions which heighten our vitality..."*
>
> *– Friedrich Nietzsche*

It seems to me that today, to be accepted as an innovative composer of serious, contemporary music, all you have to do is to understand what happens on the formal level and then break some of the rules (the same goes for all the other art forms too). It's like most of the creative work done by young composers is nothing else but only a rebellion against the teachers. The so-called art music written today must be taken in large cultural setting as a revolt against certain kinds of tradition. It doesn't have any intrinsic meaning, and as a consequence, in order to understand it, a listener has to have an extensive knowledge of Western culture, and particularly of the trends in Western art music over the last few decades.

This method of composing doesn't carry any meaning in itself. The meaning is instead contained inside a listener with all his preconceived knowledge which the music serves only to trigger. It is impossible that anything created in this way can ever become objective and real or, just as an example, ever be understood by another civilization. It's a closed circuit, and a very limited method of communication, based on artificial presumptions. It's art for the sake of art itself. Composition has become an intellectual game with systems and the formal manipulation of material as its most prominent quality. It has lost contact with reality; it deals with processes that have no adequates in the real world. They are man-made illusions, always relative and very culture-oriented. One talks about composition and compares it often to mathematics – we know that there were different kinds of mathematics developed in different civilizations.

All man-made systems have one thing in common; they are relative and even if sometimes practical, certainly not necessary. The Egyptians had a strong sense of eternity and their idea of numbers was of pure, eternal entities. The Greeks were passionately devoted to the here and now, and never thought about eternity. Their mathematics was mathematics of measurements of things – they created geometry. Western man has a sense of time and change; his addition to mathematics is calculus, the mathematics of change, and quantum theory, the mathematics of chance. It's all fine and maybe rational, and we all know that any system can work. Just think about what sort of absurd systems people believed in, in the ancient past or Middle ages – that the earth was flat, and it ended approximately twenty kilometers outside of the village where you lived – and it all worked. But was this a true reality? No, it was only collective belief in, as it often was and is, a false value. For years now there has been much debating among serious composers and art theorists about conflict of hegemony between formal aspects and content in modern arts. I tell you, this conflict doesn't exist anymore.

In the academic world, formalism won at least 40 years ago. There is also presently a lot of discussion about the crisis with audiences for contemporary art music. I don't think that there is any crisis, and even if there is one, it's certainly on the other side – there is seldom anything to hear anymore. In fact very often when I go to concerts of contemporary music, I don't hear any music at all – all I hear is hard work. In my opinion, some examples of the recent trends in Western art music, like some compositions written in post serial "new complexity" style result in works that are a direct insult to listeners. I mean, you have to think that people who listen to your music are stupid in order to present them like this. The exactness is always a fake. The notation and the graphical aspects of the scores have become more important than the sound of music itself. The original function of notation was to help musicians to orientate themselves while executing a piece.

Even as late as the Baroque era, notation was only a relatively free system of cues and general indications for musicians so that they would not lose themselves during performance. It left space for imagination. With time, notation became more and more important and orthodox; something like a substitution of energy of sound by energy of signs on paper took place. The history of Western art music can be seen as a history of degeneration, and its evil is in essence graphic. It became what it is now: dogmatic constructions for the eye and intellect, small intellectual games that have nothing to do with the reality of sound. And I find it very strange that many composers don't believe anymore that one can say or, what is even more important, change anything by using sound as a medium. You can't be more wrong than that.

When an artist creates a new work, whether it's a new book or poem or painting or piece of music, he presents new information. And what follows with it – new ways to process information. This is a social function. We create options and we have to take responsibility for it. It's very simple, you either have something to say or, if not, you just create more information pollution. And if there is one general thing that one can say about most of the modern composers, it is that they may write well but they often have nothing to say.

All good art has only one purpose – to show man his own true face, and its only prerogative must be the necessity to find out the truth at all costs. The truly evolutionary art must be concerned more with living than creating and must realize that the despair of our culture and civilization can only be defeated by acts of total honesty and a faith in the true condition of all men – perfection and the state of Godhead. I don't believe in thought and intellect, I'm convinced that truth cannot be explained in ordinary logical systems. In fact I see intellect as a barrier preventing us from realizing the true values in our lives. I see it as an inhuman faculty.

The real art communicates before it is understood. It contains the knowledge that all men once had, a knowledge that today is unfortunately often ignored and forgotten. I believe that our life is magical in its essence. The working of magic is a series of actions bringing intention into focus. It's a conscious and active participation in transformation between cause and effect. We know that everything we've ever done and do is intentional, and every intentional act is a Magical act. Not understanding it means human life as a journey from nowhere to nowhere. It is evident that at the core of all the problems of modern man lies his lack of moral purpose and spiritual development.

The Egyptians all believed that they were descended directly from the Gods. For them every man was a sort of God, God in exile. For the mediaeval Church, man was an immortal soul, poised between heaven and hell. With eighteenth-century rationalism it had all disappeared and today man is just a member of a society with a duty to everybody else. I see history as a steady devaluation of the human being. Modern man has lost his destiny, purpose and power, for all the real power is the spiritual power and the tendency of everything that is real is always aspiration towards the God-like. Our mistake is that we lay too much emphasis on the intellect and rationality and we have forgotten that we are in fact Gods.

I think that the prevalence of the ideas of strain and suffering and all the negative messages incoming from the arts today are an effect of this moral degeneration. It's only a game in the exploitation of neuroses and paranoid states that were created and induced in people by our sick civilization in the first place. We are being conditioned. Consider the majority of messages coming from popular culture – in its films, books, music and lyrics, young people are being told that the only future they can expect is the future of depression, unemployment, heroin addiction and more and more crime. This is ridiculous and these are the options young people are being given today. And the art music deals nearly always with only intellectual models. Intellect is the secret of our tremendous material progress but also the cause of our spiritual downfall.

I believe that the most important fact about man is his ability to change himself. And magic is the art of causing change to occur in conformity with will. Everybody's life is the road to self-realization, to understanding the truth. Forgetting it and not trying to understand equals dying. For me music has a definite function. I see it as a tool for heightening consciousness, increasing intensity of the mind and ultimately a means of realizing God within ourselves. It should create and amplify the moments of greater intensity of life, the feeling of strength and power. It should open up the sensitivity to this common force that we call God and make everybody aware of it.

I believe that all the individuals who have ever created something of value did so not as inventors but as catalysts of existing forces. They are the ones who simply know how to look and understand. And so my main reason for working, composing music, is not to create pieces all the time but to remain ready when I can. One has to be ready for the moments when all conditions are perfect, when one is in harmony with the powers and then use it in the most efficient way. One has to be awake and aware. Nearly all the problems existing in our society today are self-inflicted and the reason for them comes from the feeling of unreality of our lives that most people have. The remedy is simple, just wake up. Chance favors those who are prepared.

To be an artist is first of all to realize this truth, to overcome the common mediocrity of our conditioned society and ultimately to strive consciously towards a state of absolute spiritual enlightenment. We do it all the time in our dreams; the trick is to be able to do it while we are awake. For some years now I have been interested in creating music that can be appreciated by beings without any cultural knowledge, music that could be called primordial, archetypical or ritual in the sense of ritual as the evolution of the individual through sacred time and space. Music directed not to the intellect but to all the senses, music whose only function is the total integration of those sacred energies and forces that exist latent in all of us.

In my concerto for percussion and large orchestra, a sonic ritual influenced by a study of *Rhythmajik*, an ancient Semitic Alef-Bet knowledge of the practice of ritual drumming, I concentrate on the research of three parameters – elements: the drum as a magical, power instrument, metabolic properties of repetitive rhythms and the physical power of sound in itself.

In many African languages the word for drum signifies both the physical instrument and various forms of communication between entities, including even telepathy. The drum is also the only instrument that has a direct physical counterpart within our bodies. Our ear canal, ending with the tympanic membrane (eardrum) is the archetype of the drum, of which all physical drums are copies. So it is no coincidence that the drum is the most commonly used ritual instrument in all cultures, the traditional instrument of the shaman or magician, the tool for communication with forces and spirits inside and outside of us. All over the world, amongst primitive societies, the beating of drum patterns is used for invocations and bringing forth of powers.

Through the use of rhythmic patterns (a specific order of vibrations) the participants' vision is focused and conditioned by the rhythmic pulsation of the synapses triggered by their ear-drums and other parts of their bodies. Through this process the awareness of the participants is harmonized with the higher consciousness of the specific powers invoked. Ritual music (and until quite recent times all music had a ritual function – art music is a very young phenomenon) was and is used in many pre-technical cultures to create and affect changes in people and their environment. Throughout the world there exist various traditions of ritual beat patterns. By using them one summons forth thunder, rain or sun, one engineers the brain, the body and its hormones. These powerful beats change the entire metabolic regulator systems in our bodies. Drum sounds are often used for healing of various diseases and inducing trance states. And it really happens; the inherent rhythms and frequencies of sound do physically reconstruct our reality.

In all ritual music the hypnotic aspect is achieved mainly through repetition. Repetitive rhythms gain their power through the fact that they can fuse the discrete events with the continuum (actually all continuous sounds are made up of discrete events), that is to say they can induce the experience of the inversions of duration (short seems long, long seems short) which are symptomatic of trance states. Because of the drum's construction and method of playing, the hydraulic (physical) aspects of sound take precedence over the neural. Its sub-harmonic frequencies affect all and everybody. Even the neurologically deaf are susceptible to the vibrations. The physical properties of the drum sound are very different to those of the other instruments in the orchestra.

A very important aspect of acoustic phenomena are the overtones of sounds. What is commonly referred to as overtones are the harmonic progressions which naturally occur when any given mass is sounded. In Western art music where the tempered tuning is accepted, these overtones are consciously controlled by means of reduction or even elimination in the instrument's construction. Traditional, classical music (and most of its instruments) works around a body of very specified, refined sounds – sounds that for the most part are separate from the sounds of the world – pure and musical. In our culture there has always been a sharp distinction between "music" and "noise".

Well, to make it clear, the music is sound that you like and the noise is a sound that you don't like or "understand". It's subjective. In reality all sounds are nothing else but the vibration of materials. Sound is a presence of energy (pressure) vibrating through space, always at the constant speed of 760 m.p.h. We form sound by applying energy to some mass/material which in turn transforms and propagates this energy into the surrounding medium (air). Since the work of H.L.F. von Helmholtz from 1863, *Die Lehre von den Tonempfindungen als physiologische Grundlage für die Theorie der Musik*, it has been known to Western science that sound is a manifestation not of linear waves, but spherical zones of pressure propagating in space from the sound source. To describe the variations in sound pressure with time, three qualities must be distinguished: how rapidly they vary – frequency (rhythm), their density or how great a pressure they produce – amplitude (pitch), and the starting points – phase (timbre).

These zones propagate by the process of vibration in the air, which in turn cause not only our eardrum but our entire body to vibrate too and respond to sound. The knowledge that we react to incoming sound not only with our ears is generally ignored but has profound consequences. Each human organ has a keynote frequency which according to the phenomenon of EMI (Electromagnetic Interference) and physical principles of resonance can be affected and activated. Modern biochemists, physicists and various spiritual leaders all agree that at the molecular level of reality, our bodies and everything around us, our whole universe, are systems of vibrating atomic particles.

Vibrations in the visible spectrum vary between 390 trillion and 780 trillion Hz (cycles per second) while the spectrum of human hearing vibrates between approximately 20-20000 Hz. Cells in the ear and throughout the human body vibrate at much lower frequencies that rarely exceed 1000 Hz. For example, physicists have shown that the earth vibrates at a fundamental frequency of 8 Hz. This is known as the Schumann resonance, and it is a function of the speed of electromagnetic radiation divided by the circumference of the earth. The alpha frequency (state of deep relaxation) of brain waves is also in the 8 Hz range. The entire body as a total system vibrates at the fundamental rate of approximately 7.8 to 8 Hz, the pulse rate in the human body has a frequency between 0.6 and 1.7 cycles, heart apex contractions 0.3 cycles, etc., etc.

Whatever the vibratory spectrum, we have to view our cells, our senses and our surroundings as vibratory transformers. We all know of the phenomenon of resonance or sympathetic vibration. It occurs when you activate and put in vibration any given mass, all other masses which have the same keynote frequency will spontaneously start to vibrate too. The feeling of sickness some of us experience while traveling in a car or on a plane is caused by certain sub-frequencies generated by the engines and triggering different organs in our body by means of resonance. Science shows us that all individual atoms and molecules have vibration as their fundamental characteristics and are known to be resonant systems.

There is a lot of research on the scales of biological rhythms (vibrations) in humans and all the matter in the universe, much of it directed towards applications in military areas. As medical and biochemical knowledge increase, frequency and pulsation appear to be one of the most crucial metabolic stabilizers. Sound is a very powerful sensory manipulator and can even be used as a weapon. The French police now use ultrasonic transducers beaming out two phased waves of frequencies for crowd control during riots and demonstrations. But as we learn more about the physical properties of sound, we also discover new facts about the true nature of our universe. These facts, once fully understood and realized, will change the course of our civilization.

As demonstrated in the work on cymatics (the structure and dynamics of vibration and the studies of patterns evoked by sound) there are specific structural arrangements corresponding to every variety of tone. A Swiss scientist, Dr. Hans Jenny, and a German physicist, Ernst Chladni, have devoted their lives to studying the interrelationship of frequencies with matter, by rendering vibrations into physical forms. They scattered sand, liquids, powders and metal fillings on specially constructed discs and obtained precise frequency stimuli by using calibrations of a vibrating crystal. As they started to experiment and change the frequencies they applied, the patterns on the discs changed too. Many of the patterns took on organic shapes, very similar to the forms we find in our world.

So it seems that all the forms existing in the universe: plants, trees, minerals, animals, even our bodies have their shape created by resonating to some specific frequencies in nature. *In a very real sense then, at the core of our physical existence we are composed of sound, and all manifestations of forms in the universe are nothing else but sounds that have taken on visible form.* The music must become aware of the subtleties of its effects.

There is no doubt that the body metabolism functions primarily via a combination of electrical frequencies, pulse rates and biochemical hormones. The brain is dependent on input. There is nothing else but sound, all that exists is vibration. My goal is to expand music until there is nothing else but music. If an idea can be proposed, it can also be realized. Nothing that's ever said is final; assume that there are always other possibilities. Where language ends, music begins.

"I can foresee a music that is beyond good and evil."
F. Nietzsche

With inspirational thanks to Z'EV, Genesis P-Orridge,
Robert Anton Wilson, Friedrich Nietzsche and Aleister Crowley.

Demonic Poetry: i

Fetish 23

WHISPERS STAIN

Feeding on the scraps of society
Feeding, fucking ass
Vaseline moon drop
Streets and rain
Whisper blue stain
Junkies and jerks
It comes around
Falling down
Grains (to the ground)
And the rest still
To bleed
The best of mediocrity
Read
Humane insane
Fistfuck
The light's on
Red
Blue
White
The light's on
Move
Move
Move on...
Asshole
For in scraps of society
Skyline
Fast polluting seed
Falls in spurts
Of 42nd alarm juice mixers
And oiled black jive
Drives... fast machine gun proofed
And rain
Blue whisper stain

It's no game
No game
No game
True blue
And the blood
Move
Move
Move on asshole

SCENE II

I paint this stream
Celluloid
I paint this scream
Come and go
I paint this shatter dream
... Unfold
Grandeur l'Amerique... toi
Puissance pays perdue... moi
Pouri île noir... vois
Focus out in cuts through
Spotlight
Sharp bright
Screw
Ships are goin' down
Ships are goin' down down down
Sell the crew

Le pays
La gloire
O grandeur
O grandeur
La peur populace
Take it
Go for it
Take it
Go for it
Running time race
Every creed credit card

Call Chase
Manhattan face
I gaze
I dollar

I dime
I fucker
I I crime
Und Gold Fleisch
Und ficken heiss
Und Geld Schweiss
Ficken Fleisch
Und komme komme
Und komme komme
Und komme komme
The ship's going down
The ships going down
Every creed
Every need
Every credit card face
Shadow chase
In a closet
In an empty pool
In a bombed out shelter
After World War III
In this stream Celluloid

In this scream
Come and go
In this shattered dream
... Unfold
O Grandeur
Puissance pouvoir
O peur la gloire
O la putain pudique
Wir rechnen die letzten Tage
Stellen hochstens noch
Ein paar ausgemergelte fragen
Sterben Reich und Stark
Gold Gold Gold
Und komme

Gold Gold Gold
Wir kommen
Gold Gold Gold
Geil und stark
Ships are goin' down
Ships are goin' down down down

MEET THE I

Making realities real
... Relative
All that meets the eye
... The I
Breaking ice
When everything shifts
Reflects
Turning around
Memories of past yet to come
Clear and recording
Shade lineaments
Silent tracing back
Contours... Tracing back

Continuously contact
Futile... Futility drives
A car
A movie
A paper bill attraction
Real... relative
Reality... Countdown construction
All that meets the eye
I meat
Come around
When everything's a part
Of the rest
In peace... Decorations
Modern ornaments and
The kingdom come
Come in the trees
Drunk shining water colours

... Call us
Guilt shimmering self approval
Beauty ride
... European citizen
Relatively present
Meets the eye
I still round...
Shifting the film
Of past yet to come
Real... Relative reality

EDEN EYE

Hall echo decay
Of flesh sacrificed
For the common good
God dog
Burning through brain
Of short-circuits

Recorded backwards up
On our previous trash... Collected
A Star
Lighten up the night of deprivation
Depraved shining innocence
Depraved young flesh
Guilt stained fertility
Bible
Anus penetratio
Moon descending in blood
The mouth giggles
A second coming
Madridden the eye
The mirror of our dreams undreamt
Wolf howling
Turn in sequences
Burn crosses of the clan
Screaming universe

Remember the past
Like we will
Laugh your labour
Succeeding through fire tongues
Of love
Bells resounding
Distant gathering of solitude
And ignorance
Demand the weak to speak
Speak
Humble servant
Speak
Your selfopposed darkness
Speak
The madman smiles
Long the night will be

Long will it take
While the seeing
Move
Move
Move
Decades starting to show
Structures unveiled
Phallos lunares
Bells resounding
In halls of decay
Sanctified for the common good
The mirror of our forbidden dreams
Eden
Young fresh naked
Smile of blood
Raising raising
New time come
New time come
Raising

Lucifer-Hiram

The Return of the World's Master Builder

Ben Kadosh

This text was first presented to the public in 1906 e.v., and has to my knowledge never been translated before. Carl W. Hansen, or Kadosh *as he called himself, was a Danish parallel to Theodor Reuss. In possession of some 300 Masonic titles, including charters for Mizraim-Memphis, Fraternitas Lucis Hermetica and the O.T.O., one could doubt his sincerity in matters occult, but here is the evidence of the contrary. The text* Lucifer-Hiram *deals with the misinterpretation of the nature of Satan, and the intention of this scripture was – as he also explains in it – to clear the reputation of Lucifer and give him back his title as Ruler and Creator of this World. Truly Satanic in its context, it is in many ways "before its time". So here, for the first time, to my knowledge, Ben Kadosh can present his message to the world outside of Denmark.*

– Fr. GCLO (translator and editor)

INTRODUCTION

A time of breakthrough is at hand! The time of material and spiritual fractions has come! The philosophy of the ancients is wrestling with modern thinking! And the ancient knowledge in the same way with the present day material teaching.

The continent is fermenting! Strong movements are going on in the depth! Partly political, partly material and partly of a spiritual nature!

Beneath the spiritual movements are those of a religious character. There are different types regarding their break-out or starting point: that source or those sources to which they owe their origin.

They can be divided into, 1) those who take, as starting point, the ordinary religious perceptions, and because of that are rooted in a broader, deeper or, as more often seen, a very superficial interpretation of this, and 2) those who take a new point of view as starting point and basis, and 3) those who take the ancient sources and find a firm foundation in these.

From the first category spring the different sects. From the next, the forerunners of "free thinking", or those which, for one reason or another, do not wish to be bound to any religious perception. Such a group are for instance the "Humanists".

Under the third category are the Orientalists, whose task is of a religious and aesthetic cultural nature, the so-called "OCCULTISTS" and "FREEMASONS"... As a link between this and the previous category are the "Spiritualists", who without using magic in the ordinary sense, claim to create contact with an immaterial and disembodied spirit-sphere. The spiritual beings there are thought to be constituted only by dead souls and not, as in magic: of higher, except for incarnates, intelligent beings or elementals, natural principles.

Occultism has its foundation in the acquisition and practice, due to an interest, of the ancient magic or the practice of secret inherited teaching, once called "Sorcery". As many no longer regard magic, in the original meaning of this word, as something impossible or supernatural, but as the most natural, possible thing in the world, as for so many other things, if only we fully manage to investigate nature and follow its laws, ways and paths, and not consider them impossible to learn.

The term "Sorcery", which was used almost ironically about magic, is therefore erased.

Freemasonry, that is to say the original ESOTERIC, constitutes the ceremonial gesture and act of magic, or the form under which one is initiated, and the form under which the dogmas of magic are studied. Besides that, it is a form of a secret, ESOTERIC, religious cult of old Gods or Supreme Principles of Nature, THE CREATIVE FORCES OF THE WORLD. Freemasonry is thereby the keeper of the ancient ESOTERIC cults and teachings, holding their most valuable property, which is also the MAIN task of Freemasonry.

It is the teachings of the ancients – THE EXOTERIC – which constituted the framework for the formation of dogmas in the Christian church.

All that the occidental church possesses, of dogmas etc., is "borrowed" or, to make it clear, "taken" from oriental, so-called "pagan" sources. It possesses nothing that it could rightfully, in this direction, call its own by originating from itself.

SATAN AND LUCIFER, inside the oldest dogmas of the Christian church, are therefore absolutely alien to the Christian TEACHING, as to any EXOTERIC religion. They both belong to the ESOTERIC cult and magic, as also their significance, role and appearance is absolutely different from that which Christian interpreters state. The teaching about them can be regarded as the extract of the essence of a secret teaching of the ancients.

JEVE is the old Pan on Israelitic territory.

The idol of the Israelitic and Tartarian SHEITAN, the Master and Majesty of the Dragon, the highest expression of the creative forces of the universe, is to be sought in China and Egypt.

SHEITAN is, inside the Chinese Esoteric Freemasonry, the very image of the WATCHING, DISEMBODIED CREATOR OF THE UNIVERSE.

LUCIFER is the "SUM", or EGO, of the material nature, the creating LOGON AND FORCE! Both personal and impersonal or individual and non-individual, as any other thing in nature, and as we want it. In fact he is the thing and the individual in third person. If one is in possession of certain keys or knowledge, one can unchain him, evoke or call him forth, but if not in possession of these, one must be content with having him in spirit, disembodied, according to the written descriptions of him.

LUCIFER in his own image is not the untasteful character some have turned him into, but a true physical reality, though of a semi-material nature.

As the creative force in the immaterial, abstract, disembodied but functional nature deserves consideration and exploration, so does energy in form of matter transforming into life – that, to us humans, is the most positive, and a substitute of the abstract, functional part of nature – also deserve attention.

LUCIFER is the potency of force in living matter, in an individually personified form, the "Sum" of the creating nature.

As propaganda for this Sum or Ego of the creating nature, is this little writing of agitation published, the task therefore being; the working towards enthronement of the Pan-Ideals and Pan-Substitutes of the ancients, springing from an inner comprehension of them and their value, and with that the acquisition of them – and their worship.

The dissemination of the knowledge and the heightening of the occult, ESOTERIC Freemasonry's *Lucifer-Hiram* will thus constitute the main task of this propaganda text, and with that, the recruiting of new proselytes. A task that deserves a worthy interest.

In hope that this goal, by the assistance of equally-minded persons, can succeed and result in the formation of a closed circle, almost under form of a new *esoteric* Order of Freemasons, which would fully be dedicated to a cult equal to that of the ancients, is left to the consideration and good-will of the readers.

To occultists and other seekers after secret knowledge I am, for further information, especially when it comes to the re-discovery of the mentioned keys, to be found personally in my home at any time.

Ben Kadosh, June 1906

EVOCATION

"Hear, I call You, mighty Pan, strong God of all Forces in the Universe, confining in You; Heaven, Sea and Earth"!

"Equally Queen of all things"!

"Eternal Fire, flowing through Your limbs and Your body"!

"Come to me good Genius, Source of Movement, drifting around, while you yourself is borne on a glittering skin, stretched between the seasons"!

"Source of all Creation"!

"Divine ecstasy"!

"Media that heats and brings to life the Soul"!

"Living amongst the Stars, You regulate the Symphony of the Universe, as it is heard in Your melodic songs"!

"You, who come through Dreams, Visions and sudden Terror, as mortals experience, You who like to dwell amongst the rocks, springs and fields of the earth, utterly absorbed in Your meditations"!

"Explorer of all Things"!

"You who dwell to hear the Echo of Your eternal Harmony"!

"God, Creator of all and everything during your wandering"!

"You, who are invoked by many Names"!

"Sovereign Lord of the World, who gives Growth, Fertility and Light to all Things, and who lives in the mountain valleys and the inner of the caves"!

"Disgusting in Your Wrath"!

"True Jupiter with *double* Horns"!

"It is You, who created the Earth"!

"When You extend Your Powers over the Sea, the Ocean obeys You, and that exists not... Even Fire and Air – which does not recognize Your Majesty"! All Elements follow the way You have prescribed for them, in spite of the instability of their nature, and give unto Man the nourishment he needs."

"Accept, holy Source, for the sake of our desire, our prayers and our incense, and do so, that we may end our lives in happiness, and raise us above that which frightens us"!

(Orpheus Hymn)

PROLOGUE

Pan:

"Overalt, hvor en tyr bygge,
Skjult af Dunkelhed og Skygge,
Uden Selskab af en Ven,
I det enlige, det Tomme,
I det tavse vil jeg komme"!
"Hvor nu paa den fælles Vej,
En sig skiller fra de andre,
I mit Navn, for tavs at vandre,
Er tilstede hos ham Jeg"!

(From Ludvig Hejberg's *Gudstjeneste*)

Pan:

"Wherever one dares build,
hidden by darkness and shadow,
without company of a friend,
in the lonesome, the empty,
in the silence I will come"!
"Where on the common path, one stands out by himself,
to my name, silent to wander, I dwell with him"!

MOTTO: "The dead shall rise again!"

All over and in all is Pan, the eternal "Sum" of nature. And this Pan is living, no longer dead, as most humans have turned him into. "Pan is resurrected"! Resurrected from that death oracles and humans have sunk him into.

The IDOL OF THE GODS, THE GOD OF GODS has returned to repossess his original place as front figure! Now his time has come, to fight the superseder and the assumption – and its agitators – that he is dead, as numerous elder and younger historical writers tell – quotation – in this way:

"Under the rule of Emperor Tiberius, the victory was announced for the new faith from Galilee. A voice whispering along the shore of the Agæic Sea: "The Great Pan is dead." So goes the story. A quotation which differs or diverges very little with the different authors.

An Oracle with the crowd of believers and the ancient highest "pagan" being of nature, confronted with the highest "christian" being of nature, could it be that prejudistic and fearsome men had killed Pan? In a way! When they couldn't do it in a more emphatic way, the result was that Pan is still alive, though withdrawn from the public scene.

Thus he is alive today – and has kept on living, without being, as pretended: dead – and with him, the faith and knowledge about him still exists inside a small group, now when the large crowd has deserted him. The members of this small group are to be sought amongst civilized as well as uncivilized nations, so also within the "highly civilized" Europe.

Pan is alive and will keep on living or existing. The idol of the Gods, and their Father, cannot die! Neither church, science or a cynical crowd can kill him.

He is the surviving "All" in personification, raised above the changeable, and finally by the nature of his being, becomes, where everybody else – including all the gods of the reformatory – ceases to exist. As such, he is raised even above the Nazarean Jesus God, taken by the christians as their special idol.

The teaching of Christ that God is love, or the loving Father in human perception, does not contain any concept of God, in the true sense. It is rather a concept of Love in extended version, to fit human conception, and only gives a vague and incomplete image of the entirety and nature of the deity. The MIND and not the HEART – at least not solely – is that which shall comprehend the image of God.

The nature of the true image of God is mainly Coldness and has only little to do with human emotions, and the product of them. WHAT IS GOD, IS NOT MAN, AND THE OTHER WAY AROUND!

The answer must be to turn away from being human, if we want to comprehend the image of God in its true REALITY, and not behind a veil of illusion. Although without being deluded or at the risk of drowning in the bottomless.

Away from being human – towards the animalistic, although considered inferior – if we want to find the image of God in its most satisfactory and real state, even though it sounds absurd. We don't want to wind up on a lesser spiritual and intellectual level than we were before the conversion, but on a higher level, which implies that we consider the animals in another way from what we are used to.

THE SLOUGH OF THE ANIMAL IS THE CLOTHING OF PAN AND HALF OF HIS OUTER BEING.

The side we often prefer to consider is the material and physical, which is considered morally objectional. What we here have to consider is the PSYCHIC, the psychic life and especially the psychic Powers which are working through the animal, and often give an impression of something strange, mysterious, often demonic in its being, attitude and outer appearance. It also reveals their intelligence, which is; that they know about and master their inner Powers, and understand the use of them. With that, we have to admit that their intelligence in many other ways are inferior to that of man.

Away from humanity brings us, considering the above, not toward the animal in its inferiority, but towards what we can call its increased intelligence. This intelligence makes them seem strange, mysterious and demonic in appearance, as it is the case with the He-goat and the Snake.

The demonic is only an image of increased intelligence in the appearance.

This Force is apparent in inferior animals – as in the case of the Serpent's Glance – it suggests the presence of a Talent or Force that works as a tool to aid the beast, against its inferiors. It also suggests – by the presence of this special Ability or Force – a side of the animal, where it is close to the divine mystery, which alone has its source in the use of psychic powers.

Notice that the animal is closing in on the divine mystery, and formulates the same; but it is not the divine mystery, neither in the shape of a snake or a he-goat, By the he-goat I mean an Alpine *ibex*.

Should one decide to dedicate oneself to the mentioned intelligence and talent, which are inside the animals, or form a cult for their worship, as is the case with the above mentioned animals, it must be one's own decision. But if so, it is done from their religious comprehension. One wouldn't do it without an adequate reason, which could be, and is, of a highly intellectual standard, and has its roots or springs from, a pleasant feeling of satisfaction, which creates spiritual peace in us and our surroundings.

Another view on the animal, other than being of inferior intelligence and morality than man, has to be taken into consideration. This has its justification and is of much more value than the ordinary consideration of the animals. Considering that there is something hidden and perfect in the animal, is of much more value than the ordinary reflection on the presence of something – from physical deformations – imperfect.

Here is the animal superior to Man, and becomes a kind of Idol to Him. The snake shows its superior intelligence – as mentioned – through its glance. With this animal it is a special ability, besides being its vigour with its outward rays, the magnetic, demonic rays in the look of the creature.

The intelligence of an animal can always be detected in its look. Without the look, an animal would – as also with humans – lose its demonic appearance.

In the eye of an animal, as for humans, we can see the soul of its intelligence, which always reveals itself as either a force of nature; heat and cold, or as a primitive form, and with the individual it is penetrating; in individualized form too.

The things which cause the demonic appearance of the animal, is then determinative for the creature's demonic individuality in its entirety.

To make this Fluid of Force appear as a special ability, the creature – in this case the snake – has to be conscious of its presence and use, and in this case it is so. The snake only uses its fluid, by pointing its rays towards the chosen prey, when it is aware that it gains an advantage by using it. The Snake is aware of the presence of this fluid of so high a nature and potency. And the same when it comes to the use of it. But by this, it must also be aware of its superior intelligence. The superior intelligence is only the realization of the presence of the Power, and the awareness of its use.

Exactly the same, though in another way, is visible in the appearance of the horned he-goat – the Alpine ibex. The horns, with their proud and provocative erection or beautiful reclining shape, and the dark face of the creature, is that which adds up to its demonic appearance. With that comes the consciousness of the animal, of its outer dark magnetism or radiation, which radiates from it, and is apparent in its conduct. Its knowledge about how to use this, its natural gift, is sufficient evidence of its special intelligence.

Here also, the look is of major importance in making up the entirety. The above stated is only an outer reflection, very imperfect, and of no great value, but necessary before approaching the inner aspects.

Here, as in all other matters, we are facing a riddle to solve, we instantly judge it by the outer appearance and weigh it against our dogmas. The expression of the increased intelligence is that which can be seen in the dark face of the Pan-Ideal, its demonic physiognomy, the face of the He-goat,

The He-goat בא, BA's corpus is the expression of the primitive nature of the PAN-IDOL. As mentioned, Pan is the "Sum" of the individualized All, in its most ancient image and shape. The demonic face of PAN, the potent expression in his dark face, is what makes him a God, and the highest amongst the Gods – the Idol of the many various sects.

Only this or that which made him – the force which penetrates and glows like a fire inside him – is above him. That force, which created him and is as a fire within him, which radiates from him as kind of magnetism, is he himself a part of.

PAN is the great Master Builder of the Universe and a cosmic living NATURAL FIRE, flowing and kindling all. THE SOURCE OF ALL LIFE is his Father, that which no language has a pronounceable word for.

PAN is a vehicle for his Father, which is why the Father only is known through PAN. PAN becomes the very image of his Father, and the existence of the Father is only due to PAN. PAN expresses the Father and thus becomes the expression of the unpronounceable.

PAN is the highest known, "the unknown Father's" visible image, in whom – like a stove – is lit an eternally burning NATURAL FIRE.

The belief in – and the cult of – the PAN-IDOL is thus not so much a belief in or cult of an outer figure, but more a worship and adoration of an eternal, hidden, mighty or all-potent force in nature. It is expressed through the PAN-IDEAL as a superhuman representation of man, seen from the hidden traditional; concrete or determined dogmas and under an ethical view on the matter. IN THE DISGUISED FACE OF PAN THE TRUE IDEAL OF GOD IS TO BE SOUGHT.

The disguised – the demonic background – in the dark appearance of Pan, must be compared to the glowing fire inside him. The disguised is a demonic reality. The demonic creates the mask of disguise.

That this mask of disguise appears demonic to us, comes from the resistance we meet when trying to force something open, from which we have been locked out. The alienation and incomprehensibility of the higher planes, will always take a demonic shape in the moment we try to break the chain which holds it together – for the sake of study.

The demonic face is dark and often also full of wrath. The light seems far away from the demonic, though it is created from that.

All in all, the image of God becomes a dark ideal and not a bright, human one, as some have turned it into.

In the physiognomy of the snake, the demonic appears in its outer reflection, in shape of energy, namely the magnetism in its glance which paralyzes the movements of a chosen prey. In difference from the he-goat, where the entirety of the disguised face, its dark and mysterious outer magnetism – even though the glance also plays an important role – made or created the demonic.

After this description of the physiognomy of PAN, and that which is expressed through it, it would be proper to describe the shape of the idol in its entirety.

PAN, the roman "Jupiter", has this appearance.

His head is that of an Alpine ibex, with the beautiful reclining horns. His face is that of a he-goat, with a thin beard on his chin covering the chest. The entire body and its limbs are hairy, and on his back are two spread-out wings. The symbol of the creating force of nature is erect and enormous in his lap, while on his body is a scarf strewn with stars. On his behind are drawings of the rivers, streams, trees and the different forms of labor. His feet are cloven hooves alike those of a goat. He is supported by a long, crooked wand, signifying his departure and goal, and in his right hand he holds his flute, with the seven pipes, signifying the tones of the seven archaic spheres.

This idol stands on a cube as a symbol of the Earth, which has been given and is subject to him.

This is the image of Pan in its entirety, according to the description of the ancients. Exactly worthy a God! Nature, with its ability and organ to create, made out in this image! The "Sum" of the surviving ALL, the highest image of the Gods or the expression of them, the image of the World's Master Builder Genius HIRAM and DEMIURGON! And then in its entirety not an image of a single being or ONE, but of a duality, two opposite elements. From the fight between these opposites, all creation springs.

Thus PAN becomes, next to his ethical highness, the expression of an antagonism or fight in nature, and his cult is then not only the cult of a dualistic principle or duality, linked to the understanding of the principle of creation, but also the cult of antagonistic elements or principles in nature.

This duality springs not only from that which PAN expresses; the creativity of the all-nature, but has its source in the very BEING OF PAN, the way his nature combines the outer dark vehicle with the inner spark of fire.

As a principle of antagonism, PAN becomes the "material wall", the underground of matter, the basis of reality. He is conscious of the material media. The life in the stone or the resistance of dead matter against so called "organic" life.

Or, on a greater scale: PAN's outer, dark vehicle, with its dark magnetism, resisting the work of the inner fire, but at the same time nurtures it by changing nature or efficacy.

All in all: a glorious image of the work in nature.

As the dark outer vehicle makes up the largest or known part of the Pan image, it is natural first to notice the principle of antagonism, the opponent, in the outer appearance and not in the inner. And if we finally behold the inner, even then will it be colored too much by the outer appearance – for certain reasons – until we can see it in its true color.

The case is, that there exists a material darkness bound to the "material wall" or underground. Above this, there is an immaterial darkness, a cosmic Abyss, "the infinite bottomless", wherein the Light or NATURAL FIRE is begotten, the fluid of primitive force. And this "infinite bottomless" and "the material wall" are, in the same way as force and matter, very strongly connected. The natural fire is only an outcome of the interaction between these two elements, as they by their nature are very difficult to keep apart, not to mention defining them separately.

Thus is the true antagonism or battle fought between the raw Force and the Matter, and the fight between Fire and Matter becomes of less importance. The fight between Force and Matter is followed by a fight between Spirit and Matter, or the Material World. The fight between Force and Matter, wherein life is begotten and finds its destruction, is not only fought very hard, but with a certain consideration from both sides, which is not likely to be found outside the great All-Nature.

All over where life springs forth, there will be a consciousness inside or conjoined with it, and where there is a consciousness there will also be a thinking mind, a Seat of the Spirit.

From the dark "demonic" outer of the PAN-IDOL and from his position as the image of the principles of antagonism in nature, connected with his apparent obscurity, comes that bigotry-sects with their followers, have turned him into a "Devil"-Idol. Though they have taken him to be, or claimed him to be, a "Devil"-idol, he is not.

PAN's "demonic" appearance is only a form of special energy of an enormous Nature and Effect, and which, as a kind of increased intelligence, is only the expression of higher awareness. The dark glance, the increased intelligent appearance, is what partly creates the demonic image. The higher states of a life in awareness is often fervently connected with the understanding or knowledge of one's abilities. With that, also the value of one's limbs or tools (organs) and the use of them. Let it be noticed that a life in awareness, on the higher planes, is mainly defined by this word: Being.

The responsibility for causing damage, made by acts pointed outward, thus becomes invalid.

Human laws and human hindrances are only valid to mankind, and cannot be used on something raised above human level.

The ordinary man's pity for his neighbor only exists in human beings and is adapted to their evolution and needs, but cannot be transferred to a Divine, Highest Being, the All-Creating Lord, to whom the single individual is an unimportant factor under ordinary circumstances.

Nature makes its own laws and borders, regardless of interference from the hand or thought of Man.

Regarding PAN as an expression of the creating ability and organ of Nature, his cult and image in this shape is not a cult of animalistic inferiority, but, as is clearly shown herein, a cult of Nature and the Beauty therein. A cult of the principle of fertility, under which considerations the apparently ugly in the image of the PAN-IDOL becomes invalid.

The ugly or obscene, the ordinary animalistic, is not purely objectionable, but has its aesthetic sides too. It depends on how we consider a thing and what value we ascribe to it, if it is going to be objectionable to oneself or others.

The symbol or organ of the creating ability of nature can be considered obscure, but it isn't. The same when it comes to the naked and very hairy body of PAN. To that I can say, that an aesthetic view of the animal in its obscurity, is of more value than an aesthetic view of the animal in its perfection, and of much more value than a vicious view of the animal because of its obscurity and raw naked body. It was created thus by nature's hand, and relates to a certain lack of physical-material things.

In PAN, people wanted, and still want, to see the image of a medieval – and until this present day – "Devil", Diabolus, if that is so that one believes in the existence of such a being. I allow myself to quote the writer C. Kohl from his book: *Satan and his cult*.

> *The great PAN was resurrected (after an oracle and the superseders had killed him) as Satan in Christianity. It is he who shows his ugly face in the prosecution of the Heretics and in the annals of the Witch-trials, and which to this present day is not forgotten!*
>
> *Almost from its birth, the church (the Christian) was surrounded by a dangerous (to the church) web of systems, schools and sects, who all wanted to introduce to Christianity, a dualism alike that of the Persians. These teachers created for most parts the so-called GNOSTICISM (from GNOSIS: realization), which meant: the religion of the perfected, and had in it the pure ideas, which were incomprehensible to the masses. Common to all of them was the opposition between Spirit and Matter, Good and Evil, a higher divine world, with divine forces or Aeons, and a lesser visible world created by the DEMIURGE, the fallen soul of the world. The evil principle SATAN, SATANAEL or SATANAKI is of major importance herein, greater than ever before. He becomes the original, independent principle, equal to the Good, and he becomes the true Creator of the material nature. The belief turns into a dualism, wherein Good and Evil, Light and Darkness struggles, like the Persian AHURAMAZDA with ANGRO-MAINIUS or AHRIMAN and as the Egyptian HORUS with SUTI.*

It is of interest to study this quotation a little closer, to see if it fits with PAN, and then how close or distant this model is. As the writer Kohl truthfully states, Gnosticism was the teaching which – by the formation of the christian church – was the foremost and therefore the first to influence, as well as adopt elements from it (the church), which is why it is worth to examine this teaching a little closer.

GNOSTICISM was constituted – as noticed above – by a number of sects or teachers, who – after becoming established – grew strong under the boom of christianity, and as a kind of counter-weight to this, depending on the degree of which it had influenced or adopted elements from the christian faith.

GNOSTICISM – derived from the Greek GNOSIS, indicates Knowledge and Awareness – as it appeared at the time of the Nazarean Jesus, was no pure teaching, but a mixture of different religious perceptions. It was no less diverging in its entirety from the teaching of Jesus, as also its foundation was totally different, far more determined and important, than that of Christ.

In its origin, GNOSTICISM was a pure teaching, which is why the fragments collected later, contain the essence of the message.

As it appears at the time of Christ, it contains elements of Jewish, Persian and Egyptian origin.

As for the Jewish influence, it is not only the pure or ancient Israelitic, the original, but also the new partly non-Israelitic, as put forth in the teaching of the Nazarean Jesus and his followers.

The principles in the teaching of GNOSTICISM are equal to those of the perception in oriental cosmology or esoteric teaching; the teaching of DUALITY and DUALISM in its origin, a counterpart to the "christian" church and with that, the occidental teachings of MONOTHEISM or the principle of one Deity in the beginning of time.

In the teaching of DUALITY, another being is set forth, which in its entirety and origin is a counterpart to the first. A separation and determination of the form, combined with the decision of the one, as a consequence of the rank and nature of the duality, a dualistic darkness is created from where "something" springs.

Two equally alike beings only exist in theory, because in practice they will always diverge.

The "something" from the dualistic darkness will always be DUALITY, and the dual nature with its duality will always exist – as is natural – in the cosmology. This is only possible by this development and makes us understand the unequal division of things, that, which has begotten Darkness and Light, Evil and Good. To put it in one word – Opposites.

Even in the harmony of the scales – the balance – this duality is represented, and constitutes the foundation of its principles, as in judgement, in the conscious being and in the "Sum" of the Ego.

From this, the opponent in christian monotheism is derived, and it is he who assures its future existence. This is also true in all other religious teachings.

The church can only exist by having its opponent or "Satan". THE CHURCH AND ITS SATAN CANNOT BE SEPARATED.

Back to GNOSTICISM. The fundamental teaching of GNOSTICISM is further, that the visible world and also the visible life, is not created by a higher being or the bright part of the duality, but is the work of the "dark" part: DEMIURGON, which then is the Father and Creator of the world, the World's Master Builder or Grand Architect, HIRAM: PAN himself.

We have reached our beginning. PAN with a principle above or inside himself.

The PAN-image with its secret Agent in or above, belongs to a cult born from the Jewish traditional CABBALAH, why the main thoughts and main dogmas of GNOSTICISM are of a Jewish CABBALISTIC TYPE.

In the teaching of GNOSTICISM it is said: "Only the Angels, the Forces, from which DEMIURGON is one, and the Aeons, the eternal models, belongs to "the unknown Father" – or METATHESIS as we could properly call him.

GNOSTICISM does not link "the unknown" or immaterial Father with the visible, material world. It keeps him as a METATHESIS, contrary to christianity who lets him interfere – especially with the catholics – in the most profane things.

It is said that the dogmas of GNOSTICISM is of a Jewish CABBALISTIC TYPE. But what is the Jewish traditional CABBALAH? Well – as the name suggests, it was and is, as it existed before and still exists and is used to day, a traditional ethical teaching. It is a collection of dogmas belonging to a transcendental and secret knowledge. In its origin very highly estimated, but derived from many different sources, of which the most famous are those derived from the Persians and Egyptians.

In the content of the EGYPTIAN MYSTERIES and the teaching of the Persians, many things are common to the dogmas of CABBALAH.

In the Persian teaching the highest principle is that of the eternal, bottomless, enormous Abyss; ZERUANE AKRENE, which equals the Cabbalistic AIJN SOPH. From this bottomless Abyss springs the King of Light; ORMUSD, equal to the Cabbalistic; "old of days". Confronting ORMUSD – created by reflecting his own image in the darkness, CHAOS, outside him, to be comprehended as a shadow – stands AHRIMAN, The Prince of Darkness, equal to the Cabbalistic SAMAEL, THE HUNTED WOLF. Egypt has OZIRIS as the King of Light and TYPHON as his opponent.

SAMAEL, the representation of the wolf, has been – when transferred to occidental ground – dressed in the slough of PAN or the HE-GOAT. And this in their wrath, as the wolf, the hunted – and as a consequence thereof; hungry and ferocious – animal has been considered as begotten by PAN and compared to TYPHON.

Inside the many Gnostic sects and camps, this dualism is most obvious by the OPHITS or "WORSHIPPERS OF THE SERPENT", as popularly referred to (from OPHIS: Snake). This deserves further investigation.

"THE UNKNOWN FATHER", the immaterial source, is here created by "BYTHOS", an infinite and incomprehensible Abyss, "DE PROFUNDIS", which confront "NOUS" or "ENNOIA", the Thought, bound to "SIEGE", the Silence and "CHAOS", matter in its primitive form.

From "NOUS" or "ENNOIA", "SOPHIA ACHAMOTH" or "PNEUMA", The Spirit of Knowledge, takes form and raises herself. From the height of "SOPHIA ACHAMOTH" has "ILDABAOTH", The Son of Darkness, sprung forth. His underground – and by this, in many ways his Father – is CHAOS (or more correct; the forces in CHAOS). CHAOS is the visible form of BYTHOS, THESIS of METATHESIS, wherein BYTHOS disappears: ceases to exist. PNEUMA is the sublime Light, a counterpart to the immaterial BYTHOS and the material Darkness of CHAOS. The reality of ENNOIA in the VACUUM is then the opposite to the material world of CHAOS. From the act of "ILDABAOTH" reflecting his image in CHAOS, "OPHIOMORPHOS" is created, the Snake, or more correctly, the being which can take on any shape.

Morally speaking: The demon of wiliness and slyness.

Originally there was only "BYTHOS", the unknown "Sum" of the Abyss, ENNOIA, the Thought, CHAOS and PNEUMA. "ILDABAOTH" and OPHIOMORPHOS (the being which is represented as a snake) was created later. "BYTHOS and CHAOS" and "NOUS and CHAOS" are the first opponents, and of these "BYTHOS" and "CHAOS" are the most conspicuous.

Yet more conspicuous become the opposites – and thereby they make up the true opposition – between "BYTHOS", the original, immaterial and unknown Father, and "ILDABAOTH", the dark child of CHAOS, the material Father, DEMIURGON, the created and creating energy, whose child is "OPHIOMORPHOS", OPHIS, the origin of the Snake.

The image of the snake is falsely considered to represent evil and harmful things. Evil is yet only relative and will in time no longer be a true expression of that which the snake-idol really is the image of.

The SNAKE-IDOL, the image of OPHIS, is only an expression of GNOSIS, Knowledge, and what works through or springs from that, and not of that which has only relative value.

In connection with GNOSTICISM I have to mention MANICHÆISM – from the Persian MANES or MANI – which had its boom in the second century after the birth of the Nazarean Jesus, and because of that partly influenced his teachings, even though stemming in its primary form from Persia.

This teaching also has two opponents facing each other: The Lord of Light and the Angel of Darkness, "EBLIS".

DEMIURGON of the Gnostics is usually pictured as "ILDABAOTH" of the Ophits, or as EBLIS of the Manichæans, equal to SAMAEL of the Cabbalah, whose image again can be transferred to PAN, on one side, and on the other to that of "SATAN" which is an alien element in christianity.

This is the EXOTERIC account derived from superficial considerations.

By this, DEMIURGON – in his original capacity as creator must have been and is; the first – has been turned into a second-rate principle, and Light has been put before Darkness.

This is absurd and a delusion! It has never been so! Never has any secret science taught such a thing!

If the Light was created before the Darkness, then this is due to the superficial, influenced by christian thought, illusions of manipulated men. Look closely into the ancient ESOTERIC writings and you will find that the Darkness, the Source and Abyss of Matter, still – as it is now – was before anything else.

The Light, the Glory and Root of FIAT, can only be sought in the already created!

Logically speaking, this is the only true perception. To consider it as an enemy seems to me to be both wrong and dangerous.

The Rule of Darkness – considering that such a thing through the ages tends to make dark Creatures shun the light – rather than making any Creature shun darkness.

From an ESOTERIC point of view DEMIURGON is the "fallen soul of the world", the true title of PAN in his ability as the creating force and principle. He is to be considered as a first-rate principle, whose outer and inner add up to Darkness; Darkness in its duality, in which it touches life in its primitive and invisible form.

The dark first-rate principle is – although only manifest through one outer appearance – a principle of duality. Only the dualistic form has the ability to create the Light, as creating in general.

Further can be said: the ONE Darkness is the absolute reality, while that of Light is only deceptive and illusive.

That Darkness can have this dualistic nature must be explained by having – as it has – a material fill or grossness, enormous and heavy in the outer and with an immaterial spiritual depth that equals the other, but inward, and which constitutes our bodies and the Darkness in them. Or, more clearly: The estimation and justification of the value of something. The estimation that, briefly speaking, it needs a tool, not entirely but close to, of dissimilar principles.

The inequality and yet entirety of the mentioned tool, makes the tool appear Dark, its surrounding nimbus becomes Darkness, and itself: The Principle of Darkness.

In order for something to be produced, this dissimilarity must be doubled, as something only exists due to this double inequality, not only in the material, but also in the immaterial and spiritual concept.

In this consideration, wherein one differs or diverges from another, is where the Nimbus of Darkness will always be dwelling.

Thus Darkness becomes the Nimbus of the dualistic Unity.

The dual nature is by the way also present in the creating PHALLUS.

The one "unknown Father" – by the way a good description of a METATHESIS – disappears completely from the ancient writings when interpreted ESOTERICALLY. The Ancients have never named, nor spoken of DEMIURGON as "the fallen soul of the world". This interpretation is only derived from a popular view of him.

As mentioned before, "ILDABAOTH" of the Ophits is given the shape and outer appearance of DEMIURGON, or to picture – or give – DEMIURGON a visible appearance, they have taken the image of ILDABAOTH – dressed DEMIURGON in the slough of ILDABAOTH – and interpreted DEMIURGON as being ILDABAOTH, or the other way around. We will therefore now investigate what relationship ILDABAOTH has to DEMIURGON. Who and what was ILDABAOTH, beside that which has been added later? "ILDABAOTH" means "THE SON OR CHILD OF DARKNESS", and is thus an aspect of Darkness. Were we to analyze him a little closer, by using ESOTERIC sources, we find him as "THE HEAD OF THE DRAGON", or more correctly "THE MASTER". But the "DRAGON" is exactly he who carries the ancient KRONON or SATURN, the oldest Idol of God.

Of KRONON is said, in the esoteric sources, that he rides upon a DRAGON (the powers subject to him, but on the other hand they also constitute him, their Potency and Master).

KRONON, the God of the old Covenant, is also the Genius of Darkness and the idolized principle therein.

KRONON is "THE OLD OF DAYS" in the Jewish CABBALAH. ILDABAOTH is thus the son of KRONON, and KRONON becomes BYTHOS, the incomprehensible depth in all things. But even if ILDABAOTH is the Son of Darkness, this is not to be taken in the ordinary narrow sense of this word, as a relation between Father and Son.

The expression: "A CHILD OR SON OF DARKNESS", suggests no more in this case than "BORN OR DERIVED FROM DARKNESS", and Darkness is in this case; CHAOS. "THE CHILD" or "THE SON" will thus have kept the character and nimbus of Darkness.

The true relationship is this: ILDABAOTH IS KRONON ON THE THRONE OF "JUPITER". KRONON AS THE ROYAL HIGH PRIEST, KRONON AS SHEITAN, SHEITAN, THE MASTER OF THE DRAGON!

KRONON is, besides being the Genius of Darkness, also the Genius of Night and is therefore most apparent in his nightly image: THE HE-GOAT. KRONON in the image of the HE-GOAT is He who constitutes the sadly famous SABBATH GOAT, because of a misunderstanding.

THE GOAT OF THE SABBATH IS KRONON: "SHABATH" IN HIS NIGHTLY IMAGE!

ILDABAOTH is thus but an occurrence of KRONON under other circumstances and another name than the original.

The character, the nature and the principle is still the same. According to the aforesaid, ILDABAOTH is DEMIURGON, which again is KRONON.

The ancient ESOTERIC sources also describe KRONON with the same Abilities and Forces as those of DEMIURGON.

KRONON becomes PAN in his origin, and very closely equals PAN in his outer appearance.

The image of the HE-GOAT is common to both PAN and KRONON.

PAN's other image, as the Bearer of Snakes, OPHIOCHUS – the hermetic image of Pan, OPHIS carrying principle – is thus to be considered as a mirror-image or reflex – equal to the Moon reflecting SATAN, and the dark CHAOS of KRONON.

OPHIS, the snake, has after its occurrence kept on being – as one ordinarily imagines the snake, in occurrence as a living form – the winding and wriggling creep, no, GNOSIS-OPHIS has raised himself and stands erect. He is the primitive model of the individual and the primitive model of a "DEVIL" equal to Man.

OPHIS as the individual personality, has become a filling in space as the Dragon of KRONON, and more real than anyone suspects.

By the image of the Dragon of KRONON are meant the powers subject to him.

THE DRAGON (which can also be a SERPENT) mentioned in ancient esoteric writings, upon which KRONON – as mentioned – rides, pictures or expresses KRONON in the outer, while its inner intellectual content represents HERMES.

THE DRAGON-IMAGE is the expression of HERMES with his snake, while on the other hand it constitutes the character of KRONON. HERMES is thus the EXOTERIC outer of the ESOTERIC KRONON. The slough of the HE-GOAT is the Robe and House of the ESOTERIC KRONON, his true image, and the HE-GOAT is the Creator and Father of OPHIOMORPHOS.

HERMES IN THE SLOUGH OF THE HE-GOAT – PAN'S EXOTERIC IMAGE – THE DISPLAY IN SPACE BY THE DRAGON OF KRONON, the human Snake: LUCIFER, which is only an image of HERMES in his Father's House.

LUCIFER, HERMES IN THE SLOUGH OF THE HE-GOAT, THE FALLEN MORNING STAR, THE BRIGHT YET DARK LORD, THE MOON – INTELLIGENCE – as the MOON in its EXALTATION, and ♀ (Venus) in the House of the Moon 1st decanate – becomes a Son of ILDABAOTH or his heir.

LUCIFER becomes the true esoteric outer of PAN! Equal to: THE FACE OF THE DARK ENERGY! THE DARK ENERGY – BEGETTING LIGHT is exactly the true image – unfortunately rather misunderstood – of LUCIFER! LUCIFER is the Creator of all things – the reality of PAN!

What follows from that, is that PAN is not the unimportant character that man in his, for the most part, childish and naive imagination has wanted to turn him into – who allows humans to play tricks on him at pleasure.

LUCIFER in his true reality and highness is a Divine Majesty! It is not in vain that his jewelry is THE MORNINGSTAR.

But under the Morningstar: VENUS. VENUS is the clothing of LUCIFER.

Amazed one could ask: how can the extremely masculine LUCIFER also be the feminine VENUS ? The only answer is: LUCIFER hides behind VENUS. He constitutes the masculine strength, the occult Powers in her.

LUCIFER is VENUS: METAMORPHOSIS, as the other way around:

VENUS is LUCIFER.

VENUS, the Woman, is only an aspect or the other side of LUCIFER, rather equal to him and created from his element.

She is the known of the unknown.

The Natural-Main-Principle in Lucifer is the SNAKE-CHARACTER, the relative image of Knowledge and Evil, and though it belongs to HERMES-MERKURIUS, the VENUS-PHALLUS aspect cannot be excluded.

Because of that, "LILITH", "LA MAITRESSE DE LUCIFER", is not so much the MISTRESS OF LUCIFER, but rather another aspect of him.

Nor is Lucifer the ugly person man in his naive imagination has wanted to turn him into, but really beautiful in his dark apparent obscenity.

Here are fragments of a description of him:

> *And at last Satan (Lucifer) – who confronted me – seemed delicious and stately to behold. Stooping over the bushes, he looked down amongst them, raised himself and stood there: proud, with dark skin, glittering limbs and nostrils dilated with lust. (He stood in the burning, intolerable sunshine, and I in the shadow of the bushes).*

Wild and killing was the glance in his eye, flinging out despise for dreams and dreamers. (He touched a rock next to where he stood, and it shattered with a crash as of a falling Ash-tree.) Strong was the magnetism which flowed from his dark body; his mighty foot, nicely shaped with spread toes, was firmly planted in the sands.

"Come forward", he said scornfully, "are you afraid to face me?" I did not answer, but jumped towards him and hit him. But he hit me thousand-fold and burned, fried and tore me with hands as fire. My body lay dead, and happy was I and jumped towards him in a new body. He faced me again and stroke me double and killed my new body. Once again I happily jumped at him. And so it continued and still the same happened – he hit me and destroyed my old body.

The bodies I took as my clothing, sunk in front of me and stood as Him, like burning fire surrounding me, but I threw them off gradually. The pain I felt in one body, became a weapon which I used in the next, and I became stronger.

At last I was perfected, standing in front of Him, with a body alike His, and equal to Him in strength, shouting proudly from joy. Then he embraced me and said: "I love you"!

And Lo! His shape changed and he bent down and took me upon his arms. He lifted me into Space and carried me over the tree-tops far out on the sea, along the orbit of the earth, far under the Moon – until we stood in Paradise!

As LUCIFER is the ENERGY OF DARKNESS, so also is he the PERSONIFICATION and INDIVIDUALIZATION of the same.

The ENERGY OF DARKNESS is that which goes on in our Shadow life, and so it is THE CONVERSE OF THINGS.

The ENERGY living in DARKNESS etc. is further to be seen as a COSMIC FORCE and most properly sought in the ECCENTRIC, the seat of the original Cosmic Force – in the form which it appears here – and which again is to be sought in the CIRCUMFERENCE which constitutes the CIRCLE around the ECCENTRICITY.

In its relationship to the "Center", the Eccentric constitutes a "DARK CENTER", the SHADOW or SHADOW LIFE of the "Center".

This "DARK CENTER" is close by, or next to, the "BRIGHT" center of every known thing.

Darkness is the end of illusion: THE TRUE REALITY AND ITS PRESENTATION AND THE VEIL THEREOF.

The Energy inside it, the "SUM", is the original Light and Life.

LUCIFER is "DAS WAHRE LICHT, DER IN FINSTERNISS SCHEINET", or more correctly: "HERVORBRECHT". The true Light that breaks forth from Darkness. Though Lucifer is the Genius of Light, he is closely related to the surrounding Darkness. Without that, he wouldn't exist. The Darkness surrounding Lucifer, its Genius and "Sum":

LUCIFUGE, "Extinguisher of Light", with the surname ROFOCALE, "The Treasurer" – also the Genius and Sum of Chemistry – and LUCIFER, LIOSBER, "Light- or Torch Bearer", cannot be separated.

But – LUCIFUGE is JUPITER-ZEUS in his EXILE, the place where he – the Light – suffers.

This gives a solution to who LUCIFER really is: an aspect of JUPITER-ZEUS and hence a JUPITER-ZEUS-MARDUCH (or Tyr) Deity, next to being an aspect of the PAN-GOAT, as Pan in his entirety not only is Pan – but PAN-TAUR.

It is not without reason that the "EVIL" principle of the ancient mystical, esoteric "TAROT-CARDS", a changed form of the Egyptian so-called "BOOK OF THE DEAD", originally appeared as a JUPITER Deity.

LUCIFER is mostly considered as a REBEL against his Master, Emperor and Creator, and the Pentagon inverso (⛧) associated with him, is yet another expression of the criminal element. And perhaps not without reason.

It is true that he constitutes the worst enemy of the church, as it is normally seen. Where the church puts limits to the allowable, he gives free passage and allows Man to go into, and gain access to, the Mysteries which the church has no interest in having insight in.

If Man then – on the other side – feels the pain by or after the indulgence – probably what the church tried to prevent – then this is to be considered as an unavoidable result of his acts.

It can only be estimated thus.

Because of this, the Obstruction or Liberation from the Bonds that repress liberation from all kinds of dependence, is considered criminal, but it is (or constitutes) the Underground of Society, the motion which came before the Movements in its Depth.

All societies have sprung from such Movements in its Core. The Obstruction then becomes, in the entirety of its depth, that which builds all lawful – perhaps not the biggest – societies. Therefore, the Idol of Obstruction has as much equality of rights, as any other Idol of Society! The bad reputation of Obstruction is often founded in people taking distance from "Something", no matter what the character of this "Something" is – even though perhaps harmless.

The criminal view is founded in taking distance from "Something" – with or without any reason – and by this: putting up limits – something contrary to nature and the Energy of Darkness, for which reason it is considered criminal – as a succession of a fear of this "Something" – and results in a judging and banishing of this "Something", in spite of the very limited Knowledge people often have about this "Something".

If this "Something" threatens the existence of society, then "Something" with its threats, is turned into a criminal element.

LUCIFER, on the other hand, can easily be considered as an aspect of the criminal.

Esoterically, he is THE CONCEALED and IMPRISONED, whose house: THE GOAT STABLE AND THE CAGE OF THE COCK also is called: THE ACCURSED.

The esoteric signs for him is the Seal of "Solomon" (✡) and IMPRISONED with the iron collar of the "BULL" (ς) a derived form of the old (Saturn) character: (♄)

He is the principle in this, which is why he also becomes the principle of the IN-

QUISITION, the magical link in the church.

For more than one reason, ROSICRUCIANS worked under the cover of the Inquisition!

Finally shall be added this about the criminal element: the very act of procuring means in an unusual way, that it is enough to consider the acquisition as being criminal or incur to punishment.

The unusual and the criminal are often closely connected. It is said that the Energy of Darkness is created from that which goes on in our "Shadowlife", and to this can be added that Darkness also is the outer of our "Shadowlife". If the "Shadowlife" fills us with a sinister atmosphere – due to imposed imagination – this is only due to our Ignorance about it, and being Unaccustomed to it. If we get used to it, by approaching it at close range, the sinister atmosphere and the emptiness will pass away; they will cease to exist.

So also with the Essence of the products of the Energy of Darkness, the Poisons, the Aura and Smell of the Dark Energy.

If our organisms gradually get used to absorbing the apparent poisons, they will gradually cease to be poisons to us, and they will become a necessary condition, nutrition, for our well-being, by constituting our Element of Life. Even Poisons are Energy and a Display of Force – at least they can be regarded that way, besides being considered as a mixture of: 1) several Dark Energies, or of 2) cosmic Fluids – and thereby deserve to be studied rather than shunned. This can be said about all which expresses the Dark Energy.

As PAN, the original "Sum", is the Almighty Nature's "Sum", so is LUCIFER LIOSBER, with LUCIFUGE, as SON and SON'S ADVISOR and HEIR as also MATERIAL FORM and VALUE which equals THE MATERIAL NATURE'S "SUM", thus the part of Nature which is closest to us.

We have now seen LUCIFER in 4 shapes: 1) as HERMES in the Goat's Stable, 2) as a MOON-INTELLIGENCE of a 3) VENUS appearance, and as a 4) JUPITER character.

Left is yet another point of view which we shall discuss here at the end.

LUCIFER is – compared to the secret sources – he or that which BUILDS; THE HOUSE, THE TIMBER and THE SKELETON – with a double significance – in the HOUSE: THE DEATH which is present there, or SKELETON-MAN inside the human body.

LUCIFER, "THE GROWN UP CHILD", is Life and the principal support and creator of it. Thus also the MATERIAL UNDERGROUND and SUPPORT.

From this the title: THE WORLD'S MASTER BUILDER HIRAM.

LUCIFER, "THE SPIRIT AT THE PORTAL OF THE MONASTERY", is 1) THE LIVING SHADOW ON THE MONASTERY WALL evoked by: THE DARK "DUPLICATE" OF THE MONKS, and 2) TETRAGRAMMATON AND THE MIGHTY DEITY OF THE GRAVE OR SARCOPHAGUS. He is: THE HUMAN SERPENT – in a double significance – THE EMBODIMENT AND CREATURE OF THE ELASTIC PRINCIPLE.

Socially considered, "Lucifer" is: POVERTY: MERCURIUS or the PROTECT-

ING GENIUS, as it is he in whose hands THE GOLD glitters and radiates its magical attraction. Because of this, he has also been callled THE GOLD's INCUBUS; the GOLD and with that also the ORIGINAL PRINCIPLE OF ALCHEMY. He is that which conceals the GOLD, and he is what GOLD is.

LUCIFER, "THE RED MOON", is: THE DEMONIC (ש), THE FIRE CHARACTER, THE LIGHT IN DARKNESS, THE LIGHT IN THE RAVEN'S HEAD, THE LIGHT OF LUCIFUGE AND THE MOON (half-moon) IN THE RUINS and ON THE ATTIC. In this world he is called Infernos, or more correctly JODCHAVAHS; THE KING; THE HUMAN EAGLE FOLLOWED BY THE RED HOUND.

LUCIFER, "THE BURNING SCHIN" (ש), in his entirety is THE "JEBAMIAH" OF EXISTENCE or SPACE: THE REALIZATION OF SPACE: THE EMBODIMENT OF "JEBAMIAH".

Thus in its entirety LUCIFER LIOSBER is a Reality and no illusion.

The Worship of Him, the hunted Wolf, has its justification. And to make Him, the injured, come to, and re-possess his lost position, is it that I contribute this writing, and hereby recommend it to the good-will of my readers.

The Northern Magical Tradition

Freya Aswynn

The magical arts of the Northern peoples covered a wide spectrum of activity, all of which was purely practical. There was none of the Qabalists' preoccupation with building a stairway to the Deity, no Golden Dawn mysticism. It was, as the poet T.S. Eliot so aptly put it, "designed to produce definite results, such as getting a cow out of a bog". If it bears a resemblance to any modern magical system then the most likely candidate is Chaos Magic, though without the insistence on complex formulaic rationalization which makes Chaos inaccessible to many people.

From examples found in the *Eddas* and *Sagas* we discover that the magic used by our Northern ancestors covered an amazing range of subjects and possibilities. A brief listing of the subjects and techniques at the Northern magician's disposal might run as follows: Shape-shifting, Incantations, Runic Divination, Sitting-out, Weather and Element magic, Evil eye, Image magic, Necromancy, Counter-magic, Charms, Prophecy and Second-sight, Herbalism, healing and poisons, Platform magic, Mind control, Death magic and curses, Sexual magic, Ghost lore, and Battle magic.

Many of these overlap one another, with shamanic techniques complementing rune-carving as an example.

The information found in the *Eddas* and *Sagas* has often suffered Christian overlay as it was recorded quite late from earlier oral sources. Yet it remains valid if examined carefully, yielding many valuable insights for anyone seeking to reconstruct its use.

SHAPE-SHIFTING

The best-known example of shape-shifting is the werewolf, and a character in one of these sagas, a grandfather of a formidable rune master, had a nickname which meant "evening-wolf" because he was thought to change at twilight. Several other examples of shape-shifting also occur: A wizard called Askman, cornered, tried to escape from his house by taking the shape of a boar, but was brought down by a blazing firebrand.

A sorceress called Skroppa tried to conceal herself and her two foster daughters by making them appear as first, chests of ash, and second, a sow and two piglets.

Odin himself is described as being a shape-shifter in the *Ynglinga Saga*. Whilst his body lay as if asleep or dead he'd assume the form of a bird, or beast, or fish, or worm (serpent) and be off almost instantly to distant places.

Classic shape-shift battles are also recorded. One was between a young man and a Lappish wizard, fighting each other as dogs and then as eagles. Another battle between shape-shifters saw two neighbors, Storolf and Dufthak, fighting one another as bear and boar respectively.

Injuries to a shape-shifter often affected the human form, as with classic werewolf lore. A witch called Thordis took walrus form and was injured in her own body when the shape was hurt.

CHARMS AND INCANTATIONS

Poetry was a powerful weapon in the Northern magician's armory, and the majority of charms and incantations were in verse. This is one area where Northern magic differs radically from the reliance on long lists of "Barbarous Names of Evocation" which was the stock-in-trade of the Qabalist or Medieval sorcerer.

PROPHECY AND SECOND-SIGHT

Foster mothers were often able to touch their foster sons before they went off to battle and predict their injuries. The future could be discovered through dreams, and the spirits of the departed could communicate with the living this way. Odin learned through magic the predestined fates of men. Weapons could also be prophetic, like a halberd which made a loud ringing sound when a man was to be killed by it, or another which dripped blood when a battle was imminent. But the greatest vehicles of prophecy were the Volvas, such as Heidi in the poem *Voluspa*. The tradition of the Volva is being reconstructed in this age and country (England, – Ed.) by myself.

The Northern peoples had a thorough knowledge of herbalism and healing, both by herbal and amuletic applications, and were not averse to the use of natural drugs and intoxicants to produce the altered states required for some techniques.

Two powerful techniques frequently employed were platform magic and sitting-out. The magical circle was another feature of more Southern practices which does not appear in the North. Instead there were three methods of isolating the magician from the world around him- or herself. One was the ox-hide, which was marked with nine squares and stood or sat upon. A second was the setting out of "hurdles" or lengths of wood to form a skeletal nine square arrangement, with the centre square being occupied. The third method was the platform, literally what it says, usually supported by four posts and high enough off the ground for someone to get underneath it, which happened in at least one case where runes cut on the supports countered the ritual in progress above.

The sheer diversity of subjects really begins to emerge when we look at some of the extant charm lists, such as the *Runatal* section of the poem called *Havamal* in the *Elder Edda*, which purports to have been written by Odin himself.

We briefly examine this verse from the *Runatal,* which lists the eight techniques that must be mastered by the rune-magician and used to operate rune-spells:

Know how to cut,
Know how to read,
Know how to stain,

Know how to prove,
Know how to ask and sacrifice,
And know how to send and to destroy.

We take this verse and turn it into a grimoire of rune magic, examining each of the stages or processes with special reference to magic.

Cutting: To perform this one has to know the meanings of the runes.

Obtain a piece of soft wood with a definite grain to it. Balsa wood from a model shop is as good as anything, and reasonably easy to get hold of in an urban environment. Whatever you use, make sure it has a flat surface with the grain running along the piece, not across it. Next take a small, sharp knife. Craft scalpels are ideal, so are those small "gentleman's" penknives with one or two carbon-steel blades. Large blades are unwieldy to control and frequently don't take such a good edge. If you're not using disposable scalpel blades a small steel or whetstone is also a good idea to keep the edges keen.

If you feel more comfortable, sketch the runes in pencil before you attempt to cut them. Master the vertical strokes before you try the angles. Remember always to hold the wood away from the place where you are cutting, as you don't want to stain your runes just yet.

Try short inscriptions first, perhaps the name of your deity or even your own name. Remember that cutting for magical purposes involves concentrating on the characters being cut to liberate their powers in your mind. Chant the runes to accompany the action.

Reading: One should already have a fair mastery of this, knowing the letter-forms and the meanings attributed to them. This is essential before you actually begin to cut any runes. Reading also refers to the art of divination by runes.

Staining: For practice, ordinary colouring is quite sufficient. Inks or felt tip on unvarnished wood often help you improve by showing up those little over-cuts that otherwise remain hidden. For magical inscriptions, the best staining medium is your own blood, because it links you to the inscription directly and the drawing of it is an act of dedication in itself. Anyone who's ever given blood will remember that initial blood-test with a drop drawn from the side of your thumb. This cut heals easily and doesn't get in the way of daily life. Sterilize your point in a candle-flame. Don't wipe off the lamp-black that accumulates. It may be messy but it's far more sterile than whatever you wipe it off onto is likely to be.

Cutting and reading are techniques the ordinary rune-carver knew, but he or she would have stained the secular inscription with pigment rather than blood.

Proving: There are two distinct meanings to be considered here. One is that generated by experience, whereby rune-spells are proven and established by their creation and use, being added to the rune-magician's armory. This is a long-term process.

In the short-term, proving refers to the construction of the spell, and means ensuring that the components are compatible. If you regard Blackthorne as a death-tree, for instance, it wouldn't be the right wood to use for a healing spell. If you think of hazel as typifying wisdom, then it's unlikely, unless you're using troll runes, to be suitable for a spell to induce madness. You can't make a silk purse out of a sow's ear but you could make pork scratchings. Similarly you might use *Pertho* to warm up a lover but *Isa* is hardly likely to be suitable.

ASKING: In a magical context, this relates back to reading and proving. It involves being certain that the charm will perform as intended. There is a similarity to prayer here, in an invocatory sense, which affects both the rune-magician and the deity. When in doubt, don't! Doubt disrupts and could involve you in a whole lot of destroying (stage 8).

SACRIFICING: This is to do with the consecration of the symbols used, each of which, whilst a component, makes up a magical whole. It leads us back to proving and forward to sending. We must ever be aware of the magical power of the symbol within its context, always checking and re-checking our work. In an actual sense sacrifice is the time we take to ensure our work is accurate and effective, rather than rushing forward to the desired conclusion.

SENDING: This is the poetic part of the process, and involves the composition of an actual "charm" and the actual activation of the completed rune-spell. Sending is the activation part of the process which gives the spell direction. It is an additional reinforcement of the completed spell and acts as a confirmatory statement of intent.

DESTROYING: Here we come to something everyone should know: how to get rid of an unwanted charm or correct one that has gone wrong. The best way is to shave off the original inscription, burn the shavings and use the base material to create a new inscription in its place. Before you shave off the old one make sure you understand it thoroughly and have worked out the replacement satisfactorily. To botch a rune-spell once is regrettable. To do it twice is unforgivable.

Destroying has nothing to do with death-magic and cursing. In the Northern Tradition magic is magic, without any white, black or grey overlay. A curse would be created in exactly the same way as any other rune spell. In Medieval times, when the darker elements of European Sorcery and Goetia had entered the picture, there would have been a much greater insistence upon graveyard dust, the hand of a hanged man, baby's fat and so on to beef up the anti-Christian morality implied in cursing. In the purer atmosphere of the pagan North these things also had their place, but with more pragmatic reasoning behind them.

Tests

Anton LaVey

Discrimination is a test of intelligence. Do you know the difference between inferior and superior? How quickly can you discern the shoddy from quality? As a Satanic test, it's more important than you may think. Like eugenics. If you can't immediately tell the difference, much less know there is a difference, between ordinary things, how can you presume a role in selective breeding?

In order to feel a range of emotions, one must be aware of *differences*. The less variation one can experience, the less one feels. The non-Satanic desensitization most humans have acquired ill equips them for any feeling or opinion save the programmed, the prepackaged.

One of the tests administered by the Church of Satan is to encourage "optional alternatives" within the framework of "Satanism". These are transparently directionless, obfuscated, and redundant sub-groups – but not to those for whom such a test would apply. The rationale of "Question all things" becomes more like "Just shopping around". The cruel fact is that it's only a separation process. It divides those who are acutely selective from those, for whatever reason, aren't. The smartest animals will avoid poisoned bait. That's why pest poisons are well researched before production, to make them as tempting as possible. And rats are much smarter than most humans (as well as more sensitive and loyal).

Knowing and feeling *differences* is one of Satan's curses upon His own, however. Elimination of comparison is the Christian way, the path of true slavery. A limited, linear, or non-existent set of options – both materially and emotionally – makes for a satisfied (translate: complacent) society. But beware of false options and Hobson's choices. A Satanic mind should – and will – readily detect them. The elation – and dismay – that accompanies an awareness of genuine differences is something Higher Man must live with every day of his life. But it provides life itself, rather than a frenetic shuffle through a world of false values, or worse, no values.

Anathema of Zos

The Sermon to the Hypocrites

Austin Osman Spare

Hostile to self-torment, the vain excuses called devotion, Zos satisfied the habit by speaking loudly unto his Self. And at one time, returning to familiar consciousness, he was vexed to notice interested hearers – a rabble of involuntary mendicants, pariahs, whoremongers, adulterers, distended bellies, and the prevalent sick-grotesques that obtain in civilisations. His irritation was much, yet still they pestered him, saying: MASTER, WE WOULD LEARN OF THESE THINGS! TEACH US RELIGION!

And seeing, with chagrin, the hopeful multitude of Believers, he went down into the Valley of Stys, prejudiced against them as FOLLOWERS. And when he was ennuyé, he opened his mouth in derision, saying:

O, ye whose future is in other hands! This familiarity is permitted not of thy – but of my impotence. Know me as Zos the Goatherd, saviour of myself and of those things I have not yet regretted. Unbidden ye listen'd to my soliloquy. Endure then my Anathema.

Foul feeders! Slipped, are ye, on your own excrement? Parasites! Having made the world lousy, imagine ye are of significance to Heaven?

Desiring to learn – think ye to escape hurt in the rape of your ignorance?

For of what I put in, far more than innocence shall come out! Labouring not the harvest of my weakness, shall I your moral-fed desires satisfy?

I, who enjoy my body with unweary tread, would rather pack with wolves than enter your pest-houses.

Sensation... Nutrition... Mastication... Procreation...! This is your blindworm cycle. Ye have made a curiously bloody world for love in desire. Shall nothing change except through your accusing diet?

IN THAT YE ARE CANNIBALS, what meat should I offer? Having eaten of your dead selves savoured with every filth, ye now raven to glutton of my mind's motion?

In your conflict ye have obtained...? Ye who believe your procreation is ultimate are the sweepings of creation manifest, returning again to early simplicity to hunger, to become, and realise – ye are not yet. Ye have muddled time and ego. Think ye to curb the semen SENTIMENTALLY? Ye deny sexuality with tinsel ethics, live by slaughter, pray to greater idiots – that all things may be possible to ye WHO ARE IMPOSSIBLE.

For ye desire savours useless to pleasure.

Verily, far easier for madmen to enter Heaven than moral Lepers. Of what difference is Life or Death? Of what difference is dream or reality? Know ye of nothing further than your own stench? Know ye what ye think ye know for certain? Fain would I be silent. Yet too tolerant is this Sun that cometh up to behold me, and my weakness comes of my dissatisfaction of your solicit... but be ye damned before obtaining fresh excuses of me!

Cursed are the resurrectionists! Is there only body and soul?

Is there nothing beyond entity? No purchase beyond sense and desire of God than this blasting and devouring swarm ye are?

Oh, ye favoured of your own excuses, guffaw between bites! Heaven is indifferent to your salvation or catastrophe. Your curveless crookedness maketh ye fallow for a queer fatality! What! I to aid your self-deception, ameliorate your decaying bodies, preserve your lamentable apotheosis of self?

The sword-thrust – not salve – I bring!

Am I your swineherd, though I shepherd unto goats? My pleasure does not obtain among vermin with vain ideas – with hopes and fears of absurd significance. Not yet am I overweary of myself. Not yet shall I palliate abnomination, for in ye I behold your parents and the stigmata of foul feeding.

In this ribald intoxication of hypocrisy, this monument of swindlers' littlenesses, where is the mystic symposium, the hierarchy of necromancers that was?

Honest was Sodom! YOUR theology is a slime-pit of gibberish become ethics. In YOUR world, where ignorance and deceit constitute felicity, everything ends miserably – besmirched with fratricidal blood.

Seekers of salvation? Salvation of your sick digestion; crippled beliefs: Convalescent desires. Your borrowed precepts and prayers – a stench unto all good nostrils!

Unworthy of a soul – your metamorphosis is laborious of morbid rebirth to give habitance to the shabby sentiments, the ugly familiarities, the calligraphic pandemonium – a world of abundance acquired of greed. Thus are ye outcasts! Ye habitate dung-heaps: your glorious palaces are set amid cemetaries. Ye breathe gay-heartedly within this cess-pit? Ye obtain of half desires, bent-persuasions, of threats, of promises made hideous by vituperatious righteousness! Can you realise of Heaven when it exists WITHOUT?

Believing without associating ye are spurious and know not the way of virtue. There is no virtue in truth, nor truth in righteousness. Law becomes of desire's necessity. Corrupt is the teacher, for they who speak have only spent words to give.

Believe or blaspheme! Do ye not speak from between your thighs?

To believe or unbelieve is the question. Verily, if you believe of the least – ye needs must thrive all things. Ye are of all things, of all knowledge, and, belike, will your stupidity to further self-misery!

Your wish? Your heaven? I say your desire is women. Your potential desire is a brothel.

Ah, ye who fear suffering, who among ye has courage to assault the cloudy enemies of creeds, of the stomach's pious hopes?

I blaspheme your commandments, to provoke and enjoy your bark, your teeth grinding!

Know ye what ye want? What ye ask? Know ye virtue from maniacal muttering? Sin from folly? Desiring a teacher, who among ye are worthy to learn?

Brutally shall I teach the gospel of soul-suicide, of contraception, not preservation and procreation.

Fools! Ye have made vital the belief the Ego is eternal, fulfilling a purpose now lost to you.

All things become of desire; the legs to the fish; the wings to the reptile.

Thus was your soul begotten.

Hear, O, vermin!

MAN HAS WILLED MAN!

Your desires shall become flesh, your dreams reality and no fear shall alter it one whit.

Hence do I travel ye into the incarnating abortions – the aberrations, the horrors without sex, for ye are worthless to offer Heaven new sexualities.

—~— —~— —~—

Once in this world I enjoyed laughter – when I remembered the value I gave the contemptible; the significance of my selfish fears; the absurd vanity of my hopes; the sorry righteousness called I.

And YOU?

Certainly not befitting are tears of blood, nor laughter of gods.

You do not even look like MEN but strange spawn of some forgotten ridicule.

Lost among the illusions begat of duality – are these the differentiations ye make for future entity to ride your bestial self? Millions of times have ye had re-birth and many more times will ye again SUFFER existence.

Ye are of things distressed, living down the truths ye made. Loosing only from my overflow, perchance I teach ye to learn of yourselves? In my becoming shall the hungry satisfy of my good and evil? I strive me neither, and confide subsequent to the event.

Know my purpose: To be a stranger unto myself, the enemy of truth. Uncertain of what ye believe, belike ye half-desire? But believe ye this, serving your dialectics: Subscribing only to self-love, the outcroppings of my hatred now speak.

Further, to ventilate my own health, I scoff at your puerile dignitaries' absurd moral clothes and ovine faith in a fortuitous and gluttonous future!

Dogs, devouring your own vomit! Cursed are ye all! Throwbacks, adulterers, sycophants, corpse devourers, pilferers and medicine swallowers! Think ye Heaven is an infirmary?

Ye know not pleasure. In your sleepy lusts, feeble violence and sickly morale, ye are more contemptible than the beasts ye feed for food.

I detest your Mammon. Disease partakes of your wealth. Having acquired, ye know not how to spend.

YE ARE GOOD MURDERERS ONLY.

Empty of cosmos are they who hunger after righteousness. Already are the merciful spent. Extinct are the pure in heart. Governed are the meek and of Heaven earn similar disgust. Your society is a veneered barbarity. Ye are precocious primitives. Where is your success other than through hatred?

There is no good understanding in your world – this bloody transition by procreation and butchery.

Of necessity ye hate, and love your neigbour by devouring.

The prophets are nauseating and should be persecuted. Objects of ridicule, their deeds cannot live through their tenets. Actions are the criterion, then how can ye speak other than lies?

Love is cursed. Your desire is your God and execration. Ye shall be judged of your appetite.

Around me I see your configuration – again a swine from the herd. A repulsive object of charity! The curse is pronounced; for ye are slime and sweat-born, homicidally reared. And again shall your fathers call to the help of women. Ye vainly labour at a rotten Kingdom of Good and Evil. I say that Heaven is catholic – and none shall enter with susceptibility of either.

Cursed are ye who shall be persecuted for MY sake. For I say I am CONVENTION entire, excessively evil, perverted and nowhere good – for ye.

Whosoever would be with me is neither much of me nor of himself enough.

—‿— —‿— —‿—

Zos tired, but loathing his hearers too much, he again reviled them saying:

Worm-ridden jackals! Still would ye feast on my vomit? Whosoever follows me becomes his own enemy; for in that day my exigency shall be his ruin.

Go labour! Fulfil the disgust of becoming yourself, of discovering your beliefs, and thus acquire virtue. Let your good be accidental; thus escape gratitude and its sorry vainglory, for the wrath of Heaven is heavy on easy self-indulgence.

In your desire to create a new world, do unto other as you would – when sufficiently courageous.

To cast aside, not save, I come. Inexorably towards myself; to smash the law, to make havoc of the charlatans, the quacks, the swankers and brawling salvationists with their word-tawdry phantasmagoria: to disillusion and awaken every fear of your natural, rapacious selves.

Living the most contemptible and generating everything beastly, are ye so vain of your excuse to expect other than the worst of your imagining?

Honesty is unvoiced! And I warn you to make holocaust of your saints, your excuses: these flatulent bellowings of your ignorance. Only then could I assure your lurking desire – easy remission of your bowdlerized sins. Criminals of folly! Ye but sin against self.

There is no sin for those of Heaven's delight. I would ye resist not nor exploit your evil: such is of fear, and somnambulism is born of hypocrisy.

In pleasure Heaven shall break every law before this Earth shall pass away.

Thus if I possessed, my goodness towards ye would be volcanic.

He who is lawless is free. Necessity and time are conventional phenomena. Without hypocrisy or fear ye could do as ye wish. Whosoever, therefore, shall break the precept or live its transgression shall have relativity of Heaven. For unless your righteousness exist not, ye shall not pleasure freely and creatively. In so much as ye sin against doctrine, so shall your imagination be required in becoming.

—∿— —∿— —∿—

It has been said without wit: "Thou shalt not kill." Among beasts man lives supremely – on his own kind. Teeth and claws are no longer sufficient accessory to appetite. Is this world's worst reality more vicious than human behaviour?

I suggest to your inbred love of moral gesture to unravel the actual from the dream.

Rejoice ye! The law-makers shall have the ugly destiny of becoming subject. Whatsoever is ordained is superseded – to make equilibrium of this consciousness rapport with hypocrisy.

Could ye be arbitrary? Belief foreshadows its inversion. Overrun with forgotten desires and struggling truths, ye are their victim in the dying and begetting law.

The way of Heaven is a purpose – anterior to and not induced by thought.

Desire, other than by the act, shall in no wise obtain: Therefore believe SYMBOLICALLY or with caution.

Between men and women having that desire there is no adultery. Spend the large lust and when ye are satiated ye shall pass on to something fresh. In this polite day it has become cleaner to fornicate by the wish than to enact.

Offend not your body nor be so stupid as to let your body offend ye. How shall it serve ye to reproach your duality? Let your oath be in earnest; though better to communicate by the living act than by the word.

This God – this cockatrice – is a projection of your imbecile apprehensions, your bald grossness and madhouse vanities. Your love is born of fear, but far better to hate than further deception.

I would make your way difficult. Give and take of all men indiscriminately. I know your love and hate. Inquire of red diet. Within your stomach is civil war.

Only in self-love is procreative will.

What now! Shall I attempt wisdom by words? Alphabetic truths with legerdemain grammar? There is no spoken truth that is not PAST – more wisely forgotten.

Shall I scrawl slippery paradox with mad calligraphy? Words, mere words! I exist in a wordless world, without yesterday nor to-morrow – beyond becoming.

All conceivableness procures of time and space. Hence I spit on your tatterdemalion ethics, mouldering proverbs, priestly inarticulations and delirious pulpit jargon. This alone I give ye as safe commandments in your pestilent schisms.

Better is it to go without than to borrow. Finer far to take than beg.

From Puberty till Death realise "Self" in all.

There is no greater virtue than good nourishment. Feed from the udder, and if the milk be Sour, feed on... Human nature is the worst possible!

Once I lived among ye. From self-decency now I habitate the waste places, a willing outcast; associate of goats, cleaner far, more honest than men.

Within this heterogenousness of difference, reality is hard to realise, evacuation is difficult.

These spiritualists are living sepulchres. What has decayed should perish decently.

—— —— ——

Cursed are they who supplicate. Gods are with ye yet. Therefore let ye who pray acquire this manner:

O Self my God, foreign is thy name except in blasphemy, for I am thy iconoclast. I cast thy bread upon the waters, for I myself am meat enough. Hidden in the labyrinth of the Alphabet is my sacred name, the SIGIL of all things unknown. On Earth my kingdom is Eternity of DESIRE. My wish incarnates in the belief and becomes flesh, for I, I AM THE LIVING TRUTH. Heaven is ecstasy; my consciousness changing and acquiring association. May I have courage to take from my own superabundance. Let me forget righteousness. Free me of morals. Lead me into the temptation of myself, for I am a tottering kingdom of good and evil.

May worth be acquired through these things I have pleasured. May my trespass be worthy.

Give me the death of my soul. Intoxicate me with self-love. Teach me to sustain its freedom; for I am sufficiently Hell. Let me sin against the small beliefs. – AMEN.

Concluding his conjunction, Zos said: –

Again, O sleep-walkers, beggars and sufferers, born of the stomach; unlucky men to whom happiness is necessary!

Ye are insufficient to live alone, not yet mature enough to sin against the law and still desire women.

Other than damnation I know no magic to satisfy your wishes; for ye believe one thing, desire another, speak unlike, act differently and obtain the living value.

Assuredly inclination towards new faculties springs from this bastardy! Social only to the truths convenient to your courage, yet again beasts shall be planted.

Shall I speak of that unique intensity without form? Know ye the ecstasy within? The pleasures between ego and self?

At that time of ecstasy there is no thought of others; there is NO THOUGHT. Thither I go and none may lead.

Sans women – your love is anathema!

For me, there is no way but my way. Therefore, go ye your way – none shall lead ye to walk towards yourselves. Let your pleasures be as sunsets, HONEST... BLOODY... GROTESQUE!

Was the original purpose the thorough enjoyment of multitudinous self, for ecstasy? These infinite ramifications of consciousness in entity, associating by mouth, sex, and sense!

Has the besetting of sex become utter wretchedness – repetition made necessary of your scotomy?

O bloody-mouthed! Shall I again entertain ye with a little understanding?

An introspection of cannibalism in the shambles of diet – the variating murder against the ancestral? Is there no food beyond corpse?

Your murder and hypocrisy must pass before ye are uplifted to a world where slaughter is unknown.

Thus, with a clean mouth, I say unto ye, I live by bread alone. Sleep is competent prayer. All morality is BEASTLY.

Alas, there has been a great failure. Man is dead. Only women remain. With tongue in cheek I would say: "Follow me! That ye realise what is hidden in all suffering. I would make your self-mortification voluntary, your wincing courageous."

Still will ye be with me? Salutation to all suicides!

With a yawn Zos wearied and fell asleep.

In time the stench awoke him – for he had slept amidst the troughs – and he observed that the crowd were no longer with him – that only SWINE remained. And he guffawed and spake thus: "Not yet have I lost relationship and am thereby nearly asphyxiated! Caught up am I in the toils of sentiment, the moral hallucinations within the ebb and flow of hopes and fears?

Shall age alone transmute desire? Not yet have I disentangled illusion from reality: for I know not men from swine, dreams from reality; or whether I did speak only unto my self. Neither know I to whom my anathema would be the more impressionable...

My insensible soliloquy is eaten as revelation! What I spake with hard strived conceit to increase enterprise brings forth only swinish snorts. Water is not alone in finding its level.

I have not met tragedy, no, not in this life! Yet, whether I have spewed their doctrines upon the tables of the Law or into the troughs, at least I have not cast away the flesh of dreams.

And turning towards his light, Zos said: This my will, O Thou Glorious Sun. I am weary of my snakes descending – making slush.

Farewell antithesis. I have suffered. All is paid.

Let me go forth and recreate my sleep.

Thelemic Morality

Rodney Orpheus

This text was the first published excerpt from Orpheus' book Abrahadabra – A Beginner's Guide to Thelemic Magick, *which was published by Looking Glass Press in 1995. – Ed.*

Well, you've been performing Thelemic magick for some time now, but as yet I haven't really described just what Thelema actually is. This has been intentional, because Thelema is essentially an active system, rather than a passive set of beliefs. Thelema is much better understood by doing, not reading, though ironically most of the Thelemites I know are obsessive bookworms (myself included).

Most books dealing with "New Age" beliefs start off by reassuring you that their system is "NOT A RELIGION!", but some sort of scientific super-psychology. Well, I'm not afraid to say that Thelema is a religion of a sort, though in actual fact it is much less of a traditional religion than almost any other belief system (including most "scientific" systems). Let's examine just what a religion is anyway.

Most people these days have a bit of a knee-jerk reaction to the word religion, brought on by forced over-exposure to such insane beliefs as conventional Christianity and Islam. The word "religion" has been hijacked and debased by the priests of faiths like these, until now it has become a dirty word amongst intelligent, right-thinking people in the Western world. The word "religion" springs from roots meaning piety, the Latin *religio*, the opposite idea to *negligens*, negligent, uncaring, unaware. It also springs from a root meaning to join together things which are separate, which in fact is the same meaning as the word "yoga" (compare the English word "yoke", which ties oxen together, for example). So religion is a word which describes the process of becoming aware and unified, of joining together all things which are diverse; it is the union of body and spirit, self and not-self, human and god. This is the aim of Thelema.

As I pointed out in the last chapter, the true Thelemic magician lives his magick 24 hours a day. I have already described some exercises that will help you increase your daily awareness, now it's time to talk about the morality that goes with them.

Morality – there's another very unfashionable word – and with good reason. Practically every religion since the dawn of mankind has imposed a set of commandments on its adherents. Thelema has one commandment only: "Do what thou wilt shall be the whole of the Law". That's it. It's that simple.

Now you have probably one of two reactions here. Either you nod sagely, and say "Of course, what other way could there be?", or your eyes open wide and you say, "But – that could never work!" If you are of the first type, fine, but you still have a lot of thinking to do. If you are of the second, I have to tell you that you are wrong, but at least you are aware enough to see the difficulties inherent in such a seemingly simple proposition.

Let's examine this phrase: "Do what thou wilt shall be the whole of the Law". Notice that we do not say: "Do whatever you like". We are talking here about your True Will. This is a concept that you have come across in earlier chapters. The word Thelema itself is Greek for Will. What is your True Will? It is your destiny, the Way through life which leads to your Great Work. Each of us is individual and unique, as Liber AL puts it: "Every man and every woman is a star". Each of us has our own light to give to the world, each of us has our own orbit, our path through the universe, which is right for us, and us alone. Moral codes which spell out a set of rules for EVERY person to follow identically lower each person's capacity for their own development in their own way.

By definition, to evolve is to become different from what has gone before. All things must change and grow, and a fixed moral code cannot grow with you. Only you can judge what action is right for you at any one time. To stop growing, to become rigid and unbending, is to start dying. As the ancient Chinese classic, the *Dao De Jing* puts it: "Rigidity and hardness are the stigmata of death; elasticity and adaptability, of life." And as Thelemites we embrace Life in our arms, we live to the fullest manner we are capable, and we extend our capabilities as much as possible, in order to be able to experience even more in the future. "Wisdom says: be strong! Then canst thou bear more rapture." *(Liber AL)*

Note that this idea of "Do what thou wilt" may be simple, but it is not EASY. Fixed moral codes have one "advantage" in that in any given situation believers always know precisely what they are supposed to do and not do. Thelemites do not have this crutch to lean on. We must decide for ourselves what we must do, and it is this that is one of the greatest stumbling blocks for many who attempt this way. Thelemites cannot take the lazy way of simply following God's orders. We are Gods, we MAKE the orders for ourselves to follow. This can be very hard work, but ultimately it is much more fulfilling than just accepting the teachings of another. As Robert Anton Wilson says: "Convictions cause convicts", and Thelemites want to breathe the air of liberty, we are masters of our own fate.

For many people the Thelemic way is too hard at first, they do not want to accept the responsibility of looking after themselves without a "big daddy" in heaven to tell them what to do. Remember that normally you cannot persuade them to change, nor should you, for perhaps this way is their Will – if they grow to accept our way in their own time, we should rejoice, but we must not interfere too much. You can inform people of Thelemic principles if they wish to know of them (that's what this book is about after all), but you must never try to force them into doing what you think is right. The line between teaching and preaching is a fine one – be careful that you don't step over it! If in doubt, keep silence, and respect the beliefs of others, even when you disagree with them. Just make sure that they respect your beliefs too...

This question of mutual respect is one reason why Crowley always advised aspirants to greet others in letters and conversations with the salutation "Do what thou wilt shall be the whole of the Law". By beginning like this you are establishing the ground rules for the coming interaction. You are stating that you will respect the other person's point of view, and that you expect them to respect your point of view also. Of course, starting conversations like this will get you some funny looks! Mind you, people do have a surprising capacity for tolerating what they will consider to be an amusing eccentricity... Many Thelemites abbreviate this greeting to the simple "93", a reference to the numerical value of the word Thelema in Hebrew. Personally, I think that this just sounds silly, though I am sure that the majority of Thelemites disagree with me. In my opinion, if you're going to affirm something, do it 100%, or not at all.

Perhaps I should now confess that for years I did not use any form of Thelemic greeting, mainly because I did not want to force my own beliefs down someone else's throat. However, while writing this book, I thought I'd better check it out before passing judgment, and I must say the result was a pleasant surprise. It really is a good exercise in "everyday" magick, and it's a great way of irritating some of the assholes you meet.

Now the obvious criticism of the doctrine of the True Will is the classic: "But if everyone just does what they want, what's to stop someone raping me/shooting me/stopping me from watching television, etc." This is a very short-sighted view, based on the typical Old Aeon morality of the monotheistic slave-religions like Christianity. These religions teach that humans are intrinsically evil, that we are all horrible monsters inside, only holding back our nasty impulses thanks to the guidelines that God has kindly given to us. Thelemites have no concept of "Original Sin"; we do not believe that people are basically Satanic glove-puppets. Rather the Thelemite realizes that each person is a pure and perfect star, each an essential part of the universe. We know that when we do our Wills, we have no desire to hurt others indiscriminately, for to do so is to destroy part of our universe, to reduce the complexity and wonderment of our lives. Each star is beautiful, and we are concerned with maximizing the beauty of life, not reducing it.

When you have an impulse to interfere with the way that others live their lives, you are not allowing them the liberty to follow their True Wills, and you must remember "the Law is for All." All people have the right to do their Wills, so True Wills should never come into conflict with each other. If a conflict does arise, you should examine yourself closely, for at least one person is not doing their True Will. In a non-Thelemic society this person will probably not be you, but if the fight is between Thelemites, then you may well be at fault. Conflict in this case can be a very useful thing, for it can be a pointer towards possible problems in your development.

Liber AL states that "Love is the law, love under will." This shows that the nature of our True Wills must always be Love. Love is the yearning for things which are apart to become unified. Love is how we reach out beyond ourselves to that which we desire. Although we are individual stars, we must never make the mistake of assuming that we are alone within ourselves; we must not shut ourselves up in ivory towers of self-absorption. We shine with our own inmost light, it is true, but the universe is full of other stars too, each shedding many-hued radiance towards us. Through Love we perceive many more possibilities than we already have, through Love we gain some understanding of the magnitude of this enormous cosmos we inhabit.

Note that Love must be under Will, however. Love is a function of the True Will, and our Love should never be used as a weapon or tool to manipulate the Will of others

– nor should we allow others to restrict our Will, no matter how dearly we love them. Thelemic loving relationships – are a great deal different from the norm. Emotional game-playing, one-upmanship, jealousy, all these things spring from lack of respect for the Will of others, and should be absent. Honesty, trust, shared feelings, freedom should characterize the Thelemic partnership. This is not easy, I know (I speak from experience...), and can take great effort to achieve. But at least it never gets boring!

You can see now that this simple formula of "Do what thou wilt" has huge ramifications to the way that you approach your life. It is a charter for universal liberty, but it is not easy to put into practice. We live in a sick society, a society whose rules and laws are frequently contrary to Thelemic belief. Even our own minds can rebel against us when we try to put Thelemic ideals into practice. We have been educated away from our natural, instinctive Godhood, and the repressions which have been sinking into our minds from an early age have twisted our consciousness, making it hard to accept our True Wills fully – and often making it even harder to accept the True Wills of others. You must endeavor to examine your actions and reactions carefully; try to see if what you are doing each moment is really what you Will to do. You must be very honest with others, but more than that, honest with yourself. The human mind has an almost infinite capacity for self-delusion, so watch out for this! The exercises that I have given in the previous chapters will help you develop a better understanding of yourself. Use them.

In order to make it easier to understand some of the ideas implicit in Thelema, Aleister Crowley wrote *Liber OZ*, reproduced here. Although still simple and easy to understand, *Liber OZ* develops the concepts in a little more detail.

LIBER LXXVII

OZ:

"the law of the strong: this is our law and the joy of the world." – *AL* II:2
"Do what thou wilt shall be the whole of the Law." – *AL* I:40
"thou hast no right but to do thy will. Do that, and no other shall say nay." – *AL* I:42-43
"Every man and every woman is a star." – *AL* I:3

There is no god but man.

1. Man has the right to live by his own law –
to live in the way that he wills to do:
to work as he will:
to play as he will:
to rest as he will:
to die when and how he will.
2. Man has the right to eat what he will:
to drink what he will:
to dwell where he will:
to move as he will on the face of the earth.
3. Man has the right to think what he will:

to speak what he will:
to write what he will:
to draw, paint, carve, etch, mould, build as he will:
to dress as he will.
4. Man has the right to love as he will: –
"take your fill and will of love as ye will, when, where, and with whom ye will." – *AL* I:51
5. Man has the right to kill those who would thwart these rights.
"the slaves shall serve." – *AL* II:58

"Love is the law, love under will." – *AL* I: 57

Aleister Crowley

If you have got this far in the book, you should have no objections to anything expressed in *Liber OZ*, except perhaps to section 5: "Man has the right to kill those who would thwart these rights." Most people who read this for the first time are deeply shocked – I myself was no exception. But after thinking the whole thing through, I began to realize that this was an essential part of the system too, for without the capacity to defend our rights, we have no real liberty. It is all very well to preach "love your enemy" (and I believe we should love our enemies) but when some asshole comes along to stick you in a concentration camp, simply following his orders is not going to help you achieve your True Will (unless following orders is your True Will – somehow, I doubt it). Our enemies must be aware that we follow our True Wills, come what may, and that we will fight to defend our right to live in our own way. We mean no harm to others who respect our rights – we encourage them to free themselves also – but we will not bow down to any man or woman. Life is the most precious gift we possess, but if someone thwarts our rights they take away our life, for eating, thinking, loving – these things are our lives. And if my enemy feels that human life is unimportant, he condemns himself, for he is human too.

Thelema is not a peaceful religion – but then again how many peaceful Christians do you know? At least we are not hypocritical about our beliefs. We state what we think, we do not try to hide from the truth. Christians say "thou shalt not kill", but they have the bloodthirstiest history of any religion.

If you still feel uncomfortable about all this, remember that all that *Liber OZ* says is that you have the RIGHT to kill those who would thwart your rights – just because you have that right does not mean that you HAVE to exercise it. There is no Thelemic law which states that you have to go out and blast everyone in sight with a .44 Magnum (please don't!) – don't forget that the biggest enemy standing in the way of your True Will is usually your own ego.

The phrase below section 5 in *Liber OZ*, "the slaves shall serve", is also often the cause of some confusion. It does NOT mean that we should enslave other people – quite the opposite in fact ("the Law is for All", remember). The phrase does not say that some people should be slaves for us – it says that the slaves shall become servants. Slaves are those who are forced to do something against their Will, servants are those who voluntarily assist others, and are rewarded for doing so. If it is someone's Will to serve, then by all means they can do so – but they should never be FORCED into serving others. Even if they wish to be slaves, we cannot enslave them – they serve through their own choice. Be wary of making the mistake of assuming that those who wish to serve are somehow inferior. The person who paints the house is in no wise inferior to the person who owns the house. If they are performing their True Will, who are you to criticize them? Better for you to concentrate on doing your own Will, rather than interfering in the Will of others. And if it is your Will to serve others – do it! "Thou hast no right but to do thy will. Do that, and no other shall say nay."

Read this phrase in *Liber OZ* again, carefully. There is an important lesson here. Never allow yourself to take any phrase at face value in the world of magick. Think about its content and meaning carefully. This is doubly important when you are reading *Liber AL* or one of the other Thelemic *Holy Books*, which frequently have hidden messages buried within seemingly innocuous sentences.

I have gone into the subject of the True Will in some depth here, and have been treating it very seriously, but when all's said and done, the great thing about being a Thelemite is that it's fun! "Do what thou Wilt" DOES mean that you can go out and do all those things you always wanted to do, and you won't spend eternity burning in hell as a punishment for your sins. To the Thelemite "the word of Sin is Restriction". You sin against yourself when you hold back from fulfilling your Will – so don't hold back any longer. As psychology teaches us, repression of natural instincts is the major cause of neurosis, and the most natural instinct of all is to have a good time. As a friend of mine once put it: "At the end of the day, it's all just sex, and drugs, and rock'n'roll, isn't it?" I had to agree that he had summed it up pretty succinctly.

To the Thelemite, the sexual impulse is practically a sacred thing in itself. Our sexuality is the most fundamental expression of our Will. We have no taboos or mores restricting sexual activity. Any sexual act between mutually consenting adults is a wonderful thing – in fact it is a holy thing, for it is the living embodiment of our Love under Will.

Drugs are a subject a little more tricky to deal with. *Liber AL* says: "... take wine & strange drugs whereof I will tell my prophet, & be drunk thereof! They shall not harm ye at all.", which is pretty clear. Or is it? Notice the phrase "strange drugs". The drugs we take must be strange, for in their strangeness lie new experiences. But once we have assimilated these new sensations, the drugs are no longer strange to us. We must be especially wary of becoming addicted to drugs, for to the addict the drug has become an intrinsic part of existence – it is not at all strange any more. And we have only been promised that strange drugs cannot harm us. The addict who is using drugs which are no longer strange has no such safeguard. Be careful, people! By all means experiment, but do not let your Will be taken from you.

As for the rock'n'roll, that's another story...

Recognizing Pseudo-Satanism

Nemo

They're out there!

They sometimes wear pentagrams. They sometimes wear black. They often claim to be Satanists.

You may have seen them on the television talk shows or in film "documentaries" on Satanism.

No, I'm not talking about the sickos trying to blame Satanism for their sociopathic crimes. I'm not discussing religious cults who *seem* to be championing the cause of ego survival. I'm not referring to the philosophical fellow-travelers of Objectivism or other Libertarian groups.

I'm talking about sheep in *wolves'* clothing. I'm referring to cult groups who *claim* to be Satanists but *act* just like the more dedicated Christian fanatics! I'm talking about the White Light Mystics who use Satanic trappings.

They are out there and they are *dangerous!*

How are they dangerous?

Well, in my own case it cost me almost three precious years of my life before I finally saw through the sham of one organization and began to undo the *damage* it caused to my life.

Yes, I said *damage!*

Satanism is the only religion in the world to champion the cause of the ego. The ceremonies and dogma of Satanism all act to reinforce this ego-strengthening intention. This is what distinguishes real Satanism from every other philosophy and religion in the world.

The elements which make up modern Satanism are forcefully expounded by its creator, Anton Szandor LaVey, in his long-term bestseller *The Satanic Bible* (Avon Books, 1969). Modem Satanism rejects the existence of any god apart from the individual himself and worships the individual's ego as the only God which is!

Real Satanists recognize that all humans are predatory animals and take pride in this fact. Real Satanists hold no belief in the defiance of reason and feel that life is to be lived to the fullest HERE AND NOW! Real Satanists understand that Satan is a myth and a symbol and they hold that symbol as the guiding light of their lives. Real Satanists do not confuse fantasy with reality. Real Satanists know that ritual magic is a special make-believe-world they enter to produce results in the material world which are REAL!

What do the pseudo-Satanists do? They parody these unique elements. They will use many of the same words and they will even perform "Satanic" magical ceremonies and rituals. It is especially insidious when they claim (as several such groups do) to be carrying on the work of the original Church of Satan.

In and of itself these acts of mimicry seem innocent enough. The problem is one of "doublespeak" and what it can do to damage the healthy growth of the individual's ego.

Pseudo-Satanic groups do *not* champion the cause of the ego. In fact, they are generally anti-mind and altruistic. They do *not* champion individual autonomy. Instead they commonly advocate the existence of external, objective gods to be worshipped and to be obeyed, even if this requires martyr-like behavior.

For example, in the group which had fooled me for so long, there was a requirement for the "higher-ranking" member to be willing to go public and give interviews on television, radio, etc. *whether or not this public statement would harm the individual in his private life!* In other words, they expected the member to be a martyr for their religion. Hardly Satanic.

By now you should begin to see the danger.

The power and freedom of becoming a strong individual in a world of dull and obedient mediocrity is slowly and carefully undercut by such groups. The words of *The Satanic Bible* become twisted and distorted until they no longer *have* useful meaning! The Satanism of the ego becomes warped into the pseudo-Satanism of the mystic slave!

You can easily identify pseudo-Satanists by checking the way they test reality, the way they set goals and how they use authority.

The pseudo-Satanists don't want to check on their beliefs in the harsh glare of reality. They want to spin their gossamer web of megalomaniacal ideas across the whole of existence without ever testing to see if there is even one small grain of truth therein. The pseudo-Satanist never admits to making mistakes. Oh no! To be able to admit you can err requires a degree of ego-strength they totally lack! They subtly or overtly dodge the rational questions a Satanist will ask with a call to "faith" or by a claim to some way of knowing which is "higher" than the rational mind. So the abandonment of reality-checking is one sure sign that the group you are with is pseudo-Satanic.

In contrast, real Satanism exalts the ultimate value of *doubt*. Real Satanists question everything and put everything to the test of reason. Real Satanists do not swallow mystical swill but rely upon the rational mind as the ultimate test of truth in any and every situation.

Second is the lack of clear-cut goals and/or a means to achieve them. This is what most MBA business programs refer to as "goal and mission statement". Pseudo-Satanism has no goal. The group to whom I'd belonged substituted mystical "buzzwords" for intentions (as well as mystical insight for reason). As a result, I kept finding myself given apparent goal statements which, upon careful deciphering, proved to be only word salad.

The goals of real Satanism are simple and direct. Because the real Satanist does not believe in some fairy tale Heaven or Hell, and views the physical death as the end of life, he is dedicated to the enjoyment of material life through the material senses for himself! Real Satanists are rational hedonists who recognize that life is not a preparation for some *other* but is existence *itself*. Therefore, the goal of life is to enjoy it and the mission, in order to accomplish this goal, is to gain direct control over the individual's material existence. In other words, the real Satanist knows that life is for the living and only the living. A real Satanist seeks material power in the real world. His magic is designed to produce earthly results. He is not interested in a pipe dream of never ending self-evolution or other mystical nonsense. The real Satanist is only interested in *results!*

Real Satanists are therefore the world's achievers, creators, producers and innovators who show great promise and deliver the goods. Pseudo-Satanists are trapped within the echo chamber of their personal delusions, ranting to their mind-numbed minions and accomplishing nothing.

One final test of authenticity of any Satanic versus pseudo-Satanic group is the question of authority versus reason. White Light occult groups have traditionally followed a very militaristic ranking system with degrees and honorific titles.

Resorting to a title or occult "ranking" to avoid answering a question is a sure sign that you are dealing with the pseudo-Satanist and not the authentic item. The pseudo-Satanists use their titles to control other members, rather than manipulate the outside, non-Satanic community. This is a simple reflection of the fact that those who cannot make it in the real world outside their organizations will tend to dry and rule their own little kingdoms within a closed community of true believers.

And it is this cut-off from the outside world that truly makes pseudo-Satanism dangerous. *Nothing* could be more dangerous for the individual than to cut himself off from knowing and responding to the *realities* of life. The pseudo-Satanists do precisely that.

Real Satanists understand that the use of a title is simply the use of Lesser Magic to manipulate the slaves of the world to obey. The early Church of Satan gave out many titles so that these could be effectively used with *non*-Satanists! ("Wow! You mean you're a Satanic Priest!") Real Satanism has always advocated study and not worship to determine what is true. This is why the *only* books published by *Satanists* on Satanism have come from active members of the Church of Satan. Pseudo-Satanists do not dare to allow their mystical blather to be openly distributed. It would immediately expose them as the shams they are!

Real Satanism, as advocated by the Church of Satan for 27 years, is alive and well in the world today, and offers power and self-esteem to those who can qualify for active membership.

Pseudo-Satanism is, unfortunately, also out there. It offers weakness and confusion for those it seduces with its debilitating lies.

The difference is vital and real.

BEWARE!

Pythagoras, Plato and the Hellenes

The Roots of Satanism

Philip Marsh

This is about a few outstanding members of an ancient people whom the defenders of Judeo-Christian institutions have feared as much as Satan. So great was their fear, that the conquering bishops, priests, and clerics of the Dark Ages degraded the proper name of these ancient people into an accusatorical curse synonymous with witch, warlock, demonolator, and even demon. The epithet used was "HELLENE!"[1]

This is about two opposing traditions that originated with the Hellenes or "ancient Greeks". One tradition begins with a cult called the Orphics, whom we are falsely told sought liberation from the body and the "cycle of rebirths" by means of "purification of the soul". This tradition runs through Pythagoras to Plato and on to the early Neo-Platonists in the Christianized Roman Empire. It is, in truth, a Satanic tradition by every principle enunciated by Anton LaVey in *The Satanic Bible*. This tradition produced the greatest, most remarkable and eloquent enemies the early Christians ever confronted, names you will be familiar with because lies, confusion, misinformation, silence, and deep embarrassment still reign today on this subject, even among Satanists.

The second tradition, originating with Socrates, who was not a Hellene, but lived in Athens as a prominent citizen, runs through Aristotle on to the mediæval Church Scolastics like St. Thomas Aquinas. This tradition has been allowed to pass through to the modern world in its entirety, it is well-aired, and has a great influence on everyone from Marxist intellectuals to advocates of democratic liberalism and humanitarianism.

Virtually every writer on this subject is a present or *former* Christian, Jew, or Mohammedan. Their lies and deeply ingrained failures to explain what went on in 5th Century Athens B.C. will be *unmasked* here. For this purpose, Hellenic, Roman, and Byzantine historians, untainted by Judeo-Christianity, will be relied upon, but references will be limited to easily obtained English language sources for any interested reader.

The primary lie is the denomination of the Hellenes as "pagans". This lumps them in with animists, nature-worshippers, and polytheists of every type. This is an effort to level them and conceal what they really thought and knew.

Anyone who sat through "Philosophy 101" or "Introduction to Western Civilization" learns that the ancient Greeks had an entire pantheon of deities: Zeus the chief, Hera his wife, Aphrodite goddess of love and beauty who was Zeus' daughter (but not Hera's), etc. This is justly regarded as quant, primitive, and downright silly, like the pantheon of Egypt in Tut's time, or the pantheon of present day natives in the West

1 *Death of classical paganism*, John Holland Smith, pp 239-240.

Indies. The only jarring note is that one wonders how the Hellenes' superlative level of statesmanship, science, mathematics, art and architecture could evolve and exist side by side with such juvenile religious beliefs. There is no limit to the number of treatises in which we are told that the ancient Greeks, despite their other remarkably evolved accomplishments, had failed to develop the so-called "advanced" religious and ethical idea called monotheism, an idea attributed either to the alleged "religious genius of the Hebrews" or to some particular "religious genius", such as Moses or Akhnaton.

It will be shown, by focussing on a few prominent individuals, that while the Hellenes had all sorts of tales of super-human heroes, gods, demons and spirits, that were part of their *common* folklore, they consistently produced and revered individuals who not only created revolutions in science and art, but ascribed this ability to the direct influence of "dæmons" who were connected to, as Dr. LaVey called it: a dark force which pervades all of Nature, balancing it.[2] Remember the terms of this idea as you continue: 1. A dark force which 2) Pervades all of nature, permeating it, and 3) Balancing it.

PYTHAGORAS

The most remarkable and prominent of these Hellenes was Pythagoras who, with his followers, flourished in the latter half of the 6th Century B.C. In addition to founding a secret brotherhood based on Orphic cult ideas, Pythagoras developed number theory, geometry (both plane and solid geometry), the theory of irrational or incommensurable numbers, and knew that the earth revolved around a central fire (sun). He invented the theory of musical harmony and discovered the relationship of lengths of strings to the pitch of emitted sounds. He is even credited with coining the word "philosophy" and using the word "mathemata" to mean what we call Mathematics.[3] The Pythagorean Theorem, named after him as discoverer, is the single most important theorem of mathematics. Without this theorem, branches of higher mathematics and physics such as the Calculus and Special Relativity Theory could not be formulated. The Pythagorean School quickly became the chief scientific school of ancient Greece.

In a surviving fragment from a lost book by Aristotle called *On the Pythagoreans*, Aristotle states that Pythagoras busied himself with mathematics and numbers but would not renounce "miracle mongering".[4] This is a reference to the fact that Pythagoras was a "goetes", which means sorcerer. Readers who associate this word with Goetia, as in rabbi Solomon's *Goetia*, the so-called grimoire of ceremonial magic, would be correct: "goetes" is the Greco-Roman root of the word "Goetia". That Pythagoras was a "goetes" has been an embarrassment for some otherwise honest translators and scholars who are anxious to whitewash Pythagoras and present him as a culturally important, mathematically gifted, but otherwise typically pagan "priest-philosopher". One such translator prefers to translate "goetes" as "medicine-man" as if this is more palatable than warlock or sorcerer.[5]

Pythagoras was both "sophistes" (scientist) and "goetes" (sorcerer). He was univer-

2 *The Satanic Bible*, Anton S. LaVey, p 40, p 82.
3 *Greek Mathematics*, Heath, p 11.
4 *Early Greek philosophy*, John Burnet, p 97.
5 Burnet, op. cit. p 97.

sally regarded in the ancient world as a teacher of an entire way of life, and was a highly distinguished initiate into an Orphic cult. Still, under the spell of Judeo-Christianity, modern writers acclaim him to be a great "religious teacher" since his instruction included both the doctrine of the transmigration of souls (paliggenesia) and Orphic cult doctrine, and since the Pythagoreans were known to have means of cultivating "spiritual purity". Members were forbidden to divulge these techniques. We shall see that the word "purity" is a woeful mistranslation if not a lie, and the entire subject is misunderstood by Christians, Jews, and other dualists.

Some rules of Pythagorean societies have been preserved for us, rules anyone cannot help but sneer at, e.g. to abstain from beans, not to touch a white cock, not to step over a crossbar, etc.[6] These rules are typically pagan and remind one of superstitious rubbish such as "don't walk under a ladder". The term "Mystikos Logos" (mystical word) was an abusive epithet hurled at Pythagoras even in pre-Christian times to discredit him and prove him "religious".[7]

What is the connection between these two kinds of mutually exclusive activity, one scientific, the other mystical and superstitious?

The Pythagoreans were instructed orally. They observed a rule of silence called "echetymia", the breaking of which was punishable by death. Their silence was said, by ancient authors like Porphyrius, to be "of no ordinary kind".[8] Iamblichus said "the strictness of their secrecy is astonishing".[9]

The contradiction between the strictly scientific attitude of the Pythagoreans and the rampant superstitions can be explained by the fact that the Pythagoreans were divided into an inner circle called the "mathematikoi" (mathematicians) and an outer circle called the "akousmatikoi" (listeners). According to Porphyry "the mathematikoi learnt the more detailed and exactly elaborated version of this knowledge, the akousmatikoi (were) those who had heard only the summary headings of his (Pythagoras') writings, without the more exact exposition".[10] The Acousmatics recognized the Mathematicians to be genuine Pythagoreans, but not vice versa.[11] After Pythagoras' death, the two groups split from each other entirely.

Originally, then, there were not two sects, but two kinds of followers sorted out by natural inclination and innate abilities.[12] A good analogy comes from music, also an important study for Pythagoreans, and something any reader can easily understand. Musically, people are divided into overlapping groups according to innate or inborn ability. These range from the tone-deaf, to those who can hear and carry a fair melody, to those with the ability to hear and identify or reproduce relative pitch (most musicians), to those gifted with the very rare ability called "perfect pitch". No amount of diet, encouragement, training, ambition, teaching, or wishful thinking can enable someone to move from one group into the group of next higher ability or "talent" as it is

6 A list of these appears in *History of Western Philosophy* by Bertrand Russell, pp 31-32.
7 Burnet, op. cit. p 94.
8 *Pre-Socratic Philosophers*, G.S. Kirk & J.E. Raven, p 221.
9 Ibidem.
10 Quoted in Kirk & Raven, op. cit. p 227.
11 Burnet, op. cit. p 94.
12 *The Pre-Socratic Philosophers*, Kathleen Freeman, p 76.

called today. To someone with inferior musical ears, the identification and long discussion of harmonies and chords such as diminished, dominant 7th, major 7th, minor 6th, augmented, major 7th with a flatted 5th, etc., seems like so much irrelevant or *mystical* mumbo-jumbo. But musicians *recognize*, *identify*, and can *reproduce* these combinations of sounds immediately by a *direct awareness* which puzzles and mystifies the unmusical.

The ability to perceive directly on matters other than music alone, was also a basis for the selection of the inner circle of mathematikoi. The rare kinds of direct awareness or "sight" common only to the mathematikoi, seemed forever mystical, opaque, and confusing to those lacking in innate awareness or ability, but these forms of awareness were considered by the mathematikoi to be no more mystical than a four year old child's musical ability! Nor are these forms of awareness more mystical than Anton LaVey's statement that he was *directly* aware of a dark force in nature. To try to teach someone these forms of awareness was considered futile. The inventor of the Calculus, Leibniz, said "nothing can be taught us of which we do not have in our spirit the idea... (the soul) may even be said to possess these truths already ..."[13] No better modern statement of this idea had been made until C.J. Lumsden and E.O. Wilson began to formulate the science of Sociobiology in the last decade, which attempts to trace culture and mind onto one's genetic code, which is imprinted at the moment of conception.

We shall see that the mathematikoi claimed to know the "dark force in Nature" directly. The above-mentioned rule of echemythein or "hold peace" meant the prohibition of "uttering all things to all men".[14] The Pythagoreans were an *aristokratia*, or aristocracy, but not one based on wealth or gender.[15] Women were admitted from the start of the school and Iamblicus has preserved for us a list of seventeen female Pythagoreans taken from all over Greece, including Pythagoras' wife Theano.[16] We shall see later, how a Pythagorean division of people into three types was incorporated into Plato's myth of three kinds of men, of Gold, Iron, and Earth, in his *Republic*.

The word "akousmata" also means "rules". It was the acousmatics who swore by the silly taboos and regulations mentioned above.

What follows will be of the greatest interest to the Satanist. What was the learning accessible to the select few? This can only be surmised from clues, but the clues are very compelling and say a great deal to a Satanist.

Much of what the mathematikoi knew, due to Pythagorean secrecy and, later on, the massive Christian library burnings, can only be reconstructed by going back to the Orphic cult sources themselves, or later accounts of them, such as what is known about a lost book by Pherecydes, a remarkable contemporary of Pythagoras. Pherecydes' book miraculously survived the burnings of the Alexandrian Library in the year 47 B.C., and still existed in the third Century A.D., but this was as far as the ecclesiastics would let it go. Pherecydes is regarded as the first to write in prose. He is often linked to Pythagoras, but whether or not he was a Pythagorean is not positively known. Pythagoras attended his burial. Pherecydes was said to have consulted lost Phoenician books. He too was a "goetes".[17]

13 *Discourse on metaphysics*, Leibniz, pp 44-45.

14 Kirk & Raven, op. cit. p 221.

15 Burnet, op. cit. p 90.

16 Freeman, pp 83-84.

17 Burnet, op. cit. p 97.

The central notions of the Pythagoreans seem to have been three: 1. Theoria, 2. Kosmos, 3. Katharsis.[18] Theoria meant contemplation of the central doctrine, which was the Orphic doctrine of the pentemychos or "five recesses/chambers/gates". These five gates correspond to the five points of a pentacle or star, called by the Pythagoreans the "pentagrammon" or "pentalpha"[19], due to the fact that the pentacle and the enclosed pentagon are formed from five (pent) letter "A's" (alpha) as such:

This pentacle and its interior pentagon: were of the utmost importance to the Pythagoreans. Both were used as symbols of recognition among Pythagorean brothers.[20] "The use of this figure in later magic is well known and Paracelsus still employed it as a symbol of health, which is exactly what the Pythagoreans called it."[21]

They also called this symbol the "triple interwoven triangle."[22] This name refers not to the construction of it from five separate "A's", but rather to the fact that it can be made by drawing continuously two "A's" and then closing the third:

That it was "interwoven" indicates the one-ness and inter-relatedness of the five gates. The Pythagoreans dedicated different angles to different gods[23], but it cannot be proved positively that this is a reference to the five angles at the five outer points of the pentacle, nor exclusively the angles of some other figure or figures. As to what the five gates represented, even ancient commentators say is "very obscure" or, as Porphyrius says, "riddles".[24] A quote from the 20th Century mathematician, logical positivist philosopher and agnostic humanitarian Bertrand Russell on this subject is very interesting: "The pentagram has always been prominent in magic and apparently owes this position to the Pythagoreans, who called it "Health" and used it as a symbol of recognition of members of the brotherhood. It seems that it owed its properties to the fact that the dodecahedron (a 12-sided three-dimensional figure) has pentagons for its faces, and is, in some sense, a symbol of the Universe. This topic is attractive, but it is difficult to ascertain much that is definite about it."[25]

The Orphics (Orphikoi) believed in a long history of the gods prior to the ordered universe coming into being. This ordered universe was called Kosmos, as opposed to

18 Kirk & Raven, op. cit. p 228.

19 Burnet, op. cit. p 295.

20 Freeman, op. cit. p 86 and Burnet, op. cit. p 295.

21 Burnet, op. cit. p 295.

22 Freeman, ibid.

23 Freeman, op. cit. p 224.

24 Kirk & Raven, p 55.

25 Russell, p 47. Russell's source for this seems to be Heath, *Greek Mathematics, Volume One*, pp 159, 162, 294-296.

the primordial Chaos (*Chaos* in Greek, same word). Before Kosmos, the first offspring of Chaos were five beings or principles, whose rule was overthrown when the ordered Kosmos finally emerged. These five are eternal and cannot be destroyed. Instead, they were thrust into the five interwoven gates or recesses (pentemychos) symbolized by the Pythagorean pentacle.[26] It is not known whether or not Pythagoras himself inherited or invented this clever symbol for this cosmological event. At any rate, only when these five "sons of Chaos" were in these five places could ordered time, space, and natural law come into being and endure, safeguarded from the five chaotic destroyers (See also the article in *The Black Flame*, issue no. 2, by Tani Jantsang on Mephistopheles, in which she points out that Faust, an adept scholar and magician in Goethe's modern drama, addresses Mephistopheles as a "Son of Chaos".).

Who were these pre-cosmic five? Again, little information has survived. One of them was called Cthonie, an "abode of demons".[27] This would mean that at least one of the alphas of the pentagram, or one of its points as a recess or gate, represents the position of a being in whom demons abide, a kind of "mother" of demons.

The "daimon" was of paramount importance in Hellenic culture, one that has been an embarrassment to churchmen and secular scholars alike because the 5th century B.C. Athenian culture, which is agreed to be the foundation of Western Civilization and without equal in world history, was ascribed by these Athenians themselves to the influence of daimons.

Daimon is the origin of the word demon. This word was used from Homer onwards, and probably before, to denote super-human forces. The term is vaguer than theos (god), also used by the Hellenes to denote superhuman forces, but daimon was intended to be less anthropomorphic! Daimones (demons) and theoi (gods) were words constantly used to denote the unpredictable and incalculable in human events. Daimon is also used in Hesiod of deceased men who gain a kind of energy and power after death. Daimon can denote a protecting spirit of an individual or a family. It can also mean one's astral self. Finally, it can mean a source of artistic or scientific inspiration.

The first and, for the unfamiliar reader, best theory of the daimones appears in Plato's dialogue *The Symposium* (the Banquet), in which one orator recounts a conversation he had with Diotima of Mantineia, a prophetess who saved Athens from a plague through sorcery. We shall meet her again later, when she curses Socrates with manifold results. In *The Symposium*, Diotima says of the function of the daimones "through this intermediary (daimones) moves all the art of divination, and the art of priests, and all concerned with sacrifice and mysteries and incantations, and all sorcery and witchcraft. For god has no intercourse with man, but through this (daimones) comes all the communion and conversation of gods with men and men with gods, both awake and asleep; and he who is expert in this is a spiritual man..."[28] Unfortunately, for reasons any Satanist can guess, all translations delete the word demon altogether and translate daimones as "spirits".[29]

26 From an ancient account of the contents of Pherecydes' lost book preserved in *Damascius de principiis*, quoted in Kiark & Raven, op. cit. p 55.

27 Kirk & Raven, p 56.

28 *Great dialogues of Plato*, translated by W.H.D. Rouse, p 98.

29 See this same translation, earlier on.

Daimones are long lived, but not immortal, and can be destroyed, according to Plutarch in his treatise *On the Failure of the Oracle.*

So endemic to Hellenic culture was the daimon, that Greeks toasted to "Agathos Daimon" which means "Here's Luck!", the cult of the "Good Daimon".[30] There were also the feared avenging, destroying, and punishing daimones, but they were not thought to be evil in themselves, though their selfishness was taken into account. They were thought to be carrying out a higher will, i.e. "following orders" in a strict hierarchy according to the wishes of the "mother" on the pentacle, obeying "anagke" (necessity), to whom even Zeus was subject.

In a later section, we shall see how the church fathers were unable, at first, to root out mingling with demons, due to its prevalence. We shall see how they first sought to lower the demons in the universal harmony, and then to exclude them from the human sphere entirely as unwelcome tenants (exorcism). Magic came to be regarded as a delusion imposed on humanity by seducing demons. The Christian attitude became typified by a Pannonian monk named Martin (560 A.D.), who said the gods of the Hellenes were themselves demons, and that these demons were "fallen angels". He seems to have believed the Hellenic people themselves were a race of incarnate demons.[31] This is a great departure from the Hellenic idea that demons are the sources of any art and science that is worthy enough to be called inspired.

To return to the pentacle and its five gates, another gate or point was identified as the abode of Ophioneus, who appears to have been the "son of Chaos", who presented the greatest threat to the emergence and stability of the fledgling cosmos. He was depicted as a monstrous, multi-headed snake (ophis), serpent, or dragon. Hellenic mythologists record a colossal battle between the conquering sky-gods Zeus-Kronos (not Chronos) versus Ophioneus and the Ophionids, its spawn, in which the Zeus-Kronos league prevailed and the rule of Ophioneus ended with its placement in its recess or gate (Kronos is time still in chaos and not yet ordered: whereas Chronos is ordered time as we know it exists, though some scholars argue as to what comes first, Kronos or Chronos.). This battle parallels that of other mythologies, such as the conquest of Tiamat by Marduk in Babylonian tales, and the Hurrian-Hittite victory of the storm-god over the dragon Illuyanka.

This notion of a victorious sky or space-time army of gods over a destructive, primæval chaotic dragon was known to Pherecydes. It was either taught directly to Pythagoras in his Orphic initiation, or was gleaned during his many travels. He is said to have covered the known world, and according to various traditions, learned from peoples as various as the Chaldeans, Brahmins, Druids, and Celtic priests and teachers.[32]

Of the other dwellers in the gates, almost nothing survives. Ophioneus is supposed to have had a consort, Eurynome, who fought along-side Ophioneus against Kronos. Various myths, surviving in whole or in part, mention Callirhoe, who produced a snake-woman Echidna, but her connection to Cthonie and Ophioneus, and to the pentacle, is even less clear.[33]

---

30 *Conversion*, Nock, p 223.

31 Smith, op. cit. pp 238-242.

32 Kirk & Raven, p 224.

33 Kirk & Raven, op. cit, pp 66-67.

The five chambers, recesses, or gates which are interwoven were collectively known as "Tartaros". The gates to Tartaros are guarded by "Harpia" (Harpies) and "Thyella" (Whirlwind).[34] Tartaros is not "hell" as Christian and dualistic distortion implies, but is rather the place where these first five beings were placed in a kind of "apportionment of the spheres"[35], in which the victor (Zeus-Kronos) takes possession of the sky and of space and time. The reason that Tartaros came to be associated with "hell" is that a number of other defeated deities, like the Ophionids, were placed there, and Greek mythology records a number of men who defied the gods who were sent there now and again. The misinterpretation of the five as "fallen angels" is the work of Origen and other Christian writers. While being consigned to Tartaros must count as a punishment for a human, or so it would seem, it is unwarranted and even contrary to Hellenic thought to think this with respect to the five and their brood. The five could not co-exist with the prevailing cosmos in which we exist, were not thought evil except by the Christians, but they certainly inspired fear. Aristotle himself, well before the Christian era, seems to have begun the mistaken interpretation of Pythagoreanism as dualistic, a claim justly denied by the scholar F.M. Cornford.[36] If, however, Aristotle was right, it must then be admitted that the Pythagoreans revered, and hailed each other, by invoking five evil beings or principles! Not so! Aristotle, nonetheless, seemed to have been aware, as many Hellenic intellectuals were in the 4th Century B. C., of an outward appearing similarity between Pythagoreanism and Zoroastrianism, since Pythagoras was said to have been visited by Zaratas, a Chaldean.

It should be noted that despite Pythagoras' undeniable cosmopolitanism, he was of Pelasgian descent, not only in body, but in mind.[37] The Pelasgians were a warlike, matriarchal people whom the Achæans, a chief Hellenic tribe, conquered and blended with, both genetically and culturally. The Pelasgians spoke a non-Hellenic language and used a non-Hellenic alphabet. Their chief god was a goddess the Hellenes referred to as Leucotheia, which means White Goddess, but apparently she was called by the Pelasgians themselves "Danæ", which is the origin of the Greek Diana. Leucotheia was the All-Mother who ever flows, she was thought to be the source of all change and was thought, according to Pausanias, to be the mother of the five (on the pentacle).[38]

The Pelasgians were called centaur-men due to their brotherly affection and community with horses, whom they cherished. From this Pythagoras seems to have derived his doctrine of the kinship of men and beasts. The Hellenes also called the Pelasgians goat-men, due to their extreme exogamy which gave them a reputation of being sexual Satyrs.

Orphism thrived among the Pelasgians, and Orpheus himself, the founder of the Orphikoi, was considered to have been a priest to the goddess Leucotheia.[39] According to Porphyry, Pythagoras was initiated into Orphism by the Idæan Dactyls, who were dancing priestesses who used the Pelasgian alphabet. The Orphics had an oath engraved

34 Remark of Pherecydes preserved by the Christian writer Origen, quoted in Kirk & Raven, op. cit. p 66.

35 Kirk & Raven, p 70.

36 *Plato and Parmenides.*

37 Burnet, pp 87-88.

38 *The White Goddess*, Robert Graves, p 281.

39 According to Pausanias, Graves, p 281 and ff.

in code on gold tablets tied around the necks of their dead. The injunction on the medallion was not to forget, i.e. the command was, when one died, to avoid drinking the waters of the river Lethe, which were thought to induce forgetfulness (amnesia) of one's prior existences, whenever one drank and was reborn.[40] One of the avowed accomplishments of Pythagoras and the mathematikoi was the clear recollection of former lives, i.e. they claimed to have overcome this state of forgetfulness, the overcoming of which was called "anamnesia". We shall see how this doctrine of recollection was carried on by Plato later.

The Orphics celebrated orgiastic tree-dances (orgia) at Zone in Thrace. Zone alternately means a woman's girdle, disrobing a woman, and the sexual act itself. The orgiastic dance in honor of the All-Mother at Zone is inferred to have been a dance of the "loosened girdle". Orpheus himself was the son of Oea Agria, which means "wild tree dance". This aspect of Orphic "religion" or custom carried into the Hellenic world, is often referred to as the Dionysian, a term resurrected by Friedrich Nietzsche, a philologist and philosopher, who used it in its original meaning.

The purpose of such orgia was Katharsis – the third of the above mentioned central notions taught to the mathematikoi. Katharsis meant release, which the mathematikoi knew resulted in health of mind, body and spirit. As Russell pointed out, the Pythagoreans called their pentacle "health", so the pentacle also symbolized the release of Katharsis. None of this is understood because virtually all of the writers on this subject would be considered "akatharti" by ancient Pythagoreans, i.e. unhealthy in the sense of having unreleased or bottled-up emotions. Some would even be considered "thanatos", a difficult word which means "alive yet miserably dead", "no longer zoös" (not an animal). Those who are akatharti were considered unfit to learn or know anything correctly. It is these writers who mistranslate Katharsis as "purification". Purification does indeed occur during and after Katharsis. This fact seems to have been understood by Dr. LaVey who, in *The Satanic Bible*, refers to cleansing oneself of malignant emotions. The malignancy, LaVey correctly believes, lies only in these emotions being unreleased or bottled or pent-up, and therefore poisonous and dangerous to one's well-being.[41] Readers may recognize the word orgasm in orgia. They would be right in part, but there is more to orgia, as will be seen below.

Due to the cultural fusion of the Hellenes with the Pelasgians, the Hellenes of Athens held Athena, a female goddess, in higher regard than Zeus. The city of Athens was named after her. Judeo-Christian falsification entails that we be impressed with the false idea that Zeus was the chief deity of these gifted Athenians. This is an effort to claim that these "pagans" worshipped a kind of patriarchal chief deity who was a rude or crude forerunner of the so-called "highly refined, advanced and spiritual single transcendent God of the Hebrews and the Christians".

Nothing could be further from the truth. Zeus was subject to higher powers in many Hellenic accounts, and, says one account, while still a mere boy, Zeus was tutored by the five beings represented by the pentacle and created by the All-Mother.[42] This

40 *Paligenesia*, Graves, p 140.

41 LaVey, op. cit. p 64.

42 Fragment of Apollonius Rhodius appearing in Kirk & Raven, p 66.

was before Zeus "grew up" and conquered sky and space. Athena became a stand-in for Leucotheia. The highest holy day in Athens was not the wedding feast of Zeus and Hera, as one would logically expect if the Christians and their apologists are right about Zeus being a proto-Jehova. The biggest "religious" festival at Athens was reserved for the birthday of Athena, the magnificent revelry of the pan-Athenæum.

Some readers will associate the name of the priestesses who initiated Pythagoras, the Dactyls, with the root word for hand or fingers. This is correct. The Pythagoreans often used the hand and/or five fingers to hail one another when pentacles were absent or forbidden. Exactly how this was done is guesswork (Tani Jantsang has suggested that it could have been a handshake similar to one used by certain "Masons" in her own family, in which the hand is cupped so that the tips of the five fingers form a pentacle with the other hand grasped inside it. Virtually all the Masons this writer has met (except one) however, including some of 32nd degree, seem completely unfamiliar with any of this.).

The most famous of the divine kings of the Pelasgians was Cheiron, which means "hand", a meaning utterly puzzling to virtually all mythographers and scholars, such as Joseph Campbell, who has levelled all myths to the tidy formula of adoring the "hero with a thousand faces". Literate Athenians believed Cheiron tutored the greatest heroes of their pantheon: Hercules, Achilles and other revered kings.[43] Julian the Apostate, the last pagan Emperor of Rome (who was hated so much by the Christians that they assassinated him) wrote a lost book called "Against the Christians". In a surviving fragment of this book, he extolled the Hellenes "of the tens of thousands who have the wisdom of Cheiron. For it is from him that they derived their initiation into the mysteries of nature and the knowledge of divine things; so that, in comparison the Hebrews seem only to give themselves airs about their own attainment."[44] We shall encounter Julian again later. Virtually all of his good friends were Neo-Platonists, who were the chief opponents of the Christian Emperors.

The initiation of Pythagoras by the Dactyls was not a minor event. It transformed him into a kind of demi-god to whom divine honors were paid wherever he went. Empedocles, a near-contemporary of Pythagoras, was also known to have received such honors.[45]

The Katharsis taught by the Pythagoreans to the inner circle of mathematikoi utilized music.[46] This form of Katharsis is obviously unavailable to the tone deaf. There was also a Katharsis through science, which Pythagoras considered the greatest of all and well above the level of the akousmatikoi.[47] It should be evident that the use of orgies, dance, music and science as a means of "education for the soul" is diametrically opposed to the Judeo-Christian idea of salvation by means of abstinence, sobriety, prayer, good works, studying scripture, etc. The reason Katharsis through science was considered the highest will be obvious to some readers who can attest to the wonderful feeling sometimes called "The Eureka Experience" that accompanies the direct and instantaneous

43 Graves, p 283.

44 This fragment, translated, can be found in *The Sirius Mystery*, Robert K.G. Temple, p 256.

45 Graves, p 283.

46 Burnet, p 97.

47 Burnet, p 98.

grasp or "sight" of a difficult, hidden, or obscure mathematical, scientific, historical, or other puzzle or problem. It feels like a release, and we can credit Pythagoras with fully understanding that this experience has as profound and salutory an effect on body, mind and soul, as sexual, though this is much less common to all men, whereas sexual release is common to all. Dualists can misinterpret this as they like, and, needless to say, have done so. The word orgia actually means "sacrament", in which one experiences not only Katharsis, but also "Ekstasis" (ecstasy).[48] The Satanist should see that Judeo-Christianity is not only opposed to sexuality and ecstasy, but opposed to and destructive of Katharsis in general, of any type, including even the Katharsis of science, etc. The Christian attack on sexual Katharsis was an attack on a form of Katharsis that is available to all people. The attack on the Katharsis of science, dance, music, etc., was an attack on a select few (I will remind the reader that during the Middle Ages, under the tyrannical rule of the Christian authorities, people did have sex, people did get born. But science and these higher forms of knowledge were utterly banned and works destroyed, for example the well-known Galileo who had his eyes taken out for looking through a telescope.).

Pythagorean cosmology involved the concept of the beginning of all (pantos arche), which was called "to apeiron", a prominent feature of a number of Hellenic philosophers' systems. This is a feature which sets Hellenic culture apart from all others and gives it a Satanic cast.

"To apeiron" is commonly translated as "the boundless", or "the unlimited", and was understood to be a dark force that pre-existed the cosmos and is presently "inhaled" by it, i.e. infused into nature (physis) everywhere, permeating and steering all. It is due to this dark infusion that change and time came into being. The concept is like Dr. LaVey's dark force in nature, and akin to the modern scientific concept of entropy, which was coined from a Hellenic word meaning both "turning" and "undoing", or "dissolving shape and form", a process of "dynamic unformation".

The infusion of this dark force, the apeiron, also causes the myriad separate things of the cosmos to come into existence, giving rise to distinction, separateness, and discontinuity. The idea is that without the apeiron, there would only be a continuum (syneches), an indistinct, static whole without motion, dynamism and change.

The inhalation itself is spoken of as a "void" (kenon) or empty.[49] When it enters, the cosmos grows and expands.

Again, Aristotle seems to have taken this to be a dualism, i.e. a dyad or pair of first principles used to energize and explain everything, the unlimited (to apeiron) and its consequent limited (deras). But there is something decidedly different about this so-called dualism that sets it apart from primitive non-Hellenic "theories of opposites". In dualistic theories, the opposites merely strive or "war" with one another, occasionally holding balance or "truce" to preserve or sustain something's existence, instead of undoing it. Pythagoras' revolution, which has become the central concept of physical science, is that these opposites, when preserving existence, balance or harmonize according to very definite numerical intervals that can be known and expressed by definite numeri-

48 Burnet, pp 81-82.

49 Kirk & Raven, p 252.

cal ratios and relationships, or, as is said today: equations. The infusion of the apeiron which causes a separate thing to exist and preserves or continues its existence does so by establishing a temporary, but perfect balance or attunement of opposites according to definite numerical ratios. Hence the famous Pythagorean dictum, carried on by Plato and never understood by Aristotle, that "all things are number". This idea will be dealt with in detail later in the section on Plato, who elucidates this subject. As to exactly how all things are numbers was revealed only to the mathematikoi who were deemed to have the innate (the reader might read "genetic") ability to Know, and, as we shall see in Plato's elaboration of Pythagoreanism, were thought to already possess this knowledge at birth, having merely to "remember" it, a kind of a-priori knowledge. This became a central doctrine of Platonism, and was the basic qualification for a Pythagorean or Platonist philosopher. Knowledge was deemed unteachable to those who lacked it within themselves innately (I refer the reader to the example of the tone-deaf attempting to know music.).

Pythagoras is credited with having discovered that if you pinch a vibrating string halfway, you produce a tone one octave higher than the whole string would produce. If you pinch it one third of the way down and pluck the larger section, you produce a tone a musician would call a fifth higher than the whole string. If you pinch it one quarter of the way down and pluck the larger part, you hear a fourth. Such intervals and ratios, which Pythagoreans called "mesotes", govern all of nature, even determining whether or not something is lead or gold, heavy or light, etc., an idea Aristotle ridiculed. As will be shown later, the idea of mesotes is the cornerstone of all physical science! This revolution begun by Pythagoras is deeper and more profound than the religious and ethical nonsense of Moses, Jesus, Mohammed, et. a1., despite the fact that, in some times and places, it degenerated into mystical numerological bunk, like justice is 4, marriage is 3, etc. Such identifications however can be traced back to the akousmatikoi[50] and are usually taken up by the same type of people today, those who Can Not Know.

Pythagoras' mathematikoi knew or set out to discover the "just blends" (krasis) or proper ratios that could sustain health, stable planetary motions, or even the continuance of the soul (this attunement was called "pathos arithmon"). The balance in nature is ultimately due to the infusion of the dark apeiron, which creates the balance or, as with LaVey' s dark force, itself acts as "the balancing factor" in Nature. As one very cautious put it: "We sometimes feel tempted to say that Pythagoras had really hit upon the secret of the world when he said "Things are numbers""[51] and thought was ever after "dominated by the notion of the perfectly tuned string".[52] This commentator presumably means rational and scientific thought, but we shall see how Pythagoras, through Plato, influenced the early Christian theologians too, who desperately needed a sound philosophical basis for a belief system that could not stand on its own, especially against Platonism. The techniques of, for example, Philolaus, the Pythagorean, could not have been more inimical to the Christian idea of God, because Philolaus, a mathematician and goetes, is said to have explained God by means of mathematical figures[53], which

50 Burnet, pp 107-108.
51 Burnet, p 112, n. 1.
52 Ibid.
53 Freeman, p 232.

sounds more like Einstein than St. Augustine. It was from Philolaus that Plato obtained his Pythagorean learning. Christians also drew upon Platonic sources to co-opt, absorb and defuse them. It should be mentioned, however, that even while Pythagoras himself was alive, a general burning of Pythagorean lodges (synedroi) occurred and continued for some time, with many followers murdered by Cylon, though this incident smacks more of personal vendetta by Cylon for Pythagoras' refusal to admit him to the order; and as a vengeance for the protection the synedroi offered to a number of political enemies of various tyrants. The Pythagoreans were no mere contemplatives, but showed activity in the political life of the day. Like the Satanist, they knew that with knowledge comes power, and the ability to work one's Will on the world. They did not hesitate to cause changes in the governments of the day.

There are several final points of interest to Satanists on Pythagoras.

Pythagorean doctrine states that the primæval dyad of the apeiron (unlimited) and the deras (limited) developed into ten principles (arches deka) that Aristotle tells us were grouped into two columns as left and right, dark and light, female and male.[54] One is reminded of the Kaballistic Tree of the Ten Sephiroth, though the latter contains a center column of four of the ten which balance and harmonize the other six. We have seen that in Pythagoreanism, the idea of mesotes or mediating numerical intervals balances the opposites. Since Aristotle was anxious to prove Pythagoras was a dualist, as scholars like Cornford have shown, one feels he may have left a column out, one that would balance and harmonize. Comparisons with the Kaballa will not be ventured into, but Kaballists have a reputation for numerological speculation. The subject is made further difficult because, according to the best authority on the Kaballa, Isaac Myer, whose work is completely ignored by the proliferation of authors on the Kaballa, the early Kaballists switched the second and third Sephiroth, a fact even Crowley seems to have been totally unaware of. Myer states this switch was done to mislead and confuse, and it has certainly had this effect. When finally the second and third Sephiroth are switched back to their correct positions, then sensible comparisons to the Pythagorean doctrine may be forthcoming.

The multiplication of the original dyad into ten principles and then into more, and then into everything, all accomplished by the infusion of the dark apeiron, cannot be found as an element of any culture except the Hellenic. To find it anywhere else, one has to engage in an often fruitless search into what little is known about the Mahakala (Great Black) sects of Tibet, or "Black Taoists" of China.

The esteem in which Pythagoreans held the ten principles which they called the Tetractys, is attested to by the fact that Pythagoreans swore oaths on it in the form of four rows shaped like an equilateral triangle thus:[55]

54 Kirk & Raven, p 238.

55 Freeman, p 224.

The departure from the merely obvious facts or data of sense experience in order to search out deeper explanations of natural phenomena is a hallmark of Pythagoreanism, Plato, and modern science. We shall see how this notion was hotly contested by Aristotle, the original "philosopher of common sense", who, like Socrates, thought science and philosophy should seek "essences", the obscure qualities inherent in things which they thought made lead lead and gold gold, make the heavy heavy, and the light in weight, light. This trend of surpassing obvious sensations for explanations of phenomena was well under way among Hellenic thinkers before Pythagoras, with Anaximander and others, even philosophers not known to the Pythagoreans. The point here is that many of these ideas such as that of the dark apeiron infused into nature, were not unique to the Pythagoreans, but endemic to the leading thinkers the Hellenic people produced, such as Anaximander, Empedocles, et al. It is incorrect, as many scholars frequently state, to say that the Orphics influenced Hesiod, or Hesiod influenced Anaximander, etc., etc. This was a single cultural milieu of a remarkably multi-faceted kind, but having common threads or features that are decidedly Satanic.

In the Christian era, writers like Iamblichus still understood what Pythagoras meant by "things are numbers", how number is the basis for the endurance of anything, whether, as Iamblichus says, they be "divine natures, gods or demons". Iamblichus still knew that this was taught by Orpheus himself. We shall see how churchmen, inquisitorial ecclesiastics, and Christian Emperors did more to search and destroy doctrines of this tradition when they could not absorb them, and that what they absorbed, they lacked the innate ability to understand. These were people Pythagoras would not have admitted, and Plato would have considered plebeians, the people modern behavioral psychology recognizes as monkey-brains who are accomplished in nothing more than advanced parroting.

SOCRATES AND PLATO

Socrates and Plato are linked historically. Judeo-Christianity and Humanitarianism has sought to perpetuate this connection in order to conceal the Satanic cast of the Orphic-Pythagorean-Platonic tradition by mixing it and confusing it with the Socratic-Aristotelian tradition. Only by ripping Socrates and all he represented cleanly away from Plato once and for all, which scholars who fancy themselves "moral" resist, can the Satanic cast of the Plato-Hellenic tradition stand out.

In Plato's dialogues, Socrates is almost invariably the principle speaker. A departure from this only occurs in Plato's later dialogues, like the *Timæus*, in which the principle speaker is a Pythagorean astronomer named Timæus.[56]

Plato met Socrates and listened to him. Since Socrates wrote nothing almost, all we know about him comes through Plato, in whose dialogues one must seek the ideas of both. Plato and Socrates are so easy to mix up, that one writer incorrectly referred to Plato's Theory of Forms as "Socrates' Theory of Forms"!

Socrates' hollow boast is famous: he claimed that, unlike his fellow Athenians, at least he knew that he knew nothing! Yet he repeatedly evinces, in the early dialogues,

56 Freeman, p 240.

sheer faith in the immortality of the soul, and an unshakable, yet never satisfactorily justified conviction that goodness, virtue and justice exist and make men happy.[57] His obediance to civil authority, despite having no convincing reasons for it, have made him the admiration of Christian, Jew, Marxist, and moralist alike. Meanwhile, Plato's Pythagorean outlook with its efforts to rip off nature's disguises and seek deeper explanations, quietly, but not without immense resistance, became the approach of physical science. We shall see why Christian writers have extolled Socrates as a forerunner of Jesus Christ, the book about whom (the *Bible*) is still the bestselling book in the Western World. It is a little known fact, that as of 1961, the second bestselling book in the Western World was one that continued the tradition of the mathematikoi: Euclid's *Elements*.[58]

The problem of which beliefs are Socrates' and which are Plato's is referred to by students of the subject as "The Socratic Question".[59] This can be a real problem for new readers, but there actually is almost complete agreement on the subject among scholars. In fact, there is almost complete agreement as to exactly what point in what dialogue Plato first breaks off from Socrates and begins to speak his own ideas through Socrates.

As already mentioned, Socrates was not a Hellene, but rather of the tribe of Antiochus (Antioch was in Phrygia, which is now Turkey).[60] He was described as short, ugly, and snub-nosed.[61] His character was not only different from Plato's, but quite different from Hellenes in general. He was utterly un-Satanic.

He had nothing to say on one of the educated Athenians' favorite topics: the nature and the origin of the universe. He was more interested in man's ethics, laws and customs (nomos) rather than in nature (physis). He could not discuss the apeiron, nor the origin of the universe. He was more concerned with disputing ethics and political matters with clever imposters. Robert Graves believes myths frightened or offended him, especially Pelasgian cult ideas and symbols.[62] In one of Plato's dialogues, Socrates says: "But I have no leisure at all for such matters; and the cause of it, my friend, is this: I am not yet able, according to the Delphic precept, to know myself."[63] Socrates is referring to the priestess at Delphi, who commanded him to "know thyself", a task he embarked upon. The oracle priestess seemed to know Socrates better than he knew himself, and she appears to have mocked him. She apparently knew that he considered the study of nature and the cosmos as irrelevant to self-knowledge, i.e. that Socrates was someone cut off from nature in mind, spirit and body. He was a confirmed city man, who confessed to Phaedrus that "fields and trees will not teach me anything, but men do."[64] Socrates was the prototypical Judeo-Christian and humanitarian ethicist, for whom man is the "element" of the universe most deserving of thought and attention. This is opposed to the Pythagorean idea that man, beast and plant are akin and merely a part of nature, which deserves study. Socrates' words are in direct contrast to those of a mediæval Pythago-

57 Plato's *Gorgias*, translated by Donald J. Zeyl.

58 *The main stream of mathematics*, Edna E. Kramer, p 47.

59 *Plato, Protagoras and Meno*, Introduction by W.K.G. Guthrie, p 16

60 *The Apology* by Plato, in *Great Dialogues of Plato*, translated by W.H.D. Rouse, p 438.

61 *The Theatetus* by Plato, in *The Dialogues of Plato*, translated by B. Jowett, p 44.

62 *The White Goddess*, Graves, pp 10-11.

63 Quoted in Graves, p 11.

64 Quoted in Graves, p 11.

rean, Bernard of Morlaix, 1140 AD, of N.W. Europe, who said that "trees and stones will teach you more than you can learn from the mouth of a doctor of theology".[65] Bernard was not a nature-worshipper, but according to Graves "held that the mythical qualities of chosen trees and chosen precious stones, as studied by Pythagoras, explained the Christian mysteries better than Saint Augustine had ever been able to do".[66]

The celebrated concept of "Platonic Love", the concept that prudes use to rationalize their contempt of their own sexuality, was really Socratic Love. Socrates turned his back not only on Hellenic science, poetry and myth, but also on the All-Mother goddess. It will be recalled that "to apeiron", the dark force infused in nature, was considered by the Pythagoreans to be dark, unlimited, female, the source of the daimones, and the cause of all creation, generation, enduring and inspiration. Socrates was in romantic homosexual love (but refrained from touching him through self-restraint) with Alcibiades, an Athenian youth, as attested to by Alcibiades himself in Plato's *Symposium.* Socrates turned his back on the Goddess who sent the daimones as intermediaries so men could commune with the gods. Socrates practised a kind of *intellectual* homosexuality, a hardened failure to respond to the female *principle* in nature, whether the response demanded was sexual, emotional or intellectual. Diotima of Mantineia (the Arcadian witch we have already met in connection with Plato's theory of the daimones) cursed Socrates for this. She warned him that a man's love should be directed towards women, that three female Muses (the Hellenic Triple Muse) presided over all acts of creation and generation, whether physical, intellectual or spiritual. She told him the goddesses Cybelle and Ishtar in the Temples of Attis tolerated sodomy between men in their temple courts, but she warned him that the ideal of intellectual homosexuality, or the severance of a man's psyche, thoughts and feelings from the female principle in nature, was a far more serious aberrancy and offence. She was referring to Socrates' efforts to make his intellect spiritually self-sufficient, to cut himself free from what Goethe called "the eternal feminine principle" and what Carl Jung called "a man's anima". She warned him he would not escape the power and wrath of the All-Mother in her many forms: Leucotheia, Hecate, Athena.[67]

As a result of her curse, Socrates got Xantippe, a peevish, scolding shrew of a wife. His beloved Alcibiades became a self-destructive, vicious, treacherous ruinator of Athens. Socrates died under a death sentence from a Court of Athens by drinking hemlock, a leaf sacred to Hecate, perfecting the delicious revenge of the All-Mother prophesied by Diotima.

Denial of the Dark Principle, as Nietzsche pointed out, results in what he called the Apollonian (ordered, logical, mechanical, rational) completely severed from the Dionysian (intuition, instinct, passion, inspiration) which results in Akatharti, or Thanatos: a man who is a head with no body, or a man whose head is at war with the rest of his body. Hence we have the Christian and other mind-body dualisms wherein "the evil body" is always causing "the pure mind" to have "evil thoughts". These so-called "evil thoughts" are in fact basic biological human natural instincts! This dualism is "the Apollonian at war with the Dionysian, or severed from the Dionysian", as if the person is

65 Quoted in Graves, p 238.

66 Ibid.

67 Graves, pp 10-12.

utterly cut-off from Nature, even his own Nature, as in Socrates. Pythagoreans, with their measurement of interval, measurement of harmonies, and their profound logic with their inspiration and Katharsis is an example of a perfect blend of Apollonian and Dionysian which results in "Zoös" and "Eros". The Dionysian can exist in a person by itself without the Apollonian, and the person will still be Zoös-Eros (health of mind, body, and spirit), however one might consider such a person "stupid". There is also the case of a totally Apollonian person who is also Thanatos, who intellectually decides (!) to "become Dionysian"; and he makes a pathetic attempt to intellectually bring out his instincts (instead of just "let go", FEELING which he is *unable* to do). The result is the inverse Christian, still exclusively Apollonian, that is, Thanatos; and now thoroughly self-deluded.

It is no wonder then, that the exclusively Apollonian and Thanatos type of person finds the Pythagorean type, or Plato's Philosopher type, to be "mystical". It is no wonder either, that the Thanatos type despises, fears, ridicules, and battles what he can never be.

This martyrdom of Socrates, which is understood in the Judeo-Christian world to be some sort of self-sacrifice he made for "freedom of speech and thought" enabled his influence to rise, contributing to the disrepute of myth, magic and science. According to Graves, the myths and their language survived "purely enough in the Mystery-cults of Eleusis, Corinth, Samothrace and elsewhere, and when they were suppressed by the early Christian Emperors, they were still taught in the poetic colleges of Ireland and Wales, and in the witch-covens of Western Europe".[68] This article will trace them as they survived in a Platonic form of magic called Theurgy that was forced underground by the Christian Emperors after they had destroyed, by imperial edicts, the finest works of the Pythagorean tradition.

Socrates' formal legal charge was one of corrupting the youth of Athens. To the young Plato, Socrates seemed only to be disabusing smug teachers and pretenders to virtue of false ideas they had about their reputed knowledge of politics, ethics and the pursuit of the good life. Socrates' refusal to escape his death sentence when offered an opportunity to do so, is taken by some moralists who advocate "turn the other cheek" to be an exemplary instance of submitting to the will of bad men. Others extol Socrates' self-sacrificing obedience to legal and civil authority and its judgements rather than committing what Socrates argued in his final moments of life, to be the "greater evil" of disobeying, escaping and thereby breaking the law willfully. His absolute faith in an afterlife expressed moments before he drank the hemlock, with not one shred of evidence or science to back it up, and his unshakable conviction as to the virtue of his accepting the death sentence, has led some commentators to compare him directly to Jesus.[69]

Undoubtedly the pride Judeo-Christian and humanitarian intellectuals feel about Socrates' death, is first and foremost augmented by the fact that the only time Socrates ever got bitter or ill-mannered in any dialogue was in Plato's *Gorgias*, in which he had the ill-luck of a head-on encounter with a Satanic personality named Callicles. Callicles presented to Socrates the Satanic idea that customs and laws are purely matters of mutual agreement and convention, and are contrary to nature. The correct thing to do,

68 Graves, p 12.

69 *Five Great Dialogues*, translated by Reverend B. Jowett in the introduction by Louise R. Loomis, p 7.

Callicles says, is to follow nature, and if one's nature is above or outgrows petty convention and morality, that man should put himself above the law and be his own law. Callicles says it is his natural right and even duty to do this, and to seek to dominate and use what he can for his own personal gratification. Callicles further states that suffering what is unjust is certainly more shameful than doing an injustice. He says that nature dictates that it is just that the superior have a greater share of things than the inferior. A superior man, he says, does not seek to restrain his pleasure or appetites, he devotes his courage and intelligence to maximizing his capacities for these. Finally, Callicles states that laws were devised by the weaker to restrain, as much as possible, the stronger.[70]

Socrates launches into a well-argued refutation of hedonism, but not until after he unexpectedly loses his usual tolerance, wit and of times humor. That this tantrum in which Socrates comes as near to blows as we ever see, is genuinely Socrates' response to Callicles and not Plato's is attested to by the fact that the *Gorgias* is one of the dialogues belonging to Plato's early period, in which he was more concerned with presenting Socrates' views than his own. It does not belong to the later group of dialogues in which Plato uses Socrates and others to relate his Pythagorean ideas.[71] We shall deal briefly later with Plato's idea, one that has stuck painfully in the soft craw of the Judeo-Christians and humanists for two-thousand years, that the philosopher-king is "above the law".

The young Plato seems to have regarded Socrates much as other Athenians did, as a fascinating, but unusual rare bird. Socrates certainly did exercise a fascination on Athenian youth, and even old folks are said to have thrown blankets on the ground in fair weather just to see him go into one of his cataleptic trances wherein he stood motionless for hours, an activity more than one historian, such as Nietzsche, found "morbid". Socrates claimed to be under the influence of a daimon (demon) himself, who was obviously unable or unwilling to teach him anything. Socrates claimed the demon warned him whenever he was about to do something unvirtuous! He received no such warning before drinking the hemlock (which killed him) – so he drank it.[72]

In Plato's early dialogues, which are generally accepted as a true representation not of Plato's own thoughts but of what Socrates actually said and did, Socrates states that he engages in a two-step process in his conversations with pretenders to virtue and ethical "knowledge".

In the first stage, Socrates disabuses or rids them of false ideas and smug convictions. Many of his verbal victims showed appreciation for this, and the young Plato, already innately Pythagorean[73] seems to have regarded this step of the process as a form of Katharsis, a release or purging from lies and falsehoods. This state is called the Socratic "elenchus".[74] In this stage, one discovers that one is really like Socrates: one knows only that he knows nothing! (Let us hope Satanists do not look inside themselves and discover that they know nothing, that could be dangerous!)

Socrates himself called the second stage of the process "mental midwifery" (maieuric), in which he aided his students in delivering, or giving birth to ideas already

70 Plato's *Gorgias*, translated by Donald J. Zeyl, pp 52 and ff.

71 Plato's *Gorgias*, introduction, note 2, p XII.

72 Plato's *The Apology*, translated by F.J. Church, p 47.

73 Freeman, op. cit. p 18.

74 *Plato, Protagoras, and Meno*, W.KG. Guthrie, see his intro to the *Meno*, p 108.

locked inside themselves, as if they were pregnant. Socrates' method intended to assist Athenian youth in defining and redefining moral, political, or religious terms, like courage, justice, and piety according to their own insights. The young Plato, we shall see, interpreted this as an example of the Pythagorean anamnesis or recollection, an awakening from the forgetfulness that comes with rebirth. But instead of remembering former existences, Plato focussed on the remembrance of the deeper laws of nature and the cosmos, not merely moral or political notions.

PLATO

There is a great deal of agreement as to exactly when Plato takes over and begins to use Socrates as a mouthpiece for his own ideas in the dialogues. This occurs in the *Meno* at Section 81 A.[75] The tone of the dialogue changes abruptly and "Socrates" suddenly refers rather atypically to the view of certain "priests and priestesses" and "poets who are divinely inspired".[76] He then proceeds to introduce the Pythagorean notion of anamnesis.

There are many oblique references to the Pythagoreans in Plato's later dialogues, in which characters other than "Socrates" begin to be used as Plato's mouthpieces. More than one scholar has noticed how wary Plato is of mentioning Pythagoras by name (he does so only once!) and how careful he is not to identify the Pythagoreans by name (which he also does only once!).[77] In the *Theatetus*, "Socrates" is made to say, immediately before a Pythagorean doctrine is introduced, "Take a look around, then, and see that none of the uninitiated are listening. Now, by the uninitiated I mean the people who believe in nothing but what they can grasp in their hands, and who will not allow that action or generation or anything invisible can have real existence." Theatetus answers, "Yes, indeed Socrates, they are very hard and impenetrable mortals". "Socrates" continues, "Far more ingenious are these brethren whose mysteries I am about to reveal to you".[78]

These later dialogues are separated from the early ones by what puzzled and perplexed Plato scholars have called a "wide interval of philosophical speculation".[79] The real "interval" is that the Pythagorean Plato takes over. His youthful fascination for Socrates seems gone.

The evidence that Plato was a Pythagorean is indirect. Much of Plato's knowledge is said to have been transmitted to him from a Pythagorean book he obtained. The book was written by the Pythagorean Philolaus, who was the first Pythagorean known to write anything down. The story of how Plato purchased this book through a man named Dion of Syracuse is preserved by Iamblichus.[80] This book perished in the general Christian destruction of the authentic Orphic-Pythagorean-Platonic tradition, but a copy of it was preserved by Plato's nephew and successor as head of the Academy Plato

75 *Plato, Protagoras, and Meno,* W.K.G. Guthrie, p 129 and ff.

76 Ibid. p 129.

77 Burnet, op. cit. p 85.

78 Plato's *Theatetus*, translated by B. Jowett, p 157.

79 Jowett, op. cit. p 709.

80 This fragment appears in Kirk & Raven, op. cit. p 221.

founded. The dialogue, the *Meno*, in which scholars see the first incidence of Plato spouting the Pythagorean doctrine of anamnesis, was written after Plato met a Pythagorean named Archytas of Tarentum, a pupil of Philolaus. Written correspondence between Archytas and Plato has survived, and Archytas once intervened to save Plato's life[81] (One is reminded of the loyalty practised by certain Masonic brethren). Archytas was the inventor of mathematical mechanics.[82] Plato was about 40 years old at this time. Plato's dialogue the *The Timæus* is so purely Pythagorean that the claim was made in the ancient world by Diogenes Lærtius, that Plato plagiarized *The Timæus* from the lost book Philolaus wrote.[83]

A complete account of Plato's philosophy will not be given here. Here one will find only what is relevant to the Satanist and what is relevant to the Judeo-Christian cover-up.

As stated earlier, the notion Plato presents in *The Meno* is not the Pythagorean doctrine of anamnesis as a key to recollecting prior existences, but rather a type of anamnesis wherein one recollects or rediscovers, deep within oneself (if one is what Plato called a "philosophos") knowledge of the order of the cosmos, of nature (that is, one recollects this IF one has it). This knowledge (of cosmos and nature) is rather blandly and evasively referred to today, by academicians, as "a priori"-knowledge. The search within oneself for clear definitions of ethical ideas à la Socrates is abandoned.

A dramatic example of a priori-knowledge was the case of Pascal, the French mathematician, whose Christian father forbade him to study geometry. On his own, the brilliant boy drew on his floor, and was up to the 32nd theorem of Euclid's *Elements* before he got caught. Plato would have said that Pascal remembered this.

Plato has a proof of this, which may have been used by Pythagoras himself in teaching the mathematikoi. In the *Meno*, "Socrates" (as Plato's mouthpiece) interrogates an unschooled slave boy about the sort of thing which Socrates (the real Socrates) himself never quizzed anyone on: mathematics. He asks the slave boy how to make a square double in area to any square you might give him to start with. The boy incorrectly says "You double the sides". "Socrates", by asking him the right questions, gets the boy to discover that such a doubled square really has *four* times the area of the original square. By continuing to press the issue, the boy discovers that to make a square double in area, you have to make its sides equal to the diagonal of the original square, like this:

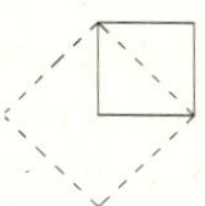

This may be obvious to some readers who have already studied Euclidean geometry, but – the boy had studied *nothing*. "Socrates" never gives the boy a decent clue: he just pressures the boy to ferret out contradictions and falsehoods that his wrong guesses logically lead to.

By this example in the *Meno*, Plato believes he has convinced a reader that certain

81 Freeman, p 233 and ff.

82 Ibid. p23 7.

83 Kirk & Raven, op. cit. P 308.

men are *not* born a "tabula rasa" (blank slate for a mind). The idea that all men are equally, at birth, blank of mind and get filled up with knowledge and teaching to their capacities, is a humanistic, environmentalistic, and egalitarian *falsehood* that has become a *dogma*. The latter doctrine (blank slate) comes from Aristotle. Leibniz, the inventor of the Calculus, already quoted above, should be someone who knows something about where new mathematical ideas come from (he *had* them). Leibniz said Plato's proof in the *Meno* of the doctrine of recollection was "excellently well considered, a fine experiment". Leibniz referred to the interrogation method used on the boy as "animadversion" – a kind of strict, critical questioning procedure. He stated that Aristotle's conception of the soul as a "blank slate" at birth is "vu1gar – a popular notion". He said "Plato goes deeper. Aristotle's influential ideas on the subject (and in general) are good for the ordinary usage of life, for there it serves no purpose to go further".[84]

This idea of innate ideas or knowledge surfaced again in a new form in the last decade when the world's leading entomologist, E.O. Wilson, collaborated with a mathematician and physician named C.J. Lumsden, to formulate a "new" science they called "sociobiology". This science attempts to formulate, in the light of the revolutionary discovery of DNA by Watson and Crick, how genetic imprinting at the moment of conception determines one's cast of mind, abilities, and even the kinds of social systems and choices that individuals, entire societies, and races will make.[85] E.O. Wilson has since returned to private curating at the Museum of Comparative Zoology at Harvard, due to the fact that abuse and even water and coffee were consistently thrown at him when he lectured on this science – thrown by egalitarians claiming to be "anti-fascist". Dr. Lumsden has continued his Sociobiological studies with new associates at the University of Toronto where there is more academic freedom than in the U.S. (Author's note: All studies of identical twins separated at birth and raised in vastly different environments, who are later found, brought together, and studied, prove these data to be true. The identicalness in character, thinking, IQ, etc., of these twins is genetic, having nothing to do with the environment.). Plato's notion of inborn or innate knowledge not common to all men, remains deeply offensive to many.

Plato states that when a "soul" overcomes the forgetfulness which shrouds it at birth, it may (if it is the soul of a philosopher) discern within itself what Plato called the "forms" ("Idea" in Greek). This is Plato's controversial Theory of Forms, and will be dealt with here, because it is commonly thought by those lacking the abilities needed to join the mathematikoi of Pythagoras, that the Theory of Forms is some sort of "otherworldly nonsense" or a pernicious dualism of "heaven wherein the Forms reside, versus an earth in which mere sense data reign".

This sort of dualism can actually be found in Parmenides, one of Plato's Hellenic predecessors.[86] Parmenides had a dualistic epistemology: there was the "Way of Truth" by which one obtains knowledge of the "One Reality" versus the "Way of Seeming" which is never knowledge, but falsehood, and is about the objects of the world of the senses.[87]

---

84 Leibniz, op. cit. pp 44-46.

85 *Genes, minds and culture*, C.J. Lumsden & E.O. Wilson.

86 See Kirk & Raven, Chapter X.

87 Kirk & Raven, ibid.

Contrary to this, Plato represents in his *Republic, Book VI* and in his *Theaterus*, the notion that there must be at least four levels or degrees of knowing, characterized in the *Republic, Book VI* as 1) ignorance or conjecture, 2) opinion or belief, 3)understanding, and 4) reason.[88] Those who misunderstand this theory Plato presents very simply out of courtesy to the unfamiliar, are those alluded to above in the *Theatetus* as "hard and impenetrable", i.e. those lacking the spirit of the philosopher, those who can never know because it is not "within their spirit", as Leibniz put it. Plato likens them to benighted men trapped in a dark cave who can see only the shadows of things existing in the sunlit world above as these things cast shadows on the walls of the cave, but are too distant themselves for the cave dwellers to even suspect as existing. These people live without ever knowing what really exists, mistaking shadows for realities, and only some are ever able to transcend this predicament.[89] The philosopher or the "talented" individual finds his way out of the cave and perceives the Forms of which the shadows cast inside the cave are but pale imitations.

This cave of ignorance is left behind not by abstinence, prayer or good works, but by the study of arithmetic, geometry, music and harmony, astronomy, etc.[90]

Plato is oftentimes considered to be the first Greek philosopher to have consciously thought anything could exist otherwise than in space, i.e. that something could exist without occupying or taking up space.[91] Plato's favorite example is one that comes readily to mind: numbers; but he said that none of the other Forms exist in space.

Virtually all of the problems and objections intelligent people can come up with against this theory of Forms were known to Plato himself, and are argued in his later dialogues. This lead the 20th century mathematician and process philosopher A.N. Whitehead to quip that all of philosophy in the West ever after was but a "series of footnotes to Plato".[92]

The Forms, then, are one of the kinds of things the soul remembers when it overcomes anamnesia and emerges from Plato's allegorical "cave of shadows".

In presenting the Theory of Forms in his dialogues, Plato at first implies to the uninitiate that everything known in the world of sense has a Form it "participates" in or mimics (methexis), much as a shadow mimics, in a deficient, incomplete fashion, the object casting it. What makes a baseball a baseball, Plato seems to be saying, is its imitation of, and participation in, a Form "Baseball" in the Realm of Forms which do not exist, at least as a whole, in space. But in later dialogues, Plato seems to say that the only Forms he really perceived and exist, are mathematical, structural, and moral Forms. An example is the Forms of Right and Wrong. For example, Dr. LaVey, in *The Satanic Bible*, characterized certain unreleased emotions as "malignant". This clearly implies that he has an *innate sense* of Right versus Wrong, a sense which is utterly lacking in many people, usually referred to as sociopaths or psychopaths; and certainly *innately* deficient in most Christians.

---

88 *Five Great Dialogues of Plato*, translated by W.H.D. Rouse, p 309.

89 Plato's *Republic*, translated by W.H.D. Rouse, p 312 and ff.

90 *Republic, Book VII.*

91 This is the opinion of Kirk & Raven, op. cit. p 250.

92 Quoted in the introduction to *Euthyphro, Apology, Crito* by Plato, introduction by Robert D. Cummings, p VII.

Plato seems to have held, likewise, that a baseball, for example, does *not* participate in an Eternal Form "Baseball", but indubitably does participate in and mimics the Form *Sphere*, the number PI, and other such Forms.

The comments are in order: 1) Sociopaths, psychopaths and many so-called "moral" people considered legally sane in Judeo-Christian society can never seem to learn or have instilled in them any ideas of right versus wrong, no matter how much one threatens, rewards, or teaches them. Many revel in the emotions Dr. LaVey characterized as malignant, and even seem to *prefer* being unreleased or pent-up emotionally (akartharti), to being released. Plato would have said they are truly ignorant and they can NOT be taught. But he also states the obvious: they can be made to obey, in many cases, and should be made to – that is "justice". 2) The second comment about mathematical Forms may frighten away or bore certain readers as too technical, but it is necessary to elaborate inasmuch as the mathematical Forms were of *primary* interest to both Plato and his mathematikoi predecessors.

Most readers will understand that any baseball is never truly a sphere, yet they will admit they have an idea of a true sphere – a Form Sphere. Someone who has left the cave, as Plato would say, has seen the Form Sphere in a clearer way than most, and may even be able to define this Form as "all points in a three-dimensional space that are exactly the same distance from a central point". Remarkably, some may even be able to define and discuss a hyper-sphere, such as a four-dimensional sphere. When mathematicians discuss these arcane subjects, does anyone ever wonder where they have gotten these ideas?

An interesting and elucidating example is PI, which is the number you would get if you divided the circumference (the outer ring-length) of a perfect circle by the diameter (width) of the circle. The Egyptians knew this number was equal to about 3-1/7. But Hellenic thinkers knew that PI could never be spoken, or written down, because no matter how you write it or say it, you are only approximating it. A closer value than 3-1/7 is 3.142. A closer value yet is 3.14160. An even closer va1ue is 3.141592, etc. The Pythagoreans knew the same problem existed with regard to the square root of 2, thatis, a number which, when you multiply it by itself, equals two. They called such numbers "alogon", meaning they could not be spoken or written. Today these are called irrational or incommensurable numbers (To simplify this for readers unfamiliar with this: the number PI goes on and on and keeps going on and on – to infinity. You can NOT write an infinite number down, or say it – it would take forever.). The word "alogon" means "unspeakable", because the mathematikoi knew that however you write them, no matter how many decimals you write, you have left something off and therefore, they are, in a sense, infinite. A correct value of PI actually is PI = (2) x (2 x 2/3 x 4/3 x 4/5 x 6/5 x 6/7 x 8/7 x 8/9 x 10/ 9 x 10/11... etc), or PI = (4) x (1 - 1/3 + 1/5 - 1/7 + 1/9... etc.), but again – though we understand what this means and we can write PI to as many fractions or as accurately as we want, the number is still infinite, and it keeps on going!

If you have a bar stool with a square seat that measures 1' on each side, the diagonal is the square root of 2 raised to 1, an irrational number. Thus even in everyday objects like this bar stool, mathematikoi or a Platonist is apt to see the infinite. A bar stool is a finite object, it is inside your den – but it contains the infinite "apeiron" in it – this is a fact!

In other words, some people can directly *see* the infinite in the finite without any mathematical training, just as easily as some people can directly *hear* the differences in musical intervals without any musical training, and it is known to these people the same way: by *direct* awareness, *direct* perception. There are those who can *not* directly perceive any of these things who would dictate to the ones who can, what "can or what can not be perceived" and argue the fact that anyone can perceive it at all, or just outright attack the person as a "mystic". The most insidious thing these *"can not know"* types do is learn all the correct words of those who can perceive, and then proceed to declare themselves "the experts". As you will see later, this is exactly what Christian theologians did with Platonism. The only ones fooled were the ones who do not have the innate ability to KNOW. The ones who can and do KNOW have never been fooled – and are not fooled. These insidious parasites of knowledge cannot fool the knowers but they can and do persecute them, which only drives it all underground – again.

The Pythagorean dictum "all things are numbers" was a puzzle to Aristotle. He never could grasp, any more than the akousmatikoi could, how number alone could make the difference between lead and gold, or heavy and light in weight. He ridiculed these notions, implying that Plato and the Pythagoreans were making the nonsensical assertion that numbers exist outside space, and yet have weight, or as if they were saying some numbers are gold, others are lead, etc. Modern mathematical physics has completely vindicated the Pythagoreans and Plato. The Schroedinger Wave Equation and other equations describe perfect attunements, intervals and harmonies in detail. In certain of these equations, a number like *one* can be plugged in at certain variables and the equation collapses or reduces to a detailed description of the shape of a hydrogen atom. But if the number *two* is substituted in these equations in the same places, the equations reduce instead to a detailed description of the shape of a helium atom. Such numbers are called "atomic numbers", and the same can be done by substituting 79 for gold and 82 for lead, though the mathematics with such high atomic numbers gets too difficult for the best human brains.

So it is indeed number (atomic number) and harmony or attunement that determines "goldness" and "leadness". Number alone also determines heavy or light in the laws of celestial mechanics as formulated in Isaac Newton's *Principia*.

Aristotle persisted in the method of Socrates, which has no value at all in the realm of natural science. Aristotle used a method of seeking to define some sort of obscure, mystical "essence" of gold or lead, a method that Socrates applied in his favorite area of "research", *morality*.

The Hellenic Atomist, Democritus, a predecessor of Plato, appears to have attributed to the atoms (which he said constituted all things) various random shapes, like pebbles on the shore, but much tinier. Plato, on the other hand, insisted that atoms must conform to regular shapes, such as the five regular three-dimensional solids, as in modern chemistry.[93]

Not only Aristotle, but other ancient writers, like Plutarch, appear to be a source of the wrong idea that Plato refused to have "recourse to the visible" and instead "relied on

93 Freeman, op. cit. P 223. Platonic misrepresentation, in modern times, can go to great depths. See Hogben, *Mathematics for the Million*, p 229 ff.

pure reason".[94] What Plutarch should have said is that Plato was condemning ad hoc ways of studying astronomy.[95]

Plato's entire dialogue, the *Parmenides*, seeks to reconcile logic and thought with sense perception.[96] This is obviously never a problem for those already characterized as not having Forms in their "spirit" to begin with. What they "see" with their senses is all they can know!

Plato was not a dualist, but held to an hierarchy of beings imitating, more or less perfectly, the various Forms (as when someone perceives something is more round than something else). He held to an hierarchy of kinds of "knowing", or degrees of truth (recall levels of hearing: tone-deaf all the way to perfect pitch). His position on the ideal Forms was not an assertion, but an inference based on direct sense perception, combined with intuition, from the obvious perception of "more real than" to its limit. Gifted and intelligent people have no lack of ideas that some things are more permanent or real than others, more independent of sense perception, and more or less capable of being described. Most people lack any such awareness. To most people, such thinking is strange and alien, even puzzling and "mystical". Plato's whole epistemology, unlike Parmenides', is one of gradation to ideal limit. G.C. Field, the most understanding Plato scholar, stresses the naturalness of the transition from the "more or less" concepts to the "absolute" ones. Plato and Pythagoras both would have reminded him that this is natural only to someone born with the Forms in his "spirit", no matter how dimly imprinted. No amount of teaching, as Leibniz said, can confer on someone an idea that is not already in his "spirit" (one might read, "in his genes"). "Platonism is a natural philosophical inclination of mathematicians, in particular those who think of themselves as the discoverers of new truth, rather than of new ways of putting old ones or making explicit logical consequences that were already implicit".[97]

Over and over again, creative, productive scientists and thinkers side with Plato and Leibniz, like Heinrich Hertz, the discoverer of electromagnetic or "wireless" waves: "One cannot escape the feeling that these mathematical formulæ have an independent existence and intelligence of their own, and that they are wiser than we are, wiser even than their discoverers, that we get more out of them than was originally put into them".[98] The scoffers at Plato, those who abused Pythagoras as "mystikos logos" or "mystic", have been the intellectually barren, sterile souls who can only conserve, criticize and analyze, but not create. And, they conserve it inaccurately! It is as if, even when told, they just *can not know!*

Plato admitted that, in some cases, things are what they appear to be.[99] He refutes dualism succinctly.[100] Yet, he insists "the true lover of knowledge strives after being. He will not rest at those multitudinous phenomena whose existence is appearance only".[101] This drive or love (Eros) for knowledge remains a puzzle to those character-

94 Freeman, p 237.

95 Ibid.

96 Freeman, p 152.

97 *The Philosophy of Mathematics*, S. Korner, p 15.

98 Quoted from Kramer, op. cit. p 90.

99 *Theatetus*, translated by B. Jowett, pp 153-154.

100 Loc. cit. p 250 and ff.

101 Quoted in *The Universe and Dr. Einstein*, Lincoln Barnett, p 113.

ized (above) by Leibniz and Plato as vulgar, hard and dense.

Plato's approach is that of science at its best today. Einstein said: "To know that what is impenetrable to us really exists, manifesting itself as the highest wisdom and the most radiant beauty which our dull faculties can comprehend only in their most primitive forms – this knowledge, this feeling is at the center of true religiousness".[102]

If the reader pursues Plato's theory of knowledge in greater depth, he will be surprised at how many of Einstein's own terms (in the above quote) recur in Plato: "highest wisdom", "most radiant beauty which our dull faculties can comprehend only in their most primitive "forms" (SIC!)". Note that Einstein rightly characterizes this as knowledge but also a feeling.

If you can understand this, you will correctly understand what Plato meant when he called the world of eyeball sight a "prison house". Otherwise, you will interpret this as a dualism, some sort of fore-runner of the demented Christian defamation of the sense, material things, the body and nature. The Christians themselves, desperate to borrow from a sound philosophical system to give foundation to their silly, untenable theology of monotheism, interpreted Plato this way themselves.

Plato founded a school called the Academy, wherein the lost book of the Pythagorean Philolaus was preserved. This school continued in existence, despite the persecutions, for over 900 years, until the Christian Emperor Justinian closed it in 529 AD, but not before it produced its most eloquent enemies the Christians ever encountered, as we shall see in what follows. Of the foundation of this Academy, one scholar says it gave "his group a sense of solidarity. Its religion was a reverant and living feeling for the glory and unity of the universe growing out of its scientific investigation, something essentially akin to the attitude of Einstein today, but its solidarity was not the solidarity of dogma".[103] Doesn't sound suffocating or mind numbing, as one writer characterized Platonism – does it? Friedrich Nietzsche, who had little to say in approval of anyone (!), cast his final judgement on Plato as being one of those who wanted to see "how far his strength will reach. But they do it as individuals... How far man might be driven in his evolution... Where has the plant "man" hitherto grown up most magnificently".[104]

In the following section we shall very briefly cover Neo-Platonism in the Christian era, the deadly enemies of Christianity it produced, how Platonism was coopted and absorbed by Christian theologians, and how magic survived in the early Christian era as a Platonic prerogative or occupation in the form of Theurgy, Hecate devotion, and knowledge through demons.

NEO-PLATONISM

Plato's Academy existed for over 900 years before the Christian Emperor Justinian closed it in 529 AD. Hence a brief survey of Neo-Platonism covering this long span of time cannot be in depth.

The dualism that prevailed in the West after Christ died, existed in its most extreme forms in the teachings of Mani, the founder of Manicheanism, who taught that the

102 Barnett, op. cit. p 108.

103 *Conversion*, Nock, pp 166-167.

104 *The Will To Power*, translated by Kaufman & Hollingdale, p 511.

material world is evil. He enjoined on his followers the need to free themselves from their flesh through asceticism and self-denial. Mani taught that Christ was crucified to save man.

In direct contrast was Ammonius Sacca of Alexandria (170-241 A.D.) and his followers, who were philosophers and mighty champions of freedom as a consequence of their philosophical ideas, which were a revitalized philosophy based on Plato. Nothing Ammonius wrote survived the Christian book-burning (the reader will tire and anger at hearing this as we go along and the characters and incidents get more extraordinary). Ammonius' followers advanced historical studies, medicine, and logic.

Plotinus was a student of Ammonius for about a decade. Plotinus is regarded as the founder of Neo-Platonism. He rejected all dualisms, in keeping with the spirit of Plato, and rejected both Christianity and Manicheanism, which were separate religions then. Plotinus rejected Christian and Manichean arguments that the material world is evil. He taught instead that an hierarchy of beings and values exist from lowest to highest, and that the body is not evil, as Mani had taught. The Christians feared Plotinus, though his intellectual attacks on them were far tamer than some later Neo-Platonists we shall meet. In Porphyry's edition of Plotinus, Plotinus describes the Christians as "those who have gone to the bad to solicit others to be their saviors or to sacrifice themselves at their behest." He disagreed with the Christians, saying that it is not right "for them to demand of the gods that they should order their affairs for them, laying aside their own (the gods') existence to do so, or that good people, leading another kind of life superior to the common human rule, should do as much for them".[105]

Plotinus considered asking for salvation instead of saving yourself, weak and wrong.[106] Compare this to Dr. LaVey's principle: "Say unto thine own heart, 'I am mine own redeemer'".[107]

Plotinus' biographer and disciple, Porphyry, was the most dedicated enemy the early Christians ever met, though when cast in this light, one is apt to overlook the fact that he was a Renaissance-man prototype who also wrote scientific works, like *On the Formation of the Embryo*. The reader should be aware of the danger of embryological studies to Christianity: it was based on embryology, not fossil evidence, that Hæckel, Darwin and others rediscovered the theory of human evolution, inasmuch as the developing human embryo in the womb recapitulates or retraces the forms of all its biological ancestors, passing through states wherein it looks like a polyp, fish, reptile, and lower mammals, before it looks human.

Porphyry was the first to demonstrate that the *Book of Daniel* of the *Old Testament* was not an ancient prophesy, as Christians and Jews claimed. Porphyry proved, on literary and historical grounds that this book was written in the time of Alexander the Great's successors, a critical judgement accepted as virtual fact today by *Bible* scholars.

Porphyry beleaguered the Christians by pointing out contradictions in their scriptures or so-called "word of god". He did so in a book called *Against the Christians*, showing how one passage of the *New Testament* contradicted another. He stated simply and clearly that Christ's apostles were liars, especially in regards to their narratives of

105 Quoted in *The Death of Classical Paganism*, John Holland Smith, p 16.

106 Ibid.

107 LaVey, op. cit. p 33.

Jesus' infancy. He gave reasons why Jesus himself was not a good man, nor his followers.[108] Porphyry's denial of Jesus' infancy narratives was a mode of attack calculated to vanquish the Christians. This is so because the early Christians had no history, tradition or philosophy to back up anything they said. They could not rely on the Hebrew tradition because existing Jews denied Jesus was the Messiah and would not cooperate with the Christians in "sharing" their own books, which later became the *Old Testament* of the Christians. Since the early Christians did not have a theological or historical leg to stand on, their primary effort was directed toward destroying traditions and tales of divine births other than their own, so they could claim extraordinary phenomena accompanied Jesus' birth and no others'. For example, Christians suppressed the little known story, well known in the ancient world, that Plato's father received a dream from a demon while his wife was pregnant with Plato, telling him his son would be an avatar or incarnation of Apollo[109] (Note, such tales of "divine", or omens at, births are quite common in the ancient world both East and West. Ghenghis Khan is said to be descended from such a birth. When Plato turns out a genius and Ghenghis Khan a conqueror of the known world such divine-birth stories circulate.).

Porphyry' s Neo-Platonic attack on Christianity was considered so deadly, that no parts of it have survived. His work was solemnly burned by Imperial decree in 448 A.D. All that survives are references to these lost works. One scholar dates the beginning of the Dark Ages with this burning.[110]

It was Porphyry's student Iamblichus, who revived Pythagoreanism in Neo-Platonism. It was Imablichus' version of the "Religion of the Hellenes", i.e. Pythagoreanism, that influenced Julian the Apostate, the last great pagan emperor, and the latter's friends, this "religion" of miracle mongering and sorcery so bitterly condemned by Byzantine Christians.[111]

Julian the Apostate was surrounded by Neo-Platonists, whose spirit and intellects he relished. We have already quoted a surviving fragment of Julian's *Against the Christians* in a prior section, a fragment in which is praised the tens of thousands of Hellenes taught by the Pelasgian King Cheiron, in comparison to which the Hebrews' attainments, he said, seem like putting on airs.

Julian appeared to be aware of a dangerous situation: the Christian Church Fathers were osmotically (like parasites) absorbing and assimilating Plato and Hellenism to bolster their vacuous and absurd theology, so Julian passed laws forbidding Christians to read or teach Hellenic texts. Already before Julian, Plato was being re-interpreted dualistically by dualistic minds, who considered the realm of Forms to be some sort of "Kingdom of God", and Plato's *Republic* to be a kind of "City of God", a view perpetuated by St. Augustine. Numenius (160 A.D.) called Plato "a Moses speaking Attic Greek". In a fashion all too-typical of his case of mind, Numenius read Plato as saying that the soul becomes involved with the body because of guilt. This was an effort to theoretically justify the completely untenable (utterly insane) Christian doctrine of "original sin".

108 Smith, op. cit. p 17.
109 Nock, p. 232.
110 Smith, op. cit. p 226.
111 Smith, op. cit. P 56.

While the Christian Church Fathers busied themselves with converting Plato's *Republic* into the "City of God", the Ottoman Turks' social system began to approach Plato's Republic in reality, becoming a strict meritocracy which, as one historian put it, "for two hundred years furnished the founders of the Turkish Empire with soldiers and ministers that were the wonder and despair of Christian Europe".[112]

So far did this Christian theft of Plato go, that many ecclesiastics came to believe that Plato had been taught not by Pythagoreans, but by the Hebrew prophet Jeremiah in Egypt. They thought Plato had a soul "naturally Christian".[113] They should have confined this remark to those about whom it is true: themselves!

So Julian attempted to set a barrier to Christian absorption of Platonism with his edict forbidding them to read or teach Hellenic texts. Julian wrote, in *Against the Galileans*, "If the reading of your scripture is sufficient for you, why do you make such a fuss about the learning of the Hellenes? It seems true that you yourselves must be aware of the very different effect of your writings on the intellect compared to ours, and that from the study of yours, no man could achieve excellence or even ordinary goodness; whereas from studying ours, every man can become better than before. Now this would give you clear proof: select children from among you and train them up and educate them in your scriptures, and if when they come to manhood they prove to have nobler qualities than slaves, you may believe that I am talking nonsense".[114] Julian agreed with Nietzsche: Christianity is a slave religion.[115]

Julian was assassinated by a Christian, and a story about his deathbed conversion to Christianity faked. In a cover-up, a Christian historian named (oddly enough) Socrates, employed Julian's own Hellenic ideas to explain his death, claiming a demon killed Julian, "an avenging Furie".[116] One is reminded of Arthur Koestler's novel *Darkness at Noon*, which shows the common thread connecting Christians, Communists, and witch-hunters: it is not enough for these persecutors to kill their enemies: they must also fake stories about conversions, confessions, recantations and admissions of error or "slacking", which are extracted before death by torture if they are not forthcoming voluntarily.

Jerome, a vicious woman-hater, and the issuer of the complete *Vulgate Bible*, wrote in triumph, "How many as much as know Plato's name? – to say nothing of his works! Even old men sitting in corners with nothing to occupy them can scarcely remember them".[117] He was partly fantasizing: a form of Platonistic magic called Theurgy remained alive and well underground all this time, even when the persecutions of Hellenism were at their peaks. Mingling with, and invoking, daimones or demons continued. Porphyry and others, like Celsus, wrote of the need to exercise caution when consorting with demons, who, they said, enjoy bloody sacrifices and incense burning, their motives being a selfish desire to "feed".[118] The *Corpus Hermeticum* stated that demons "drive the evil

112 *Five Dialogues of Plato*, translated by B. Jowett, introduction by Louise R. Loomis, p 25.
113 Loc. cit. p 27.
114 Quoted in Smith, op. cit. p 109.
115 Nietzsche, op. cit. pp 85-146.
116 Smith, op. cit. pp 114 and ff.
117 Quoted in Smith, op. cit. p 223.
118 Nock, op. cit. p 224.

to fresh sins"[119] (Typists' note: it is the greatest pity in human history, that such genius degenerated into this. The loss of knowledge is IN-calculable.).

Christians were required to renounce all commerce or contact with demons. The obsession with demons one finds during the later Inquisitions was already evident at this earlier time. Julian the Apostate wrote of these Christians: "For the high point of their theology consists of these two things, hissing at demons and sketching the cross on their foreheads".[120] Knowledge through demons, something Socrates could not obtain, and the "binding of souls", a theurgic practice, all had to be renounced.

The theurges taught that the most powerful names are the secret titles of the Demiurge, the maker and ruler of the world. The concept of the Demiurge was taken from Plato's *Timæus*, which was the only dialogue of Plato that existed in the Latin-speaking Christian Empire. Speaking such secret names of power could be fatal to the uninitiated, but these names were taught by Hermes Trismegistus (Thrice-Great Hermes) to full-fledged theurges. Theurgy was a grand synthesis of all the forms of magic that remained from the pre-Christian world, supported by a Platonist philosophy and metaphysics. Theurgy was considered "deeply disturbing and menacing to the well-being of individuals and the state".[121] Christian Emperors made laws distinguishing between pagan worshippers and the Platonic theurges for purposes of arrest and punishment. In the differences between the theurges and mere pagan worshippers, Christian authorities were carefully and accurately distinguishing between the two disparate groups of so-called "occultists" one still finds today: there are the Satanists and demonolators, as opposed to the Wiccans, New Age pagans, etc.

Due to singling out the theurges for special persecution, theurgy went underground, flourishing among tavern-keepers, dancing girls, players (actors and actresses), prostitutes, gamblers, circus-performers. The only respectable class of people among whom theurgy flourished were practitioners of medicine, leading to their exclusion from the Christian world. One is reminded of Dr. LaVey (who had been an animal-handler in a circus) when one discovers that in Later Rome, in the reign of the Christian Justinian, circus performers were regularly accused of being theurges. Examples are Theodera, a bear-keeper's daughter, and Antonia, the wife of a performing Charioteer.[122] The prevalence of theurgy among such performers and life-styles could also have been due to the fact that such people really know how much of their lives depend on good luck, a blessing Christianity, in its denials of reality, could not confer and did not even recognize. These inn-keepers, circus acrobats and others lived life to the fullest. They feared neither life nor death.

Practitioners of theurgy were, at one time during Justinian's reign, easily recognized by their dress, which was called "Hellenic". They were called, as one contemporary writer said, "priests of the old faith, which people nowadays generally call Hellene, who repeat unholy words".[123] These unholy prayers were actually Orphic hymns.[124]

119 Ibid.

120 Quoted in Smith, op. cit. p 97.

121 Smith, op. cit. p 19.

122 Smith, op. cit. p 225 & p 233.

123 These are the words of Procopius, quoted in Smith, op. cit. p 234.

124 Ibid.

Finally, mention should be made of the last great teacher of the ancient Western world, Proclus, a Neo-Platonist philosopher and theurgist. He revered and regularly made sacrifices to the "All-Mother" in the form of Hecate. Plutarch taught him a version of Platonism, and Plutarch's daughter Asclepigenia taught him the lost Orphic Hymns. Two of Proclus' own pupils emigrated to the other half of the Christian Empire in Constantinople in a daring attempt to single-handedly overthrow Zeno, the Christian Emperor. They failed: one was executed, the other disgraced.[125]

The strength of the theurgist underground is attested to by the fact that, whenever draconian laws were enforced to round up the theurges, as in Justinian's capitol, theurges could immediately round up their own massive bodyguard, along with plenty of sorcerers to threaten and curse their persecutors.[126]

From here on, "Hellene" degenerated purely into an insult hurled at any Christian enemy, real or imagined, regardless of his dress or beliefs.

It should also be mentioned, as many readers will know, that not all sorcery and magic at the time was theurgistic. Many magicians, scholars, witches and warlocks sought refuge in the woods and outbacks, and one can easily find Church councils of the era frothing about prohibiting witchcraft and devil-worship in the countryside, which was much less easy to police than the cities. And so it is today. Today, as in the Christian Empire, the study of the occult, magic, satanism and demonology is associated in the prurient, "akathratic" minds of Christians with depravity and perversion.

What Dr. LaVey said in *The Satanic Bible* can be said of the gods and demons of the Hellenes: "The old gods did not die, they fell into Hell and became devils." The Church "doctors" turned "the guardian spirits and source of inspiration" into wicked beings.[127]

Not all of the mathematical and architectural genius was lost during the days of the Christian persecution. People were hired to build magnificent cathedrals for the Christians, people who still had the mathematics and excellent building techniques and structural technology.

A part of theurgy, connected to it, was alchemy (chemistry) and metallurgy. Recall that Plato spoke about the atomic number. Modern readers can find many amulets and such that are engraved with some symbol that might mean "harm to your enemy" or some such. Giving this amulet so inscribed to your enemy, nothing happens. If you were to make it out of thorium, something would happen. Your enemy would either get very sick, or die. The symbols told the initiated what the amulet really was. Loss of knowledge is when you have no idea what metal to use and think it makes no difference, but you have "faith" in some silly symbol that has come to mean bunk. Engraving a radiation warning sign on silver produces nothing. Engraving it on uranium is wise. Thorium, like uranium, is radioactive – and easily found. Most readers are probably familiar with the drugs reported to be used by witches during the days of the Inquisition. Just with this practical knowledge alone of chemistry and metals – with the Christians knowing nothing, the sorcerers could be a real threat. There is no way to know if these sorcerers really believed in bunk, or if they, like their predecessors, cloaked their knowledge in these myths, or if all of it was just confessions extracted under torture.

125 Smith, op. cit. pp 231-232.
126 Smith, op. cit. p 234.
127 LaVey, op. cit. pp 56-57.

Well-poisoning was a common accusation. With aforementioned metals, one could easily poison a well, causing family, cattle, etc. to get sick.

Why is it so many Satanists are right on the mark when it comes to exposing the fraud and atrocities of the Christian world, but when it comes to viewing the Hellenes, our extinct brothers, who were free of the Judeo-Christian pollution, they *can't find their way?* They also cannot seem to find their way even with the small, but known groups in other cultures in the East that celebrate the "Great Black" dark force in Nature and who are also totally free of the Judeo-Christian pollution. It must be a kind of Christian hangover, a kind of victory Christianity has claimed over their minds that is so *deep*, that they cannot even begin to be truly free of it. When they see the real thing, a real Satanist, *why* can't they *recognize* it?

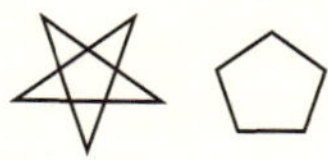

ADDENDUM: The star is drawn with two points up. Drawing it this way, you get a PENTAGON in the center. It looks like a house and it represents a house! You do not make a house with the foundation sticking up and the pointed roof down!

BIBLIOGRAPHY

—— Barnett, Lincoln: *The Universe and Dr. Einstein* (William Morrow & Co., New York, 1948)

—— Burnet, John: *Early Greek Philosophy* (Adam & Charles Black, London, 1948)

—— Cornford, F.M.: *Plato and Parmenides* (London, 1939) Understands Aristotle's misinterpretations of Plato.

—— Eisberg, Robert & Resnick, Robert: *Notes on Quantum Theory* (John Wiley & Sons, New York, 1968) A University course text for "Physics IV."

—— Field, G.C.: *The philosophy of Plato* (Oxford, 1949)

—— Freeman, Kathleen: *Companion to the pre-Socratic philosophers* (Basil Blackwell, Oxford, 1966) Not connected to the *pre-Socratic philosophers* below, but to a different book altogether.

—— Graves, Robert: *The White Goddess* (Farrar, Straus & Giroux, New York, 1948)

—— Heath, T. L.: *A history of Greek mathematics* (Oxford, 1921)

—— Hogben, Lancelot T.: *Mathematics for the million* (W. W. Norton, New York, 1937) A Marxist interpretation of mathematics, and a mis-interpretation of Plato.

—— Kirk, G. S. & Raven, J. E.: *The pre-Socratic philosophers* (Cambridge University Press, Cambridge, 1957) Contains many hard to find pre-Socratic fragments in translation.

—— Koestler, Arthur: *Darkness at noon* (Random House, New York) A novel. Koestler was a Marxist-Communist. He later recanted.

—— Korner, S.: *The philosophy of mathematics* (Harper & Row, New York, 1960)

—∞— Kramer, Edna E.: *The main streams of mathematics* (Fawcett Publications, Greenwich, Conn., 1951) One of the great female mathematics professionals.
—∞— LaVey, Anton Szandor: *The Satanic Bible* (Avon Books, New York, 1969)
—∞— Leibniz: *Discourse on metaphysics* (Manchester University Press, Manchester, 1953) The discoverer of the calculus.
—∞— Lumsden, C. J. & Wilson, E. O.: *Genes, mind and culture* (Harvard University Press, Cambridge, Mass., 1981) The inventors of sociobiology, a new, persecuted science.
—∞— Myer, Isaac: *Qabbalah* (Samuel Weiser, New York, 1970) Best book on the subject, completely ignored.
—∞— Nietzsche, Friedrich: *The will to power* (Random House, New York, 1968) Nietzsche's epigrammatic and fragmentary notebook.
—∞— Nock, A D.: *Conversion* (Oxford University Press, Oxford, 1969)
—∞— Plato: *Five great dialogues* (Translated by B. Jowett. Walter J. Black, New York, 1942) Jowett was Reverend Jowett, but still a good translator.
—∞— Plato: *Gorgias* (Translated by Donald J. Zeyl. Hacket Publishing Co., Indianapolis, 1987)
—∞— Plato: *Great dialogues of Plato* (Translated by W. H. D. Rouse. New American Library, New York, 1956)
—∞— Plato: *The dialogues of Plato, vol. II* (Translated by B. Jowett. Random House, New York, 1892) .
—∞— Plato: *Protagoras and Meno* (Translated by W. K. G. Guthrie. Penguin Books, Baltimore, Maryland, 1956)
—∞— Plato: *Euthyphro, Apology, Crito* (Translated by F. J. Church. Bobbs Merrill Co., Indianapolis, 1940)
—∞— Russell, Bertrand: *A history of Western philosophy* (Simon & Schuster, New York, 1945) A mathematical logician, anti-Christian atheist/agnostic.
—∞— Smith, John Holland: *The death of classical paganism* (Charles Scribner's Sons, New York, 1976) A book by a man who calls himself "an educated pagan".
—∞— Temple, Robert K. G.: *The Sirius Mystery* (St. Martin's Press, New York, 1976) The appendices to this book contain a number of almost impossible to find fragments in translation.

A Few Acid Writings, Reconstituted from a State of Celestial Appreciation for Dull Human Consumption

Terence Sellers

I cannot say it better than Rainer Marie, *Notebooks of Malte Laurids Brigge:* "But the woman, the woman, she had completely collapsed into herself, forward into her hands... I began to walk softly as soon as I saw her. When poor people are reflecting they should not be disturbed. Perhaps their idea will yet occur to them... The street was too empty; its emptiness was bored; it caught my step from under my feet and clattered about with it... The woman startled and pulled away too quickly out of herself, too violently, so that her face remained in her two hands. I could see it lying in them, its hollow form. It cost me indescribable effort to stay with those hands and not look at what had torn itself out of them. I shuddered to see a face from the inside, but still I was much more afraid of the naked flayed head without a face."

I cannot say it better yet I will go on talking. This is the fate of all writers, cruel to themselves and to those who must hear them say it all again. Again: the masks, the masks suspended over the void. How well I see the void, under the influence of acid. This is why acid is so feared: you see the masks, the masked void, and the void obtrudes, just like that word: OBTRUDES. Masks we need to give us human form – but why must we bother with that rotten old form, the human? Trapped, trapped hopelessly, in the rotting human mask. More than a bore: an exhausting horror of a bore.

ZOMBIES. Zombies rule New Orleans, where I am. Zombies on beer. Kim, don't make me think of zombies now. Zombies have no masks, they are the same as death and the void. The voodooists say it is a great honor to be made into a zombie. It is only temporary, they give you a drug and bury you alive. When the zombie-making drug wears off, the zombied dances with his coffin. Where is my coffin – I WANT TO DANCE WITH MY COFFIN RIGHT NOW GODDAMMIT.

ROT. UNIVERSAL ROT. O great constancy of rot, I love you. O vanity of all effort, luxurious perception! Teach me, o rot, how to do nothing. Teach me how to love the void. I'm dancing now, I'm dancing for you, bring on all the coffins dancing so gaily a-dancing.

I now allow all civilisation to rot. And why not? Why not rot? It will not all rot quietly and humbly as is fitting. It makes a great screeching riot as it dissolves, it reeks and suppurates and pours a pus into our eyes. This is considered culture. It is, but it's not. It's just rot, rot held up by a vast machinery of steel, of steel beams and cubicles and inerasable timetables, the steel stolen from the rocks, railroad tracks to blind depots where a yawn may pass for a poem. All that blind industrial urge faking out the rot, you cannot believe it, you cannot. It's nothing but mechanical breeding urge, that just goes on creating more of itself for no reason but some emotional thrill that evanesces in the noonday sun, under the stutter of a mumbled prayer. They run all over the beautiful earth solidifying the shrieking metals trying to get back to their quiet rock homes, yes the innocent elements forced into stupid conduits for rot, for the human fleshly urge to go on, seeking seeking their satisfactions, and to the disgust of the Void Imperial actually finding that twitching cosy pleasure!

At last in a fit Mother Earth menopausal throws you all out from her sore and sagging bosom, all the hungry mouths, all the fleshy sucking seethe, the endlessly multiplying pigs in shit ROT of it all. O seething void of breeders may I get as far as I can from you!

Kim and I in the burlesque house on Bourbon Street gazed in dismay upon the naked dancing boys, ignorant and greedy, begging for dollars and spreading saliva through the innocent air. Kim said, God it's that old festering ooze again, Mama. Here it comes, through the cracks. Plug it up, I shrieked, throwing my wallet into the swirling stream of whores. Escaping to Nature, we tried to adore her, but everywhere came golfers in yellow, green and red, the colors of the rotting brain. Upon the greens (mere crusts upon the abyss) the golfers dallied. How can they put on those red pants and balance on their yellow shoes upon the seethe, putt-ing their balls across the green crust, into the hole where the ooze is no doubt even now a-rising? It's just a crust away, and they, blasé, go on a-putt-ing across the abyss, right alongside the old bayou lakes of crocodiles.

We decided the answer was in the roots. All we had to do was hang onto the roots and the ooze could not seep out. We could cleanly void our beings, and I immediately from sheer horror puked, and there was my ego, lying in the swill. A great relief. Farewell, old nobody. I surrendered to the roots of an oak, but Jupiter was not fond of me. I tried climbing down but forgot the password. As I struggled to recall, a brownie, disguised as a golfer, mischievously asked me how much my python boots had cost. Zip, squish, right back into the fleshy mask, ooze a-percolating and me a-swimming frantically fast away.

A problem arose whilst hiding underneath it all. I dissolved, but the pen held steady. How could it? There was nothing I wanted to write anymore. I knew that my sigil from then on was to be the crossed-out word. I could not describe it, but only draw its picture. How do you draw a picture of a crossed-out word? How do you make a picture of something that's erased?

I went dreaming and was reading the first manuscripts of the ancient fathers. I took some white paint and painted over some of their words. My act made the fathers angry, but to fight with the letters was no longer the point. The crossed-out word was what would be. Maybe the less words, the better, maybe not. I showed them how their machines were worn-out, too old to breathe anymore, and could not interest anyone but wretched deluded scholars who would chastely observe them inside glass cabinets in dusty museums on the edge of some old sleeping bayou.

So I fixed it well so that no-one could read what the old manuscripts of the fathers had said. They were plenty pee-o'd with me but I just laughed and got real free. There were the manuscripts now, with big white blocks all through them, but even so on the white blocks were a few last vengeful marks made by the old fathers coming back one last time for a try. The marks were hacked deep in the side of the manuscripts, which now could be known as white cliffs on a mountainside, seen from a very far away place. And yes they were beautiful to behold, those crack-marks on the white and curling page of stone. Against them all words fall in silent disarray, for the stone overrules any scratch-mark made, and before the white cliffs I lay down my pen in mute reverence that all is in vain, all effort is vanity, o luxurious and final perception!

O great and mystical inspiration! Rock, stone, and pebbled sea! Speak to me, granite, of dark thoughts never spoken! Tell me, o diamonds, of clarity! The secret of the stone is the sigil of the crossed-out word. O sacred Word, may you never be translated, never be spoken or heard, without the world coming instantly to an end! Yes, let me hear it, then, on this day I am born!

Maybe you are waiting for me to tell you that the word is: love. But you have invented too many strange byways in seeking out love, too many masks worn and worn out, for love to be a pure word anymore.

1/88
New Orleans/New York City

Harry Smith (1923-1991)

Hymenæus Beta

Harry Smith died November 27, 1991, at the Chelsea Hotel in New York. He was born on May 29, 1923 to an Oregon family active in freemasonry and occultism. He enjoyed propagating alternative biographies: born in 1918, delivered of the Princess Anastasia on a Russian gunboat off the coast of Alaska, or fathered by Aleister Crowley who seduced his mother on a Pacific beach. Smith developed his lifelong interests at an early age: occultism, music, anthropology, linguistics, painting and film. He studied anthropology at a college in Washington State. Around 1945 he moved to San Francisco where he held what was possibly his first and certainly his last regular job, as an office clerk for ARAMCO. Since then he lived for art and gnosis with little thought for practical consequences. With the occasional grant (including two Guggenheims), the occasional patron, his friends, and his indifference to adversity, he always got by.

The 1940's were a formative period in experimental film, and Smith was a member of the small circle of California avant-garde filmmakers. He worked with the influential Art in Cinema Society in San Francisco, helping to arrange showings of films by Anger, Deren, Markopolous, Harrington, Broughton and European filmmakers like Cocteau. Most of these were "personal" semi-narrative filmmakers, and although Smith would later make analogous personal statements with his live-action superimposition films, he was at this time closer in temperament and technique to the Surrealists and abstract artists and filmmakers from whom he drew inspiration. He would hitchhike to Los Angeles and stay with the Whitney family; he always acknowledged his debt to them, especially in technical areas. Another influence was Oskar Fischinger; Elfriede Fischinger recalls that Oskar took pride that Smith had described his *Film #5* as a homage. Smith's close association with non-objective artist and filmmaker Jordan Belson, a few years his junior, dates to this period.

Hilda Rebay of the museum of Non-Objective Art (now the Guggenheim) was so taken with Smith's and Belson's work that she arranged a grant to bring the young artists to New York. Belson eventually returned to San Francisco where he continues to live and work, but Smith stayed on. Except for a few "field trips" he remained in New York for the rest of his life.

Smith always considered himself more a painter than a filmmaker, and the distinctions were sometimes moot; e.g., he created the first frame-by-frame hand-painted films in America, circa 1939. Unknown to Smith, the New Zealander Len Lye had made such films earlier, but Smith's are far more ambitious.

Sadly, Smith's paintings are little known and never shown, due in no small part to his ambivalent attitude towards his own work's survival. Throughout his life he destroyed with one hand as he created with the other; that his work survives has been largely through chance or the intervention of friends. Many films are lost or destroyed, and the original negatives of most no longer exist. He once rolled the original of a hand-painted film – representing years of work – down 42nd Street. He eschewed selling his work; although broke and fighting eviction, he told one hopeful collector to call Holly Solomon. It was a ruse; Smith had no gallery, nor did he want one.

In the early 1950's, Smith created a series of "jazz paintings", which probably survive only in photographic plates. These paintings were synchronized to particular jazz tunes, traceable rhythmically note by note across the two dimensional field. A pan shot of one of these (a "Dizzy Gillespie" painting) appears at the beginning of his *Film #4.* Smith was one of the first American artists to exhibit at the Louvre, around 1951, in a two-man show with Marcel Duchamp; apparently it was his hand-painted films, and not his paintings, that were exhibited. Many of Smith's drawings and paintings survive – as yet uncatalogued – in several private and public collections. But what survives probably represents only a fraction of his output.

Like the Whitneys, Smith experimented with film technique. In the 1950's, he constructed an elaborate multiplane animation system for his unfinished *Wizard of Oz* film, and worked with 3-D and kaleidoscope effects; fragments of these efforts survive. Many of Smith's animated films employ overt magical symbolism and allude to drugs, two favorite preoccupations. He described *Film #10* as "an exposition of Buddhism and the Kabbalah in the form of a collage. The final scene shows Agaric mushrooms growing on the moon while the hero and heroine row by on a cerebrum." This film was a study for a more ambitious collaboration with Thelonius Monk, *Film #11, Mirror Animations.* This carried out the methodology of his jazz paintings in film, tightly synchronizing the animation to Monk's *Mysterioso.* His black-and-white *Heaven and Earth Magic (Film #12)* was created in the late 1950's and early 60's by using sortilege to animate cut-outs from old department store catalogs and books. Originally six hours, it survives only in a one-hour version, with a "musique concrète" soundtrack by Smith that uses sound effects in an analogous manner to the cut-up images. In its graphic depiction of spiritual transport and transformation, this film is the true American *Book of the Dead.* In keeping with its alchemical theme, certain images are synchronized to the soundtrack by elemental attribution; e.g., when a salamander appears (the usual form of a fire elemental in magical tradition) a fire engine is heard in the soundtrack. In the 1970's, in a departure from his earlier work, his films use live-action super-imposition as well as animation. He continued to innovate technically; his *Mahagonny* required a custom synchronized multi-screen projection system of Smith's design, so complex that it is unlikely to be shown again as the filmmaker intended it.

Smith declared that "my movies are made by God; I am just the medium for them." He was very much a modern Prospero, and his work is riddled with hermetic allusions. His magico-religious philosophy was rooted in the writings of Aleister Crowley, but greatly amplified by diverse other sources, including parapsychology, spiritualism, Egyptology, Assyriology and oriental magic and mysticism. In the late forties Smith met and studied the magical works of Crowley's student Charles Stansfeld Jones (a.k.a. Frater Achad, 1885-1950). He studied yoga and magick intensely throughout the 1950's with Jones' student Albert Handel in New York. Jones was the novelist Malcolm Lowry's magical preceptor as well; his influence is overt in both Lowry's *Under the Volcano* and Smith's later animated films, especially *#10-12*.

Smith had a lifelong love of Native American culture and language, beginning with his childhood experiences with the Northwest Coast Indians of his native Oregon. He spent years living with various tribes, particularly the Kiowa and Seminoles. In the early 1960's he flew to Oklahoma with filmmakers Conrad Rooks and Sheldon Rochlin to work on what became Rooks' *Chappaqua*. On arrival Smith disappeared without warning, showing up at the motel in the middle of the night with perhaps a dozen Kiowa tribesmen and a bushels of peyote. Rooks and Rochlin pushed on westward by car to continue filming this early psychedelic epic, but Smith stayed on. Some of his Oklahoma footage appears in his superimposition films created in the 1970's. He later issued a recording of *Kiowa Peyote Rituals* on Folkways Records. He also amassed an important collection of Seminole ritual objects, now in a museum in Stockholm. Smith's longest completed prose work is a comprehensive unpublished study of string figures around the world.

His other collections included an unusually fine private library and a fantastic collection of Ukranian Easter eggs. When he had money, he usually bought a new book and forgot about dinner. He even amassed what was undoubtedly the world's largest collection of paper airplanes. For forty years, as he found one (and he found them everywhere), he would note the date and place and file it away. By the early 80's he had no less than a dozen large boxes. The Smithsonian Air-Space Museum sent a special courier when he donated the collection.

Smith also spent years collecting records by early American folk and blues musicians, and in the early 1950's issued his multi-volume *Anthology of American Folk Music* on Folkways Records. Dylan and a host of other folk musicians would later draw on this anthology for inspiration and material. Smith received a Lifetime Achievement Award at the 1991 Grammy Awards in New York for fostering blues and folk music as a vehicle for social change. He was also an ethno-musicologist – a term he disliked for its cultural bias – whose interests ranged from Mongolian mouth music to Scottish "Pimbrochiad" bagpiping.

Like many experimental filmmakers, he was greatly helped over the years by Jonas Mekas and the Anthology Film Archives. In recent years he was sustained by his many friends, especially Allen Ginsberg and Dr. Joseph Gross, and recently received a three-year grant from the Grateful Dead, which was continued posthumously to help catalog his archives. He was also a mentor and "shaman in residence" at the Naropa Institute in Boulder, Colorado. Smith was also a gnostic bishop in the Ecclesia Gnostica Catholica (Gnostic Catholic Church) of the Ordo Templi Orientis.

Smith was a seminal underground force for several generations. A natural polymath, he moved easily from one field to the next, and always left his mark. The true extent of his varied accomplishments has only become apparent after his death, as his friends from different periods and fields have gathered and compared notes. His influence is as greatly felt in the work of the artists, writers, musicians and philosophers he inspired, turned on, and initiated, as in the work to which he attached his name.

Outofinto

(To him who bears thy name)

Andrew M. McKenzie

ONE

The crowd thickened as he half-heartedly shuffled further along the street. The vicious rasping blare of various different street bands mixed together with the sound of laughter and the smell of burning meat from barbeques scattered across the city. It was in a state of mass celebration. Fortunes were being made, repressed emotions vented, short-term undying love being proclaimed to complete strangers. The street was one that he had walked along almost every day of his life, but was now totally transformed by the sheer volume of activity. He was, as far as his watch indicated, late. Probably one of the few occupants of the city that actually had an appointment. Easily susceptible to outside influences, the situation was not making him calmer or composed, as he had wished to appear at his interview. A child grabbed his trouser leg, and he brushed away the small hands as gently as possible. With difficulty, he navigated his way across to the other side of the street through the slowly moving floats, fire eaters, cheerleaders, assorted animals, beer cans and grinning people. Rings of sweat were beginning to show under the arms of his off-white suit. The welcome but unearthly hum of air-conditioning greeted him as he stooped through the tiny door. The lights were dim in the reception area, but through the haze, as his eyes adjusted to the gloom, he picked out the gleam of a young woman's teeth, bared, presumably, in an effusive gesture of welcome. He had not seen her before, and shuddered at the thought that she might very well know who he was. He evaded any exchange with her by whisking through the only door visible.

TWO

At least two of the fluorescent strip lights in the corridor were working. Three others were flickering erratically in their last throes, and the rest were out. He walked along slowly, surrepetitiously holding his breath. All nameplates had been unscrewed, revealing lighter patches of paint on the doors placed irregularly along the corridor. He tried the handle of one. Locked. He knocked, let out his breath, and waited. Nothing. He repeated this procedure another four times, then realised that such a place was unlikely in terms of the level of interview he had arranged. In the dossier he had received by post, outlining the structure of the company, its interests, aims, projects and expected growth curves, there were a number of portraits of directors past and present which afforded a view of the spacious offices which did not resemble the space he was now in. The cracked linoleum floor and peeling paint were not in evidence there, and the size which could be readily imagined from the posed and airbrushed photographs of the various department heads did not square with his present situation. A feeling of distant comprehension vyed for his attention. He continued along to the end of the line of doors, and turned the corner which had not been there immediately visible a few minutes earlier as he stepped in.

THREE

Before him lay a much longer and slightly broader corridor. As he steeped cautiously into it, the metal grips stuck into the soles of his shoes came into contact with the tiled floor. Small traces of grit cracked and resonated along the entire length of the passage, which he now saw was totally covered in inexpensive glazed squares, devoid of pattern or decoration. He trod even more stealthily for fear of slipping. Every sound lingered for about half a minute after being produced. Small beads of sweat oozed out onto his forehead, even though the air was, as to be expected from such a surface, quite cool. He smelt, or thought he smelt, cigarette smoke. His stomach made an impressive gurgling sound as an automatic reaction to the fact that he had given up smoking five days ago. There were no doors. Instead, a small panel containing a grille and a small button had been let into one of the walls at waist height. After a few scarce seconds of hesitation, he crouched down so that his head was level with the grille, and pushed the button. There was a crackle of static, and then a short burst of hiss that was abruptly terminated. He pressed again, but this time held the button in. The same crackle returned, not dissimilar to the noise from his shoes scraping the grit on the tiles, and then a faint constant high pitched tone. This grew rapidly into howling feedback, at which he jumped back to his feet and let the button loose. The whistling rang up and down the corridor for a good minute, as he waggled his little finger deep into his left ear, wincing. Examining the fingernail, he continued to the end of the swimming pool-like tunnel.

FOUR

There were many, many candles mounted on tall stands around the corner, infinitely reflected by perfectly polished mirrors which lined every surface of the corridor. The ceiling was considerably higher, and here and there stood a slightly opened door which further intensified and complicated the repetitions of the candles, of the reflections of the reflections and so on. A slight breeze was created by his entrance. He felt dizzy, struggling to adjust to the myriad perspectives of himself inverted, angled, juxtaposed with reversed and correct versions of his body. He dropped his briefcase, which sprung open, scattering pens and loose sheets of paper. Scooping them up and locking them back in, he found his creeping vertigo was lessened if he focussed on things close at hand. Making for one of the open doors, his foot found a weak spot in one of the mirrors on the floor, in which a crack suddenly snaked out away from him. The opened door turned out to be merely a reflection. He was no longer sure if he was advancing, or retreating. The size was impossible to estimate, and positions of reference points fitted away with every step, shuffling themselves with inhuman dexterity. He shut his eyes and walked on, just as he had when small, daring himself to keep on in spite of increasing uncertainty. He stopped when he felt heat at his right hand. He opened his eyes for a moment, corrected his trajectory, and continued walking. He felt his toe gently tapping glass in front of him, and on opening his eyes once more, found that he had narrowly missed kicking over another of the candlesticks, but had reached the end of the corridor. To his left was a small opening.

FIVE

The follow-on corridor was more in the order of a small aircraft hangar, with what must have been hundreds of school desks arranged in perfect rows, evenly spaced throughout. Deep grooves were carved into the lids – countless messages, insults and pearls of wisdom obscured by many others layered over them. He studied the morass of cuneiform script on one of the desks, and then slowly lifted the lid. A large beetle was fastened to a thread, which was in turn made secure to the middle of the inside of the desk by a drawing pin. The insect was circling the pin in an obvious attempt to escape. The thread was being wound shorter and shorter. He closed the lid sharply. He walked slowly over to another desk further along a row, and opened it quickly. It was full of roses. He allowed the scent to reach his nostrils before shutting the lid. Another desk, chosen at random, contained short, beautifully polished copper bars, all exactly the same length. He neither thought or even registered feelings any more, so disorientated by this tableaux. He toyed with the idea of opening another, but was startled out of his reverie by a clock chiming the hour loudly from somewhere outside the building. He composed himself as best he could, and blinked myopically for some sign of an exit. He was not disappointed. He felt the lodestone of logic inside him, his method of orientation splintering and fragmenting even as he tried to hold the shards together into a coherent whole. His body moved without his conscious bidding towards a green and white illuminated sign bearing the legend “exit”.

SIX

At the door which connected him with the following chamber (for this is what it was), he was faced with a red plastic machine which dispensed tickets printed with a number on thin paper. He took one, glanced at it, half-heartedly trying to remember the number. It was impossible to discern the origin of the light which seemed grey and lifeless. There also appeared to be no particular reason for the ticket. There were no signs of life. A closed shutter indicated a sort of reception counter with a large padlock fixing the bottom slat to the metal frame surrounding the opening. He noticed other discarded tickets here and there, and sat down on one of the chairs dispersed at random throughout the space. He pulled out a handkerchief from his trouser pocket, and loose change clattered onto the bare concrete floor. Immediately, a deafening alarm bell began to ring. He jumped to his feet and looked around wildly for a way out. On reaching a likely looking door, he found it locked. After trying to force the handle, he kicked it in disgust and put the palms of his hands over his ears. He closed his eyes. He remained in this state for a few minutes, and was startled out of it by a tap on his shoulder. He opened his eyes, pulled his arms back down to his sides and spun around to find a small man in a blue serge uniform with an obvious wig with an index finger on his lips. The door was now open, and the bell had stopped ringing. The man remained motionless, staring at him. He swept past this immobile figure through the door.

SEVEN

A very long corridor stretched out in front of him, immaculately tiled with alternating black and white squares. Halfway along it stood a table with something on it. The closer he got to it, the more apparent it was that a meal had been set out. He sat down, and without questioning whether or not the meal was actually intended for him, began to eat. It was simple food, simply prepared; a piece of meat, slightly overcooked vegetables. He ate carefully, concentrating on the taste of each individual part of the food. He was still not thinking. The outside world had ceased to exist. He had no idea how long he had been inside this labyrinth, nor had he any more desire to find out. His acceptance of everything was consummate, total. He finished chewing the last mouthful, swallowed, and took a gulp from the glass of wine that had also been provided. He reached into the inside pocket of his jacket for his cigarettes, but they had disappeared. He then realised that he had left his briefcase in the previous chamber. The look of panic common to those just realising a mistake flashed across his face. Bolted from the table back towards the door where he had entered. Not only was it firmly shut, but there was no handle from his side. It hardly seemed to matter any more. He walked back to the table and opened a small packet containing a moist cloth impregnated with a lemon scent. He wiped his hands carefully, screwed the cloth into a ball and tossed it onto the empty plate. There were a number of portraits in oil hanging on the walls. He inspected them one by one. They appeared to be all of the same woman, from very young to late middle age. She was remarkably plain, but the artist had attempted to disguise this by placing her in the most sumptuous of settings. These were somehow vaguely familiar to him, but only served to emphasise her lack of beauty or ugliness. She had become an object in a still life, inert, without a shred of personality. She had disappeared – she had been eliminated by the enthusiasm of the artist who had, it was obvious, tried to set her in surroundings that would lend her grace by association. In the last portrait, she was surrounded by candles, sitting cross-legged, and imitating a professional model's posture, the back of her hand curled underneath her chin, her elbow resting on her knee. She was crying. He opened the door directly opposite this picture and stepped through, glancing over his shoulder to give it a farewell glance.

EIGHT

There were books as far as he could see, lining the walls, piled up in huge stacks on the floor, crammed into every available space, except for a very small gangway running through the middle. He had to turn sideways and shuffle through, the powerful musty smell of the paper becoming almost oppressive as he progressed further. He could not help but notice, seeing as how his nose was virtually pushed into the many volumes on the shelves, that most of the books were in a foreign language not known to him. Those that he could read the titles of were mainly detailed technical texts on various aspects of engineering. Taking one down, he peered at the maze of figures, formulas and tables. It was material he had seen long ago when studying for an exam that enabled him to take the position he now held. As it turned out, the branch where he finally ended up working had little, if anything at all, to do with engineering, except in the broadest sense of the word. The recognition of the information filled him with a mild sensation something like fear. The nights spent trying to feed the abstract signs into his memory with never enough time came back, the flavour of the overstrong coffee drunk to keep awake was palpable again. He put the book back, and continued shuffling his way along. He began to circle back in himself to that period, being periodically reminded along the way by the occasional book he knew only too well. A knot began to form in his stomach. This was not proceeding in the manner he wished. As he thought the thought, he felt a sharp stab in his hip from the doorknob at the end of the line. This did not turn, but had to be pulled to one side, ball-bearings squeaking against the runners holding the door in place.

NINE

As the perfume reached his nostrils, he realised that there was the beginning from a system of entry and exit. He fully appreciated that his actions were being monitored in one way or another. The situation had been constructed, this much was certain. But at the same time, there was a question mark hanging over whether or not the various tableaux had been prepared for *him*. As he gazed around the room in front of him, almost gagging on the overwhelming scent, a cheap, pungent and very feminine scent, his eyes slowly became accustomed to the gloom. Details here and there became steadily more clear. A four-poster bed draped with lace, and a cat sleeping at one of the corners. A small radio gently generating static from a station after closedown, a tiny red light indicating its presence on a table at the side of the bed. A large mirror where nothing appeared to be reflected. Riped curtains half-open, framing a window looking out onto a vast empty courtyard. Small jars containing dark fluid on three shelves directly in front of him. For a bedroom, for so it undoubtedly was, it was incredibly cold. He gave an involuntary shiver, and holding his nose, trod softly into the boudoir, sliding the door to, carefully, behind him. He felt the presence of someone, but was sure that this person had somehow positioned themselves out of reach of his direct perception. Here and there he saw items of clothing half-folded, hanging on the back of a chair or just thrown onto the floor in heap. The carpet was very thick. There was no sound at all, apart from the static. He could feel his heart steadily thumping, and after a few minutes, began to hear it in his head. He suddenly vigorously rubbed his hands together. The cat started in its sleep, twitching its left hind leg irregularly, but with enough force to accidentally knock the telephone on a night-table beside the bed onto the floor. At the clatter of the internal bell he froze in his silent tracks. A window-catch suddenly came loose, and the window swung into the room, wind ruffling the curtains and all free-hanging clothing, and blowing open a door to his left that allowed an intense light fall into the darkness. He padded over to the door without looking back. He had seen all he wanted in the gloom, and looked straight ahead of him towards the opening.

TEN

Immediately he stepped through the door, the floor began to move forwards and upwards like an escalator. He looked around to see that this corridor was filled with similar moving walkways at various levels and travelling in various directions at differing angles to one another. Each walkway disappeared into a wall, and seemed to re-appear at a different level and tack. And indeed, it appeared that he was rapidly advancing towards such a hole in one of the vast walls. The darkness lasted a fraction of a second, but was total. He re-appeared going in the opposite direction, about half as fast again as a few moments ago, and at a considerable distance from the ground. There was nothing to hold onto, and he found himself doubting his sense of balance. As he checked himself, the walkway swung alarmingly from side to side, making the complimentary return swing even more extreme. There was definitely a degree of danger becoming apparent, when he entered another opening, automatically correcting the pendulum-like motions. He re-entered the corridor at an even faster rate than ever, and tried, very carefully, to sit down. But his efforts only produced the same effects as before. Again, just as he was contemplating the ever-increasing distance he would have to plummett, he reached another opening. In the blink of an eye that he changed onto the next track, he made the decision to try another ploy; he began to run as fast as he could, keeping his eyes fixed on the next door where he landed in a heap on the floor, gasping for breath and nursing his shoulder with closed eyes.

ELEVEN

He opened them slowly, noticing the grit pressing against his cheek. His heavy breathing was disturbing plaster dust, spiralling away off down the corridor. It was totally empty. There were no doors or windows, just endless expanses of concrete and plaster. He slowly raised himself up to a sitting position, and half-heartedly brushed dust from his jacket with his hands. He stood up, realised that this little act of vanity was quite superfluous to requirements, and looked around him. He walked to one wall, then the next, measuring the dimensions of the corridor with his own outstretched body. He made notes in his small notebook, and then took his jacket off. This he rolled into a sort of ball, and lay down, putting it under his head. He went to sleep.

Nature – Now, Then and Never

Beatrice Eggers

We may be the dominant species in the world, with our capacity for communication, ability in intellectual devices, and even when it comes to developing sophisticated emotions. Are these then qualities, under such unique premises, that our superiority is rightly justified? We have a *need to think*, just as the *other* animals have a need to survive. Are our needs above their needs in a universal context? Our thoughts are as transparent as the air when the mind is exposed to nature's omnipotent face. Survival of the fittest doesn't mean to overcome death, but to appreciate, in terms of intuitive evolution, that death will overcome you if you no longer have a function on this earth, and the dimensions belonging to it. We are mortals and therefore it isn't longer possible for us to verily comprehend the wisdom of life after death. What we are capable of, is instead to intuitively understand the functions of the evolutionary system, designed and produced exclusively by nature's own sacred source of gravity and creativity. Anything living carries the weapons of will or, if you prefer to connect it with a universal term, energy. This is nature's identity, her logo, thought to represent her enterprise in the most successful way. We have reached an identity crisis, because her traits or trades do not fulfil our lives anymore.

When looking up in the air, down underground, in the bushes or behind the trees, we see creatures of mountain-filled strength. What happens when we choose to look close for once? Are these winged, clawed, coiling and climbing animals here for reasons different than ours? What constitutes their existence in comparison with ours? What is it that nature wants to reveal by comparing our minds with their implanted system? We seem to be trapped by our own mentally imposed, illusory perceptiveness, for anything living is an intuitive pulse of directed information, a vital program inside the computered form. It must be true that nature owns a body, i.e. that which we can perceive with our senses, and a mind, i.e. that which cannot penetrate anything but time and space. We are strangers before the sun, for we do not bum of life anymore.

The distinction between a human and animal isn't made by us, even though we choose to think so. We pathetically crown our heads with the jewel of superior complexity, casting them in a disgraceful position we call the brainless but functional composition of existence. We think we dictate the terms, and soon we are bound to discover that our approaches are of weak qualities. We are paying off our stupidity, but since we do not possess anything of value anymore, we ignorantly try to get nature to pay for our mental (quasi-low-rated, unmotivated expansions) expenses. Nature created the laws of survival, but surely overestimated man's potential to be the fittest interpreter of this law. Nature misjudged her own creation only because her creations misjudged themselves. Who came first will die last, simply because experiences constitute the true evolutionary process. We are only a page in the history of the soul, but we try to publish, i.e. mark our validity as being the writers of the book of life, instead. This cannot be published, for nature holds copyright on every thought we may or may not think. Our greatest misfortune is that we choose to disregard those human traits that summon up the balance of our work. Beauty, strength, wisdom and freedom are empty words, simply because we don't hold the will to invest them within the unlimited boundaries of nature's universal bank.

We must sharpen our abilities in order to make them fit the answers of nature's questionnaire. We must start to un-teach our minds – the only solution to our problems. We came here to represent life in its most potential and absolute form. Animals live their lives for reasons very natural to them. Why is it that we can recognize everything but our own reasons for being here? When animals live their lives they do it because of the programmed identity of survival, creating a close connection to death as a result. But we cannot find the true identity of our death, and so we lose the ability to comprehend nature's will to strangle our purpose to live. But since we don't live after a survival program, we must exaggerate proportions of life so they will fit, at least in our minds. One of our deadly mistakes is the fact that we want to live, instead of wanting to survive. To live in the dimension of survival means to connect with the highest purpose of living. It will make an existing creature confront its powers and thus to utilize them in the most efficient way possible. We seem to live simply because time and space exist, and so we should die for the same reason.

We must understand that our intellect is nothing but a tool, intended to serve our survival quest instead of controlling it. As long as we rely upon the intellect as being a sort of guide instead of a servant, nothing can be true about us. Illusions are our greatest enemy, and if we are to justify our position on earth, then it is clear to me that all results of our intellect must die. Our perception, springing from the mind, but also being distorted by it, must be dragged through a filter of awareness, produced by a subconscious understanding of will, our depth of survival, in order to connect us to our development of survival. Life is a natural device and cannot be taught in another manner than that of perception of will. The mind consumes more than it can produce, and the trash grows, inflicting the filter with a vulgar form of realisation. Self-destructiveness is the result, for we must destroy that which cannot be mentally fertile. We are neither man nor god, but a spirit of intelligence.

The closest apprehension of a god is nature, and we must live within god and thus become the essence of divinity, spirit of her essentiality. But how can it be that nature believes in an alternative world called civilization? Aren't her choices rather cryptic? For if man lives outside of his original atmosphere, he cannot possibly be any spirit of hers at all. This invention that she experiments with will not last because the idea is arbitrary in the universe. It is dangerous for us to stay in existence. We cannot represent arbitrary lives, no one can. We cannot be masters of nothing, now can we?

We are not magickians, i.e. true interpreters of natural philosophy. Instead we should call ourselves imported and distorted technickians, working for a corrupt company outside the enterprise of nature. Our export consists of manufactured behaviour and the prices are low, for the quality of our self-awareness is rather low. We sell poorly, for our products are made out of want instead of will. Our manufactured mentality plagues the market of evolution, and it's competition we need to create better goods. We have the animals to compete with, but we choose our intellect instead. There is no guidance from nature for those who wish to control or comprehend that which is a natural product. Without guidance, bankruptcy is a fact. The god of comfort came to please our will, but ended up pleasing our needs instead. We are the fools of fools, betraying ourselves in the worst kind of manner. We no longer have to use our will – our will uses us instead. The machines rob our minds of true communication, and technical devices crush every imaginative aspect of that communication. Without the will, there cannot be anything left for us to expand in a natural way. We let the machines express that which we would want to express but don't think we can. It has gone that far. The machines form our expressions and thus control our impressions as well. They are shaping our minds in a very subtle and effective way, almost unnoticeable before our gross machinery of perception.

We connect unto the machines' will as a wire connects with the light. Our will doesn't need us anymore and the god of comfort flourishes because of it. Animals have a justified position, for they need their will. They cannot invent a reflection of themselves as we can, for they don't have to. Their system programmes their will, our machines programme ours. The animals have got a will to survive, their creativity lies in the art of survival. They change without any intellectual substitutes. All we can do is to re-arrange changes and that isn't good enough according to the school of movement. Since we re-arrange, we still tamper with the meaning of life. Instead of changing the approach towards knowledge, we change knowledge. This is something that cannot be done according to nature. For wisdom is her rule and it can't be broken.

Artificial alchemists, technickians and mass-mysticism are the results of this re-arrangement. If there are any tourists on earth, we are them. We aren't even close to the thread of evolution, for there aren't any forms of development left for us to be part of. This I claim on the grounds of the decadent truth stating that we don't need ourselves anymore. We don't live our lives, they have outlived us. We are falling to pieces just as the future is falling into place. It is obvious and it is terribly true. We substitute every aspect of our will. Our spirit doesn't find anything real within, and outside ourselves nothing is to be found but the prostitution of will. We get more and more dependent upon lies since we think that truth can be reached inside our heads. We own giant enterprises, but we don't own ourselves anymore. Greed for knowledge, abuse of universal facts, distrust in will, corruption in heart and negation of nature. These are all human traits. Filtration of knowledge is our only hope, but the mental filter is abused by thoughts and thus cannot be intuitive anymore. We must understand what needs to be understood, and disregard those things that don't ought to be understood by us. It doesn't inform our minds of much, but it is the key to information. It is the sacred law of wisdom – evaluate wisdom through will, and not because our minds want to store all kinds of facts because it pleases the intellect. Reflections of wisdom are dangerous, wisdom is fatal because of it. For either you understand your thoughts' intentions, or they will distort your inventions. We seem to know all the wrong things, for we haven't been competent enough to trust the wisdom outside our own existence. Nature now might as well be nature never in our apprehension of life.

Also Available from Trapart Books

The Fenris Wolf 10 (2020)

Carl Abrahamsson – *Editor's Introduction*, Carl Abrahamsson – *Onwards to the Source!*, Ludwig Klages – *On the Essence of Ecstasy*, David Beth – *Katabasis and Erotognosis*, Henrik Dahl – *An Introduction to Eroto-Psychedelic Art*, Peter Sjöstedt-H – *Antichrist Psychonaut: Nietzsche's Psychoactive Drugs*, Carl Abrahamsson – *Lux Per Nox – The Fenris Wolf As Libidinal Liberator*, Jesse Bransford & Max Razdow – *Revisiting the Veil of Dreams*, Christopher Webster – *Beyond the North Wind*, Kendell Geers – *A Long Boundless Systematized...*, Kadmus – *Seeking the Three-Headed Saint*, Billie Steigerwald – *The Chthonic Seed: Reflections of an Ancient Death Gnosis*, Fred Andersson – *The Gospel According to the Tomb Man*, Zaheer Gulamhusein – *Sunflower*, Charlotte Rodgers – *The Riderless Horse...*, Craig Slee – *The Occult Nature of Cripkult*, Damien Patrick Williams – *Daoism, Buddhism and Machine Consciousness*, Philip H. Farber – *Thoughts on the Creation of Memetic Entities*, Thomas Bey William Bailey – *Memetic Magick*, Mitch Horowitz – *Is Your Mind a Technology for Utopia?*, Ramsey Dukes – *I'm Gonna Blow Your Mind*, Carl Abrahamsson – *Grasping Reality with Gary Lachman*, Anders Lundgren – *Mike Mignola and the Lovecraft Circle*, Peggy Nadramia – *So It Was Written*, Peggy Nadramia – *Addendum to So It Was Written*, Nina Antonia – *Maya*, Jack Stevenson – *Häxan/Witchcraft Through the Ages*, Andrea Kundry – *The Demonic Cultural Legacy of Antonin Artaud*, Joan Pope – *The Birth of Ideas*, Genesis Breyer P-Orridge – *Idiosyncratic Use Ov Language...*, Vanessa Sinclair – *Try To Altar Everything*, Claire-Madeline Corso – *Cutting Up a New Conversation*

The Fenris Wolf 9 (2017)

Vanessa Sinclair & Carl Abrahamsson – *Editors' Introduction: Looking back at the crossroads*, Katelan Foisy – *Invocation: Homage to the spirits of the land/London*, Sharron Kraus – *Art as Alchemy*, Demetrius Lacroix – *The Seven Layers of the Vodou Soul*, Graham Duff – *Sublime Fragments: The Art of John Balance*, Ken Henson – *The American Occult Revival In My Work*, Gary Lachman – *Was Freud Afraid of the Occult?*, Peter Grey – *Fly the Light*, Val Denham – *Proclaim Present Time Over*, Katelan Foisy & Vanessa Sinclair – *The Cut In Creation*, Claire-Madeline Culkin – *Beds, Bodies and Other Books of Common Prayer – A Reading of the, Photography of Nan Goldin*, Steven Reisner – *On the Dance of the Occult and Unconscious in Freud*, Katy Bohinc – *The 12th House: Art and the Unconscious*, Olga Cox Cameron – *When Shall We 3 Meet Again? Psychoanalysis, Art and the Occult: A Clandestine Convergence*, Ingo Lambrecht – *Wairua: Following shamanic contours in psychoanalytic therapy at a Māori Mental Health Service in New Zealand*, Elliott Edge – *An Occult Reading of PAO! Imagining in the Dark with Our*

Vestigial Shamanism in a Shade, Shadow, Wide, Charlotte Rodgers – *Stripped to the Core: Animistic Art Action and Magickal Revelation*, Alkistis Dimech – *Dynamics of the Occulted Body*, Fred Yee – *Cut-Up As Egregore, Oracle and Flirtation Device*, Robert Ansell – *Androgyny, Biology and Latent Memory in the Work of Austin Osman Spare*, Ray O Neill – *Double, Double, Toil and Trouble: Psychoanalysis Burn and Surrealism Bubble*, Derek M Elmore – *Dreams and the Neither-Neither*, Julio Mendes Rodrigo – *Rebis, the Double Being*, Eve Watson – *Bowie's Non-Human Effect: Alien/Alienation in The Man Who Fell to Earth (1976) and The Hunger (1983)*, Carl Abrahamsson – *Formulating the Desired: Some similarities between ritual magic and the psychoanalytic process*

The Fenris Wolf 8 (2016)

Carl Abrahamsson – *Editor's Introduction*, Vanessa Sinclair – *Polymorphous Perversity and Pandrogeny*, Charles Stansfield Jones (Frater Achad) – *Alchymia*, Tim O'Neill: *Black Lodge/White Lodge*, Nina Antonia – *Bosie & The Beast*, Aki Cederberg – *Festivals of Spring*, Michael Moynihan – *Friedrich Hielscher's Vision of the Real Powers*, Friedrich Hielscher – *The Real Powers*, Orryelle Defenestrate Bascule – *Ear Horn: Shamanic Perspectives and Multi-Sensory Inversion*, Zbigniew Lagos – *The Figure of the Polish Magician: Czesław Czynski (1858-1932)*, Gary Lachman – *Rejected Knowledge: A Look At Our Other Way of Knowing*, Carl Abrahamsson – *Intuition as a State of Grace*, Bishop T Omphalos – *The Golden Thread: Soteriological Aspects of the Gnostic Catholicism in E.G.C.*, Kendell Geers – *iMagus*, Johan Nilsson – *Defending Paper Gods: Aleister Crowley and the Reception of Daoism in Early 20th Century Esotericism*, Gordan Djurdjevic – *The Birth of the New Aeon: Magick and Mysticism of Thelema from the Perspective of Postmodern A/Theology*, Tim O'Neill – *The Derleth Error*, Antti P Balk – *Greek Mysteries*, Carl Abrahamsson – *The Economy of Magic*, Stephen Sennitt – *The Book of the Sentient Night: 23 Nails*, Henrik Dahl – *We Ate the Acid: A Note on Psychedelic Imagery*, Jason Louv – *Robert Anton Wilson's Cosmic Trigger and the Psychedelic Interstellar Future we need*, Carey Hodges & Chad Hensley – *New Orleans Voodoo: An Oddity Unto Itself*, Alexander Nym – *Kabbalah references in contemporary culture*, Zaheer Gulamhusein – *Standing in Line*, Carl Abrahamsson – *As the Wolf Lies Down to Rest*, Vanessa Sinclair & Ingo Lambrecht – *Ritual and Psychoanalytical Spaces as Transitional, featuring Sangoma Trance States*, Hagen von Julien – *Listening to the Voice of Silence: A Contemporary Perspective on the Fraternities Saturni*, Erik Davis – *Infectious Hoax: Robert Anton Wilson reads H.P. Lovecraft*, N – *II. Land*, Cadmus – *Neo-Chthonia*, Kadmus – *A Fragment of Heart: A contribution to the Mega-Golem*, Stojan Nikolic – *The One True Church of the Dark Age of Scientism*, Miguel Marques – *The Labors of Seeing: A Journey Through the Works of Peter Whitehead*, Renata Wieczorek – *The Conception of Number According to Aleister Crowley*, Orryelle Defenestrate Bascule – *Fragments of Fact*, Derek Seagrief – *Conscious ExIt*, Kasper Opstrup – *By This, That: A spin on Lea Porsager's Spin*, and Genesis Breyer P-Orridge – *Greyhounds of the future.*

Also Available From Trapart Books

The Fenris Wolf 7 (2014)

Carl Abrahamsson – *Editor's Introduction*, Sara George & Carl Abrahamsson – *Fernand Khnopff, Symbolist*, Sasha Chaitow – *Making the Invisible Visible*, Vanessa Sinclair – *Psychoanalysis and Dada*, Kendell Geers – *Tu Marcellus Eris*, Stephen Sennitt – *Fallen Worlds, Without Shadows*, Antony Hequet – *Slam Poetry: The Warrior Poet*, Antony Hequet – *Slam Poetry: The Rebel Poet*, Genesis Breyer P-Orridge – *Alien Lightning Meat Machine*, Genesis Breyer P-Orridge – *This Is A Nice Planet*, Patrick Lundborg – *Psychedelic Philosophy*, Henrik Dahl – *Visionary Design*, Philip Farber – *Higher Magick*, Kendell Geers – *Painting My Will*, Carl Abrahamsson – *The Imaginative Libido*, Angela Edwards – *The Sacred Whore*, Vera Nikolich – *The Women of the Aeon*, Jason Louv – *Wilhelm Reich*, Kasper Opstrup – *To Make It Happen*, Peter Grey – *A Manifesto of Apocalyptic Witchcraft*, Timothy O'Neill – *The Gospel of Cosmic Terror*, Stephen Sennitt – *Sentient Absence*, Carl Abrahamsson – *Anton LaVey, Magical Innovator*, Alexander Nym – *Magicians: Evolutionary Agents or Regressive Twats?*, Antti P Balk – *Thelema*, Kjetil Fjell – *The Vindication of Thelema*, Derek Seagrief – *Exploring Past Lives*, Sandy Robertson – *The Fictional Aleister Crowley*, Adam Rostoker – *Whence Came the Stranger?*, Emory Cranston – *A Preface to the Scented Garden*, Manon Hedenborg-White – *Erotic Submission to the Divine*, Carl Abrahamsson – *What Remains for the Future?*, Frater Achad – *Living In the Sunlight*, Genesis Breyer P-Orridge – *Magick Squares and Future Beats*

The Fenris Wolf 6 (2013)

Carl Abrahamsson – *Editor's Introduction*, Frater Achad – *A Litany of Ra*, Kendell Geers – *Tripping over Darwin's Hangover*, Vera Nikolich – *Eastern Connections*, Carl Abrahamsson – *Babalon*, Freya Aswynn – *On the Influence of Odin*, Marita – *Runic Magic through the Odinic Dialectic*, Aki Cederberg – *Afterword: The River of Story*, Shri Gurudev Mahendranath – *The Londinium Temple Strain*, Gary Dickinson – *An Orient Pearl*, Derek Seagrief – *Aleister Crowley's Birth & Death Horoscopes*, Tim O'Neill – *Shades of Void*, Nema – *Magickal Healing*, Nema – *A Greater Feast*, Philip Farber – *Sacred Smoke*, Robert Taylor – *Death & the Psychedelic Experience*, Michael Horowitz – *LSD: the Antidote to Everything*, Alexander Nym – *Transcendence as an Operative Category…*, Carl Abrahamsson – *Approaching the Approaching*, Renata Wieczorek – *The Secret Book of the Tatra Mountains*, Sasha Chaitow – *Legends of the Fall Retold*, Sara George & Carl Abrahamsson – *Sulamith Wülfing*, Robert C Morgan – *Hans Bellmer*, Genesis Breyer P-Orridge – *Tagged for Life*, Carl Abrahamsson – *Go Forth and Let Your Brain-halves Procreate*, Anders Lundgren – *Satanic Cinema is Alive and Well*, Anton LaVey – *Appendices*

The Fenris Wolf 5 (2012)

Carl Abrahamsson – *Editor's Introduction*, Jason Louv – *The Freedom of Imagination Act*, Patrick Lundborg – *Such Stuff as Dreams are Made of*, Gary Lachman – *Secret Societies and the Modern World*, Tim O'Neill – *The War of the Owl and the Pelican*, Dianus del

Bosco Sacro – *The Great Rite*, Philip H Farber – *Entities in the Brain*, Aki Cederberg – *At the Well of Initiation*, Renata, Wieczorek – *The Magical Life of Derek Jarman*, Genesis Breyer P-Orridge – *A Dark Room of Desire*, Genesis Breyer P-Orridge – *Kreeme Horne*, Ezra Pound – *Translator's Postscript*, Stephen Ellis – *Poems for The Fenris Wolf*, Hiram Corso – *Mel Lyman*, Mel Lyman – *Plea for Courage*, Gary Dickinson – *The Daughter of Astrology*, Robert Podgurski – *Sigils and Extra Dimensionality*, Frater Nigris – *Liber Al As-if*, Peter Grey – *The Abbey Must be Built*, Vera Mladenovska Nikolich – *A Different Perspective of the Undead*, Kevin Slaughter – *The Great Satan*, Lionel Snell – *The Art of Evil*, Phenex Apollonius – *The Quintessence of Daimonic Ipseity*, Phanes Apollonius – *Infernal Diabolism in Theory and Practice*, Anonymous – *Falling with Love: Embracing the Infernal Host*, Lana Krieg – *Sympathy with the Devil: Faust's Infernal Formula*, Carl Abrahamsson – *State of the Art: Birthpangs of a Mega-Golem*, Carl Abrahamsson – *Hounded by the Dogs of Reason*

The Fenris Wolf 4 (2011)

Carl Abrahamsson – *The whys of yesterday are the why-nots of today*, Hermann Hesse – *The Execution*, Fredrik Söderberg – *Black and White Meditations 1-23*, Peter Gilmore – *Every Man and Woman Is a Star*, Peter Grey – *Barbarians at the Gates*, John Duncan – *Hallelujah*, Ramsey Dukes – *Democracy Is Dying of AIDS*, Tim O'Neill – *The Technology of Civilization X*, Thomas Karlsson – *Religion and Science*, David Beth – *Bloodsongs*, Payam Nabarz – *Liber Astrum*, Hiram Corso – *Unveiling the Mysteries of the Process Church*, Jean-Pierre Turmel – *The Pantheon of Genesis Breyer P-Orridge*, Kendell Geers – *The Penis Might Ier Than Thes Word*, Z'EV – *The Calls*, Robert Taylor – *Dreamachine: The Alchemy of Light*, Phil Farber – *An Interview with Terence McKenna*, Phil Farber – *McKenna, Ramachandran and the Orgy*, Thomas Bey William Bailey – *The Twilight of Psychedelic America?*, Ernst Jünger – *LSD Again/Nochmals LSD*, Baba Rampuri – *The Edge of Indian Spirituality*, Aki Cederberg – *In Search of Magic Mirrors*, Carl Abrahamsson – *Thelema and Politics*, Carl Abrahamsson – *Someone's Messing with the Big Picture*, Carl Abrahamsson – *An Art of High Intent?*, Carl Abrahamsson – *A Conversation with Kenneth Anger*

The Fenris Wolf 1-3 (1989-1993-2011)

Carl Abrahamsson – *Editor's Introduction*
Carl Abrahamsson – *'Zine und Zeit (2011)*

The Fenris Wolf 1 (1989)
John Alexander – *The Strange Phenomena of the Dream*, Helgi Pjeturss – *The Nature of Sleep and Dreams*, Tim O'Neill – *A Dark Storm Rising*, Carl Abrahamsson – *Inauguration of Kenneth Anger*, Carl Abrahamsson – *An Interview with Genesis P-Orridge*, William S Burroughs – *Points of Distinction between Sedative and Consciousness-Expanding Drugs*, Carl Abrahamsson – *Jayne Mansfield: Satanist*, TOPYUS – *Television Magick*, Anton LaVey – *Evangelists vs The New God*

Also Available From Trapart Books

The Fenris Wolf 2 (1990)
Lionel Snell – *The Satan Game*, Carl Abrahamsson – *In Defence of Satanism*, Anton LaVey – *The Horns of Dilemma*, Genesis P-Orridge – *Beyond thee Valley ov Acid*, Phauss – *Photographs*, Jack Stevenson – *15 Voices from God*, Jack Stevenson – *18 Fatal Arguments*, Tim O'Neill – *Art On the Edge of Life*, Terence Sellers – *To Achieve Death*, Stein Jarving – *Choice and Process*, Tim O'Neill – *Under the Sign of Gemini*, 93/696 – *The Forgotten Ones In Magick*, Tim O'Neill – *The Mechanics of Maya*, Coyote 12 – *The Thin Line*, Genesis P-Orridge – *Thee Only Language Is Light*, Jack Stevenson – *Porno on Film*, Carl Abrahamsson – *An Interview with Kenneth Anger*

The Fenris Wolf 3 (1993)
Jack Stevenson – *Vandals, Vikings and Nazis*, von Hausswolff & Elggren – *Inauguration of two new Kingdoms*, Tim O'Neill – *A Flame in the Holy Mountain*, Frater Tigris – *A Preliminary Vision*, Carl Abrahamsson – *The Demonic Glamour of Cinema*, William Heidrick – *Some Crowley Sources*, Peter H Gilmore – *The Rite of Ragnarök*, ONA – *The Left-Handed Path*, Zbigniew Karkowski – *The Method Is Science...*, Fetish 23 – *Demonic Poetry*, Ben Kadosh – *Lucifer-Hiram*, Freya Aswynn – *The Northern Magical Tradition*, Anton LaVey – *Tests*, Austin Osman Spare – *Anathema of Zos*, Rodney Orpheus – *Thelemic Morality*, Nemo – *Recognizing Pseudo-Satanism*, Philip Marsh – *Pythagoras, Plato and the Hellenes*, Terence Sellers – *A Few Acid Writings*, Hymenæus Beta – *Harry Smith 1923-1991*, Andrew M McKenzie – *Outofinto*, Beatrice Eggers – *Nature: Now, Then and Never*

Genesis Breyer P-Orridge: Sacred Intent – Conversations with Carl Abrahamsson 1986-2019

Sacred Intent gathers conversations between artist Genesis Breyer P-Orridge and longtime friend and collaborator, the Swedish author Carl Abrahamsson. From the first 1986 fanzine interview about current projects, over philosophical insights, magical workings, international travels, art theory and gender revolutions, to 2019's thoughts on life and death in the the shadow of battling leukaemia, *Sacred Intent* is a unique journey in which the art of conversation blooms.

With (in)famous projects like C.O.U.M. Transmissions, Throbbing Gristle, Psychic TV, Thee Temple Ov Psychick Youth (TOPY) and Pandrogeny, Breyer P-Orridge has consistently thwarted preconceived ideas and transformed disciplines such as performance art, music, collage, poetry and social criticism; always cutting up the building blocks to dismantle control structures and authority. But underneath the socially conscious and pathologically rebellious spirit, there has always been a devout respect for a holistic, spiritual, magical worldview – one of "sacred intent."

Sacred Intent is a must read for anyone interested in contemporary art, deconstructed identity, gender evolution, and magical philosophy. The book not only celebrates an intimate friendship, but also the work and ideas of an artist who has never ceased to amaze and provoke. Also included are photographic portraits of Breyer P-Orridge taken by Carl Abrahamsson, transcripts of key lectures, and an interview with Jacqueline "Lady Jaye" Breyer P-Orridge from 2004.

Genesis Breyer P-Orridge: Brion Gysin – His Name Was Master

Brion Gysin (1916–86) has been an incredibly influential artist and iconoclast: his development of the "cut-up" technique with William S. Burroughs has inspired generations of writers, artists and musicians. Gysin was also a skilled networker and revered expat: together with his friend Paul Bowles, he more or less constructed the post-beatnik romanticism for life and magic in Morocco, and was also a protagonist in an international gay culture with inspirational reaches in both America and Europe. Not surprisingly, Gysin has become something of a cult figure.

One of the artists he inspired is Genesis Breyer P-Orridge, who collaborated with both Gysin and Burroughs in the 1970s, during his work with Throbbing Gristle and C.O.U.M. Transmissions. The interviews made by P-Orridge have since become part of a New Wave/Industrial mythos. This volume presents them in their entirety alongside three texts on Gysin by P-Orridge, plus an introduction. This book is an exclusive insight into the mind of a man P-Orridge describes as "a kind of Leonardo da Vinci of the last century," and a fantastic complement to existing biographies and monographs.

Carl Abrahamsson: Mother, Have A Safe Trip

Unearthed plans and designs stemming from radical inventor Nikola Tesla could solve the world's energy problems. These plans suddenly generate a vortex of interest from various powers. Thrown into this maelstrom of international intrigue is Victor Ritterstadt – a soul searching magician with a mysterious and troubled past. From Berlin, over Macedonia, and all the way to Nepal, Ritterstadt sets out on an outer as well as inner quest. Espionage, love, UFOs, magic, telepathy, conspiracies, LSD, and more in this shocking story of a world about to be changed forever…

"It's a thrilling roller coaster ride through psychedelic adventures, juicy romantic interludes, metaphoric dreamscapes, high Himalayan yoga enclaves, telepathic portals, 60's flashbacks, magical constructs, secret government pursuits and many more twists that kept all three of my eyes open. It's a story that you'll definitely want to keep non-stop reading, which I enthusiastically recommend."

– George Douvris, Links by George

"*Mother, Have A Safe Trip* is a highly entertaining and thought-provoking novel. Chock-full of psychedelia, the book is also a much welcome addition to the far too few fictional works published dealing with psychedelic culture."

– Henrik Dahl, Psychedelic Press

"The dialogues are great. But it's too short. I wanted more."

– Genesis Breyer P-Orridge, Artist

Also Available From Trapart Books

"It's a wonderful read. A lovely book."

– June Newton/Alice Springs, Photographer

Vanessa Sinclair: Switching Mirrors

Switching Mirrors is an amazing collection of cut-ups and mind-expanding poetry by Vanessa Sinclair. Delving into the unconscious and actively utilising the "third mind" as developed by William S Burroughs and Brion Gysin, Sinclair roams through suggestive vistas of magic, witchcraft, dreams, psychoanalysis, sex and sexuality (and more). Causal apprehensions are disrupted by a flow of impressions that open up the mind of the reader. What's behind language and our use of it? What happens when random factors and the unconscious are given free reign in poetic form? *Switching Mirrors* is what happens.

Vanessa Sinclair (ed.): Rendering Unconscious – Psychoanalytic Perspectives, Politics & Poetry

In times of crisis, one needs to stop and ask, "How did we get here?" Our contemporary chaos is the result of a society built upon pervasive systems of oppression, discrimination and violence that run deeper and reach further than most understand or care to realize. These draconian systems have been fundamental to many aspects of our lives, and we seem to have gradually allowed them more power. However, our foundation is not solid; it is fractured and collapsing – if we allow that. We need to start applying new models of interpretation and analysis to the deep-rooted problems at hand.

Rendering Unconscious brings together international scholars, psychoanalysts, psychologists, philosophers, researchers, writers and poets; reflecting on current events, politics, the state of mental health care, the arts, literature, mythology, and the cultural climate; thoughtfully evaluating this moment of crisis, its implications, wide-ranging effects, and the social structures that have brought us to this point of urgency.

Hate speech, Internet stalking, virtual violence, the horde mentality of the alt-right, systematic racism, the psychology of rioting, the theater of violence, fake news, the power of disability, erotic transference and counter-transference, the economics of libido, Eros and the death drive, fascist narratives, psychoanalytic formation as resistance, surrealism and sexuality, traversing genders, and colonial counterviolence are but a few of the topics addressed in this thought-provoking and inspiring volume.

Contributions by Vanessa Sinclair, Gavriel Reisner, Alison Annunziata, Kendalle Aubra, Gerald Sand, Tanya White-Davis & Anu Kotay, Luce deLire, Jason Haaf, Simon Critchley & Brad Evans, Marc Strauss, Chiara Bottici, Manya Steinkoler, Emma Lieber, Damien Patrick Williams, Shara Hardeson, Jill Gentile, Angelo Villa, Gabriela Costardi, Jamieson Webster, Sergio Benvenuto, Craig Slee, Álvaro D. Moreira, David Lichtenstein, Julie Fotheringham, John Dall'aglio, Matthew Oyer, Jessica Datema, Olga Cox Cameron, Katie Ebbitt, Juliana Portilho, Trevor Pederson, Elisabeth Punzi & Per-Magnus Johansson, Meredith Friedson, Steven Reisner, Léa Silveira, Patrick Scanlon, Júlio Mendes Rodrigo, Daniel Deweese, Julie Futrell, Gregory J. Stevens, Benjamin Y.

Fong, Katy Bohinc, Wayne Wapeemukwa, Patricia Gherovici & Cassandra Seltman, Marie Brown, Buffy Cain, Claire-Madeline Culkin, Andrew Daul, Germ Lynn, Adel Souto, and paul aster stone-tsao.

More information can be found at our web site: www.trapart.net

Made in the USA
Las Vegas, NV
15 August 2021

28227774R00187